The Three Legends

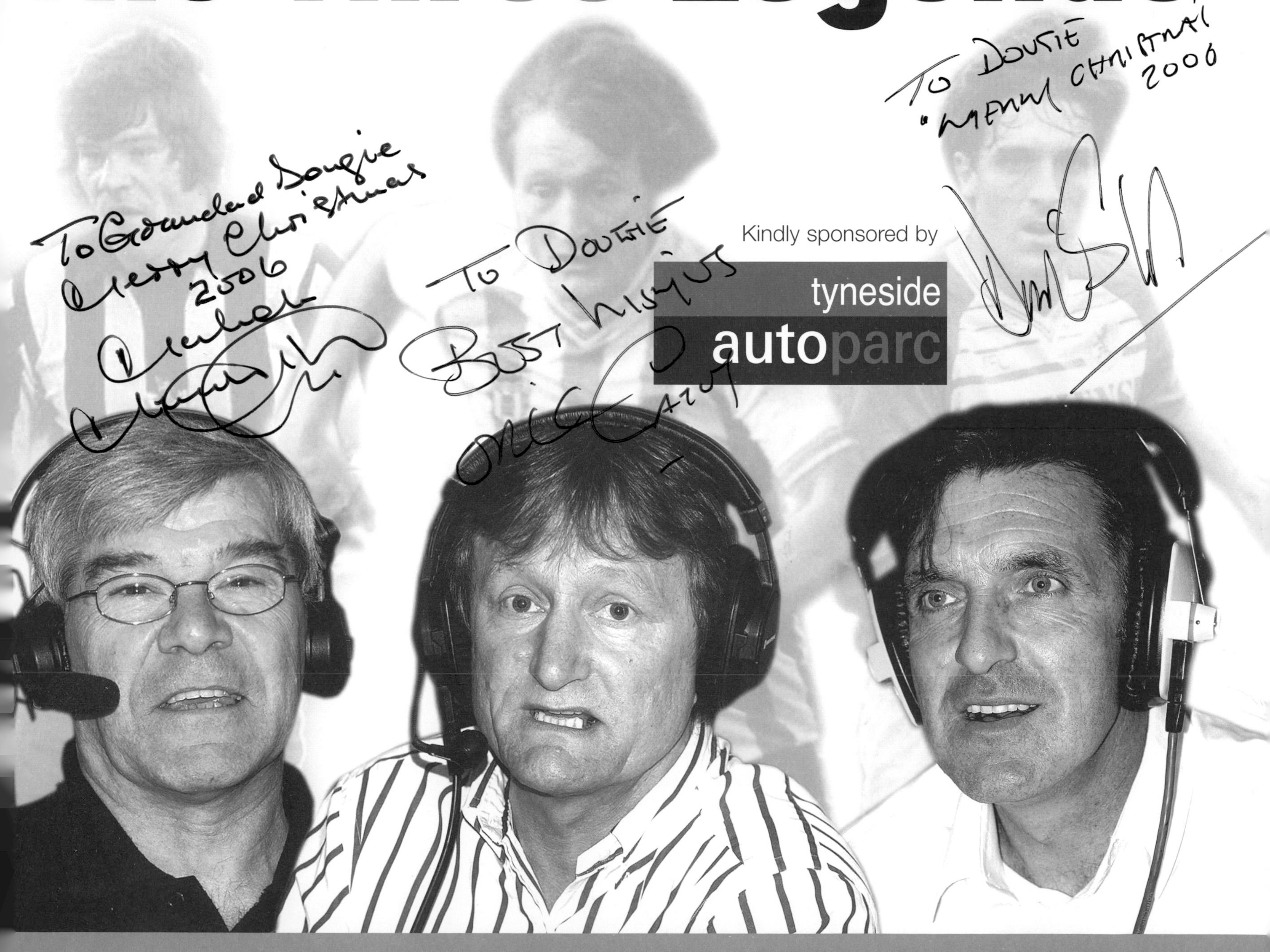

To Grandad Dougie
Happy Christmas
2006

To Dougie
Best Wishes

To Dougie
"Merry Christmas"
2006

Kindly sponsored by

tyneside
autoparc

Malcolm Macdonald, Eric Gates and Bernie Slaven

First published in Great Britain in 2006 by The Three Legends & Linthorpe Publishing, c/o 38 Westwood Avenue, Linthorpe, Middlesbrough, TS5 5PX

ISBN 978-0-9553363-1-7

Designed and printed by Hillprint Media,
Prime House, Heighington Lane Business Park, Newton Aycliffe, County Durham.
Tel. 01325 245555. www.hillprintmedia.com

Photo credits

The authors and publishers are grateful to the following for permission to use photographs in this book: Blades Sports Photography, North Eastern Evening Gazette, North News & Pictures.
Other photography by Hillprint Media.

Bigger than Bernie's Quiff.....
Bigger than Malcolm's Moooo.....
Bigger than Gatesy's Gob.....

But with 1200 quality used cars on one site every day

is the biggest by far

Big is beautiful

www.tynesideautoparc.co.uk

Sandy Lane, Gosforth, Newcastle
(just off the A1 at Gosforth Park)
9am - 8pm Mon-Fri 9am - 6pm Sat 10am - 5pm Sun

contents

	Page
The Legend of The Three Legends	01
Eric's Story:	
The Luckiest Lad Alive	23
Coming Home	33
Retirement by the Pool	42
Stabbed in the back	45
Malcolm's Story:	
Bring Me Sunshine	53
Talk of the Toon	59
Highbury Highs and Lows	66
Man of Many Talents	72
Bernie's Story:	
Strikingly Different	77
Boro Barmy	85
Vale of Tears	93
Radio Ga-Ga	96

	Page
Eric's Legends 'n' Leg-ends	102
Sunderland	105
Malcolm's Legends 'n' Leg-ends	118
Newcastle United	121
Bernie's Legends 'n' Leg-ends	136
Middlesbrough	139
The Three Gaffers	154
Bernie Banged Up	156
Three Legends, Three Lions	158
Bernie's Rant	159
Scotching a Legend	161
Who You Gonna Call?	165
The Secret Lives of The Three Legends	227
Question Time	235

ACKNOWLEDGEMENTS

A big thank you to everyone at Century fm who has helped to make our programme what it is. We are grateful to Century for the bravery they display in giving us the license to put on air some of the things that we do! Particular thanks must go to Owen, Kathryn and Rod at Century.

But our biggest thanks must, of course, go to the people of the north-east who listen in such great numbers and call, text and email us in such a big way. Not only do you make The Three Legends show – without you, there is no show.

Particular thanks for his advice and input in taking this book from bright idea to reality goes to Dave Byrne. We are also grateful to Alastair Brownlee for all of his advice and enthusiasm.

Special thanks to John Alderson and Chris Bartles-Smith at Hillprint for their excellent input on design and imagery. Also to proof reader extraordinaire Mike McGeary for his many hours of work. Finally to Fr. Paul Farrer for his technical skills.

Bernie, Eric and Malcolm

To Sophie and Grace

DEDICATIONS

To my family, who stuck by me through the good times and the bad times.
I hope the good times I brought helped make up for the bad times I gave you.
Thanks for everything.
Eric

To my boys, Dominic and Ryan.
I hope they grow up to be as proud of me as I am of them.
Bernie

To all listeners of The Three Legends.
Thanks for listening.
Malcolm

THE LEGEND OF THE THREE LEGENDS

THE THREE Legends Football Phone-in has been on air since the start of the 2000-2001 season and has now racked up more than 1,500 shows. The voices of Malcolm Macdonald, Eric Gates and Bernie Slaven have become more familiar to north-east football fans than any of their modern-day heroes at St James' Park, the Stadium of Light or the Riverside. But the tale of how three such contrasting and demanding characters have stuck together through all the ups and downs is an intriguing one.

All three had enjoyed wonderful football careers that most players, let alone those of us not fortunate enough to have such skills, can only ever dream of. All three had enjoyed glory days in the north-east. And all three already had considerable experience of radio work when Century hit on the idea of a football phone-in with a difference during the summer of 2000. How three fans' favourites who hardly knew one another were forged into the legend that is The Three Legends phone-in is one only they can tell.

That summer, as seventh-placed Sunderland enjoyed a rare season as the regions top dogs, ahead of Newcastle and Middlesbrough, the three clubs came together on-air too, though initially confidence in the show's prospects of being a success was far from unanimous. But doubts were cast aside, as Malcolm gave up plans to return down south, Eric made the switch from Metro Radio and Bernie increased his links with Century that already involved commentating on every Boro match as Alastair Brownlee's sidekick.

All three of them were contacted by Century officials to consider the idea of being part of a revolutionary show that would prove phenomenally popular with football fans throughout the region. It was Century's plan to update their phone-in show, then hosted by former Newcastle and Sunderland skipper Bob Moncur and Alastair Brownlee, with a completely new format.

As he was already on the radio station's books, Bernie was the first to be contacted. 'I had a meeting with the Century gaffers at The Tall Trees Hotel in Yarm,' he recalls. 'They told me they had an idea of putting three ex-players together for a phone-in show, representing Boro, Sunderland and Newcastle – in order, the north-east's three biggest football clubs. Century wanted me to be the Boro man. Naturally, I was up for it.

'They told me they were considering Peter Beardsley and Gary Rowell as the respective representatives of Newcastle and Sunderland. I understand Beardsley was approached but didn't fancy it. I said that if for any reason Gary Rowell couldn't do it then Eric Gates would be good at it, but Gatesy was at Metro and everyone thought that wouldn't change. Although we weren't mates back then, I knew Gatesy was a bit of a character as I had bumped into him from time to time. It's history now that they eventually lined up Gatesy and Malcolm Macdonald.'

With Bernie in the bag, Century approached Eric and Malcolm, though it is the subject of some debate if The Three Legends might otherwise have been completed by Gary Rowell and Peter Beardsley. Malcolm, for his part, does not believe his fellow Geordie hero Beardsley was ever seriously considered.

Century approached Supermac knowing he had worked with them in the past but was now planning to leave the north-east behind. 'Having done my own thing for a couple of years since leaving my previous role with Century, I got a phone call from Steve Mackie at the station, asking me to come in,' says Malcolm. 'I told him I didn't want my time wasting but he assured me that wouldn't be the case. Century had been taken over by Capital and he wanted me to meet Nick Davidson, the new managing director.

'A few days later, I sat down with Nick and he told me that he had this idea in his head. He said he had talked to people who knew the industry and the north east and that everybody kept throwing two names at him to get on the payroll. One was Mike "The Mouth" Elliott, and the other was me.

'He told me that they wanted to revolutionise their phone-in show to cover the three Premiership clubs. He said that they had Bernie Slaven lined up for Middlesbrough while he mentioned Gary Rowell in terms of Sunderland. I hadn't met Gary but I knew him as a player and knew the way he thought. Nick asked me how I saw it going.

'I told him that we could be three ex-professional footballers trying to be radio presenters and make a right hash of it - or we could be three ex-professional footballers who go into a radio studio but treat it like a dressing room. He sat up and his ears pricked like a cat's. I pointed out that the first and last thing that happens in a football dressing room was that everybody took the p***. Nothing like what I was suggesting had ever been done on radio before. I saw us going into the studio with nothing written down at all, just to let footballers' humour propel it and see where it went. On hearing this, Nick said he wasn't now going to get Gary but Eric Gates. No offence to Gary, but it was a great decision by Nick because Eric has a brilliant but dry sense of humour.'

The fact that Eric had been on the books of rival radio station Metro until his shock departure is also likely to have been an influencing factor in Century's thinking. Eric was still reeling from his sudden exit when he received a similar call to the one Malcolm had taken from Steve Mackie.

'Eric, I've heard you're not at Metro anymore,' said Mackie. 'Would you be interested in coming to Century?'

'What have you got lined up?' asked Eric.

Once again, Mackie explained the planned format for the show but Eric was bemused. 'Two hours, Monday to Friday?' he shrieked. 'It won't work!'

Recalling the conversation, he says, 'I thought talking football two hours solid every night would bore the pants off people. I felt maybe half an hour would work. But I was out of work, so I asked which other players they were thinking about. He said Bernie Slaven was nailed on, while Newcastle they hadn't decided but it would either be Peter Beardsley or Malcolm Macdonald.

'I asked them to call me back the next day while I thought it over. I think they were offering me £60 a show. I knew it would cost me £20 a night in petrol. But with my Metro work down the pan, I had little else on so I agreed to do it show by show through to Christmas with no contract. If I wasn't happy I would walk away.'

So while Malcolm and Bernie were convinced the show could be a success, Gatesy was sceptical but enthusiastic. But none of them could have guessed just how popular the phone-in would prove to be.

'Bernie was full of enthusiasm because it made him a six-days-a-week employee' explains Malcolm. 'He could focus the radio station with his life. I could see that it could be a success but it had never been done on radio before. It was so refreshingly new and we were being given a blank canvass. Gatesy didn't think it would work but he decided to suck it and see.

'We had an informal agreement that we would do it until Christmas and see how it went. But very quickly the figures in terms of the number of listeners were sensational. From there, protracted negotiations began because in those first six months we did it for peanuts and we needed contracts if we were to commit to it. Radio is not television, it's a quite different market. There's a lot less loyalty in radio than there is in television so the contracts were important for us.'

By then, even Eric's initial doubts about the show's potential had been swept away on a tide of phone calls, football and fun. 'Come Christmas we all agreed it was going great,' he says. 'The figures went crazy. It surprised me because I never imagined it would be such a success. But the three of us just gelled. I knew of Bernie and Malcolm but didn't know either of them well. I had played against both of them, of course, while I used to meet Bernie at the "grab a granny" night at Hardwick Hall. Malcolm was a great player and it was brilliant to play against him. I was in awe of him. He was a big name and I thought what a great name to have on the show.'

Bernie believes a key to the show's success was the way the trio took the winning mentality that had made them such a success as players into the studio. He explains, 'As strikers who scored the best part of 500 career goals between us, we had always believed in setting ourselves ambitious targets. Our philosophy didn't change once we went on-air, telling the gaffers at Century that we aimed to eventually overtake the station's breakfast show as the most listened to programme. At any radio station, the morning slot is the top show, usually boasting the most listeners. At Century, Paul "Goffy" Goff was the breakfast show's high-profile presenter, but we had no interest in reputation. People within the organisation laughed at us, believing we had no chance of achieving our aim, but we were deadly serious.

'During our first few shows those who had written us off must have felt as smug as Malcolm after a rare victory by the Geordies. We were lucky if we had a couple of callers each night so the three of us had to do most of the talking. We were new to the game but we were determined to get better. After a slow start, things began to pick up and our listening figures became increasingly impressive. Nowadays, we'll have had 40 callers and there's still another dozen who can't get on.

'What's more, we've achieved what we set out to do. The Three Legends phone-in is now Century's most popular show. We take pride when people who know far more about radio than we do express their astonishment that we can attract 250,000 listeners a night, especially between 6pm and 8pm in the evening. That means we've trebled our listener figures since our earliest shows. Even more impressive is our audience share. One in four people listening to the radio in the north-east region between 6pm and 8pm weekdays listen to our phone-in. When you think of the multitude of national and local radio stations out there, those figures are unbelievable. To put them into context, our audience share when we first started out was just 8 per cent. I think there is resentment from some radio presenters that three hippies have walked off the football field into the studio and achieved listener figures they could only dream about.'

So what makes the show so popular? The Legends themselves point to the humour and passion of north-east football fans, but there can be little doubt that the decision to bring Bernie, Gatesy and Supermac together on-air was an inspired one. Although they are all very different characters, they have bonded together in a way that makes the show a must-hear experience from many of the region's football

faithful. And there can be little doubt that their banter – brought from the dressing room into listeners' homes and cars via the power of the radio – is a major factor in the Three Legends' ongoing popularity.

Every night the trio devote much time and energy into winding each other up, often forcing their fellow presenters into a corner on the latest issues at Newcastle, Boro and Sunderland. But what do the trio really think about each other?

Let's talk about Gatesy first. Malcolm certainly has plenty to say about Mr Gates. 'Gatesy was one of the most cunning, clever players that I ever came across,' he smiles. 'He was sly so you didn't know what he was going to do next. He was very clever on the ball, had a fabulous touch and was a very good passer. Gatesy was a 'selfish' player, as Bernie and I were, not purely to score goals but to play people in all of the time. He was brilliant at it. He was always looking to play the killer ball. I don't think he's changed much because he's always looking for the killer punchline on the show. There are times when he'll say something and you know you can't say it any better.

'But Gatesy is a very difficult character to work with. He is very aggressive and I think he makes enemies wherever he goes because of it. He'll probably call me stubborn but, my God, a lot of the time it's his way or no way. He's all shouting, screaming and bluster. But a dressing room is a great experience and prepares you for many similar situations in life. It's all very well knowing the weaknesses of players but you have to ignore them, find their strengths and play to them. That will make him a better player and, in turn, it will make you a better player. In a similar way we look for each other's strengths in the studio. So when Eric goes off on one while we're off-air I just go away and sort emails out or whatever. I've learned to live with him.

'Eric also has a short attention span. I have always enjoyed debating different issues in detail but I used to notice that while something was being discussed he would be getting frustrated and angry. I can go on about things and Gatesy and Bernie would cut me short. I wouldn't show it but Gatesy could sense that, in turn, I would start to get annoyed. But the more I thought about it and the more I saw him wanting to move on to the next issue or the next call, I realised it was perhaps better for the programme not to get too deeply into issues, at least not too often. Eric's style is wham, bam, thank you ma'am. I realised that maybe I was wrong and that it was actually a strength of the programme that he would say, "Right, that's enough, next subject, let's move on". That way we can cover a huge gamut of subjects. But Gatesy is a moaner, without any shadow of a doubt. He could go into paradise and find fault all over the place!'

There are few things that Malcolm and Bernie agree on – but one is that Eric is Premier League champion at whining. 'He's an unbelievable moaner,' nods Bernie. 'He is always moaning. It gets you down listening to it every night. But it's not our fault the team he supports have been so crap. Unfortunately, it got to the stage where he didn't want to talk about Sunderland any more. He was bored with them. He wanted to do the Ten Grand Fan instead. He loves the quiz, he's more into that than he is doing the phone-in. He lights up at quiz time, while I'm the opposite and find it a turn-off because I've never been into quizzes. I can only presume he was into pub quizzes when he was younger.

'But I love working with Gatesy. Like a good goalscoring partnership, we complement each other. He is a real character and we get on well, both during the phone-in and away from the show.

• A BIG IMPROVEMENT ON MALCOLM! Eric and Bernie enjoy a pre-show chat with Century's Maddy Briggs.

'Mind you, there is no disputing that he's got a face for radio. I'm not surprised the audience figures were down after the phone-in was shown on Tyne-Tees TV a few times! Eric's a nice guy, but that face just isn't made for television.'

Before we move on to our next victim, it's only fair that we give Eric a chance to respond to Malcolm's accusation that he is aggressive. In his own defence, he claims that his bark is much worse than his bite. 'I've fallen out with everybody at Century,' he admits. 'People don't know how to take me. I'm like a Jack Russell. I speak my mind and shout at people. I think I scare people but I don't mean to. I'm harmless really. I was like that in the dressing room as a player. I've always had the attitude that if there's something to say I'll say it.'

Now for Bernie! First up with his views on the Boro man is Malcolm. 'Bernie is the wacky one of the three of us. Bernie and Eric have created a madcap relationship and when it starts to spark between them I just let them go and see where it takes us, even if the clock is running over. That's when you get the very best radio. I am happy to just sit back and let them. Bernie sparks a lot of that off.

'I will take my hat off to Bernie. I probably give him more stick than I give Eric simply because I think Bernie opens himself up to it. He sets himself up, playing the jester by saying things like, "I'm not Scottish, I'm Irish". But he never takes umbrage with all the stick he gets. He will laugh at it and see the funny side even though the joke is on him. I admire him for that. He never gets vengeful about it; he just carries on in his usual way. He gets his own back in the natural process of things so he doesn't have to make a concerted effort. That is an important key, that we've got a good sense of humour.

'Bernie is daft but some very funny things come out of his mouth. He often makes me sit up and think, "Where the hell did that one come from?" Now and again the cleverness of what Bernie says gets lost in his daftness. But I realised a long time ago that, like Eric, Bernie has a very short attention span. However, while Eric would get annoyed and demand to move on to another topic, after about 90 seconds Bernie would just switch off and disappear onto another planet!'

The point Malcolm makes about allowing his fellow presenters to enjoy their madcap moments is seen in a rather different light by Eric, who says, 'I always thought Bernie was a Jack the Lad but I liked his character and we get on like a house on fire on the phone-in. Bernie is always up for having a laugh, so we click as a partnership. We can laugh at each other, we can take the Mick out of each other and we bounce off each other. It all goes over Malcolm's head because he's too slow to get our jokes.

'I always thought I was a bit hyper, but since getting to know Bernie, I've realised I'm relatively normal. Bernie is ten times worse than me. He is so scatter-brained that he doesn't know what he's doing from one day to the next. In Bernie, I have found someone who is worse than me for lateness, not wanting to do things and that you can't rely on. He is murder, he's such hard work. His mind wanders throughout the show and half the time you think he's not involved in it. For two hours, he will read the papers, pick his nose and pick his toenails. He's unbelievable.

'We all need to listen in to calls but Bernie seems to switch off and pick a paper up if it's not about Middlesbrough. Then somebody will him ask a question and he'll say something off the top of his head that tells you that he hasn't been listening. Other times, when a question is suddenly directed at him, he'll look up from the paper, take his headphones off and ask, "What's he been saying, Gatesy?" and I'll have to whisper in his ear. But you won't change him, that's just the way he is. He's a one-off.

'What's more, he doesn't do anything when it comes to planning the show. If you try to plan anything, he doesn't want to know – and he's always first out of the studio as soon as the show's over. But Bernie's got a heart of gold. The charity thing he did with his autobiography, raising over £30,000 for sufferers of multiple sclerosis, you just can't knock him for that.'

Now it's time for Eric and Bernie to have their say on Malcolm – and it's no holds barred. Bernie goes first. 'Malcolm is selfish, obnoxious, arrogant, sarcastic and smug. He does my head in. In his mind, he is infallible. He believes that what he says is gospel and that he is never wrong. Of course, as all right-thinking listeners to the show know, that isn't true. I didn't know Malcolm before The Three Legends show, but he's had quite a life. He's been through the mill in his lifetime

and has come through the other side. Basically, he's done it all, while me and Gatesy are still trying to do it.

'Me, Eric and Malcolm work well together, probably because we are three different animals. I see Malcolm as the headmaster. He is prim, proper and well educated, with a posh London accent. Me and Gatesy are the pupils, acting like children, having a laugh and talking about any subject that comes into our heads.

'Malcolm's a different generation to us two. I'm the baby out of the three of us. I'm in my mid-40s, Gatesy is 50-odd and Malcolm is 85. He is as deep as the ocean and tries to belittle us two, looking down his nose at us. He's got his posh accent, while me and Gatesy are rough. He likes to use these long words that I would have to look up in the dictionary. Gatesy and I look at each other and wonder what he's talking about, but the truth is I don't think even Malcolm knows what some of the words he uses mean. There is a warm side to him too, but if I was a listener at home, hearsay what he says, I think I'd have thrown my radio out of the window by now.

'But the great thing about all three of us is that what you hear is what you get. I know some radio deejays who come off-air and they are totally different people - they are an act. If you bumped into us in a bar, you would recognise the very same personalities that you hear each night on the phone-in. On air, what you hear is three former professional footballers being themselves, talking just as we would if we were sitting around a table in a pub. People know we've got no airs and graces. Fans can come on, call us names and generally hammer us. We accept it as banter and give as much back in return.'

Before we discover what Eric has to say about Malcolm's character, let's give Supermac a chance to respond on the issue of his long words. 'I do play up to it because I know it irritates the other two,' he insists. 'I look for opportunities just to throw in as big a word as I can because it brings out such brilliant reactions from them. Bernie says I don't know what they mean but I can tell him that I do know the meaning of the words I use, but I always use them for effect.'

Now it's Eric's turn to have his say on Malcolm. 'I always thought Malcolm was arrogant – and he is. It seemed to me that he had a chip on his shoulder. What came across loud and clear was, "I'm the greatest thing and I know everything." He is an arrogant b*****d but I can honestly say this about him – he's a nicer man than people realise. I feel he's a better person now than he was when he joined the show. He's had great times in his life and he's had some bad times as well, but he's come out of it at the other end. Malcolm's all right and I respect him. Having said that, there is no doubt that he offends people and gets their backs up.

'And it's got to be said that Malcolm is far too slow. Maybe me and Bernie are too quick but Malcolm waffles on and you think he'll never make his point. If he was a record you'd think it was stuck. Sometimes Bernie has read the whole paper by the time Malcolm has read out an email – mind it's usually *The Sun*, so it doesn't take that long. When it's clear Malcolm is going to go into one, Bernie lifts the paper up and I'm on my own with Malcolm. I do give Malcolm a hard time for it but I think he can see the funny side.'

While the Three Legends are undoubtedly a crucial ingredient to the show, Eric believes the callers are even more important to the show. 'It's not us three that make the show,' he insists. 'It's the listeners and the callers. We help, of course, but a lot of it is down to the football and the passion of the people. The different characters that call us up really make the show. And it always amazes me how many people say they don't really follow football but they always listen to the show because they like the craic. They might not understand the game but they can still listen in and have a laugh at the banter and the jokes.

'The importance of humour on the show is total. I wouldn't be doing it if it didn't have any humour in. We couldn't just sit and talk football for two hours every night without it. It would bore the pants of people if we just sat and talked football, tactics and formations. I've had people say to me, "That show last night was the funniest thing I've heard." We will take the Mickey about Malcolm sounding like a cow when he's going "Mmmmm" when he's considering a point that's been made. And we all know that Bernie sounds like Rab C. Nesbitt and plays the bagpipes brilliantly. It is strange how he can suddenly be Scottish again when Scotland win a couple of games!

The humorous calls are the ones that people remember and that's what makes us stand out from other shows. I do

deliberately wind up Newcastle and Boro fans. I have to, because I'd have topped myself if I had tried to just talk about Sunderland for the last few years. I leave myself open to get ridiculed back in return but I've got to do it, if only to deflect the attention away from Sunderland. Sunderland's results have been so bad at times that there has been no banter at all among their fans. They have had no fight left in them because there was nothing they could say anymore without being shot down.'

Malcolm agrees that banter and humour are all-important. 'What is key is that out there in the north-east the sense of humour is absolutely brilliant, and that's reflected in the callers. Fans hear the banter between the three of us and want to take part and have their say. We could have made the most horrendous of cock-ups when we first went on-air. The reason we didn't – and this is a key reason why the programme has become so successful – is that we took the p*** out of each other and we took the p*** out of each other's clubs. Then, when the callers came on, one of us would be critical and the other two would be the person's friend. On a constant basis we will push callers into a corner of having to make a choice on whatever subject they have called to discuss.'

It's clear that the show would die a death if the calls dried up so the three have devised different tactics on how to turn listeners into callers. 'If there have been no games over the weekend, it can initially be quiet,' says Bernie. 'We know people are listening but they're just not calling. Hit on the right subject and the switchboard will light up. It doesn't have to be football, sometimes it's a quiz question, sometimes it's an outrageous statement designed to get up the noses of the fans of one of our clubs. Offering a signed ball to anyone who comes on usually works too.'

Malcolm agrees that they find provoking a reaction with outrageous comments or actions has a tendency to get the callers flooding in. He recalls, 'The night after Portugal knocked England out of the World Cup, Bernie played the Portuguese national anthem. That's Bernie showing his nationalistic tendencies - not that he knows what his own nation is - but he is taking the p***. The more people hate him for it, the better it is for the show. It makes them call, email and text, telling him to shut up or reminding him of the fact that neither of his countries of choice, Scotland or Ireland, were even at the World Cup.'

The quality of the callers varies vastly, from the straight talking to the nonsensical, from the boring to the whacky. Eric summarises the worst in a typically succinct fashion. 'I have to say some of the fans talk dire sh**!' he moans. 'There's many time where I think, "What a clown this guy is."'

Bernie goes into more depth. 'The callers are a completely mixed bag. Some guys that come on are clearly clued up, they know more than they should, probably because they've been talking to someone at one of the clubs. Others talk such utter tripe you would think they had just arrived in a spaceship from Mars. Then there's the punters that think they're Jose Mourinho, that they are some sort of master tactician. Others are plain funny, while some just like the sound of their own voice.'

But it's a case of saints and sinners, welcome all, as Malcolm explains. 'There is an absolute unity between all three of us - and that is the belief that everybody – and we mean everybody – is entitled to their opinion. They might talk absolute rubbish - that is immaterial. Our programme is their vehicle to voice that opinion, no matter what it is.'

So why do people call the show? Bernie thinks he has the answer. 'I see the phone-in as being like a confessional box for north-east football fans. It's their chance to get things off their chest. Apart from the pub, there's nowhere else for them to do that so it's an outlet, a platform for them to feel like their views matter. That can only be a good thing for fans and north-east football in general. Those who come on the show to let off steam probably go to their team's next game less frustrated, having said what they need to say.'

Malcolm and Bernie believe that many supporters call the show as a way of giving indirect feedback to the football clubs. Malcolm says, 'What we get is an awful lot of people who talk to us hoping and praying that somebody at their club is listening and that the message gets through to the decision-makers. We always say, "Don't worry, they're listening". Of course, not all of them will be listening but somebody from the club will be. I think people feel that by communicating with us they can get a message across. It's

the only forum the fans have. They can write a letter to their local paper but it doesn't mean they are going to get it published. If they phone our programme, they know they are going to go out on air.'

Bernie picks up on this point, adding, 'Some of our callers phone up in the hope that their team's manager or players might be listening to the show. They want to let them know how they are feeling, especially when results aren't going well. We do know players and managers listen to the phone-in, though they don't always appreciate what the fans or the three of us have to say.

'I know some people think such detailed scrutiny of our clubs can be damaging but I personally believe a little criticism can be a good thing. I would even go as far as to recommend that the managers of our local sides make a point of tuning in occasionally. As a manager, you're in a cocoon in which you only get to hear a watered down version of what people really think. It would be easy to believe that everything in the garden is rosy when, in truth, there are justifiable grumbles. Most fans would be too intimidated to tell their team's manager their honest views if they met him face-to-face, so the phone-in presents a real opportunity.'

While all fans desperately want their team to be successful, it is a well known fact that local newspapers and fanzines sell more copies on the back of bad results. It's human nature to want to read the views of like-minded, disappointed fellow fans. By the same token, some of the best Three Legends shows come off the back of disastrous results for the north-east's big three.

'There's no denying that the phone-in is at its best when teams are having a bad time,' admits Bernie. 'Bad results translate to more and better calls to the phone-in. People find it easier to have a go than to praise. Many of them know what they're talking about and are spot-on with their views. They know the game and are frustrated by what they are seeing.'

Malcolm agrees, saying, 'Fans will always find it easier to create conversation when things are wrong. I think calling us is a way for fans to show their desire to make things better. When things are right they don't necessarily understand why they are working but they can often see the faults when things are going awry. I think football just mirrors life in general. That's why football is so popular. It's a simplified version of life.'

So are critical calls the best calls? 'No,' replies Malcolm. 'I think they're important, but I think the most important calls are those when a supporter might have a very valid point, it might even be critical, but he or she comes on and has a right good

•SHOW TIME:
The Legends, pictured here with Century's technical wizard Rod Hardisty, have their own specific seats for the phone-in.

laugh and brings across a humour. I think that is the whole basis on which the show works. They can talk about any serious points but the humour is underlying.'

As much as poor results can turn angry fans into Three Legends callers, too many bad results can go beyond the pale, where sarcastic humour or even anger gives way to resignation. That, in turn, means fewer calls to Century. To twist a well-known phrase, you can have too much of a bad thing, as the Legends discovered during Sunderland's awful 2005-06 Premier League campaign.

'It went too far for Sunderland in their relegation season because there wasn't anything more to be said,' Malcolm reflects. 'I felt sorry for Eric. It was the equivalent of laying in a coffin and being told to write a comedy script. It was dreadful. We were trying to bring Eric into the programme but long before the end of the season he was just repeating himself. There was just nothing else left to say. It got to the stage

where the callers wouldn't take the p*** any more. I don't think I've ever witnessed a football club and all the people involved hitting rock bottom quite like that. Even die-hard haters of the club, like Newcastle fans, stopped taking the Mickey. In the good times when they were successful, Eric had said that if the club took it for granted they would go the way that Sunderland had gone so many times before. He went on record as saying there was an arrogance creeping in. He prophesised the disaster that was waiting to happen but he never gloated when he was proved right. When it all went wrong again, he could so easily have gone "I told you so," but I felt he retained a certain grace through it all.

'Gatesy will be praying that Sunderland top the Championship and that Newcastle and Middlesbrough have bad seasons in 2006-07 because he had the greatest misery any radio presenter has ever suffered during his club's awful season, facing 10 hours a week of utter p***-taking until even Newcastle supporters felt it cruel to go on.

'There were times when I did wonder if Gatesy might just jack it all in. I could well have understood it if he had done so. But one of Bernie's strengths is his empathy for hurt and sick animals so his heart went out to Gatesy! Nurse Slaven really came to the fore during the latter part of their relegation season.'

Eric readily confesses he got little satisfaction out of co-hosting the phone-in during Sunderland's disastrous return to the top flight. 'I find it tough going when the team are struggling. I want the club to do well because the town is buzzing when the team are winning games. But for too long the Sunderland fans have had nothing. Last season they gave up the ghost. If you're having a bad time you get more callers, but Sunderland have been so bad that it has gone too far and, as a result, we hardly get any callers. Last season as we lost game after game it got to such a low level that there was nothing more to be said. We beat the Boro away and I played on that one for about a week but apart from that there was hardly a thing. It went past the point of banter or giving views on what could have been done differently. The place was flat as a pancake.

'There have been times when I haven't fancied going on the show. The bad run in 2005-06 even affected my matchday routine. I've always enjoyed arriving at the ground about an hour before kick-off, having a drink and a chat with people, and then staying around after the game and enjoying the banter, but I started arriving about 10 minutes before kick-off and shooting off straight after the game. The place just became depressing.'

The rivalry between fans of the three clubs is another issue the Legends play on. Bernie says, 'Like the three opposing teams we represent, me, Gatesy and Malcolm try to come out on top each night. Some nights you win, other nights you get hammered - by the other two and by the callers. I love trying to wind up the callers – especially the Newcastle fans. It makes my weekend when I know Newcastle have been gubbed and Boro have won. Equally, if we get walloped and Newcastle do well it does my head in because I know what's coming during the phone-in. Malcolm will be as smug as he likes.'

Being smug is an accusation Bernie frequently throws in Malcolm's direction, so now is a good time to ask Supermac if it's a fair description. 'Am I smug? Yes, I suppose maybe it comes over as a smugness' he answers, with a knowing smile. 'Sunderland can't be relied upon to maintain their status, while Middlesbrough have always struggled even to be bridesmaids of north-east football. They've just managed to overcome that hurdle in recent years, but in the eyes of Geordies everything is a test for Middlesbrough. Newcastle have the better record and we are the ones that go out and buy the top names. All of a sudden, Middlesbrough are getting ideas above their station but whatever they do they are never going to be as good as Newcastle. I will perpetuate that feeling and go out of my way to find every smug thing that I can say because I know that gets Bernie's back right up and p***es him off – and I like to see him p***ed off! Plus, of course, I know it gets callers.'

One of Malcolm's favourite taunts is that Bernie often sits on the fence with Boro issues. It's an accusation Bernie strongly refutes but Malcolm is sticking with it.

'Bernie does sit on the fence,' he states. 'He is closer to Middlesbrough Football Club than Eric or I are to our respective clubs. I think the way that Middlesbrough chairman Steve Gibson goes about his business is absolutely brilliant.

He makes friends where most chairmen make enemies. It's clever and it's a gift. Nevertheless it still leaves the latitude for opinions to be given. But Bernie will not have a go at Middlesbrough because it might sound as if he's having a go at Steve Gibson. So he is careful of criticising people at the club because they are Gibson's appointments.

'I am critical of Bernie in that respect but I understand that there is a greater connection between him and his club than with myself and Newcastle. It's two-fold. Bernie has always lived in the Boro since he came down from Scotland while also the club went bust when he was there as a player and he has seen the thing disappear in a pit of flames before the club made its phoenix-like recovery. That has given him a unique affinity that Eric and I can't have because we haven't experienced anything like that.

'I do wind him up about his relationship with Steve. I will push him and he gets defensive and a little bit stroppy with me. But what it usually prompts is callers coming on and defending Bernie and defending the club. There is nothing to create a bit of patriotism that wasn't there than a foreigner having a go. And I am the "foreigner" having a go at Middlesbrough that makes Boro supporters call up to defend their club and have a go at me. But I have never known such critical supporters as Middlesbrough's are towards their club. I think it's the Yorkshire element in their thinking; their pots are half-empty rather than half-full.'

Eric agrees. 'Bernie definitely sits on the fence. He's got a closeness with the club, partly through Ali Brownlee, his Boro co-commentator. I think that in the early stages of the show he was frightened to upset people at the club. To be fair to him, I think he came out of his shell and he says it like it is now. He does sit on the fence quite a bit and we will tell him that he's got splinters in his backside. He doesn't like us saying that!

'Having said that, I think Malcolm wants to keep in with Newcastle and is quite loathe to have too much of a pop at the main regime there, but he's not frightened to have a go at the players. Let's put it like this - half of Bernie's backside sits on the fence, a quarter of Malcolm's does and there's only Eric's that is either on one side of it or the other. I've never been accused of sitting on the fence – never!'

The implication that Bernie avoids making controversial comments about Boro is one he is keen to contest. 'Gatesy and Malcolm have accused me of sitting on the fence on certain subjects, but I also get Boro fans telling me I'm over-critical. It's a no-win situation. I don't go out of my way to upset anyone but I won't say something I don't believe just to avoid rocking the boat. I've learned over the years on Century that you have to be you. You have to say what you see. That's what I try to do. I know some things I say might upset or even offend players, but I am simply giving my view of what I am seeing on the pitch.

Thousands of football fans throughout the north-east listen to the Three Legends show every night and we owe them to at least be honest with our views. If a player is having a bad time, his touch isn't right or he is missing chances, I will say so but I will also try to point out that he's still a good player. If a player is crap on any particular day then I'll say he's crap.'

Bernie's 'special' relationship with Steve Gibson led to the Boro chairman making a memorable guest appearance on the phone-in October 2005. Gibson joined Bernie in the press box at the home ground of Swiss side Grasshoppers as Boro prepared for a UEFA Cup tie, determined to tackle growing disquiet among supporters at the team's inconsistent form.

Bernie recalls that Gibson came to appear on the show after the pair chatted during the flight from Teesside to Switzerland. 'I said to Gibbo that if he wanted to come on the show that would be great. When he said he would like to come on, I asked him if he was talking about taking a few calls but he insisted he would be happy to come on for the full duration of the show. Beforehand, I told him "Don't forget, Gibbo, nothing's scripted. We don't know who's coming on or what questions are going to be asked. You just have to deal with it." Mike O'Neill, his business partner, assured me he would be fine – and he was right.

I thought he was great and he dealt with the callers brilliantly. He got all the plaudits and I felt he came up smelling of roses. In fact, he should have given me a few quid for letting him go on our show! In all honesty, I was hoping there would be a few tougher questions. If I had been a fan I'd have given him a harder time. We asked him some serious questions, but I think some fans froze. But the upshot was that they felt he

was one of them.'

But Bernie was stunned to hear Gibson inform Boro fans that he had told manager Steve McClaren that the club had to go on the attack when playing at home. 'He said that he had told McClaren that there would be no repeat of playing one up front at home. I thought that was a bit bizarre. Gibbo has always backed his managers but I felt that was overriding his position as Chairman. If I'd been manager and he'd done that to me, I'd have been unhappy. I'd have told him that it was my job to decide formations. I can imagine McClaren wasn't happy, though it might have woken him up and made him realise how fed up the fans were at seeing us play one up front at the Riverside against mid-table sides.'

The following February, with Boro suffering a mid-season crisis and many fans calling for McClaren to be sacked, the club's chief executive Keith Lamb followed Gibson's lead by appearing on the show. He answered many difficult questions, defending McClaren's record and explaining why the club had decided to give him an extended contract. But the show's final call resulted in Lamb making a startling revelation – that McClaren had not yet signed the contract, several months after it had been claimed he had done so.

Bernie smiles as he remembers the moment. 'The show had gone very well and Keith was great. Then a caller asked him a question about the contract and Keith revealed that he hadn't actually signed it, that there was some technicality still to be sorted. To be fair to Keith, he could have lied. Instead, there was a silence, and then he told the truth. I couldn't believe it.

Looking back, I think it was a good move by Keith because it made McClaren sign the contract. If he had been offered the England job and had still not signed the contract it would have cost the club money because he could potentially have just walked away without the club getting a penny in compensation. So it was clever and shrewd of Keith.'

While Sunderland and Newcastle appear reticent to acknowledge the show's existence, Boro's policy of having officials call and even guest on the show is one that Malcolm applauds. 'Middlesbrough FC are prepared to work with us and I have to say they go up in our estimation because of that.

Steve Gibson goes, "Hey, I've got something to say, I want to come on your programme." Terrific, he is welcome. We asked him pertinent questions and he answered them. He goes way up in our estimation. Keith Lamb did the same and others from the club phone up time and again and say, "I've heard a discussion. Can I just put you right on something?" We will still be critical towards Boro but we finish up saying well done to them more than we do to the other two. We struggle to praise Newcastle and Sunderland because they have this aloof, arrogant attitude towards us.'

Gatesy admits he would have preferred to have received the occasional call from those in charge at the Stadium of Light. 'I think people from the executive side from the club could have come on the show over the years and I think it would have done them a favour, but some people resent the show, possibly because it is too honest. I think Middlesbrough were like that to start with and Newcastle are still like that. It would be nice for the new regime at Sunderland not to be totally against the show. I hope they will recognise that we are behind the club, we want them to do well but that if it's not good we'll say so. Certainly I'd like to think that I personally would have a better rapport with the club than I have had in the past.'

There can be little doubt that many of the Legends' no-holds-barred comments about north-east football go down like a lead balloon within the walls of St James' Park, the Stadium of Light and the Riverside Stadium. But neither Eric, Bernie nor Malcolm will bow to any pressure they come under to temper their comments.

'I do think we p*** them off,' reflects Malcolm. 'We weren't chosen for our diplomatic skills. Although we rarely all agree, all three of us can be controversial in our different ways. None of us beat around the bush. I call a spade a spade, Gatesy is very much that way, while Bernie can sit on the fence and then suddenly jump off and come out with the most alarmingly extreme view that makes you wonder, "Where did that come from?"

'We don't go out of our way to be controversial because I think we are naturally that way inclined. We haven't got axes to grind. When something is good we will say it's good and applaud them. But when we have got an honest viewpoint to

be made, we will make it, regardless of whether any football club, official or player likes it or not. People often complain about TV pundits who are basically told what to refer to and what not to mention. We're not like that. One of the strengths of our show is that it is unscripted and we won't dodge topics just because they are controversial.'

Malcolm believes all three clubs should look on the Three Legends show as a great positive. 'It's free advice for them, both from us and their customers, the fans,' he explains. 'Far from the show damaging north-east football, it's wonderful free advertising for the clubs. It's promoting their brand 10 hours a week. The clubs should pay us! They might not be prepared to say this publicly, but in their heart of hearts, I think the clubs would begrudgingly admit there's a lot of common sense spoken on the show and it's a great way to get feedback about how their supporters are feeling. Enough comes back to us that we know that people at the clubs are listening. If we were insignificant, they wouldn't be listening, nor would they be worried what we said.

'Fans call the show not just to criticise but through a genuine desire to make their club and team better. What the football clubs sometimes fail to appreciate is that the criticism they hear isn't the be all and end all. Yes, it might touch raw nerves at times but that's not really the issue at stake. Football clubs make that the issue but the truth is that humour is key first and foremost.

Two years after The Three Legends began we were shifted out of Century's sports budget into the entertainment budget. That's how the radio station sees us and that's how the football clubs should see us as well. They have to listen to the fans and take seriously what they say but they shouldn't take the three of us as seriously as they do. Let's face it, if there's a problem at the football club, it will be discussed in minute detail for two hours on the Monday night but by the following night it's often forgotten. There's a saying that goes today's news is tomorrow's fish and chip paper. You can't make radio shows into fish and chip paper but the same principle applies and we move on to new issues.'

But Malcolm reiterates the importance of clubs taking seriously the views of their fans. 'I said this as a player and I'm still saying it now all these years later that the north-east clubs

11

have incredible support. They can rely on the people to come in no matter what but that's not necessarily a good thing. The supporters go through thick and thin, no matter what, which means they sometimes get taken for granted. I think Steve Gibson has started to change that trend. He truly wants to create a success there for the supporters, but I haven't been convinced at all by Sunderland and Newcastle and all that they have done. The clubs should be prepared to work a little more with us than against us. I just wonder if the take-over with Niall Quinn could pre-empt a better relationship with Sunderland. I'm sure it will.

'The show gives the fans a voice they've never had and that is vitally important. We say to them they've got to have a voice, they've got to stand up for themselves and not be treated like fodder. They're not just supporters of a football club, they are a business's best customers and every customer has rights. We have told them they have been taken for granted for too long and that they shouldn't be happy to accept second best. If Marks and Spencer or any other businesses treated customers the same way, they would just say, "I'm sorry, I'm not going to shop here again." But because it's a football club and you are dealing with issues of the heart people wouldn't go elsewhere. Sometimes some might say is enough is enough and not go at all but the majority will keep going.'

Bernie, meanwhile, believes The Three Legends show should be essential listening for any Newcastle, Middlesbrough or Sunderland manager – at least on an occasional basis. 'I think it would be enlightening for our managers to hear the real views from fans. I know there are some idiots who call the show but there are far more who make some excellent points. I accept that if you're the manager of one of our sides and the team is on a bad run it's not going to do your confidence or spirits any good to listen to your fans publicly slaughter you for two hours. So I'm not advocating that they listen in when their team has suffered a bad defeat, but it would do them a world of good to have a wee listen every now and then just to get an idea of what the fans are thinking and saying. That can only be of benefit.'

Malcolm reveals that comments made on the show have occasionally brought the Legends into conflict with the clubs.

But he insists the clubs have to learn to live with it. 'Trying to convince us to say other than what we think won't work,' he insists. 'It doesn't wash with us and is more likely to send us the other way. I've had journalists ring me up and pass on little messages from the club that I've gone too far or been unfair. On one occasion, a television screen in front of my seat in the press box at St James' went missing. Usually there's a mini TV screen for everyone in the press box to see action replays of key moments but the fella had been specifically told not to put one on my seat. Pathetic! If they do petty things like that, I'll lambaste them and find other things to criticise. It is pointless them trying to stifle us like that. It would be far better for them to work with us.'

Bernie upset Bryan Robson, Terry Venables and Steve McClaren with his comments during their spells in charge at Boro, but it was Peter Reid, during his time at Sunderland, that struck back at him. 'To this day, I'm still not sure what Peter's problem was,' he says. 'The first I knew of any problem was ahead of a north-east derby between Boro and Sunderland when Boro TV attended Reidy's pre-match press conference at the Stadium of Light. Reidy spotted the Boro TV logo on their camera and immediately insisted that the cameraman and reporter were ejected from the stadium, apparently because of their association with me. At the time, I was still working for Boro TV as well as Century.

'I readily admit that I don't sit on the fence when it comes to doling out the criticism but I also like to think that I am balanced in my views. So I was gobsmacked that I could have upset Reid so much that he would take his fury out on two innocent people. The truth is that when Sunderland fans were having a go at Reidy during the Century phone-in I usually stood up for him. He was obviously a listener to the show, if not particularly a fan, as something he had heard had put his nose out.

'I couldn't help but wonder if he had heard something second hand and it was a case of my words being twisted. I readily admit that I have never watched either Sunderland or Newcastle play on a regular basis, nor would I want to, but I do make plenty of comments about both teams and the various personalities, simply because it's all part of the banter we have between the three of us and the listeners. But I have always defended managers, especially when they have been under pressure and callers are insisting they should be sacked. Basically I like to play the devil's advocate.

'I put the incident to the back of my mind until months later when we both took part in a charity game at the Stadium of Light along with other former Boro and Sunderland players. Before the game, Reidy made a point of shaking hands with each player apart from me. He was letting me know how he felt in no uncertain terms, which I didn't have a problem with. At least no one could accuse him of being two-faced. We were actually in the same side and I noted he didn't stoop to refusing to pass to me. As we waited in the centre circle for the second half to begin, the referee was nowhere to be seen so I decided to take the opportunity to try and break the ice.

'I told him he had got it wrong about me and that I had constantly stuck up for him on our radio show. He looked me in the eye, shook my hand and said, "You're right - it's the other f***ing idiots!"

'If I believed that was the end of it I couldn't have been more wrong. The following derby match, Boro TV returned to the Stadium of Light, believing that they would now be welcome as I had assured them there would no longer be a problem. But lo and behold, he threw them out again. So he was two-faced after all. I would rather he had told me his honest opinion when he'd had the chance. I certainly would have respected him more for that.

'One problem with the medium of radio is that people only tend to listen to part of the programme. Only by listening to the full two hours of The Three Legends phone-in will you get the full picture of what we are trying to say, but it's human nature for people to form their opinions based purely on the few minutes they have heard. Unfortunately, it's very easy to get completely the wrong impression by listening into a conversation when so much more may have been said beforehand. That's the downside that I don't like about radio work. People tell their mates or family what they think they heard one of us say on the radio, it gets distorted or they have heard only part of the story, and before you know something that's far from the truth is being reported as fact. It's like a game of Chinese Whispers.

'I would hope anyone who had a problem with what I said about them or what they think I said about them on air would tell me to their face so I could give them my opinion and make sure they know the truth about what exactly I said, as opposed to some twisted or sensationalised version of it. I would be happy to be challenged if I was wrong. I would rather they did that than snub me or call me behind my back. I'm always up front with my views and like others to be up front with theirs in return.'

Malcolm makes an important point about the way listeners can get the wrong end of the stick. 'We read out text messages and emails from fans that may state views which may be geometrically opposed to our own. But to someone who is only half listening, the owner of the opinion as well. Criticism follows'.

While Peter Reid was clearly no fan of The Three Legends, not everyone connected with Sunderland has taken such a negative stance against it over the years, as Malcolm remembers. 'Kevin Phillips was the first player to call the show. He had just completed his move from Sunderland to Southampton and called us to thank the Sunderland supporters for the backing they had given him over the years. He was on for a long time and was prepared to answer all sorts of questions, which we appreciated. My first reaction was well done to him. He clearly understood the people and what the game means to them.

'If nothing else, our programme is the forum of the people. Most players choose to ignore us but that's the worst thing they could do. If I were a player I would not ignore this type of programme and I would be happy to go on any time. But too many modern day players want distance. They don't want to take part in society and they don't relate to the fans. Phillips showed the common touch that day. What it showed was that he understood the fans, something that too many footballers aren't even willing to try to do. What annoys me is that a lot of them give me the impression that it is them that are doing the fans the favour by playing in front of them. In truth, the fans are doing them the favour by paying good money to go and watch them play.'

Eric remembers the call by Phillips with particular affection, as do many of the show's listeners. 'To be fair, there was only ever one or two Sunderland players that seemed to resent the show, though Kevin and Alex Rae were the only ones ever to come on and talk to us,' he explains. 'Kevin was always good with us. Me and him weren't great mates, but we always got on. Kevin's call was arranged through a mutual friend, who said he wouldn't mind coming on to thank the fans for their support. I thought it was brilliant of him. It says a lot about the affinity he had with the Sunderland fans. In the end it caused a bit of controversy because he said that he wouldn't have minded signing for the Boro. That was picked up on by some of the tabloids who twisted it and suggested he had said he would rather have signed for Middlesbrough than Southampton. He didn't say that, as such, because as a professional he was 100 per cent behind his new club, but he was being honest because I'm sure he would have gone to Boro as I know he was settled up in the north-east.'

Criticism, of course, can be a two-way street. Among the accusations launched in the direction of the Legends are that they are vindictive, bitter or both. Bernie strongly refutes these suggestions. 'I do get accused of being vindictive towards players I don't like or that I am somehow jealous of modern day footballers, but that's utter garbage. I stick to my opinion and don't let my personal feelings about individual players cloud my judgement. If a player has done well I will say so, if he hasn't I will say so. Whether he's a friend, enemy or someone I've never met in my life is irrelevant. I pride myself in being honest. If people think we are vindictive that's up to them but I'm not setting out to hurt anyone. I just give my view and people can accept it or reject it, that's up to them.

'I have no envy at all that there's such big money in the game now that wasn't there when I was playing. If players are earning it, then good luck to them. But it annoys me that so many modern day footballers don't have the hunger. That's because they are getting the rewards even though they've not done it. I don't begrudge the top players getting big salaries but a lot of very average players are now on £10,000 a week and more, but some of them couldn't trap a bag of Blue Circle cement. They've got the flash cars, the big house and the holiday homes so how can we expect them to be motivated about playing the game?'

'We are far from being bitter,' insists Malcolm. 'Some people think we should be bitter but the three of us are anything but. What we try to get across is that ours was a completely different type of era. It was so different that it's beyond comparison. People want to make the comparison but the money now is beyond comprehension for the three of us or for anyone taking part in the programme.

'But I also look on it from the viewpoint of supporters. I remember one person came on to criticise a particular player and said "I love my team with all of my heart, but I'm struggling to raise a family and pay my mortgage. My annual salary is a quarter of what that fella earns in a week - and he can't be bothered." That's where the bitterness is and I think it's entirely understandable. I think footballers have been removed from the real world and that is a bad thing.

'It's the ordinary man's game. It's not the possession of hugely-paid super stars. If we are bitter, it is that the last few years have seen footballers able to lock themselves in a type of ivory tower and remove themselves from public life. They have created a bubble. We get the impression at times that the footballers think that it's the public who are the lucky ones to be able to go and watch them. That's arrogance and it does make me feel bitter.'

But Kevin Phillips clearly isn't the only player who has understood the power of the Three Legends show, as Malcolm reveals. 'A few years ago, one of the top names at Newcastle – and I'm not going to name him because he spoke to me in confidence – phoned me and said that a rumour that was doing the rounds was completely wrong. The suggestion that had been made by the Newcastle *Chronicle* was that there had been a rumpus between Bobby Robson and this player. He asked me if I would let it be known that nothing of the kind had ever happened. I did think that the whole thing didn't sound at all like Bobby. So we put it out and we created a bit of a conversation, poo-pooing what had been suggested in the newspaper. When I switched my phone on at the end of the programme, the message came through from the player in question, "That was great. Thanks very much."

'Journalists occasionally approach me to give me information that they daren't use themselves. I use that info on the programme to inform the fans of things I think they ought to know. If it's something I don't feel comfortable saying, there are some occasions when I get Eric to say it and we'll create a conversation around it. He'll say that he has heard something on the grapevine, then it's out in the open and I give my opinion on it.'

On-air disagreements between the Legends are commonplace but the perception that all is peace and harmony off-air can be highly misleading. 'We sit in the same three chairs,' says Malcolm, 'And I have a button next to mine that fires the break. So I will say, "Call us on 0191 477 2000," and this button then plays the 10-second piece about the phone-in before it cuts to adverts. During the break, we have a rabbit about whether there's anything we can pick up on and go for.

'But that's also when the effing and blinding starts, not from me, the other two. I don't tend to swear. I do an awful lot of public speaking where I set out everything I'm going to say and there's the absolute minimum of foul language. I don't swear gratuitously but Eric does. He does it right up until 6pm, then switches into a new mode where he continues to talk with a passion but cuts out all the foul language. Bernie is much the same, but I have to ensure that I don't get sucked in with their flow because I don't have that switch-off. I guess Malcolm Allison didn't either. He swore on air during a Century commentary and has never worked in the industry since. His voice has never been heard on radio again.

'Fortunately, I was taught radio etiquette and microphone technique from an early stage. There's a saying that is legion in all broadcasting that goes "Mics are live at all times." What that means is that even if you are meant to be off-air there is the possibility that your mic might not have been switched off. That's what infamously knackered Ron Atkinson when he started to make some outrageous comments when he thought he was off-air but in fact his mic was picking up everything he was saying and broadcasting it across the Middle-East. Bernie and Eric don't have the background I have with radio so forget about that golden rule of mics are live at all times, so we have to be very careful to ensure the mics are off.'

Had the microphones been left on during a number of fiery ad-breaks then The Three Legends show would have gone

out in a blaze of four-letter publicity, never to be aired again. Tempers have flared between the trio on more than one occasion. Despite Eric's infamous temper, the two occasions when things threatened to get completely out of hand both involved Malcolm and Bernie. The reason for their first major fall-out still baffles Supermac.

Malcolm explains, 'Bernie always goes away for a month or so over the summer. Every year Gatesy and I put together the questions for our Ten Grand Fan quiz, which runs throughout the close season, while Bernie gives us an offering. It could be 200 questions, it could be 20 questions, we never know. Gatesy and I would write the questions onto paper and these would be typed into a computer to the point where we had about 1,400 questions. I realised that we could stick them all together and they would make a quiz book. Gatesy liked the idea, so did Century and we agreed to make it official. I phoned a publisher I new in Leicestershire who do that kind of book and everything happened in the month that Bernie was away. There was a few quid to be made but Bernie got upset about it.'

The fact that Bernie, who had written hardly any of the questions, got so angry with Malcolm, who he says had written only a few more, still puzzles Eric. 'Bernie got upset with Malcolm about the book thing but it's me who does the quizzes. I come up with nearly all the questions. Malcolm will try to come up with some Newcastle questions but, like his comments, they are usually too long. Bernie does next to nothing. I asked him to contribute and he came up with a few questions but didn't know the answers to them!'

Bernie takes up the story at this point. 'I have to admit that I've not always seen eye to eye with Malcolm. We often have a go at each other during ad-breaks. We ask each other why we made a particular comment or I might accuse Malcolm of being up Freddy Shepherd's arse! More serious was the time Malcolm went behind my back to produce a book about the show without my knowledge.

'I had been away from the show for a few weeks during the close season. On my return Gatesy asked me if I'd heard about the book. I didn't know what he was talking about so I pulled one of the staff and asked them. She told me it was going to be called 'The Three Legends' but that I wouldn't be involved as it was all about the Ten Grand Fan football quiz that Gatesy and Malcolm had run during my absence. The fact is that the quiz had been part of our phone-in and I would clearly have been involved if I hadn't been away on holiday at the time. I was incensed.

'The following day I stormed into the office of Century's gaffer and told him I had found out second hand that Malcolm was bringing this book out but there was no way it would use the name, 'The Three Legends'. I pointed out that I wasn't involved in it, so they could call it 'The Two Legends' or whatever they liked, but they weren't calling it that. I finished by telling the gaffer that he could tell Malcolm my opinion. I wasn't going to tell Malcolm personally because I wanted him to know how it felt to be kept in the dark and not be spoken to by someone you work with on a day-to-day basis. When he arrived, the gaffer pulled him aside and told him what I had said.'

Malcolm recalls, 'I told Bernie it was a moneymaking idea. I said, "You don't really get involved in the Ten Grand Fan, you're not interested, so it's mostly based on the work Gatesy and I have done." But I assured him that I had a bank account set up in the name of The Three Legends so we weren't trying to rob him and he would get his cut.'

But Bernie wasn't in any mood to be reassured. 'Seconds before we went on air with that night's show, Malcolm asked me why I hadn't spoken to him instead of going to the gaffer. I didn't need a second invitation to let rip. I told him he was f***ing sneaky and that he had treated me like a leper. I have a month off and he goes behind my back to get a book printed. I couldn't believe it.'

As Bernie launched into an all-out tirade against his fellow presenter, the show's introductory sounds kicked in. 'The Three Legends Football Phone-in. The legends are Newcastle and England legend Malcolm Macdonald…'

'We got on with the calls for the next 20 minutes as if we'd never had a cross word,' laughs Bernie. 'Then into the show's first ad-break, Malcolm started trying to explain himself. I just said, "F*** you!" I wasn't interested in listening to his feeble excuses. I hardly let him get a word in, I was so furious. This continued during each ad-breaks throughout the rest of the show until I felt I had made my point.'

But it wasn't long before Bernie and Malcolm fell out again. This time there were very nearly more serious consequences as the pair threatened to turn the Century studio into a boxing ring. Eric still shakes his head when he recalls the incident that saw him acting as peacemaker between the two.

'It's a brilliant show but believe me some of the best bits are off-air,' he grins. 'Malcolm had got us involved in doing some work at a factory that was closing down. He told us it was for a government department so we would have to wait 120 days before we got paid for the work. But one month, two months, three months went past and nothing happened. It got embarrassing. Every night we kept wondering why Malcolm wasn't saying anything. The money was one thing but it was the principle of it. Eventually it got to six months and still there was no sign of the money and Malcolm didn't even try to explain. We thought he probably had the money and had spent it!'

Malcolm insists that the situation was out of his hands. 'It all stemmed from a day's work we did for the electronics company, LG Philips,' he explains 'They had closed a big plant at Belmont industrial park, just outside Durham and something like 800 workers had been laid off, many of them having worked there for many, many years. I had done some work for the Durham Job Centre in the past and my contact there, Janet Kelly, had been seconded to the LG Philips site to help people who had lost their job to move on and find new openings. As part of this, they had a careers day with a whole host of prospective employers and educational organisations in attendance. To lighten the serious mood, they put food on and asked us to go along and mingle with the people there.

'Afterwards, I sent an invoice for the agreed fee for all three of us. I had told Bernie and Gatesy at the outset that we wouldn't be paid within the usual 30 days and that it was more likely to be something like three months but I assured them that we would eventually get our money. Unfortunately, this thing dragged on and on and we still hadn't been paid after five months as LG Philips and the government debated who was meant to be paying us. Janet was pulling her hair out but she wasn't to blame and neither was I.'

Whatever the reasons for the delay, Bernie's patience eventually reached breaking point, resulting in a Three Legends ad-break showdown. All three have differing versions of exactly what happened next.

Eric recalls, 'Before the show, Bernie asked Malcolm when we were getting paid. Malcolm's response was, "Oh Bernie, what's the matter? I told you it would be three months. Everyone knows it's 120 days with the government." We'd never heard of this. Bernie was getting more and more agitated. He said, "I want my f***ing money, you're messing us about. Are we going to get it or not?"

'I told Malcolm he was out of order, that he had said f*** all and demanded to know when it was going to get sorted, out but there were no apologies. Malcolm is aloof like that.

'When the 7pm break came, it was earphones off and Bernie said, "Are we going to sort it out?" Malcolm lost it. He went over and got Bernie by the scruff of the neck and pushed him against the wall. Bernie was throwing punches and trying to get Malcolm off him. If I hadn't been there, god knows what would have happened. Unbeknown to thousands of listeners, all this was going on during a Three Legends ad-break. It was three minutes that felt like three days and then we had to go back on air.'

Malcolm's recollection of the incident is, not surprisingly perhaps, different to Eric's. 'What happened with Zinadine Zidane in the World Cup final was very similar to what happened to me with Bernie in the Three Legends studio. Just as Zidane walked away, thought about what had been said to him and then saw red, so did I. As we went into a break, I recall Gatesy saying something about the money and that stoked Bernie, who suddenly ripped into me. Ever the diplomat, Bernie shouted, "Yeah, where's our f***ing money, you c***?' I just said, "Oh, don't start on that again. I'm doing my best to get the money." I tried to simply walk away to avoid the row. As I walked out of the studio door, I was trying to get my head around the fact that I had just been called a c*** by Bernie because I had made efforts to make him money. Now

he was calling me that because he wasn't getting the money quick enough.

'Suddenly, it was like being back on a football pitch again. I didn't lose my temper. I was ice cold and expressionless. I just turned, walked over to Bernie, got hold of him by the scruff of

•THE FOUR TOPS: Like Rod, Kathryn Humphreys is an unheard but crucial member of the Three Legends team.

the neck and pushed him up against the wall and pulled my fist back ready to throw a punch. Gatesy jumped in and Bernie reacted, though there was no risk of him striking me because he would never have reached me because of the way I had hold of him. Gatesy thinks he stopped me from swinging but I'll leave them both to think that. I had made my point. I let go and walked out of the studio.

'I didn't need to calm down. I was cold. I just walked out and stood in the other studio next door to ensure there was no further exchange of words. Ten seconds before the ad-break finished, I walked back into the studio, sat down and got back on with the show as if nothing had happened. Nothing further was said and I have never discussed it again – with anyone – since that day until now. I had made my point. It left a thought, that seed, in other people's minds that Malcolm wasn't that placid, laid-back fella that they all thought he was.

Bernie himself recalls that he told Eric that he was going to demand answers from Malcolm before the scuffle occurred. 'I was tired of Malcolm's excuses about where the money had gone to,' he says. 'So I turned to him and said, "Look, where the f*** is the money? If you've got a problem retrieving it, give me the woman's phone number and I'll phone her".'

But Bernie was infuriated when, instead of answering his question, Malcolm walked past him and headed for the door. 'When I realised he was going to ignore me I shouted, "Where are you going, you c***?" I just wanted an answer to my question, having asked him ten times already over several months. But to just walk past me was damn ignorance. I don't use the word c*** usually but it's a terminology I use when I'm angry with someone. Malcolm took offence at it but it was just the first word that came to mind. He turned and tried to go for me. He had me by the jumper, tried to push me back towards the wall and I think he threatened to throw a punch. But then Eric came between us and Malcolm stormed out, still giving no answers.

'Eric had to act as referee. In fact, looking at his face, it makes me wonder if it is a result of taking a few punches when breaking up too many fights!'

So does Bernie think Malcolm might really have thrown a punch? 'I will never know what was in Malcolm's mind so I don't know if he would have hit me, but he shouldn't think he could have tried without getting a bit back. In his heyday he might have been able to handle himself but he's getting on and I like to think I'm still fairly fit. I'm sure I'd have given him as good as I got, if not better.'

Malcolm believes he put lessons learned in the dressing room and on the training pitch to good effect that day – both in looking after himself and in putting the incident behind him. 'Football taught all three of us wonderful lessons for real life,' he explains. 'I had to deal with the likes of Tommy Smith, Don Murray, Norman Hunter, Terry Yorath, John Roberts and Kenny Burns, the sort of fellas who would kick their grandmother if it would give them a chance of a win bonus. So you learn to deal with it. You learn how to react and how to put fear into other people if necessary.

'I had a few fights in my time, especially with my present day Century colleague Bob Moncur when we were both at Newcastle. We tended to be against each other in training and we would finish up in confrontation. We also viewed life, football and just about everything from totally different poles so we always clashed in terms of our views. Bob was the skipper, Mr Solidarity, dependable and reliable. Not only did he not rock the boat, he was captain of the boat. He was a very, very good captain but while many of the players were happy to go along with whatever Bob said I didn't feel everything he said and did was right. If I felt there was another way of doing it then I'd say so. By my very nature, I was more gregarious and flamboyant in my attitude. Bob and I never actually exchanged punches with each other but we would both grab hold of each other and threaten to do so. I saw Bob hit people but he never hit me and I never hit him.

'I did hit a few opponents but only for a very good reason. I would never be the initial aggressor but if someone had been out of order I would make recompense, either with my boot, my fist, my elbow or my head. I was only ever caught once and I was sent off for it. I can't ever remember the ref's name now but he was absolutely right to send me off.

'Arsenal were playing Coventry City. I was 20 yards into the opposing half with my back to goal and Liam Brady played the ball into me from our half and made an angled run. I could feel the centre-half behind me so I checked a bit and put my body into him to get myself a yard or two of space. I dropped the ball off into Liam's run who played it down towards the corner flag for an overlapping Graham Rix. Then Coventry's Terry Yorath hit me with a tackle. He has done me right on the ankle with his full weight. The 'tackle' is so late that Brady has gone beyond me and all eyes are on his pass to Rix. He has knocked me right off balance and back towards my own goal.

'As I turned, Yorath was down on his backside. Just at the point Rix was knocking the ball in the area, I was running past Yorath so I punched him with all my might without breaking step. I caught him right on the jaw. He was spark out! I carried on sprinting into the area, believing I had got away with it. But the referee blew his whistle, walked over to me and sent me off. After the game, I confronted the ref and asked, "What the hell were you doing looking over your shoulder to see me do that? Why weren't you following the ball?" He replied, "Well, I knew that Yorath had caught you real bad." I suppose he had allowed the advantage to be played but it struck me that he had taken no action against Yorath while I got sent off.'

So maybe Bernie got off lightly that night in the Century studio? Malcolm shakes his head. 'The truth is I wouldn't have hit Bernie, but I did make him think. Put it this way, he has never called me a c*** again! Our relationship could have been destroyed, but what will always stand us in good stead is the experience we have as footballers in the dressing rooms. You have incidents like the one Bernie and I had in the Century studio all the time among team-mates and you know you have to put them behind you. All sorts happens in our ad-breaks that sometimes have to be seen and heard to be believed, but we get on with the show because we know how to deal with it.'

This is one point on which Bernie will agree with Malcolm. 'We had these big bust-ups but the next night we were back to talking like it had never happened. I didn't hold any grudges. Footballers are brought up like that. In football, it's given that you say things to one another in the heat of the moment and then it's all forgotten. It was the same for me and Malcolm, though I remained adamant that there would be no reference to The Three Legends in the quiz book, which was eventually called 'The Ten Grand Fan'. But we buried the hatchet to such an extent that I later agreed to join Malcolm and Gatesy at signing sessions to promote the book.

'Give him his due, he came in a couple of nights after our fight about the money he owed us and said that it would be sorted. These things happen in work places and I accept that some people get the sack for such things. But afterwards we were professional and got back on with the show as if nothing had happened.

'If punches had been thrown it could have affected our relationship, but I like to think that I can argue with the best of them without resorting to punches. My father would have knocked Malcolm out before he was out of the door but my way is to try to talk my way out. I'm not scared of a fight if I have to but I like to think that no matter how wound up I am I will never punch anyone. There's loads of f***ers I'd love to punch, mind.'

What comes across is that Bernie tends to save his biggest fall-outs for Malcolm, enjoying a more harmonious relationship with Eric, but he insists that isn't always the case. 'I've had my tiffs with Eric because it's his way or nothing. He sees things

from his point of view and no-one else's. There have been one or two occasions over the years when I've had to walk out of the studio because Malcolm and Eric have done my head in. But we've all experienced these situations through football and know how to avoid falling out too badly in the main.'

Despite the language used by the Legends themselves when off-air, the use of the F-word – and any other expletives – is strictly off-limits on the show. 'There's many a caller I'd love to tell a few home truths to and tell them what I really think about them,' admits Bernie. 'But I can't - not unless I want to go the same route as Malcolm Allison! Despite the temptation, I've never hidden or deliberately not turned up for the phone-in just to avoid a verbal onslaught. I've learned to accept that there'll be bad weeks, but revenge will be all the sweeter when Boro are on the up and our rivals are struggling. I can tell you that it takes some time to wind down after the show, especially if callers have been having a go at me. I'll say what I think about them during an ad-break or once the show has finished but never on-air.

'Some people that come on are genuinely hurting, others are furious. A small minority lose it completely and start swearing. I remember one caller who must have used the word 'bloody' 50 times – it was bloody this, bloody that and bloody everything - until we finally got fed up and cut him off. Fortunately, there is a seven-second delay between what is said and its transmission on air, which gives us a short window of time to cut them off and avoid their foul language being aired early evening into living rooms and kitchens across the north-east.'

Malcolm explains, 'Off to my left is an orange rectangular button. It's called the dump button. If a caller swears or says something that we can't allow to go out on air – if it's racist or bigoted – I dump them. I've done it a few times, though not as many as you'd think. There was a guy I phoned for the quiz over the summer who will never get back on-air again. I called him and said, "You're our next caller on the Ten Grand Fan." Without thinking, he responded, "F***ing hell!" There was no way I could keep him on so I hit the button. The button takes you back SEVEN seconds in time so any listeners would probably have heard me saying, "You're our next contes..." Then it would have been back live with me saying that he

19

must have had a problem with his phone or something.

'I do get irritated with some callers but it's only people who go too far who I dump and put on a black list. I have no problem with people who seek to antagonise me. All three of us are prepared to get emotional with callers, so it's a two-way street. If we feel someone is a real stickler on a point, we will get emotional and go against them. We push them to get a reaction.'

It's a fact, of course, that heated debate is one of the reasons why The Three Legends show is such must-hear radio. 'The three of us argue on-air all the time,' reflects Malcolm. 'We regularly have differences of opinion and fall out but we know we can always jump out of the debate by putting it to the listeners. We will debate an issue and make our own stances clear, then we'll put it to the fans. *Call us on 0191 477 2000.* Straight away the switchboard will light up.'

Bernie enjoys a good debate as much as anyone but reveals that there are times when some fans go too far. 'I've angered a fair few Newcastle and Sunderland punters with my comments over the years – probably a few Boro fans too. I regularly say things to deliberately wind fans up, just as all football fans do when they're enjoying a bit of crack with their mates. Most understand that it's all just banter and forget about it, but a minority take it to heart and think I'm their enemy. The majority accept you for what you are but I think a few would kill you if they could.'

In a close-knit place like the north-east that can lead to the occasional bit of trouble, as Bernie reveals. 'It was as a direct result of my comments on the phone-in that I nearly got done in when Boro won 3-1 at the Stadium of Light back in 2003 as Sunderland were heading for relegation. Boro were two-up by half-time so it was all over bar the shouting. A couple of the local morons decided they would take out their frustrations on me.

'As he does for Boro's games against Sunderland, Gatesy had joined Ali Brownlee and me on commentary duties. When the half-time whistle blew Gatesy suggested we went down to the press room for a cup of coffee. As he headed off ahead of me, I began following him along the press box gangway towards the concourse. I hadn't gone far when a wee lad of about 35 started giving me it.

•FINGER ON THE BUTTON: The dump button is only to be used in emergencies.

'He was shouting, "Hey, Slaven, I've heard you on the radio slagging us off," trying to confront me and be generally aggressive. This was obviously pretty brave of him to do when surrounded by 35,000 other Sunderland fans. He was ranting, "You're not so brave now, are yer! I'll give you something to think about."

'I had no intention of getting into the debate he was hoping for so I told him, "You can f*** off," and simply kept on walking. Gatesy might have been able to diffuse the situation but he had now disappeared into the crowded concourse ahead of me. As I tried to avoid the first idiot, another guy joined him. Eventually, I was surrounded by three guys – all of them head-bangers - but I put my head down and kept walking along the gangway. They were clearly drunk, out of their skulls and up for a fight.

'Just before I reached the concourse a copper spotted me with my three unwanted guests and intervened. He advised me to go back to my seat in the press box for my own safety. With another 2,000 Sunderland fans to get through on the concourse before reaching the press room, I wasn't going to argue. Having said that I'm certainly not tarring them all with the same brush and I was grateful to other Sunderland fans who were embarrassed by what they had seen and told me they weren't all like that. Even so, it wasn't a pleasant experience.

'So, before Newcastle played at the Stadium of Light a couple of weeks later. I made a point of advising Malcolm to avoid going for a half-time coffee. Malcolm being Malcolm, however, he ignored my warning and headed off through the concourse at the end of the first half. His appearance amid the home fans resulted in several of them throwing pies at him. In all honesty, he was lucky it wasn't punches.'

Despite the fall-outs, there is no doubt all three appreciate how lucky they are to talk football for a living. 'I love doing the show,' says Malcolm with enthusiasm. 'I think we all enjoy it. We are just so lucky. We've been paid for playing the game that we love and then, when that has stopped, we are being paid just to talk about it. And we've been looked after all the way.

'I occasionally do motivational speeches and a while ago I went down to deliver one at Alton Towers. There was this huge room with about 300 people in it. They were all technical wizards who made and sold this software. They had to know how the machine worked and how it was put together. It struck me the amount of learning that they had to do just to be able to do their job.

'I couldn't help but reflect how lucky we were in comparison. To do our job, we don't even have to know how to use a computer, let alone how it works. There's no real preparation for it. We go and watch a football match on a Saturday afternoon and then talk about it for two hours. We've got it down to a fine art!

'We all enjoy it. If we didn't enjoy it then I think that would come across. Yes, we fall out but what's better is that we fall out on air. I think that gives it drama. But I think it's a great shame that in future there probably won't be talk-ins and after-dinner speeches from people who used to be top players because these guys are so far removed from society, in such a different financial bracket, they won't need to do it and they won't want to do it. We have this love of taking football to the ordinary man and I can't help but think that today's big money superstars won't share our enthusiasm.

'As for how much longer The Three Legends show continues, I'm not sure. I'm forever thinking about it. We're now into our seventh year. In radio, everything is figures driven, so some time ago I asked Giles Squire, formerly a senior guy at Century who had radio running through his veins, how you can tell when a programme is peaking. His answer surprised me but I have no reason to disbelieve him. He said in radio nothing ever peaks until its tenth year at the very earliest. So do I see us getting to 10 years? In our time, we've had several different owners and I know radio is the most volatile of industries infamous for its lack of loyalty, so who knows?

'But it is quite amazing that Eric and Bernie have stuck with the show for so many years, given their short attention spans. It is testament to how much they enjoy it that they have done so. Personally, I think we've got an awful lot more to do, so as long as we're enjoying the show and north-east football fans are tuning in then we should continue with it.'

Bernie's view on continuing as one third of the Legends is simple – as long as he is enjoying himself and the listeners are still tuning in he will keep going. 'I love the show. If ever I'm having a downer and have got a few problems, I go on the show, have a laugh and forget about them. It takes me an hour to get up to the studio every night and I do moan about that, but I never moan about doing the show. As long I'm treated right, I'm happy.

'I've been with Century 10 years now – six on the Legends - and hopefully there's a lot more to come. If the ratings and figures are good then I can see us going on for a long time yet. Having said that, I know Century have thought about getting rid of us before, even though the Legends show along with the match commentaries are probably their most prized possessions, so you never know what's round the corner.'

The final word about the show goes to Eric. 'I'd be lying if I said I looked forward to the show every night because there have been times when it's been a grind trying to find something new to say about Sunderland these last few years. But the show's popularity never ceases to amaze me. I remember going to a Boro match two or three years ago and the crowd were shouting "Gatesy, Gatesy, what's the score?" There were 22 Premiership players on the pitch and the fans were singing about a radio phone-in!

'I count myself as the luckiest lad alive to have played professional football for a living. Nothing could beat that. But aside from playing this show is the best thing I ever did. So to the people involved in Sunderland Football Club who brought about my demise at Metro - of which, more later- I'd like to say thank you very much. You helped my career!'

Eric's Story:
THE LUCKIEST LAD ALIVE

I'M THE luckiest lad alive. That's my honest opinion when I look back on my life and think how lucky I've been to enjoy such a long and successful football career, full of the sort of experiences most can only ever dream about. I get fed up of hearing footballers moaning their lot. They need to take a reality check because, I tell you what, there's a heck of a lot worse off than them in the real world, outside the cosy environment of professional football.

And I know some of you will be reading this, thinking 'What's Gatesy on about? He's the biggest moaner of the lot!' You're right, I do moan. I moan when I hear players complaining about money or injuries and the fans having a go at them or when managers use the excuse for bad performances on their players being tired because they had to play three games in a week. Do me a favour! I loved playing three games in a week and was gutted when I missed any of them, as were most of my team-mates. So, yes, I do moan and complain about modern day football, but I'd like to think I do it with a passion that comes from the fact that I love the game and I think the people who pay good money to follow it deserve better than that.

But what I will never do is bemoan what I did or didn't achieve in my football career. Yes, I had disappointments, just like anyone does in any walk of life. Yes, I had disagreements and fall-outs – probably more than most, because I've never been one to keep my opinions to myself. But I was *lucky*. Lucky to have had the talent to play football. Lucky to have enjoyed 21 years in the game. Lucky to have won things. Lucky to have played for a club as good as Ipswich and for fans as brilliant as Sunderland's. And now lucky to be getting paid to talk about the game I love.

If I'd been unlucky I might have spent my life doing the sort of job my dad and my granddad before him did, working down the pits day after day. That very thought was something that drove me on throughout my career, particularly my younger days when the possibility remained that I might not actually make it in the game.

Just like his father and the vast majority of the local men, my Dad, Jimmy Gates, was a coal miner down the pits. I can still remember him coming home from a hard day's graft down the Dean and Chapter pit, black as the ace of spades and getting a wash and scrub in a tin bath in front of the living room fire. It was only 40 years ago but, looking back, it seems like I'm talking about ancient times. As most mothers did back then, Mam – Nancy to her friends - stayed at home to look after their five sons in our terraced house, 16 Neal Street, Dean Bank, Ferryhill. It was into that typical working class background that I was born on June 28 1955. I was the second youngest of five brothers. Bill was the eldest, and then came Jimmy, Peter, me and finally Alan.

I loved my young life in Dean Bank, seven of us living in that little house. Loved it. One of my abiding memories is playing with all the kids of a similar age that lived on Neal Street. As its name suggests, Dean Bank was built on a hill which made it perfect for kids to roll down on anything that had wheels. Nowadays, it would probably be roller blades, but back then we made do with a book on top of a roller skate. We'd take turns sitting on the book, feet up in the air, getting a push off one of the other kids and going flying down the street, trying desperately to keep balance to avoid falling off. It was simple but great excitement for us and thankfully there were few cars about back then.

It was my eldest brother, Bill, who got Dad out of mining because he knew it was on its way out. There was no future in it. He persuaded them to get a village shop in Staindrop, near the town of Barnard Castle, about 20 miles from Ferryhill. It was a big decision to make, particularly for Dad because he didn't understand anything but mining. But it was the right decision and the best thing my brother could have done for them. Mam and Dad still live in Staindrop to this day and I

ERIC'S STORY

always think about them. They've been brilliant to me. But moving to Staindrop broke my heart. I was eight years old and distraught about leaving behind all that I loved about Dean Bank for a very different way of life in the backwaters of County Durham. I cried my eyes out for weeks.

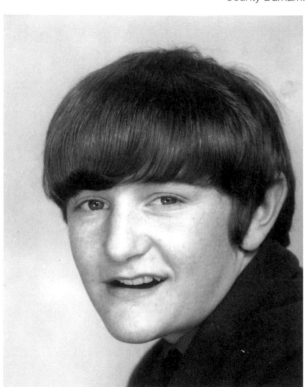

•LOOKALIKE: In my John Lennon phase as a young lad.

But football had already become the love of my life and would soon distract me from my heartbreak. Football was my passion from as young as my memory can take me. I first honed my skills as a toddler in Granddad's house, over the road from ours in Neal Street. He would take candlesticks off the mantelpiece and put them on the floor as makeshift goalposts. He would go on his knees as goalkeeper and I would bray the ball in an attempt to score goals past him. My Granddad used to love it, but the best thing for me was if I could knock the candlesticks over. Later, as a I grew up in Neal Street, I played football in the cobbled street and 'gatey' in the backstreets. And I loved nothing better than 'keepy-uppy'. If I kept the ball up twice I wanted to keep it up four times. I loved that challenge and I was proud as punch when I knew that I was improving.

After we left Ferryhill, I switched schools from Dean Bank to Staindrop Church of England School and my football ability really started getting noticed. A memory I'll always have is my photograph appearing in the local paper when I was about nine years old because Staindrop C of E beat Barnard Castle RC School 5-0 and I scored all five. From Staindrop junior school, I moved to Baliol secondary school where all the talk was of a talented young lad who had just left the school called Dave Thomas. Dave went on to enjoy a fantastic career with the likes of Burnley, QPR and Middlesbrough for a brief spell, while also winning England caps.

While I became a regular for the school team, by the time I was 13 or 14 I was also playing in a local men's league for Newton Aycliffe Sports Club alongside my elder brother

Jimmy. So as a kid of 14, I was doing something that would be frowned on nowadays, playing for my school on a Saturday morning and then holding my own in a men's league on the same afternoon.

And I was still only 14 when I made my debut in the Northern League, which back then was respected as one of the best amateur leagues in the country. The local side before our move to Staindrop was Ferryhill Athletic, who were members of the Northern League for many, many years. They always attracted fairly big crowds but I would get in for free, sneaking in through broken parts of the fence around the ground or going down at half-time when they'd let you in for nothing.

I made one Northern League appearance for Spennymoor United against Ashington and we won 4-0. I was probably the league's youngest ever player and was proud as punch that Bill was among the crowd of probably 500 there that night. I only played that one game because if I'd played more regulations stipulated that I wouldn't have been allowed to carry on playing for Newton Aycliffe. It was another step up in my development and it certainly did me no harm. I got kicked but it toughened me up. That's maybe why I won't have this tiredness lark and arguments about kids playing too much football. As a kid, all you want to do is play football, the more games the better.

There were always a few scouts at Newton Aycliffe's games so it wasn't long before I got picked for Bishop Auckland Boys. I was always a midfielder or forward, quite skilful and scored goals, though I was never big enough to be an out and out centre-forward. And I hated defending even then. But I wasn't the one the scouts from the Football League clubs would usually come to see. That honour fell to a lad called Peter Hampton, who was picked up by and played for Leeds United. Another of my Bishop Auckland Boys team-mates was a lad called John Peddelty, from Evenwood, who went to Ipswich with me and played for their first team before I did.

But my first trial with a professional football club came not through a scout but through our Bill's links with Middlesbrough. While Dad had been a decent local player, there was clearly football talent in the blood in the Gates household, though Bill was a rugged, hard man defender rather than the skilful little forward that I was. Like me, Bill carved out a career in professional football, though it was his venture into sports retail that made him a fortune and now allows him to enjoy a lifestyle that includes a home in the Caribbean. I was only six when Bill made his first team debut for Boro as a 16-year-old who had already won England youth caps. Although I can't remember his debut, I do remember going to Ayresome Park with Mam and Dad to see him play with the likes of Gordon Jones, Hugh McIlmoyle, John Hickton, Ray Yeoman and people like that. Because of Bill, my allegiance as a kid was definitely to Boro. I have never been particularly close to Bill. He left home at 16 or 17 to marry his girlfriend, Judith, and I really don't remember him living with us, only of him visiting. In many ways, we are opposites as characters and as players, but it was his success with Boro over a 13-year period into the early 1970s that drove me on. It's a fact that I wanted to follow in his footsteps.

And our Bill certainly helped me on my way to getting my first breaks into professional football. But my first trials did not go well and ensured a swift end to my previous allegiance to Middlesbrough. Bill got me a couple of games for the Boro when I was about 14. I played a couple of trial games at their Hutton Road training ground but I didn't get any good feedback. There was no enthusiasm from them to get me to sign then or in the future, nor any encouragement to come back for them to take another look at me. Quite simply, they didn't fancy me as a player.

I was disappointed but I soon had a chance to turn the tables on Boro - and I didn't hesitate to take it. It turned out that Aston Villa, Wolves and Ipswich were also interested in me, so I went down to all three for trials. When I left school at 15, I had a choice of which of those three clubs to join. Only when they heard this did Boro decide they too wanted to sign me. But I wrote Boro off because of their initial rejection. They had turned me down so I turned them down. I left the final decision between Villa, Wolves and Ipswich to our Bill, telling him that I didn't mind which club I went to, whichever one I'd be best suited to.

People often ask me why I chose Ipswich, in the football backwaters of Suffolk, the club based furthest away from home. It helped that they were always signing on young lads from the north-east, thanks to the excellent work of the regional scout, John Carruthers, who spotted me playing for Bishop Auckland Boys. When I went down there for a trial, I was one of two busloads of lads from the area. Right throughout my early years at Portman Road they were always bringing down young lads from up north. In fact, a few years after me they took a look at Paul Gascoigne but turned him down! But the main reason I plumped for Ipswich is that Bill got a deal for me that meant I would actually get substantial bonuses if I played a certain number of first team games. Bill knew what was going on, knew the game and did his best for me in financial terms. He actually spoke to the managers at the three clubs before doing the deal with Ipswich.

As a 15-year-old apprentice at Portman Road, I was on £5 a week, a sum that had raised to more like £19 a week by the time I was making occasional first team appearances three years later. But Ipswich also agreed a written deal that meant that when I made the first team's starting line-up I would get paid a lump sum of £2,000. That was a phenomenal amount of money in those days, especially for a young kid. But as time went by I started to believe that what had looked like a great financial agreement was holding back my career. I was substitute 16 times over two seasons for Ipswich without ever making a first team start, despite the fact that I felt I was doing well and setting up goals.

Imagine as a kid that happening to you and you would come to the same conclusion I did – that Ipswich weren't picking me simply to avoid having to pay that £2,000 sum. Unbeknown to me, our Jimmy actually phoned up Ipswich manager Bobby Robson and asked him why I wasn't playing and whether the financial agreement was holding me back. Jimmy said that if it was the money holding me back then they should just forget about it. Bobby assured him that it was nothing to do with that. He said it was just a good side that I was trying to break into – which it was - but it still seemed strange. To this day I do still wonder if that agreement was in Bobby's mind when he was picking the team but I've never got round to asking him.

After all those sub appearances, getting increasingly frustrated with it all, my first start finally came against the reigning champions Derby on a wet, muddy pitch at the Baseball Ground. I travelled with no expectation of playing but four Ipswich players failed pre-match fitness tests. 'Gatesy, you're making your debut,' I was told, and I was in. I couldn't believe it. Unfortunately, in a midfield role, I didn't play at all well that night and I think Bruce Rioch scored the winner in a 1-0 Derby win.

Maybe I can knock Bobby Robson for not picking me all that time, but when I first moved down to Ipswich that same fella actually put me up in his house. I went down from the north-east and moved in with the manager of the club, his wife Elsie and their three sons, who were all a bit younger than me. How many managers would do that for a 15-year-old kid? In fact, John Peddelty and I both lived with Bobby for about a month. That's the kind of guy he is. I always say that I taught his sons how to gamble, drink and pull a bird – and Bobby never thanked me once!

Bobby's wonderful gesture didn't half help me because it broke my heart to leave home. Just as I had when I left Ferryhill for Staindrop, I cried my eyes out after moving to Ipswich, not just for an hour but every night. I missed home so much, I was on the phone to my parents every day. But I didn't want to let them down so I stuck with it.

After a month with Bobby, I went into digs which was an arrangement that never worked out. I lived with a woman of about 70, an old widow. Every night dinner would be on the table at six. When I sat down, she would put a little table in front of the television and put the budgie cage on it so I couldn't see the TV. Incredible. When I complained, the club got me out and I moved into a hostel with 12 or 13 other young players. That was great for a year or two but eventually we didn't get on. And all the time I was homesick. I used to love going home whenever I could. Every summer right up to my mid-20s I would cry my eyes out on the way back to Ipswich after spending the close season back with my parents.

Bobby Robson was and always has been a very good man. Back then, he was 'Mr Ipswich'. The club's owners, the Cobbold family, were great people, real characters, but it was Bobby who ran the club. When he spoke he made sense, whether it was on the training pitch or during his half-time team talks. And he knew how to man-manage players as individuals. I learned a lot from him, whether he was kicking

me up the arse or patting me on the back – and he did plenty of both.

People often ask me if Bobby was a great tactician but I've never been sure about tactics any way. I think the game is just about common sense. As the saying goes, football is a simple game complicated by fools. And a big part of management is about knowing your players, what they can do and what they can't do. I played in a great side at Ipswich but every one of them had their faults. Bobby just knew how to get the best out of the lads he had at his disposal.

When he got the Newcastle job many years later, people used to say he was going senile, he's forgetting things. I would tell them he used to forget things 25 years ago. He called me Eric Sykes for 10 years! His team talks were a lark. They would last two hours and were so boring that people would be falling asleep, but then he would unintentionally say something funny and the place would erupt with laughter.

After finally making my first start against Derby, I didn't go on to establish myself in the team as I would have hoped. I don't think the coaching staff could make their minds up about me as a player. I wasn't a big lad up front, even though I could play there, and I wasn't a workhorse type of midfield player. I was a lazy b*****d, if you like. Attacking wise I'd break my neck to get in the goalmouth, but when it came to getting back I was crap. I didn't want to chase back and defend. So I wasn't really a midfielder or a forward. The free role between the forwards and midfield was probably my best position. I started that role in many ways, because it had never really been seen until then.

But over the next couple of years I was in and out of the side to the point where I got so frustrated with it all that I actually walked out on Ipswich. I was 22 years old and still hadn't established a regular starting place, even though I felt I merited one. I was doing brilliant for the reserves and felt comfortable in the first team. The likes of Brian Talbot, Trevor Whymark, Clive Woods and Roger Osbourne were usually picked ahead of me. It was upsetting me and eventually I'd had enough. I decided if they weren't going to play me regularly then I was p***ing off. I came back to the north-east.

In some ways it was a spur of the moment thing but the

situation had been building up for a while. I felt I should have been in the team. I was knocking on Bobby's office door, saying, 'I deserve to be playing. Are you going to play me?' I used to play hell. Players too readily accept not being in the side nowadays. It wasn't a case of being big-headed. I just had belief in my own ability and have always be one to speak my mind. Though I had plenty of arguments and fights with Bobby in my years at Ipswich, I got on well with him but I was determined to let him know how I felt about being left out.

The straw that broke the camel's back was a UEFA Cup game against Wacker Innsbruck. Ipswich were losing 1-0, I went on, made one of the goals and we won 2-1. I thought I was a certain starter for the league game the following Saturday but Bobby made me substitute and didn't even put me on. That was it. Afterwards I got in my car and drove home to Staindrop.

I was back home with my parents for a week without the club knowing where I was. They eventually tracked me down. Bobby sent his scout, Ron Gray, to see me.

'Come back, son,' he pleaded.

'Bollocks, stuff the club,' I replied. 'I'm not going back unless Bobby is going to give me a regular game – they can play me or let me go.'

It was a strategy that was a little bit risky because they could have let me rot. In truth, I was on fairly safe ground because I knew other clubs wanted me. Terry Venables, who was in charge at QPR, wanted to buy me, as did Brighton. If Ipswich weren't going to play me, I would have been happy to go somewhere I could establish myself.

I eventually agreed to return to Suffolk and three or four days' later I was picked to play an away game at Man United. We lost 2-1, but you know what? I never ever got dropped again. In the remaining eight years of my Ipswich career, if I was fit I played. Was my walkout a brave or a daft thing to do? Well, it worked, I got in the side and I stayed there, so there's nothing more to be said.

But things didn't always run smoothly from that moment on. In fact, at the end of that very season, 1977-78, I suffered the disappointment of being left out of our FA Cup-winning team. I think I played in the first two rounds before getting injured.

There was only one substitute allowed back then and I thought that would be me in the final, but Bobby made Micky Lambert sub because it was his testimonial season. It was a huge disappointment for me. It was brilliant to see Ipswich beat Malcolm Macdonald's Arsenal, thanks to Roger Osbourne's goal, but I was gutted to miss out. Call it a selfish attitude if you like but, while everyone else was celebrating, I was as sick as a parrot. I tried to console myself that I would get back another year, but in fact I never did.

That season was a strange one for Ipswich because, although we won the Cup, we didn't do so well in the league. But we were actually one of the country's best sides throughout most of the 1970s and into the early 1980s. In fact, it's incredible to think that that cup-winning season was the only year in nine that we finished outside Division One's top six. We were European regulars and acknowledged as one of the country's most entertaining sides. Only Liverpool consistently finished above us.

It was an amazing achievement for a country bumpkin club. Much of the credit for that must go to Bobby Robson. What Bobby did was get a fantastic youth set-up going. I grew up with the likes of Kevin Beattie, Alan Brazil, Russell Osman, John Wark, George Burley and Terry Butcher. For several years, those players – every one of them products of the club's youth development system - were the heart of the club, combining with some brilliant signings to make a successful team. George Burley and I were members of the team that won the FA Youth Cup in 1973 and the likes of Wark and Brazil were in the side that won it again a couple of years later.

I've got so many tales about Bobby but a daft one I always remember followed an away game against Sunderland at Roker Park. Whenever Ipswich played in the north-east I would stay over for a couple of days, rather than travel back to Suffolk with the squad. I'd have one of my brothers waiting to take me back to my parents' house after the game. I'd get my bags off the bus and jump in a car with my brother back to Staindrop.

On this occasion, Bobby had told the players no drinking in the bar after the game, he wanted everybody back on the bus by quarter past five. 'If you're not on the bus, we're leaving without you,' he warned. The team were due to travel to

●THE GATES BOYS: In a picture taken to mark my first hat-trick for Ipswich, My four brothers are pictured (from top) Bill, Peter, Jimmy and Alan.

27

ERIC'S STORY

Durham by coach under police escort before catching a train to Peterborough, where another bus would meet them and transport them back to Ipswich. It was a long journey so the club were naturally keen to ensure they didn't miss the train. So the message was clear – the bus had to be away bang on time.

• A GLIMPSE OF MY FUTURE: in action against Sunderland, as Joe Bolton looks on while Sam Allardyce challenges

Having got showered and changed after the game, I got on the bus to get my gear. Team-mates were shouting to me to get off the bus, the usual banter that players exchange with each other. As I climbed back off, carrying my suit and bag, the driver asked, 'All right then?'

'Yes, you can go now,' I said, without even thinking.

With that, the bus started to move off from Roker Park, while I made my way to my brother's car. I could hardly believe my eyes when running out of the stadium reception comes Bobby, shouting, 'Where's that f***ing bus?' It had gone without him! I told him it had just turned round the corner. He ran like crazy up the road and disappeared round the same corner. I got in the car, told my brother what had happened and wondered how long it would be before they realised they had left the manager behind. What I didn't know was that the players sitting at the back of the bus had seen Bobby running behind, shouting for it to stop. This was manna from heaven for footballers, who thrived on childish humour at the best of times. 'Drive on!' they shouted, sending Bobby into panic that he was really going to be left behind.

But I knew nothing of this and forgot all about it during my stay back home in the north-east. It was Tuesday before I returned to training on pitches we had just outside the Portman Road ground. As I warmed up with the rest of the players, out of the corner of my eye I spotted Bobby limping towards us. I couldn't help but laugh. 'What's he f***ing done?' I asked. Bringing me quickly up to date, the lads told

me how he had pulled a muscle while running after the bus after Saturday's game.

As Bobby limped towards us, we were all laughing, but I wasn't prepared for what happened next.

'And you, you little c***, I've got a right mind to fine you a week's wages,' he shouted through gritted teeth, pointing straight at me.

'Me?' I questioned, incredulous. 'What the f*** for?'

'You were the b*****d that told the bus driver to drive off without me,' he said. It transpired that, on catching the bus, he was understandably furious to have pulled a muscle and had demanded to know whose idea it was to leave without him. 'Oh,' replied the bus driver, 'It was the guy with long hair that got off the bus.' Unbelievable!

But Bobby wasn't the only character in charge at Portman Road. The Cobbolds, the club's owners and directors, were unique. John and Patrick Cobbold were brewery people and Eton-educated, I believe. And it is fair to say they liked a drink. In fact, the saying went that if there was a crisis at Ipswich then we'd run out of wine! Bobby used to tell us players to keep away from them because he didn't want us drinking at their pace. John in particular loved the club. He wouldn't tell Bobby what to do. Whether we won, lost or drew, he was happy. You simply wouldn't see the likes of the Cobbolds nowadays.

My favourite story about the Cobbolds involves Patrick, after Bobby Ferguson had succeeded Bobby Robson as Ipswich manager. The new boss had said to me, 'Eric, your contract's up. What are you looking for?' I told him I was naturally looking for the best possible contract and discussed money with him. They ended up offering me a four-year contract on £650 a week with a £12,000-a-year loyalty bonus. I was happy with that but I asked for 24 hours to think about it. The next day I went in and Bobby asked me if I was going to sign the contract. I said yes, I would. But then, after training, I started to wonder why I hadn't asked for a five-year contract.

So at the bottom of the stairs, as Bobby and I were about to join Patrick Cobbold to sign the new deal, I said, 'Bobby, look, it would be best if I had a five-year contract, not four.'

He blew his top, calling me all the names and insisting he had put his neck on the line to get me a four-year contract. 'Two hours ago you had agreed it,' he snarled. 'So if you want five years, you're on your own.' My attitude was that they could only say no, but five years would be brilliant. So we went upstairs and joined Patrick Cobbold and the club secretary in the boardroom.

'Look, Eric's not happy with four years now,' said Bobby, 'He wants five.'

The secretary started explaining that who would mean another £12,000 loyalty bonus plus all the additional salary in five years' time and it was impossible to say what sort of financial situation the club would be in by then. I explained that I wanted something that would take me to football pension age when other payments would kick in. I always intended to sign four if I had to but I was determined to do the best for myself, because I never had an agent throughout my time in football.

All this time, Patrick Cobbold was sitting in the windowsill, quietly sipping a glass of wine. He listened to the argument for some time before bringing the meeting to a rapid conclusion, piping up, 'What are we f***ing arguing for? Just give the boy what he wants and let's finish this bottle of wine.' And that's exactly what we did.

As much as I loved Bobby Robson, I owe a great debt of gratitude to Bobby Ferguson. He was the club's youth coach as I was coming through the ranks, working with me from being a kid of 15. He made me the player I was. Bobby was like a sergeant major and the young lads were frightened of him, in awe of him. When he spoke, you listened. You did it Bobby's way or no way at all. If you did it, he loved you. He bullied me into fulfilling my potential.

And it was Ferguson, rather than Robson, who pushed me towards the first team, telling the manager to get me in the side. He knew what I was like as a player and how to get the best out of me. And it was he who got me the free role behind the main forward or forwards. I could play up front pretty well, but this was my ideal role.

The way Ipswich played had to be altered to accommodate me in that position because they had always played with a winger, usually Clive Woods, two front men and three midfield players. But they had to drop the winger to enable me to play in the hole. It was a formation and position that suited me down to the ground. I saw so much of the ball and absolutely loved it. What's more, it caught a lot of teams on the hop. For the next two years people didn't know how to mark me. Teams couldn't decide whether a centre-half or midfielder should be picking me up. We played Manchester United one year and big Gordon McQueen came out of the back four to chase me around midfield. We beat them 6-0 at Portman Road despite missing three penalties! They just didn't know how the f*** to stop me.

We changed football by playing that way, with two forwards up front and me in the hole behind them. The next few years were unbelievable, with little old Ipswich challenging at the very top of English football – and deservedly so. Most of the team were rewarded with international call-ups but the success our football truly deserved proved frustratingly elusive.

The FA Cup success apart, of which I have such bittersweet memories, our only silverware came in the wonderful shape of the UEFA Cup in 1981. A long European run, packed with goals, ended with us beating Dutch side AZ67 Alkmaar in a two-legged final, 3-0 at our place and then a 4-2 defeat at theirs, to give us a 5-4 aggregate victory.

One of my abiding memories of that cup run was a crazy game we played in the snow against Widzew Lodz out in Poland. Having beaten them 5-0 at home, we went over there confident that we were already through. But there was about four feet of snow on the pitch and it was clear it wasn't going to disappear in 24 hours. Because we were confident that we were as good as through, we agreed to allow them to steamroller the snow down to about two inches thick. In the event, we got beat 1-0. After the game, we were laughing and throwing snowballs at each other, but Bobby Robson didn't see the joke. Spotting us laughing back in the dressing room, he asked 'What do you think's so f***ing funny?'

In answer, Alan Brazil made reference to the tights and body stockings we'd worn to protect us from the biting cold. 'Well, Gatesy's just told me it's the first time he's ever had a hard-on for 90 minutes!'

ERIC'S STORY

•STRIKE FORCE: Training with Ipswich, watched by my two fellow front men, Alan Brazil and Paul Mariner.

As good as it was to win the UEFA Cup, I think everyone was genuinely deflated that we didn't win either the FA Cup or, better still, the League title itself that season. We had genuinely thought we could win all three. We were certainly a better side than Aston Villa, who eventually pipped us to the title, while it still rankles with me that we didn't win the FA Cup. I felt we were stone cold certain to win the Cup that season. Instead, it was Tottenham who beat Manchester City in a final that is remembered for Ricky Villa's amazing goal in the replay. It was City who beat us in the semi-final. We went into the game full of confidence but we had a rare off day, while Kevin Beattie broke his arm. It was 0-0 after the 90 minutes and looked like going to a replay, only for City's Paul Power to bend a 30-yard free-kick into the top corner about a minute from the end of extra-time. I was as sick as a dog, gutted. Every year I thought we could win it but that was the nearest I ever got, barring my disappointment in 1978.

I look back with regret that we didn't win the League that season. With Liverpool having a rare off-season, it was between us and Villa for the championship. We beat them 3-2 at Villa Park with a few games to go and thought, 'We've won it now.' But it all went wrong in the last game at Middlesbrough. Villa were losing at Arsenal at half-time that day, while we were one-up at Boro. We were 45 minutes away from being champions. But we threw it away in the second half. Yugoslav striker Bosco Jankovic scored two to give Boro the points, a win made all the worse when we heard that Villa had lost as well. If we'd held onto our lead, we'd have been champions. We actually beat Villa four times that season – twice in the league and knocking them out of both the League Cup and FA Cup – but it counted for nothing in the end.

Over a period of six or seven years we were on a par with the great Liverpool side of that era, but the difference is that they have the titles to show for it. We had to make do with being runners-up twice and third a couple of times. But it's important to keep that in context. Can you ever again see Ipswich achieving what we did? Looking back, I was privileged to be part of it and that whole set-up. It was a joy to be there. Maybe that's why I'm so critical about players now. I experienced and was part of the heights that I don't see a lot of now. OK, Man United, Arsenal and the like are often brilliant but what I see at Sunderland is woefully short of what I came to accept as the norm. I don't want to sound bitter but it is hard to accept second best, having been a part of that wonderful Ipswich side.

We had good players in every position and the team almost picked itself for several years, with Paul Cooper in goal, Mick Mills and George Burley as full-backs, and Allan Hunter and Kevin Beattie succeeded by Russell Osman and Terry Butcher in central defence. Then there was John Wark, Arnold Muhren and Frans Thijsen in midfield, myself in the hole and Paul Mariner and Alan Brazil up front.

Paul Cooper was a very good friend of mine and still is. At one time there was only me and him among the Ipswich regulars who weren't internationals, but he was the first one to call to congratulate me on the good news when I got my first England call-up. Paul was a penalty-saving expert and one season famously saved 10 out of 12 penalties he faced. He was a big, strong lad, who wasn't short of football skills for a goalkeeper. I believe he played up front for Shrewsbury reserves and was always comfortable with back-passes because he knew how to pass the ball. He is manager of a golf course in Spain now.

I grew up with our right-back George Burley, as we joined Ipswich at the same time. If you want to talk about attacking full-backs, George was one of the best. Technique wise, he was brilliant, always able to pick me out with a perfect pass. I'm not at all surprised he has gone into management because even back then he always wanted to be a manager.

Our left-back and captain was Mick Mills. Bobby Robson just loved Micky, who could do no wrong in his eyes, but I don't think he was a great player. I don't want to knock him because he was a reliable player and another great example of how Bobby could get the best out of everyone. Mick won a lot of England caps, which I think is amazing for a player who wasn't a good passer of the ball and didn't have great control.

On the other hand, Kevin Beattie was without a shadow of doubt the best player I ever played with. I tell you, that lad was absolutely brilliant. Bobby always classed him up there with England legend Duncan Edwards. The thing is there were no airs or graces about Kevin and he didn't know how good he was. He was incredible. He was a towering, powerful player but I never saw him foul opponents, he always looked to win the ball cleanly. By the same token, he was an athlete and yet he didn't look after himself because he always liked a drink.

Kevin's central defensive partner, Allan Hunter, was a good footballer and a good man – though, again, not a total professional off the training pitch. I remember he used to go and sit with the groundsman for a sneaky cigarette whenever he had the chance. Beattie and Hunter were replaced by another two of our youth team products, Osman and Butcher, who both won England caps. Russell and Terry were great mates and did very well for the club as our central defensive partnership, but I have to say that neither were fit to lace Kevin Beattie's boots. I can only wonder when I think that Terry won about 70 caps while Kevin won only nine. That's nothing against Terry, who was respected as a player and a leader, but Kevin was a gifted man-mountain.

Then there was our case of Double Dutch – Thijsen and Muhren. We thought we had a good side but Bobby went over to Holland and got these two players we'd never heard of. We wondered why we needed them but Bobby was right because they improved us. Frans Thijsen was a dribbler - give him the ball and you couldn't get it off him. He was a good fella too, who mixed well with the British players, coming out and having a drink and a bet with us. Arnold was the opposite, much more of a family man who kept himself to himself. He was very quiet and soft as sh**. He was all left foot, couldn't kick with his right, couldn't tackle and was often a liability away from home. On the other hand, on his greatest days Arnold had a brilliant left foot and would pick me out time after time.

The other thing about Thijsen was that shooting wise he wasn't a good clean kicker of the ball. He was a bit like Newcastle's Keiron Dyer is now. Dyer can't kick the ball properly and Thijsen used to scuff his shots. Some players, like Bobby Charlton and Alan Shearer, can strike the ball but others aren't clean kickers.

In the middle of the park we had a lad called John Wark, a brainy player who was good at everything. People talk today about the need for defensive or holding midfielders. We had Muhren, Thijsen, me and Wark in our midfield. Three of us didn't have a defensive bone in us and Wark, our so-called anchor man, scored 38 goals one season! You didn't have to have a defensive fella in front of the likes of Kevin Beattie or Terry Butcher. Deep down, you have to trust your defenders. It's about players having brains. If John Wark made a run into the penalty area, Thijsen, Muhren and even Gates would think, 'Well, Warky's gone' and we would sit back a bit and cover for him. Warky fitted into a team pattern that enabled you to see the best of him. He was good defensively, was a brave and strong tackler and a good passer. He also had a knack of arriving in the box at the right time. As a penalty expert, he always loved me, because I won a load of penalties for him.

Up front, we had Alan Brazil and Paul Mariner. Technique wise, Mariner was the best centre-forward I ever played with. He was brave, strong, and confident, could hold the ball up and lay it off. He was a good footballer but if I had to pick a fault I would say he didn't score enough goals. Brazil, on the other hand, couldn't head the ball, wasn't brave and had no right foot. But put the ball over the top and get it on his left foot and you knew he would score. For two or three seasons, he was great on his day – and those days came along regularly.

And then there was Eric. I had my faults, but all the players did. Bobby accepted them and concentrated on getting the best out of all of us. He realised what I could do for the team – and what I couldn't. I hated defending, that's why I could never have been an out and out midfielder, because that role is all about getting forward and getting back too. I could get forward no problem. Few were better than me in the creative role. I thrived on creating and scoring goals.

That was the core of the Ipswich team for several seasons, with a few other others like Steve McCall, Kevin O'Callaghan and Mich D'Avray also playing their parts. There was very little chopping and changing. We gelled as a team and knew each other's game inside out. I think I played in 61 of our 67 games in that incredible season of 1980-81, and several others played more than that. That's why I have such a gripe about this daft thing about modern day players supposedly being tired because they are playing too many games. I'm sorry, but that's just bull. I can't have it that players are tired or don't want to play. It's an excuse used by managers more than players, especially Steve McClaren when he was with Middlesbrough. The truth is that if you're doing well you want to play. If you're in a winning side – and let's remember, only the winning sides play a lot of games – you want to play football and you look forward to the next match. And playing the same starting 11 as often as possible can only be of benefit because the players get to know each other's game.

Although we might have achieved more, those were great days at Ipswich and I still look back and recall what a great team we had. I don't go back down to Suffolk a lot but maybe once a year we have a reunion. I was last back there in April 2006 when we celebrated the 25th anniversary of the UEFA Cup win. That success is still recalled and celebrated in Ipswich all these years later in a similar way that Sunderland people mark their FA Cup win in '73.

One of the great knock-on effects of our successes at Ipswich was the fact that so many of our players won international call-ups. Butcher, Osman and myself followed Mariner and Mills into the England squad. My first cap was a World Cup qualifier against Norway at Wembley in September 1980. Kevin Keegan got dropped and I got picked. I thought, 'This is it, boy, I'm on my way. I'll win a hundred caps now!' But it didn't happen for me. We won 4-0 that night but I was to play only once more for my country.

A month later I played again, in another World Cup qualifier, against Romania in Bucharest, but I was taken off at half-time in a shock 2-1 defeat. I shouldn't have played. I had spewed up in bed and had flu. I didn't train on the Monday or the Tuesday, only training on Wednesday, the day of the game. Afterwards, Ron Greenwood, the England manager, asked me if I was all right. I said yes, played, had a bad game and never got picked again.

It was ironic that I won my only England caps under Ron Greenwood because Bobby Robson took over from him and I always thought he would pick me, but he never did. Perhaps Bobby knew he would have to change the way England played to accommodate me and I guess he wasn't prepared to do that. It was a strange thing but, as privileged as I felt to play for the national side, I didn't enjoy being part of the England squad. I don't know what it was. I had several Ipswich team-mates there with me but I just didn't feel 'at home'. I was comfortable in the surroundings of Ipswich, in a sort of comfort zone, I suppose, and I didn't feel right when I joined up with England.

But far from feeling bitter about not having played more for my country, I feel privileged to have won two England caps. I look on myself as having been lucky to have achieved what I did. There were a few better players than me that didn't win any caps at all. Pop Robson, who scored hundreds of goals, many of them for Sunderland and Newcastle, for instance, or Billy Bonds, who played a thousand games for West Ham but never got a cap. Having said that, there's a lot worse players than me who won more than two caps. I think of Carlton Palmer, Emile Heskey and Keiron Dyer. It's frightening to think how many times they played for England. And then I look at someone like George Burley, who won about 13 Scotland caps compared to Mick Mills, who won 42 for England, and yet George was twice the player that Mick was.

Eventually that great Ipswich team started to split up and the club began to fade. Bobby Robson leaving for England was probably the catalyst. My old mentor, Bobby Ferguson, took over as manager but it didn't work out for him. I personally got on great with Ferguson but others didn't. He was a passionate, hot-headed geezer, and that was fine when he was working with kids, but I think he found it hard to man-manage senior players. I had chances to join Liverpool and Everton, who both made bids of something like £1 million but Ipswich turned them down. Instead, my future was back home in the north-east.

Eric's Story:
COMING HOME

I ALWAYS wanted to come 'home' to the north-east to finish my playing career. Throughout those great days of European football and title challenges at Ipswich, I always said I would come back. Ipswich Town was a lovely club with a family feel to it and I'll forever have a special affinity with the place but I love the north-east, so throughout my career it remained my intention to come back and live here. If I could come back and play for one of the big three – Newcastle, Middlesbrough or Sunderland – I thought that would be great, but I might otherwise have gone to Hartlepool or Darlington if the timing had been right.

As it turned out, Boro were never really on the agenda, especially with all their problems in the mid-'80s, but both Newcastle United and Sunderland came in for me during the summer of 1985. By that time, Ipswich had left their glory days behind and the club was on the slide. Bobby Robson was long gone and so were many of the stars who had made us so successful, most of them to the so-called bigger clubs. Paul Mariner had gone to Arsenal, John Wark to Liverpool, Manchester United had signed Arnold Muhren and Spurs had bought Alan Brazil. Ipswich had built this big new stand that cost them a lot of money, so they had a lovely stadium but then the results stopped coming and they weren't getting into Europe, so they had to sell players to keep their heads above water. The players who had made the club a success a few years earlier were on big contracts comparable with the Liverpools and Evertons, but Ipswich couldn't sustain that sort of expenditure any more.

The club were struggling and we nearly went down in 1984-85. As the financial problems continued, it was made clear to me and any others on top wages that it was best if we left. On £650 a week and a £12,000-a-year loyalty, I was a top earner, especially as I recall we were on £200 a point on top of that. To make matters worse for Ipswich I was on a five-year contract, so they needed me to leave.

One day Bobby Ferguson called me into his office and told me, 'Jack Charlton has been on. He wants to buy you for Newcastle.' Bobby knew I wanted to go back to the north-east if the chance arose and he knew he had to get rid of all the big-earners, so he wasn't going to stand in my way.

That same day I drove all the way from Ipswich to the north-east to meet Jack Charlton at the Scotch Corner Hotel. I fully expected to become a Newcastle United player but I was in for a shock. I got there first and sat down in the hotel lounge. When Jack arrived, he was less than enthusiastic.

His first words to me were, 'Have you eaten, son?'

'No,' I replied.

'Right, I've got time for a quick sandwich and a cup of tea,' he told me. 'Then I'm going fishing in Scotland. We'll see if we can do a deal, eh?'

This was the first time I'd ever met Jack and I was underwhelmed. There was no 'Pleased to meet you' or anything and I thought, 'You're really bothered about signing me, aren't you?'

He sat down and bluntly asked, 'Do you want to come to Newcastle.'

'Yeah,' I said.

'What do you want?'

'Well, I want exactly the same contract I'm on at Ipswich.'

'What's that?'

'I want a five-year contract.'

'No problem there,' he replied.

'And I want £650 a week basic wage.'

Jack nearly choked on his sandwich. 'F***ing hell! The top earner at Newcastle is on £500 a week.'

When I told him about the £12,000 a year loyalty bonus, he

nearly dropped through the floor. 'F*** me!' he said. 'We can't manage that.'

'Well, what do you mean, you can't?' I asked him.

He told me they could afford my basic wage but not the bonuses. So I asked him what he thought the incentive was for me to leave Ipswich to join Newcastle.

'Coming back to the north-east, that's the incentive,' he told me.

I just thought, 'F*** off!' There was no suggestion of Jack going back to the club to see if he could better the deal, so I told him there was no chance.

'Well, my offer's the five-year contract and £650 a week. You know I'm going to Scotland. If you change your mind and you want to do the deal, phone Joe Harvey up at the club and he'll do the deal with you.'

I told him I wouldn't be phoning anyone up. 'You've wasted my time,' I said.

My parents' house was a few minutes away from the hotel but I was so sick and annoyed that I drove the four hours straight back to Ipswich.

But if I thought I was back in Suffolk for good, I was in for a shock. The telephone was ringing as I walked through the door of my house back in Ipswich. I answered it.

'Hi Eric, it's Lawrie McMenemy,' came the greeting, in deep Geordie tones.

'F*** off, Coops!' I shouted back. I thought it was Paul Cooper, having a laugh at my expense – and I was no in mood for pranks.

'No, it's Lawrie, it's the truth,' came the shocked response.

And he *was* telling the truth. I could hardly believe it. Lawrie, who had recently been appointed Sunderland manager to great fanfare, told me that he knew I'd been to see Jack Charlton and asked me how it had gone. I told him the proposed move had fallen through.

'Are you interested in coming to Sunderland?' he asked.

'Well, yes,' I replied. 'I would be interested.' Sunderland had recently been relegated from Division One, which in those days was still the top flight, but I knew the club had a massive potential.

'OK, get yourself up to Sunderland straight away.'

I told him I had only just returned to Ipswich after having had my time wasted by Big Jack, so there was no chance I was coming back again just like that. 'We'll talk money before I come anywhere,' I said. I told him what I was on and that I wanted the same if I joined Sunderland.

'Just put your boots in the car, son, and get up here tomorrow for half past ten. The money won't be any problem.'

I thought, 'You'll do for me, boy!' Those words were music to my ears – and, as it turned out, the most sensible thing I would ever hear Lawrie say.

I signed for Sunderland on exactly the same salary and bonuses I was on at Ipswich, even though they were in Division Two while Newcastle were in Division One. A few weeks later, Jack Charlton got slaughtered off the Newcastle crowd in a pre-season friendly and threw the towel in. In one of his books, he wrote that one of the reasons they turned on him was because of his failure to sign me. I suppose that's a compliment but I'm not so happy with something else he has said. Apparently, in his after-dinner speeches in future years, he would tell people that the reason he didn't sign me was because I turned up at our meeting with a brown paper bag that I wanted him to fill as my signing-on fee. I'll go on record to say it didn't happen that way. I didn't even ask for a signing-on fee, let alone one in a bleedin' brown paper bag.

If I thought the people of Sunderland would welcome me with open arms, I was in for a rude awakening from the very start. The morning after my conversation with Lawrie McMenemy, I jumped in my car early doors and headed back up north, aiming to be at Roker Park for half past ten. It was quarter past on a wet and miserable day by the time I left the A19 and headed towards the city centre, not knowing how to get to the ground. Realising I would have to stop and ask someone for directions, I spotted a potential good Samaritan as I passed Vaux Breweries and made my way onto Wearmouth Bridge, the main gateway into Sunderland.

'You'll do,' I thought to myself as I pulled up and wound down my window to get the attention of this Andy Capp lookalike, cloth cap, overcoat, fag hanging out of his mouth and black and white mongrel by his side.

'Scuse me, mate,' I called. 'Can you tell me the best way to get to Roker Park please?'

The guy stopped in his tracks, looked at me, stubbed out his fag with his foot and walked over to my car, all the time taking me in.

'You're a footballer, aren't you?' he asked, ignoring my own, more urgent question.

'Yeah,' I answered. I was thinking, 'Well, I'm the club's new star and you don't know who I am.'

'You're that lad, Gatesy.'

'Aye,' I nodded.

'Best way to get to Roker Park?'

'Yeah, I've got to get there by half past ten so I've got less than 15 minutes,' I explained. I was not expecting the reply.

'You keep practising, son, you'll get there one day.'

Without another word, the t**t just walked away! That was my first experience of Sunderland as their big new signing but, as I have come to recognise over the years, it was typical of the dry sense of humour so many in the north-east have. Fortunately, two old dears further up the road pointed me in the right direction, so I did eventually get to Roker Park in time. But there were times over the next two years when I wished I had taken the hint from my cloth-capped friend and got the hell out of there.

The next two years for me personally and for the club were a disaster. Terrible. I was 30 years old and felt I should have been at the peak of my ability but little went right for me or Sunderland for a period that seemed to go on forever. I've always said that if you do it in the north-east you are a god to the supporters. Bernie and Malcolm are living proof of that, thanks to their successes at Boro and Newcastle. The passion of the people for football is second to none. But if you don't do it then be prepared for the bullets. I'll be honest enough to say that I didn't do it and, boy, I was faced with a constant barrel of verbal shots for the next two years.

The aim, of course, was to bounce straight back up following

the previous season's relegation under Len Ashurst. But to say what followed was a big disappointment is an understatement of the highest order. My first year at Sunderland was horrendous. The fans gave me some terrible stick, deservedly so, but my heart was in the right place. Having made my name outside of my native north-east, I had wanted to come back to the region and do well. I wanted to finish my career on a high by helping Sunderland back into the First Division. That would have been brilliant but it didn't work out like that. We played badly from the start and things just went from bad to worse.

I accept that neither I nor any of the other players pulled up any trees in the months that followed but we didn't get any leadership whatsoever. I've got to say that I thought Lawrie McMenemy's knowledge of football was nil. Maybe having Bobby Robson as manager for so many years had spoilt me. Bobby and Lawrie were worlds apart in their abilities as managers. When Bobby spoke about football, you listened. In comparison, Lawrie was a clown.

And yet I had always had the utmost respect for Lawrie. I had played against his Southampton teams many times over the years and respected him for what his club had achieved with similar resources to Ipswich. He had attracted many of the game's top players to The Dell and they'd had several good seasons. I thought he must be a great manager. Of course, I'd never been in a dressing room or on a training pitch with him, but he was a regular TV pundit and he always came across very well, full of humour and the sort of guy who would charm your granny. But I honestly wondered what he was talking about when I finally got to hear him in the Sunderland dressing room.

When it came to talking to players either in the dressing room or on the football pitch, Lawrie was clueless. When Bobby walked in the dressing room at half-time, he would kick you up the arse if you weren't doing it and pat you on the back if you'd done well. He would change things around if things weren't right. He'd give out advice to certain individuals and

•CALM BEFORE THE STORM: All smiles with Lawrie McMenemy on the day I joined Sunderland - but I thought he was a disaster as manager.

35

everyone would go back out for the second half knowing exactly what was expected of them.

At Sunderland, we'd be 3-0 down at half-time and Lawrie would walk in and ask, 'What do you think lads?' We'd be getting hammered and he would ask us what we thought! As a result, the dressing room would descend into chaos. I'd maybe have a go at Alan Kennedy and ask, 'Why doesn't Alan pass to my feet?' He'd have a go back at me and arguments would ensue around the room. We'd spend the entire 15 minutes fighting amongst ourselves and all the time our manager would just sit and listen, never offering one piece of advice or analysis. Then, when the bell rang that indicated it was time for the second half to start, he'd say, 'You've done some talking, lads. Go and prove it now.' Unbelievable. It was no wonder we struggled.

If anything, training was worse. For starters, I rarely saw a ball on the training pitch. If we lost 1-0, he'd tell us to run five miles. If we lost 2-0, he'd tell us to run six miles. It was crap but that was his attitude to training. As a result, I'd never been fitter in my life but I was playing the worst football of my career and my team-mates were no better. We were all crap. That's not to say we were all crap players, but we certainly didn't perform. Lawrie can't take all the blame for that but in my opinion his non-existent style of leadership was the source of most of our problems.

One particular tale of Lawrie really sums up how lax it was when he was manager of Sunderland. After the first six games of the season we hadn't scored a goal and hadn't won a game. We were running five miles, ten miles, whatever it took, but training was always crap. Friday, the day before a match, was the only day we would see Lawrie on the training pitch. Training would start at half ten in the morning with all 35 players warming up by running around the Roker Park pitch. Our trainer, 'Miserable' Lew Chatterley, would stand next to the tunnel and chuck a bib at you as you ran past. 'Put that on,' he'd snarl, giving out bibs to so many of the players and always looking like he'd rather be anywhere else than at Roker Park. 'Lawrie will be down in five minutes. We'll have a bit of a practice game and look at what he wants you to do tomorrow.' That was about as professional as our training sessions ever got.

The manager would eventually emerge and we'd have a practice game, with the following day's starting line-up taking on a team of players who would be missing out. This particular morning, as usual Lawrie stopped the game every five minutes to organise a free-kick. He'd tell one of the players, 'You've got a good left foot, so I want you taking all the free-kicks from this side tomorrow.' The game restarted and after a few minutes he stopped and talked about corners. This went on, stopping and starting, for maybe 40 minutes. He finally blew his whistle, brought an end to the game and asked all those wearing green bibs to gather around.

'That'll do us, lads,' he said. 'Obviously you know this is the team I'm playing tomorrow.'

My best mate at the club, Frank Gray, looked surprised. 'We can't play that team tomorrow, boss,' he piped up.

'Why not?' asked Lawrie.

'Because it's got 12 f***ing players in it!'

Still not believing Frank, Lawrie counted the players gathered around. 'One, two, three, four…'

Seconds later, he nodded, turned to us and said, 'You're right, Frank. I got mixed up. You're not playing tomorrow, son.'

But that wasn't the funny bit. What was funny – or would have been if it wasn't so bloody ridiculous – was that Lawrie had just had Frank taking all the free-kicks and corners for the previous 40 minutes and yet he wouldn't even be on the pitch for the following day's game!

On another occasion, even the manager's attempts at giving us a bit of confidence ended in farce. Lawrie decided to have us play a game of 'shadow football', whereby the team go through the motions of a game with an imaginary ball. I know it sounds bizarre to a lot of people but it's a system used by lots of managers to allow players to run through exactly what is expected of them. We were doing awful, bottom of the league, so he thought a shadow game could only help. Basically, you 'kick off', one of the strikers plays the imaginary ball out wide, the winger runs down the wing, pretends to beat the opposition full-back, crosses the 'ball' and the centre-forward arrives in the box to head it into the net. Easy. Or so you would think…

This day, I 'kicked off', passing our invisible ball to my fellow striker Dave Swindlehurst, who kicked it back to Gary Bennett in central defence. He, in turn, passed it to the full-back, Alan Kennedy, who just goes 'F*** ya!' and kicks the 'ball' back to the goalkeeper Iain Hesford without even looking. It was incredible enough that without opposition we'd played the ball all the way back to the 'keeper, but far worse that Hesford was actually in the back of the net putting his cap on at the very second Alan played the back-pass to him. We must have been the first side ever to go 1-0 down in a game of shadow football! I just fell on the floor in complete bewilderment. All that our esteemed leader, Lawrie, could say was, 'Well, I thought it couldn't get any worse.'

People often say to me that Lawrie must have had something about him or Southampton would never have done so well for all those years under his management. If he did, I never saw it. Maybe the players just gelled for him there and he got away with it, because when things were going wrong Sunderland needed a strong leader at the helm and he wasn't it. At Southampton, he had a lot of older players like Kevin Keegan, Mike Channon, Peter Shilton, Dave Watson and my old Ipswich team-mate Mick Mills and it worked for him, though by all accounts Alan Ball did all the coaching.

He tried a similar trick at Sunderland, buying plenty of older players like me, Alan Kennedy, Frank Gray and another of my friends from Ipswich, George Burley. Anybody old, he bought them. Actually, anybody who was a full-back, he bought them. Gray, Burley and Kennedy were all good players in their own right but they were all full-backs. In addition, young full-backs Nick Pickering and Barry Venison were already on the club's books, so we had five full-backs competing for two places so he was playing them in midfield and anywhere other than their best position. Surprise, surprise, we were totally unbalanced. We just didn't gel. All this time Lawrie was trying to push out lads like Pickering and Venison, who understandably resented it. He wanted his own men in.

We stayed up by the skin of our teeth that year, finishing 18th in Division Two when we had hoped to press for promotion. It was so disappointing but there was no sign of improvement as the following season began. I couldn't believe it when, at the end of that awful season, the fans stayed behind for us to

do a lap of honour. Things were no better off the pitch either, with directors fighting and constant talk of boardroom takeovers. Behind the scenes, there was hell on and the boardroom battles hardly helped. The whole club was in a mess. I came from a so-called country bumpkin place like Ipswich that had been run professionally by Bobby Robson and I had expected Sunderland to be run in a similar professional manner, but it was an amateurish club, badly run from top to bottom. After years of knowing only a happy atmosphere at Ipswich, finding myself surrounded by all that animosity was a real culture shock.

But in my heart of hearts, I didn't regret the move. Yes, I regretted not playing well. I had a nightmare and I was upset with myself for that. It hurt me that I wasn't playing anything like as well as I knew I could, though no one played well. We should have been a good team but we weren't. I deserved the criticism I got from fans. To be fair, I wasn't just criticised, I was slaughtered. I accepted that from the fans. It was fair enough because I wasn't doing it.

But what I didn't accept was when one or two local journalists at *The Journal*, *The Evening Chronicle* and *The Northern Echo* started suggesting I was some sort of money-grabbing b*****d who had only come to the club for a big payday or that I didn't even care whether I was playing badly or not. That was wrong and it hurt. I didn't mind them saying I wasn't playing well but I was angry when they wrote bull about me only being there for a pot of gold. I had come back to the north-east desperate to do well when it would have been easy to stay at Ipswich and I was as frustrated as anyone that it wasn't going to plan.

I have broad shoulders and can take stick but these journalists made it a personal crusade against me. Where as at Ipswich people had accepted me for what I was, suddenly I was a lazy b*****d, and yet I hadn't changed my game. I sometimes wonder how I would have reacted if there had been a Three Legends show on the radio in my playing days. I probably wouldn't have liked it but I hope I would have tried to get to know the lads involved. The press people that had it in for me certainly never did that, otherwise they would have known that I wasn't the sort of person they were trying to make me out to be.

I actually won the player of the month award in *The Journal* but they didn't present me with the trophy because the people concerned were so against me. Another guy at *The Northern Echo*, Frank Storey, always seemed to be having a go at me. On one occasion, when Sunderland were on the way back up, we beat Southend 7-0 and I scored four. In the paper the next day, most of the team had been given marks of nine out of ten. But Eric Gates, who scored four of the goals, was given seven! It was pathetic. I'm not like that. I might give stick to someone one week but if he then plays well the following week I will bull that lad up to the hilt.

But all that served to drive me on and I didn't forget their actions when things improved after those first two difficult years. It was great for Eric two years down the line to ram it up their arse by playing well and then snubbing them when they wanted interviews. I made it clear there was no chance they'd get anything off me.

It didn't help that Lawrie didn't understand how to get the best out of me. He never played the system that suited me. Sometimes I played in the centre of midfield, sometimes I was up front, but I was always just trying to fit in. Having said that, I scored nine goals that season, which is no great shakes but we had a centre-forward at Sunderland last season, Jon Stead, who scored his first goal in April and people were saying he had done quite well. I can't get my head around that.

As the bad results continued to follow in my second season at Roker, the atmosphere on matchdays became increasingly worse. The crowds were a far cry from the attendances Sunderland have attracted to the Stadium of Light in recent years but there were still enough people there to make you feel pretty bad about yourself if you were having an off-day.

It got so bad that players really didn't want to go out and play. A perfect example of that came in a home game we lost. We were 1-0 down at half-time, as usual things weren't going well and we had three injured players limping around the dressing room. I had suffered a dead leg, someone else had a twisted ankle and a lad called Steve Hetzke said he was injured as well. Again, these were the days of one sub but all three of us reckoned we needed to come off. Lawrie made the decision to take me off, probably because he had a forward on the

bench, combined with the fact that my thigh injury meant I couldn't run. But it was a decision that didn't go down well with Steve. In fact, he was so furious that he came running at me, put his hands round my throat and screamed at me, 'You b*****d! I'm injured, you're not!' He was six foot three, couldn't play the game and was trying to make out that I wasn't really injured. He was that desperate to get off. When teams are winning no-one wants to come off but it's always different when you're on a losing streak.

One of the worst moments that will always stick in my mind until the day I die came in yet another home defeat. We were losing 2-0 with about 10 minutes to go when a dog ran on the pitch. Out of all the people on the pitch, the bloody thing came sniffing at my feet. The referee stopped the game while we got the dog off the pitch but I certainly wasn't going to volunteer to chase it and drag it away. Instead, I just tried to ignore it, to shoo it away because all the focus was on me while it was sniffing at my feet. The wags in the crowd were shouting, 'Gatesy, you can't even kick the f***ing dog, never mind the ball!'

Eventually, Lew Chatterley jumped out of the dug-out, raced onto the pitch and grabbed the dog by the scruff of the neck. The crowd gave a few ironic cheers because this was about as good as the entertainment had got all night but I was just glad the focus wasn't on me anymore. But then, clear as a bell, somebody behind the dug-out shouted out, 'Chatterley, you stupid b*****d, leave the f***ing dog on and take Gatesy off!' There was laughter all round and the joke was on me when my confidence was already at its lowest ebb. All I wanted at that moment was for the ground to eat me up but I had to play the last 10 minutes of the game listening to the crowd on my back, slaughtering me.

But none of the players did it. Yes, I had a nightmare, but our forwards, David Swindlehurst and Ian Wallace, didn't do it either. They had both done OK at their previous clubs but not for Sunderland. Wallace had been signed by Len Ashurst the previous season and probably thought Lawrie didn't want him, which may well have been the case. Swindlehurst was a McMenemy signing but he was from London and I honestly don't think he really wanted to be in the north-east. Yes, he wanted his move to Sunderland to work out for him and for the club to be top of the league, but when the results went against us how much did he really care? When it didn't go well, he wanted to get back down south. It was no surprise that neither player stayed around long.

Things just got worse and worse. Of course, at the time you hope you'll fight your way out of it but we weren't unlucky to go down. We deserved to be relegated. The club sacked Lawrie McMenemy with seven games to go and Bob Stokoe, a Sunderland legend, took over as caretaker manager for the run-in but it was too late for him to make any difference. We went down to Division Three for the first time in the club's history. It was embarrassing. To come back 'home' and play a part in a low point like that was horrible. In my 21 years playing football, that was my worst moment. I had never experienced failure until then and it was hard to take.

That could so easily have been the end of the story for me and Sunderland. Bob Murray, who had eventually taken over from Tom Cowie as chairman, called me in and said, 'Look, Eric, you're on big money, so if we get an offer over the summer, we're going to let you go.' I'm not too proud to admit that I was in tears. I understood their predicament but not being wanted for the first time in my career was an awful feeling.

But the winds of change swept through the club that summer, with Denis Smith appointed as manager and Viv Busby his assistant. They told me that they knew what had gone on before, that I'd had a nightmare, but that they also knew what I was capable of. 'You do the business and we'll look after you,' was the clear message. I tell you what, I never looked back.

Denis and Viv were like a breath of fresh air. The greatest tribute I could pay Denis is that I would put him on a par with Bobby Robson. He was cocksure and arrogant but I respected the geezer. He made training enjoyable and when he spoke he made sense. The difference in our performances and results was immediate and we won the Third Division title easily.

Denis made a few new signings but the most important one came a few games into the season. That was when he teamed me up with a lad called Marco Gabbiadini. They told me they had bought a young striker from York City. When they

•JOHNNY ON THE SPOT: I celebrate as Marco Gabbiadini shows why he earned that nickname with another important goal.

told me he was called Gabbiadini, I said, 'Oh, we'll be all right for ice creams then!' I had never heard of the lad.

I don't think we trained together before our first game as a partnership, at home to Aldershot, as I'd been injured so I still had no idea what he was like. After about five minutes he had this shot at goal that missed the target by about four yards. I shouted to him, 'Good shot, Marco, son.'

But I wasn't ready for his reply. 'Sorry, Eric, I was trying to trap it.' I hoped he was joking but he was serious! His control always was sh**. But right from the start we clicked as a partnership. Marco has gone on record to say that I made him as a player, which is nice of him. But the truth is he helped me as well. He was my runner, if you like. I was the supplier and he was the goalscorer. Having said that. Gabbers was such an exciting player, strong, fast and powerful. He wasn't the best centre-forward I played alongside, because he wasn't as good as Paul Mariner or Alan Brazil, but he was as exciting as both of them. Marco scored goals, of course, but you often didn't know where you were at with him. He would get on the end of balls you didn't expect him to. Sometimes he would

•NO PAL OF MINE! Taking on Boro's Gary Pallister at Roker Park early in 1989-90 season. Bernie put Boro ahead - but Sunderland won the game.

trap a ball and stick it in the net, but the ball was just as likely to bounce 20 yards off him. By then, I didn't run any more. I had lost my speed, I couldn't out-pace opponents like I'd once been able to, so I had to adjust my game accordingly. I still had good technique and a football brain, so I would just stand still and ask for the passes to come to me. I would find space and it was up to the others to get it to my feet.

The whole team did that brilliantly under Denis Smith. Implanted in their minds was to look up and think, 'Where's Gatesy?' Because I didn't move much, they instinctively knew where I was. My first thought was always to look for Gabbers. What I always used to say to him as we went onto the pitch was, 'I just want to see your big fat arse running towards the goal.' I would be facing play, ready for passes from others, but I wanted him running on so that I could just help the ball on to him first time. We did that a lot and it inevitably ended in a goal. I used to call Gabbers 'Johnny on the spot' because he would score goals out of the blue. Later, Kevin Phillips had that same ability. For me, Kevin had a bit more technique, though Marco had the explosive power.

I was pleased with my effort of 19 league goals on our way to winning the Division Three championship. We had a lot of young lads, like Gordon Armstrong, Gary Owers and Gabbiadini. Eager and hungry, they would run through a brick wall for the team if that was what was asked of them. Winning the title was great but I have to be honest and tell you that a little part of me was saying, 'So what?' I'd experienced the highest level of football at Ipswich, won the UEFA Cup and played for England. Topping Division Three ahead of the likes of Walsall, Northampton and Chester City just wasn't the same.

The following year we didn't do badly in Division Two, finishing mid-table, but my last season with Sunderland, 1989-90, could not have ended more dramatically. We finished sixth to claim a place in the play-offs, as fate would have it against our fierce rivals from up the road, Newcastle United. Having finished fully six points ahead of us, narrowly missing out on automatic promotion, they were disappointed to be in the

play-offs, while we were delighted to still have a chance of going up because we'd never really looked like getting one of the automatic promotion spots.

The first leg at Roker Park ended nil each. It was a hard-fought game and naturally neither side wanted to get beat, but we really should have won the match.

Paul Hardyman had the chance to give us a one-goal advantage to take into the second leg but he missed a penalty in the last minute of the game. Newcastle goalkeeper John Burridge saved it and then got kicked in the head by Paul as we challenged for the rebound. It resulted in a mass brawl between players of both sides and Paul being sent off.

There was no doubt that it was a great result for Newcastle. In the bar after the game, their players like Micky Quinn and Mark McGhee were very cocky and you could sense that they thought they had done it. That same feeling came across from the local press, with their build-up to the second leg making it sound like a Newcastle win was just a formality, as if we were going to St James' Park like lambs to the slaughter. But we didn't see it like that. We felt we had a chance because we were a better team away from home, able to catch teams on the break, thanks mainly to Marco's amazing pace.

Arriving at St James' on the team bus two hours before kick-off reminded me of a few hair-raising experiences in Europe with Ipswich. Our coach was stoned and the windows smashed in Italy and I had a gun held to my throat by a Greek police officer after a game against Aris Salonika. The hostility we faced from the Newcastle fans that night was a throwback to those days and I couldn't help but notice that much of the hatred was directed at me. I don't think the Geordie fans had forgotten that I had turned them down five years earlier so I got the brunt of it.

Before the match, Denis told us to make sure none of us got carried away with the rivalry and got ourselves sent off with silly tackles or overreacting to situations. Equally, we were warned not to incense the crowd. During our pre-match warm-up half an hour before the game we could feel the hostility. It was an intimidating atmosphere. I can't say that I was frightened because I thrive on the feel of a big game but a few of us were a bit worried about our families who were there to see us. I thought to myself, 'There's going to be hell on here tonight if we win this match.' I wasn't wrong.

In the very first minute of the game, I got embroiled in an incident with their supporters. The ball went out of play and I ran off the pitch to retrieve it from next to the fence in the hope of taking a quick throw-in. But as I leant down to pick the ball up, one pair of hands came through the fence and grabbed my long hair and another started twisting my nose! With the ball in my hand, I was trying to pull away but I was being dragged towards the fence, making me an easy target for all the b*****ds who wanted to spit at me and throw oranges in my face. It's funny now, looking back, but it was horrible at the time. And this was the first minute of the match! I eventually managed to pull myself away and gave them a few words, telling them what I thought of them. But I was glad there was a big fence between us.

Midway through the first half, I got my last ever goal for Sunderland, sliding in to score past Burridge. From that moment on I knew something was going to happen. We were no better than Newcastle on the night but we wrapped up a massive win when Marco Gabbiadini scored after playing a one-two with me. There were just four minutes left but an amazing sequence of events meant that the final whistle wasn't heard until well over half an hour later.

As Newcastle kicked off again from the centre spot, a noise erupted from behind me. I turned around to see that the Newcastle supporters had broken down part of the fence behind the goal and there were about 300 of them charging onto the pitch towards us. It was like The Alamo. I've never been so frightened in all my life. I ran like hell towards the safety of the tunnel. I always remind Gary Bennett, our big, brave central defender, that he was the only f***er that beat me up that tunnel, the soft t**t! The truth is that Gary heard the fence go and saw the fans racing onto the pitch but wasn't bothered until somebody booted him up the arse. As he turned around to punch whoever had done it, he could see the eyes of dozens of angry Newcastle fans on him. He didn't need a second invitation to get the hell off the pitch.

There was hell on in the tunnel, with players, police, referees, linesmen and coaches all saying their bit about what should happen next. The Newcastle staff were desperately trying to get the game abandoned, which is probably what their fans had had in mind when they invaded the pitch. Can you imagine it if that had happened with four minutes left? Thankfully, the referee, George Courtney, made it quite clear that abandoning the game wasn't an option. 'Whatever happens, we're going back on the pitch,' he said. 'This game is getting finished tonight.' We knew we had won so it was a surreal atmosphere while we waited for the pitch to be cleared so we could play those last four minutes. It was probably 30 minutes before we got back out there.

I did two things in those final four minutes that I'd never done before. First of all I played on the left wing because that was right next to the tunnel. I was making absolutely certain that I would be down that tunnel like a shot if the fans came on the pitch again. And for the last minute of the match, I marked someone for the first time in my career. The person I marked was the referee, George Courtney! Wherever he went, I went with him, ready for him to blow the whistle so I could get off the pitch as quickly as I possibly could.

Twelve days later we went to Wembley for the play-off final, only to lose to Swindon. We got beat 1-0 but that didn't reflect the game. We got battered, out-played and were fortunate to come away with only a single-goal defeat. Beating Newcastle had been our cup final and we weren't able to lift ourselves again. It looked like promotion had gone begging but it was then ruled that Swindon had breached 36 League rules, many of them involving illegal payments to players. Their punishment was to be denied promotion and, despite defeat at Wembley, Sunderland were promoted to the top flight instead.

That Wembley defeat was my last game for Sunderland. I'd had a decent season and was touched to win the club's Player of the Year award at the age of nearly 35, but I knew I would be no good for Sunderland in the top flight. My contract was up and I just felt it was the right time to hang up my boots, going out on a high, having helped the club rise from Division Three to Division One. Given those difficult first two years at the club, we parted in the way I would have wanted. There were no ill feelings either way. I left with my head held high.

Eric's Story:
RETIREMENT BY THE POOL

•VIV BUSBY: My boss at Hartlepool.

AS FAR as I was concerned my playing career was over the day I left Roker Park, having helped them back into the big time. But I got talked into playing on for another year. I got a phone call at home one day that summer from a guy called Clive Middlemass, asking me if I would be prepared to go and play for him at Carlisle. He said they were a good club, played football the right way and had a good chance of winning promotion, having just missed out the previous season. More interestingly for me, Clive promised that if I did well he would make me his assistant at Christmas. I didn't know Clive but he was a lovely chap and he talked me into signing a two-year contract.

With hindsight, I can say it was a mistake. I should have stuck to my guns and packed up. Instead, I found myself in a struggling side and found it harder and harder to motivate myself to play at a level that was nothing like the football I had taken for granted in those great days at Ipswich. The truth is that I would get frustrated with the ability of my team-mates, but I did that even when I left Ipswich and played for Sunderland. That's not being big-headed. It was just hard to accept that lesser level, having played at the top. So Sunderland had been a drop down, but to then go to Carlisle and drop another level, especially when we weren't doing well was really difficult. It got to me.

I had my pride and went out and did my best, scoring a reasonable amount of goals, but people at Carlisle won't have particularly fond memories of me because I was the big name and we didn't do as well as we had hoped. But the way it works if you're an old pro who goes to a new club and does well and the team wins games is that everyone says your experience is vital, but if it goes the other way and the team is struggling then you're an old has-been who is too slow and can't run. In the eyes of Carlisle fans, the latter was probably the case with Eric Gates, but I accept that.

One memory I do have of my time at Carlisle was finishing the season as the club's joint top scorer with Paul Proudlock, a good player who should have played at a higher level. Thanks to a local manufacturer, the prize for the top scorer was a bed, so we were left with a question when me and Proudy finished on the same number of goals. Do we share the bed? I quickly decided that Proudy should get it. We could have shared it, of course, but although he might be that way inclined, I never have been! (Only kidding, Proudy) I could sleep easily at night in my old bed knowing that I had shared the goalscoring honours.

I retired from the professional game that summer, taking an option to end my two-year contract halfway through, knowing that I had carried on for 12 months longer than I should have. It could have turned out differently, of course. Carlisle could have won the league and I could have been appointed assistant-manager and gone on to better things. But I wasn't bitter in the slightest. Football had given me a great life. The game doesn't owe me anything and I don't think I owe football anything.

Since then I have played the occasional charity games, even turning out for local village sides at times because I was still fit and have never lost my love for the game. My brother was manager of West Auckland and whenever he was short of players he would give me a shout. Again, this is not meant to sound arrogant but playing in the Northern League was a doddle for me. I would play centre-half or sweeper and enjoyed it. In a way it had brought my playing career full circle, because having played in the Northern League with Spennymoor at the age of 14, I had returned there with West Auckland right until my mid-40s.

But it wasn't too long after leaving Carlisle before I was involved in League football once again. I'd been out of the game for a few months when, out of the blue, I received a call from Viv Busby, who had been Denis Smith's assistant at

Sunderland. Viv had recently taken up the job of managing Hartlepool and told me about the challenge he had on his hands.

'There's nobody else here with me,' he said. 'No assistant, no coaching staff, no youth staff, nothing. Will you come and help me?'

If Viv was trying to put me off the idea, he was succeeding. But he wasn't finished yet.

'I can't give you a salary. All I can promise you is your petrol money.'

Jack Charlton would have been proud of Viv's negotiating skills, but I thought, 'What the hell?' I wasn't a great pal of Viv's but I respected what he had done in the past and he clearly felt similarly towards me. With nothing else on offer, I decided I had little to lose by giving it a go. But life coaching a basement club proved to be very different from the career I had enjoyed with Ipswich and Sunderland. For a starter, the facilities were desperate.

On my first day, Viv asked me if I would take the youth team down to Rotherham for a match the following day.

'Yeah,' I replied. 'Do you think the mini-bus could pick me up at Scotch Corner?'

Viv shook his head and smiled knowingly. 'I don't think so, Eric, because you'll be driving the f***er!'

I couldn't believe it. Viv hadn't mentioned he needed a bus driver as well. I'd never driven a bus in my life but I soon got the hang of it. Not only did I drive the youths down to Rotherham the next day, I was their chauffeur and coach for the rest of my time there. To this day I don't know if was I supposed to have a licence for the bus.

For the final few months of the season, I was a full-time member of the Hartlepool staff in return for my petrol money from Barnard Castle to Hartlepool every day. All in all, it went pretty well. I looked after the youth and reserve sides while Viv took care of first team duties. That summer, Hartlepool chairman Gary Gibson offered us a year's contract and we accepted. It was good to be back in the game and we were enjoying it. We had some decent players in the likes of Brian Honour, Nicky Southall, Ian McGuckin, Micky Tait and a former

Manchester United reserve called Paul Wratten. There were some tough characters but they all wanted to do well. I trained them hard and we won a few games, though we were never going to be world-beaters.

But it was a couple of episodes with the locals, rather than any particular games, that stick out in my memory. For instance, there was the occasion when I was sitting in Viv's office with Gary Gibson when we saw one of the balls the lads had been training with bounce over the fence and onto the main road. That probably happened on a daily basis but this time we watched a woman stop her car, jump out, grab the ball and drive off with it at her side.

Gibson shouted to me to get the ball, and I - like a daft t**t – raced out of the office and chased down the road after the car. As luck would have it, our thieving female's car was stuck at the nearby traffic lights so I quickly caught up.

Tapping on the window, I breathlessly asked, 'Excuse me, can I have the f***ing ball back?' She handed it over without debate, but afterwards I couldn't help but wonder what might have happened if some big fella had been in the car when little Eric came demanding his ball back!

That wasn't the only time I chased after the locals without thinking. Another time we arrived for training on the council park a few miles away from the Victoria Ground just as three kids shot out of the back door carrying three footballs that they had obviously decided to pinch. As we yelled at them, two of them dropped the balls but one ran up the road with the ball under his arms. Without a second's thought, I ran after him. He led me a merry dance down the local streets before finally disappearing through the back door of his house. It was only when I started banging on the door that I thought about what might happen if some big chap came out and belted me one. My heart was racing by the time the door opened and I was grateful to see the face of a woman, obviously the lad's mother, who gave me the ball back.

But stolen footballs were far from the club's only problem. Financial difficulties were mounting, though we were initially kept in the dark by Gary Gibson. I don't want to go into too much about Gibson, but let's just say he wasn't someone I trusted. Anyway, the first month of our new contract we got paid fine. There was no problem the second month either. The third month our cheques bounced. We were promised it would be sorted but, sure enough, it bounced again. Wondering what was happening, we went to see Gibson, though we were far from confrontational. 'Don't do that,' we told him. 'There's no need to give us cheques that will bounce. If you can't pay us, don't pay us until you can.' We told him not to worry about it. We loved what we were doing so we were prepared to go without pay for a while if it made things easier for the club.

Sadly, it turned out that the players weren't getting paid either. These lads were training and playing but not getting paid their wages that were hardly a king's ransom in any case. It became increasingly harder to motivate them and there were often rumpuses with players demanding their money.

But there was no sign of any improvement. After a third and fourth month of us not getting paid, Viv called me one day and told me, 'Eric, we've been sacked for financial reasons.'

Financial reasons? We hadn't been paid for four months! How could it be for financial reasons? If Gibson had said he was sacking us because of the team's form he might have had a point because we weren't doing great, but this was just taking the Micky. I've had more arguments with anyone in my time in football, but I like to think I'm straight. If I don't like something I'll say so, but I won't bulls**t anyone. Gibson simply hadn't been honest with us. But my disappointment wasn't about the money. What made me so disappointed was that I had lost an opportunity to get on the coaching bandwagon.

As I was due to take the youth team to a game the next day, I had two sets of strips in the back of my car, but I kept them. I never went back to the club again. After we left, the club nearly went to the wall, while it was about another six months before our unpaid wages were covered by a payment from the Football League.

To this day that remains my last direct involvement with a professional football club. And yes, I do miss it. What I miss most is the dressing room banter. People talk about the money but it was the laughs I had that was the best thing about being a footballer. We were all like big kids, constantly messing around from the age of 13 to 36.

I look back on my life and know what a lucky lad I was. I was paid for doing something that I loved. I was equally lucky never to suffer a serious injury. The worst I had was a twisted back that caused me problems for about six months until I had a manipulative operation. The next day I was right as rain. Not everyone is so lucky. Injury finished my team-mate Kevin Beattie in his prime. I didn't make a fortune but my life wasn't all about making money. Yes, I wanted to be well paid and do well for myself but that certainly wasn't the be all and end all.

Eric's Story:

STABBED IN THE BACK

IT'S DAFT in a way but I desperately wanted to get away from football when things didn't work out for me at Carlisle and Hartlepool. After playing non-stop for 21 years, I had been keen to get into coaching but when things turned sour I decided I needed a total break from the game. For quite some time I wasn't involved in the professional game at all. I was quite happy doing nothing very much, attending the occasional game or watching a match on the TV. There had been times when I thought I couldn't live without football, but I really didn't miss it.

The truth is, taking a backseat probably didn't help my case because when I wanted to get back into the game I couldn't. Having said that, I didn't try too hard. I didn't send my CV here and there or apply for any jobs. My attitude was people knew what I had achieved as a player and they knew where to find me. If someone had come knocking on my door to offer me a job, that would have been great, but it just wasn't me to go around asking to be given another chance.

That's not to say I did no coaching at all. For about 18 months I spent a lot of time coaching local kids, running football courses and just passing on my knowledge of the game to the next generation. I loved working with kids but even that came to an end when new regulations were introduced stipulating that you had to go and get badges to show you were qualified to coach. My attitude was, 'Why should I do that?' Why did I have to go on a course for three or four weeks to tell me how to teach kids to play football, learning off someone who couldn't even play the game? I'm not a big head but what can some administrator teach Eric Gates, who played professional football for 21 years and won England caps? I could have bitten my tongue, done the courses and qualified for the badges, and maybe I should have done. At least then I could have done what I wanted to do, which was coach children. But I don't regret it. I stood by my principles and refused to bow to ridiculous rules.

But for a twist of fate that might have been it for me and football. Believe me, I never ever thought I would get involved in radio work or have anything to do with the media. Even in my playing days I wasn't one for writing columns or courting the press and I never did many interviews. If someone asked me to do a presentation, I would say, 'Fine, I'll sign autographs but I won't speak.' I just wasn't comfortable with speaking in that kind of situation or airing my views to the public. I was more outspoken than most in the surroundings of the dressing room, but I wasn't one for shouting my mouth off to the media. I was probably resentful of reporters, especially those in the north-east who made their attacks so personal when things went badly for me at Sunderland.

So I was far from interested the day I got a phone call from a guy called Charles Harrison, who had commentated on Sunderland games for many years on Metro Radio.

'Eric I'm looking for someone to help me tomorrow,' he said. 'I need a former player to come to Reading to commentate on the match. Would you be interested?'

I thanked him for thinking of me but made it clear I wasn't interested, giving him the names and numbers of a couple of my former Sunderland team-mates like John McPhail, thinking it might be up their street.

'Try them first, Charles,' I said. 'If they can't help you, then come back to me and I'll do it. I won't let you down.'

I hoped that would be the end of it but an hour and a half later he rang me back. None of the former players I mentioned were available. As I'd promised I would, I reluctantly agreed to travel with him to Reading the following day. But I surprised myself by finding that I enjoyed my first ever co-commentary so much that I readily agreed to carry on when Charles asked me if I was interested in joining him every week.

Who would have believed that game would have been the

ERIC'S STORY

•MEETINGS: Talking to chairman Bob Murray convinced me Sunderland were heading into trouble.

start of what is now more than a decade of Eric Gates on the radio? Certainly not me, that much I can tell you. I was Metro Radio's commentator on Sunderland games for five years, during which time the figures for the number of listeners we were getting went through the roof. They were unbelievable. That's not to say it was all down to me or any one individual. The truth is that the team started doing well, twice winning promotion under Peter Reid and then starting to do well in the Premier League as well.

When Charles left the station, his replacement as commentator was a guy called Guy. Guy Mowbray was my new co-commentator, a smashing lad and a very good commentator who has gone on to greater things with *Match*

of the Day in recent years, while we were also joined by another guy called Tony McGill, who so happened to be a good friend of Peter Reid. 'The Guy, Gilly and Gatesy Show', as it became known, was very popular with Sunderland supporters.

Right from the start, I had a straight-talking style that the fans appreciated but the club hated. The simple fact is that I spoke more for the fans than I did for the club. I was doing a job for the radio station that involved trying to give an honest assessment of the games I saw. I felt I had a responsibility to relay to those supporters who weren't at the game what it was really like. I wanted to give the sort of straightforward report that a fan would give to his mates back in the pub, so if any players had a bad game I would say so. On the other hand, if somebody did well I'd shout it from the rooftops. So there was no bulls**t and I certainly didn't kiss the backsides of the manager or the players. There are always plenty of hangers-on around any football club but I have never been like that and I wasn't interested in being anyone's friend so I was comfortable telling it like it was.

Unfortunately, this caused a lot of problems with Sunderland Football Club and initially the man who suffered wasn't me, but my sidekick Guy. I first started to hear rumbles that people weren't entirely happy with me after Sunderland got beat 4-0 at Reading in a First Division match in October 1997, the season they ended up narrowly missing out to Boro for an automatic promotion place. But they'd made a bad start to the season and the Reading game was awful. During my commentary, I said words to the effect that the performance reminded me of the Lawrie McMenemy days when Sunderland really were a bad team.

I thought they were fairly innocuous comments to make that no-one could really disagree with but within days I heard that my thoughts had got back to some of the Sunderland players. Their response was to stop giving Guy interviews for Metro. Nobody wanted to speak to him because they had heard that Gatesy had apparently said this and that.

I bumped into Richard Ord at the Stadium of the Light the following week. Richard was one of the players who appeared in the game at Reading. I took my opportunity to let him and the other players know exactly where I stood.

'What's your f***ing problem, not doing interviews?' I asked.

'Well,' he replied. 'Last week you said we were poor and that it was like the McMenemy days.'

'What did you think of the performance? Was it like I said?

'Yeah, we weren't good but that's not the point. You shouldn't be so critical. You are one of us.'

I made it clear that he had me all wrong. 'No, that's not the way it works,' I said. 'I'm not in the dressing room any more, Richard. I'm paid by Metro to tell the fans what I honestly think about the game I see. It's not my job to defend you when you're poor and I won't do it.'

Then came a twist to the tale when I got a call out of the blue from Lesley Callaghan, Sunderland's public relations chief. 'Bob Murray wants to see you,' she said.

Having known Bob from my playing days, I had always got on great with him and I felt he appreciated me as a player and now as a commentator. I was intrigued that the club's chairman wanted to speak to me, but I couldn't help feeling a bit reluctant as I didn't want to waste my time. 'What's it about?' I asked.

'I'd rather not say,' came the response.

'Well, is it to my benefit to come to the meeting?'

'It might be,' came the reply. Lesley told me that Bob wanted to take me to the Black Bull at Malton one night for a chat.

I agreed a date to meet but couldn't help wondering what exactly it was he wanted to say to me. The more I thought about it the more I started to think he was going to offer me a job at the club. I had heard suggestions that he wasn't entirely happy with the club's PR and, as I was on the radio, I wondered if he had started to think that I might be a good guy to have on board. I even told people close to me that I thought I was going to be offered a job at the club, maybe some sort of PR work or liaison between the football side and Bob. I couldn't have got it more wrong!

A few nights later, Bob arrived at the restaurant in a chauffeur-driven car. We sat down, ordered drinks and food and chatted away. He asked me my opinions about the club and we talked about Peter Reid, the players and generally how the season was going. All the time I was thinking, 'Where's all this leading?'

Finally, he got to his point. 'It's a great radio show, Eric, but you're not speaking enough for the club. We want you to say more in favour of the club, to get over just how much progress is being made.'

I couldn't believe what I was hearing. I could feel my blood boiling as I told him, 'If you've brought me all the way down here just to say you want me to start licking your backside and changing how I am to suit you, then you've wasted your time and mine. That's not the way I work and it never will be. Bob, thanks for a lovely meal.'

With that, I stood up and walked out of the restaurant, without even shaking his hand. I was disappointed, angry and deflated. I had gone into the meeting hoping the club wanted to utilise my skills and experience, but instead it was just an attempt to control what I was saying on the radio. I would have loved to help the club and to have been the person Bob could have bounced ideas off. Whether it would have worked, I don't know, though I do know I would have done a lot better job than a lot of people there. Bob clearly had too many 'yes' men around him and no one apart from Peter Reid who was big enough to stand up to him.

From then on, there always seemed to be a barrier between me and the club. At the same time, I wasn't enjoying commentating as much as I once had.

Thankfully, things improved for a while after that, both on and off the pitch in terms of my relationship with the players, as Sunderland only lost three more league games all season and were desperately unlucky not to go up, finishing a point off automatic promotion and then losing the play-off final to Charlton in unbelievable fashion, going down 7-6 on penalties after a 4-4 draw.

I have some wonderful memories from Trafalgar Square in London the night before the play-off game against Charlton at Wembley. That night Guy, Gilly and me helped Sunderland fans take over Trafalgar Square. By midnight, one or two of the supporters had jumped in the fountain. I stood back and laughed, while Guy and Gilly got closer and closer before finally taking the plunge and joining the growing number of fans in the water. People were chatting to me and asking me if I was going to join them, but I was having none of it because I was wearing my best gear. Suddenly, a group of them grabbed hold of me and threw me in, actions that drew laughter from all the fans stood around. Looking like a drowned rat, I stood on the edge of the fountain as water dripped from me and shouted, 'Call yourself Sunderland fans? You're not real Sunderland fans until you've been in the fountain!' In a flash, nearly everyone there, probably 400 in all, leaped into the water. It was like the Alamo! I'll never forget a guy who was stood next to the fountain with his little boy, who was probably aged only about six. The father was desperately trying to encourage his son to join in the fun but the young lad just stood there trembling with cold in his knickers. But as soon as I shouted my challenge to prove who was a Sunderland fan, that young kid's dad just pushed him in! It was brilliant and so funny. That whole occasion summed up the great rapport I had, and hope I still have, with the Sunderland supporters.

The following year everything clicked into place and Sunderland won promotion by a mile. But it wasn't long before the old problem came to the fore with players not liking me telling the truth if I thought they were bad. This time the problem kicked off after a 1-0 FA Cup win at Lincoln City in January 1999. It was an uninspiring performance but a win is a win, no matter what the opposition. At the end of his commentary, Guy said that it had been like a Sunday morning game in the park. I replied by saying, 'Yes, it was a crap game and nobody will remember it but we won so we can't be too hard on anyone.'

Once again, my thoughts got back to the players and there was a bit of friction as a result. I would see them every week at the stadium but none of them ever said a word to me. Again, they simply made their feelings clear by denying Guy any interviews. If I had become personal in my comments then fair enough, I might have understood their reaction, but I never did. It was garbage and a terrible way to react to a bit

of honest assessment, but Sunderland were doing well and a lot of them were getting a bit too big for their boots. I was doing talks to fans alongside the likes of Alex Rae and Kevin Phillips and got on great with them but it was clear that others resented me.

I couldn't help think that some of them were a little bit jealous of how popular the show was becoming. They probably thought, 'Who the f*** is Eric Gates to criticise us?' It was daft, but I know Bernie has had similar problems at Boro in the past. It was clear that either I could go in the players' camp and make myself look a fool to the fans or go in the fans' camp and upset the players. It was an easy decision to make.

I always said that I would be happy to go in the dressing room, talk to the players and apologise if I had said something out of order, but I never felt that was the case so that day never arrived. It's a dressing room rule or tradition that everyone sticks together and keeps their feelings about other players within the dressing room, never to go slagging team-mates off to the outside world. But the point the players didn't understand was that I wasn't in the dressing room any more. If I had still been in the dressing room then I'd still have been speaking the same language as them but I wasn't a player now and I wasn't one of them. I don't go for this 'once a player, always a player' bull but the Sunderland players couldn't get their heads around it. It got to the point where I felt sorry for them, not for me. It wasn't really my problem.

Then I started to hear that the manager himself, Peter Reid, was less than happy with me. I never got to know Peter beyond saying, 'How are you?' and giving him a quick shake of the hand if I saw him around the stadium, but he started to get a bit funny towards me and I heard that out of my earshot he was saying a few less than complimentary things about me.

It was amid a background of all this bitching going on that I made the decision to take events into my own hands and go and have a one-to-one chat with Bob Murray, the club's chairman. So I phoned Bob up, asked if I could come and see him about things that were being said and he readily agreed.

When I got to the Stadium of Light, Bob greeted me, took me

to the boardroom and asked, 'Eric, would you mind if John Fickling sits in with us?' I didn't know John, the club's chief executive, but I was to discover that he was on the same wavelength as I was.

'No, not at all,' I answered.

But once John had joined us, Bob had another question. 'Would you mind if I go and get Lesley Callaghan?' I agreed, but I couldn't help thinking this wasn't quite how I'd planned it. I had gone down there for a one-to-one chat with the chairman to tell him where I was coming from and to ensure there was no more friction but it now felt more like three against one.

I'll never forget what John Fickling said to me while Bob was getting Lesley Callaghan. Stretching out his hand across the boardroom table, he said, 'Eric, this is about babies, isn't it?' He was referring to the way the players were behaving, reacting like spoilt brats because someone wasn't saying nice things about them.

'John, you're on the same wavelength as me,' I said, starting to believe that the meeting could go a long way to getting things sorted. It was good he said that but sadly it gave me a false impression of how the meeting was going to go. Although he had invited John and Lesley to join him in the meeting, over the next half hour Bob made it clear he stood right behind the players. I told him where I was coming from and he put a few things to me, but what he said was a big disappointment. He made it clear that they weren't prepared to listen to any criticism of Peter Reid and his players while the team was doing so well.

His summary of it all was that no one was bigger than the club, he didn't want anyone upsetting the dressing room and he certainly didn't want any friction caused by me or anyone else at the radio station. Much of that was fair enough, but he had saved his full backing to last. What he said – and I'll never forget this – was, 'Eric, if Peter Reid says black is white, then we are going with Peter for the sake of the club.'

'Are you serious?' I asked, disbelievingly. 'Whatever Peter says is right? What he says goes and if he says jump then everybody jumps? You can't do that.'

Murray replied that Reid was the manager and he had the full backing of the club.

I had heard enough. I told him, 'I am wasting my time here if that's what you think.' I got up and left the room without another word. I lost respect for Murray after that. It was a case of yes, Peter, no Peter, three bags full Peter.

After winning the Division One championship, finishing 18 points clear of their nearest rivals, Bradford City, Sunderland surpassed themselves by finishing seventh on their return to the Premier League, though it could have been better still, as we were second mid-season. But my meeting at the stadium with Murray and my refusal to water down my commentaries was to come back to haunt me. Both Metro Radio, my employers, and Sunderland, the club I loved, knifed me in the back.

As usual, my work with Metro Radio finished for the close season over the summer of 2000. I heard nothing for most of the summer, apart from the occasional call from Mick Lowes, who was Metro's commentator on Newcastle games.

Mick assured me that, despite rumours that I had heard, my job was safe. 'Eric,' he said. 'We don't know what's happening yet, but you'll be all right because they know you're good at what you do. You're the goose that laid the golden egg.' I thought that was good of Mick to say and his words reassured me that I would simply continue my role of the past five years alongside a new co-commentator when Sunderland kicked off the 2000-01 season back in the Premier League.

But then I started hearing rumours that while the new anchorman would be a lad called Simon Crabtree, his sidekick was going to be former Sunderland striker Gary Rowell. I didn't know if these rumours were true or complete fabrication but it left me wondering where I stood. My work with Metro was a major part of my income so I need to know if I still had a job with them or not but nobody had the good grace to ring me. The more it went on, the more I thought there was something going on.

A week before the season was due to begin, I decided to bring things to a head and get it sorted. I got in my car and

ERIC'S STORY

•ALWAYS RIGHT? Well, that was Bob Murray's view of Peter Reid.

drove up to the radio station's offices in Swalwell, near the Metro Centre. My role at Metro didn't involve me ever going to their studios or offices so I hardly knew anyone there but I had heard that the two guys in charge who were supposed to be sorting out who was commentating were called Tony McKenzie, the programme controller, and his senior, Mel Booth. I'd never met either guy before but knew I had to get a straight answer from one of them.

I strolled into Metro's reception area. 'Hi, I'm Eric Gates. I want to see Tony McKenzie.'

'He's not in yet,' said the receptionist.

'Well, when he comes in tell him I'm waiting here for him,' I told her, taking a seat on some chairs in the reception.

When McKenzie arrived soon afterwards, it was pointed out to him that I was there to see him.

He came over to me, shook my hand and asked if I would give him five minutes and he would be happy to sit down for a chat.

I was in no mood for being messed about any further. 'I'll give you five minutes but if you're not down here I'll be up to your office, because I'm not sitting around here waiting for you.'

Five minutes later we were sitting in his office. 'What's happening?' I demanded to know. 'Am I doing the f***ing commentary or not?'

Incredibly, he reckoned he still didn't know as the final decision was being made by his colleague, Mel Booth. I found that hard to believe.

'You don't know and there's a week to go? I've heard Rowell and Crabtree are doing it. Is that true?'

Now the truth started spilling out. 'Well, it looks that way.'

'And you haven't had the balls to tell me! I have one question

to ask you. Why?'

'Sunderland Football Club don't want you to do the commentary any more.'

The truth was getting more painful. 'Why?'

'There's nothing that you have to apologise for,' he said. 'But I understand they feel you speak too much for the fans and not enough for the football club.'

I shook my head, trying to take it all in. 'So you are going to go with Sunderland rather than Eric Gates, who has been with you five years and has only ever given his absolute best at the job he has done for you?'

'Business is business, Eric.'

I was determined to walk out of the room with my head held high. 'You can't sack me,' I snarled. 'You can stick your job up your arse.'

So that was me, out of a job. I'm not too proud to admit that I drove home feeling sick as a parrot, rejected and dejected. After all I had done both for Sunderland and Metro Radio they had stabbed me in the back. I know football owes me nothing but they had taken away my livelihood and I felt it was particularly nasty of the people at the football club to do the dirty on an ex-player who genuinely wanted them to do well and had no axe to grind. I won't forget what they did in a hurry.

After returning home from Metro, I chatted the situation over with a few people close to me and slept on it. The following morning I knew exactly what I had to do. I got up and shot straight back to the station and back into Metro's reception.

'I want to see Mel Booth.'

As with McKenzie the previous day, Booth wasn't in yet but he was due in soon. 'When he comes in, tell him I'm sat here,' I told the receptionist.

A while later, she said, 'That's him coming in now.' I had never seen this geezer before but all I could think was, 'This is the fella that's sh*t on me.'

He came in, the girl told him Eric Gates was here to see him and he looked over just as I stood up, staring him in the face.

He must have been surprised to see me because no doubt his colleague had told him that I'd been given the bad news the previous day.

As he walked towards me, he asked, 'What do you want?'

'I just want to see your f***ing face so that I know what you look like. Next time I see you, I want to make sure there's no way you can put a knife in my back.'

He tried to act all innocent, asking me what I meant.

'You know what I mean,' I said, staring him right between the eyes. 'You've done it once, you'll not do it again. Now f*** off!'

I'm not saying whether what I did was right or wrong, but that's the type of the lad I am and I certainly felt better for it. The first day I drove back home feeling sick. The second day, after saying what I had to say, I drove home feeling much better. And, best of all, I would be on the dole for only 24 hours! The call from Century came the next day...

Malcolm's Story:

BRING ME SUNSHINE

THE NORTH-EAST has been my home for the last decade, just as it was in my football hey-day, and I expect it to remain that way for the rest of my life. I love the place and feel like I belong here. But my early life in London could not have been more different from the idyllic, countrified lifestyle I now enjoy when I'm not co-hosting The Three Legends show.

I was born in Fulham on January 7 1950, the first of four sons to my parents, Charles and Florence Macdonald. A Yorkshireman, born just outside Hull, my father was a talented sportsman, who played both football and rugby and turned out for Hull City as an amateur at centre-half as well as centre-forward. He also had a spell with Blyth Spartans while working as a paint-sprayer in the Tyneside shipyards. And it was from my father that I got all my pace that was to become such a key part of my game. Something of a speed merchant, he was so good that he ran in high-class races for professional athletes. He served the RAF during the war, working as a wireless operator on a Catalina flying boat out in Ceylon, after being turned down as a fighter pilot as his eyesight wasn't good enough.

My mother was born in Chelsea and met my father while serving in the Land Army at Wollaston in Northamptonshire. He had been stationed near there on his return from the Middle East. After failing to settle in Hull, they returned to London's West End. Any football fan who has ever been to Craven Cottage, the famous old home of Fulham Football Club, will have probably walked past the house in which I spent the first 17 years of my life, 33 Finlay Street. I was later joined in the world by my younger brothers, David, Neil and James. We were fortunate enough to have two parents who always had time for their children, time to sit down with them and communicate. That's the clearest memory I have of my childhood. My mother and father were devoted to each other and would sit talking for hours and hours. I remember us getting our first television when I was about 10 and we

watched it for the first fortnight until the novelty wore off, after which it was almost never turned on.

While many footballers talk of playing their first football in the backstreets, I was lucky to have a park just 50 yards up the road. My greatest thrill as a kid was playing football in Bishop's Park, next door to Craven Cottage. Crazy about the game from the start, I was always up the park playing football, from first thing until dark.

My father, who by then ran a painting and decorating business, took me to see my first professional game when I was four. We went to watch Blackburn play Fulham at Craven Cottage. I went regularly after that, usually pestering my father to take me.

The first footballer to really make an impact on me was Blackburn's England international Bryan Douglas, who could play outside-right, outside-left or go through the middle. But then a young man came into the Fulham side and, wow, he was the best thing I've ever seen on a football field. His name was Johnny Haynes. He'd get the ball in the middle of the field and he would spin around until he'd got the right angle and half a yard of space. He would then ping it, knocking a pinpoint pass 50 yards to one of the wingers. He was quite phenomenal.

My father would also take me to watch the other professional club in west London, Chelsea. Later, I would join friends to 'bunk in' to Stamford Bridge, though my blood runs cold when I think back to the risks we would take to do so. We had to hop over about six live electric lines of the London Underground railway before squeezing through a hole in the railings.

My semi-idyllic existence, and that of my family, was rudely shattered when my father, at only 48, had a massive coronary, followed two weeks later by a cardiac arrest. I remember it all vividly. Dad, having come in late from work, had gone to get washed and changed. He then went out to the toilet – we had an outside loo – and he must have been in there for more than half an hour before any of us realised something might be wrong. It was a good thing I was there to help my mother and my Aunt Connie, who had come round to see her, because he was just slumped in the toilet and we had to break down the door. That was the start of one of the most difficult but most character-building periods of my life.

Dad was in hospital for months and it was quite a struggle for us to survive. His business collapsed because he was in no position to give his men any work, so we had to live on the sickness benefit my mother received. To help out financially, I took on a paper round, weekend jobs and deliveries for the greengrocers and butchers. I started working for WHSmith at Putney Bridge station and had to be there at five o'clock in the morning to do the marking-up of the newspapers to be delivered by the paperboys. That usually took me two hours and then I had a paper round of my own to do. The trouble was, I was always late for class at Sloane Grammar School, opposite the Chelsea ground. It meant I was forever in detention on a Friday.

When Dad eventually came out of hospital, he was a semi-invalid for a long time. He was forced to take an office job at the Pitman School of English in the West End, but that meant standing on a crowded tube train every day and we could see him just slowly wasting away. He had five heart attacks during this period and was forever in and out of hospital. Towards the end of 1966, four years after the initial coronary, it was becoming increasingly obvious that Dad didn't have long to live. When there was nothing more that the hospital staff could do for him, he was brought home by ambulance on Christmas Eve and carried on a stretcher to our living room settee to spend his last Christmas at home. We got up on Christmas Day to find him in a coma. Dad died in hospital later that morning.

Before his passing, Dad had gone through the process of selling our house in Finlay Street and beginning the process of purchasing a small shop in the Sussex village of Forest Row, near East Grinstead, believing that he and the family could run it as a business despite his deteriorating health. When he died we were already committed to carrying through the purchase,

so my mother and I, just turned 17, set about trying to run the shop as best we could. We didn't really know what the hell we were doing but rolled up our sleeves and said, 'We've got a family to keep together and we are going to do it.' My mother continued to run the shop until she became my personal assistant during my days at Newcastle, keeping tabs on my fan mail, sponsorships, media interviews and diary engagements.

Sadly, my father never saw me make it as a professional footballer, but nobody did more to push me in that direction. It was he who took the decision to let me leave school at 16 to pursue a career in football despite the fact that he was a great believer in the importance of a good education. Between the ages of 13 and 16, I had established myself as the best player at Sloane Grammar and had represented London Grammar Schools. Having my heart set on being a professional footballer, I neglected my lessons because I felt that nothing else mattered. It all came to a head when I was invited to go for a trial with Barnet FC by Terry Casey, one of the coaches of the London Grammar Schools XI, who was also captain of Barnet. They wanted to assess me in their reserve team in the Metropolitan League, so they applied to Sloane Grammar for permission to do so. But not only did the school refuse, they banned me from playing in the school team because I was not concentrating enough on my academic work, which I have to admit was correct.

When Dad discovered this, he arranged a meeting with the headmaster to see if he could find a compromise between the school and his strong-willed son. But he found it impossible to establish a rapport with the guy, who was a bit of a pompous so-and-so to put it mildly. He finished up having a full-scale row with him. 'You are the most pompous, ignorant man I have ever met!' Dad yelled at him. Then, having turned angrily on his heel and opened the door to walk out of the room, he left with the parting shot of, 'My son is leaving this school to find a career for himself.'

I left school without taking O-levels, partly because I wanted to become a professional footballer and partly to help the family out financially. I started with Alec Brooke Ltd, a sports and clothing shop at King's Cross, then spent a few months helping out a plumber. Even before Barnet, I'd trained with

Fulham and QPR, but I was always small for my age and didn't really fill out until I reached my late teens, so when I was 13 or 14 I found it a bit difficult playing against 15 and 16 year-olds at QPR. I was continually brushed aside all too easily, but it just made me all the more determined to succeed. It didn't help that I would occasionally turn up late, or not at all, for training sessions. Unfortunately, some days it was physically impossible to go to school, do my jobs and get to training. So perhaps Fulham and QPR might have interpreted that as me not being totally reliable.

I was 15 when I joined Barnet as a left-back, which was the position I had opted for when I went for the London Grammar Schools trials and the position in which I began my professional career. At school, I'd play centre-half, centre-forward or maybe in midfield. It really depended on where I was needed to play most of all because I was their star and had become a sort of utility player. But it was at left-back that Barnet's Terry Casey saw some potential and recommended me to his club. Although I trained with Barnet for some time, I never got to play for their first team, partly because I wasn't physically ready and partly due to my father's death and our move to Sussex.

For a while, there was no football at all, apart from the odd game for the local village side, but then I played a few games for a team called Knole Juniors in the Sevenoaks League before being recommended to Harry Haslam, the manager of Tonbridge, the Southern League club just down the road. I was a regular in the Tonbridge team by the start of the following season, though I was switched to right-back as the club already had a good left-back in Vic Akers, who has more recently been kit man for Arsenal and manager of their ladies' team.

Harry Haslam, known as 'Happy Harry' because he was always laughing and joking, was like a second father to me. He would always be very open and honest with my mother when she called to ask him how I was getting on. 'Look, I think the boy's got something,' he would tell her. 'I'll try everything in my power to get him in as a full-time pro. Then we'll see how he goes. But I'm not making any promises beyond that.'

At the end of my first full season with Tonbridge, he

engineered an invitation for me to go to Holland with Crystal Palace's under-19 team to play in a tournament there. They had a tasty team that included Stevie Kember, who later played first team football for both Palace and Leicester. We eventually beat Ajax 1-0 in the final at the Feyenoord Stadium in Rotterdam, with the winning goal coming from one of my long throw-ins. Palace manager Bert Head wanted me to sign for the club, actually agreeing a fee with Tonbridge and offering me terms. I was concerned that I would struggle to make an impact at Palace because they had something like

56 professionals on their books, but any quandary I might have had vanished when Harry phoned me to say he had left Tonbridge to join Fulham's new manager Bobby Robson as their chief scout. As a former Fulham player, Bobby was one of my heroes, while Craven Cottage was obviously a place I knew well. So I made my mind up to make the move back to west London.

Having made my choice, I quickly discovered that I'd been better off financially playing for Tonbridge. The terms I

●EARLY DAYS: My first team picture. This was the Queen's Manor Primary School, Fulham, side, and I'm on the far right of the front row.

•LONG-THROW SPECIALIST: An early sign, at Sloane Grammar, of the ability that won me a BBC TV long throw competition in the 1970's beating Tottenham's Martin Chivers in the final.

accepted at Fulham, £20 a week, were identical to the ones I'd been offered by Palace, but it was a flat rate that came down to £15 after tax. Then I had to bear all the costs of travelling between London and Sussex, a round trip of about 70 miles a day. So I'd been earning £17.50 a week in the Southern League and was now earning £15 in Division Two of the Football League!

I started my career with Fulham, aged 18, as the reserves' left-back, but that season, 1968-69, an injury crisis hit the first team, particularly in attack. That September, Harry Haslam urged Bobby Robson to play me up front, telling him that I'd always scored goals when he'd done so at Tonbridge. So that's how I started playing as a centre-forward. But I was rough, raw and my ball control left an awful lot to be desired. I was still playing like a Southern Leaguer, in fact. Nevertheless, once I got into the penalty area it was almost as if I became a different type of player, a different person even. I made things happen.

With the first team having failed to score for four games, Bobby put me in the team for the next match away to Oxford. I had the ball in the net twice, only to have both 'goals' disallowed for offside in a 1-0 defeat. The following Friday I made my senior home debut against Crystal Palace, of all teams, and I was delighted to score the only goal of the night. After scoring, I missed an absolute hatful but our goalscoring hoodoo was broken.

I played in four more games for the first team and scored in all but one. As our home game with Blackburn was on *Match of the Day*, I rushed home to sit down in front of the television, never having seen myself play before! Then, just after this little six-game run, during which I'd amassed five goals, Bobby Robson was sacked. I knew Bobby had been having problems with the senior players. As I was still only a kid, a lot of it went over my head, but I was certainly aware of the animosity being shown towards the manager by certain members of the team. What brought everything to a head and prompted Bobby's sacking, I believe, was the training session the day before his departure. He made it clear that many of the youngsters in the squad would be playing the following Saturday, resulting in many of the seniors treating that day's practice match almost as a joke. The following day, Bobby

was gone. I'm sure it was because of pressure brought to bear on Tommy Trinder, the Fulham chairman, by the old guard of players, who knew full well what was in the offing. More fool Trinder for bowing to their wishes because it was the old guard that had been responsible for the fact that Fulham were bottom of the old Division Two.

Bobby was guilty of trying to do nothing but good for the club, yet it seemed a lot of other people were hell-bent on committing professional suicide. He would have been 35 then, which was young for a manager. Johnny Haynes was about the same age – and that was basically the problem. In fact, if that episode taught me anything, it was never to try to manage players who were formerly your team-mates. Gareth Southgate, beware!

I was not at all surprised to see Bobby go on to become a very good manager. He had a very deep strength of will; one could sense it in him. In those days he would let his anger show. It was a lot more controlled by the time he was in charge of Newcastle United, although it was there on occasions. My abiding memory of the Fulham training field was not so much the good work of Bobby Robson, but the blatant sabotage. The training session having gone wrong, half the people involved would start to laugh. And there was Bobby, going red in the face and wanting to break people's necks. But, without doubt, Bobby helped my development and gave me a platform that allowed me to prove to myself that all things were possible.

My boyhood hero Johnny Haynes was made caretaker-manager following Bobby's dismissal, but you are mistaken if you think that sounds like a tale for *Roy of the Rovers*. One of his first acts in the role was to tell me I wasn't playing the following day.

'But I'm your highest goalscorer! I'm the only goalscorer!' I protested.

In response, Haynes said coldly, 'As far as I'm concerned, you can't play and you'll never make a career for yourself in the game. And while I'm at this club, you won't play here again.'

So, along with a number of other players, I was thrown straight back into the reserves. Despite what Haynes had said, I was dragged into the seniors a couple of times as a substitute, and I even got on once as an outside-left at home to Middlesbrough. But there was nothing anybody could do to save Fulham and the club were relegated into Division Three.

In the summer of 1969, having been told I was being retained, I requested an increase in my salary, which I felt I deserved. But my request was met with a blunt refusal. So there I was, being told I had to continue living for at least another year on £20 a week.

'I can't do it,' I said. 'It's just not possible.'

In response, I was reminded we had just been relegated.

'That's not my fault,' I replied. 'I've done all that was ever asked of me. I cannot live another year on £20 a week. It's kids' money.'

I desperately needed a rise because, having been married to my first wife, Julie, we had got a small flat in Wimbledon that was costing me £8 a week. So that summer I decided to go and get myself a second job. I found work in a factory that made supermarket shelves. It was my responsibility to take them off the production line and store them in the warehouse, so in the process I also became a forklift truck driver of some expertise!

With no improvement in the situation at Fulham, I was delighted when I got the opportunity to sign for Third Division Luton, thanks to the efforts of my old mentor Harry Haslam, who had left Fulham to become the Hatters' chief scout. Alec Stock, the Luton manager, did a deal with Fulham for £17,500. More importantly for me, the terms he offered me were £35 a week, which was music to my ears. Then he added, 'You'll also get a three-bedroom club house for as long as it takes you to sort out your own arrangements. We'll charge you a nominal rent of £2.50 a week.' On top of all this, he confirmed that I was due a signing-on fee. I couldn't believe it. After all my troubles, here was a guy who was doing everything he could to help me.

When the pre-season friendlies started, Stock wasn't quite sure where to play me, with the result that I was used in one position, then another. Finally, on the eve of the opening match, he not only confirmed that I would be the team's number 10 but set me a target of 30 goals for the season. I was stunned. I just thought, '30 goals in 46 matches? I can't

do that! That's a nonsense total!' But when I'd recovered from the shock, I thought, 'You've got to build yourself up for this and go for it. You've got make scoring opportunities for yourself.'

I was absolutely beside myself, however, when I failed to find the net in our opening game, despite our comfortable 3-0 home win over Barrow. The 30-goal challenge now had to be achieved in 45 games instead of 46! A whole weight was lifted from my shoulders the following week when I scored the only goal of the match at Bournemouth. From then on, the games couldn't come quick enough for me. Luton were neck-and-neck with Leyton Orient throughout the season, both clubs swapping first and second places. We were eventually promoted as runners-up behind Orient, though I found myself apologising to Alec Stock for finishing the season one short of my 30-goal target! His response was to set me the same target before the following season's Division Two campaign, after switching me from number 10 to number 9.

I would be first to admit that I was not technically gifted as a footballer, but nobody worked harder than I did to make myself better at what I was good at - scoring goals. Although the teamwork training with Luton was fine, I always wanted to hone my goalscoring skills. Unfortunately, there was nowhere to do this at the Vauxhall Motors sports ground they used for training, so I found a small room above a souvenir shop that was meant to be a stock room. I would practise in there using a plastic football, on which was an autographed picture of Johnny Giles, then Leeds' gifted little midfield playmaker and occasional enforcer. Giles kicked me a few times in my career, but that was about the only time I ever managed to give a good kicking back!

When I had to find alternative premises because I was driving the people in the shop below mad, Harry Haslam found me an empty warehouse the Co-op no longer used. Harry set out exactly what I needed to do to improve. 'What you need to work on is getting the ball, turning and shooting,' he said. 'Get it, turn, shoot; get it, turn, shoot.' So what I'd do is drive the ball against one wall of the warehouse and, no matter how it rebounded to me, control it with one touch, turn and shoot against the other wall. Get it, turn, shoot! Get it, turn, shoot! I'd repeat the exercise over and over again, until I was so dizzy with exhaustion I nearly blacked out. I used to do it for two hours, sometimes four, on at least two afternoons a week.

My reputation for goalscoring was built at Luton. I continued scoring at the higher level following our promotion, by which time my strike partner was Don Givens, one of four players signed from Manchester United. He was a bit special. He was extremely long-legged and brilliant in the air. We had a reasonable season but any hopes of a second successive promotion faded over Easter. Towards the end of the season, Alec Stock told me that, with promotion out of the window, the club needed something in the coffers and were ready to sell me. He went on to explain that three clubs had been showing an interest in me - Manchester United, Chelsea and Newcastle. He added that Newcastle had easily been the most enthusiastic.

I went into Luton's final game of the season against Cardiff having already matched my 29 goals of the previous campaign. I hit the 30-mark with the opener that day before adding two more in the second half. The following Friday Alec told me he had agreed a fee of £180,000 for me to join Newcastle United, instructing me to go to the Great Northern Hotel at King's Cross where Newcastle manager Joe Harvey would be waiting for me.

On meeting him at the hotel, I said, 'Good morning, Mr Harvey. My name's Malcolm Macdonald. Alec Stock has asked me to come and meet with you.'

I was a little taken aback when his first words to me were, 'So, you're the little b*****d who's just cost me another 35 grand? What the hell did you think you were doing scoring a hat-trick in your last game? Do you realise the deal was already done for £150,000 before your manager, with you scoring that bloody hat-trick, whacked the price up?' It was the perfect icebreaker. We sat down and got on like a house on fire. I loved Joe from the very start.

Football memories aside, another reason I have to remember my time at Luton with affection was the recruitment of Eric Morecambe, one half of the celebrated and much-loved comedy duo, as a director of the club. In fact, Luton became nationally famous overnight because Eric, who lived just a few miles south in upmarket Harpenden, was persuaded to join

the board. When Eric was introduced to the players, he was in his element. I think he was far happier there with the lads, joining in the quick-fire banter, the rapid humour and the Micky-taking, than he was up in the boardroom with the other directors. But the players were in for a surprise when, in a complete reversal of a footballer's usual situation, they started to pester him for tickets for the recording of his Morecambe and Wise shows.

Eric kept putting them off and putting them off, until finally he said, 'Look, I'm going to have to talk to you lot, aren't I? Please try to understand when I say to you that I work very hard and the last thing I want is you bunch of p***-takers in the audience when I'm trying to work.'

In retaliation, we said in that case we didn't want him in the stand when we were playing. How dare he come and watch us work when we couldn't go and watch him! This brought on an immediate flurry of pipe-sucking from Eric, but he was adamant that none of us would be allowed to join his TV studio audience - and none of us ever was. But while Luton had Morecambe, I knew I was wise to make the move north to a club where the passion of the support was something to behold.

•MAD HATTER: Comedian Eric Morecambe was a big hit as a Luton director.

Malcolm's Story:

TALK OF THE TOON

I WAS given the most fantastic welcome to St James' Park that left me in absolutely no doubt that I had arrived in the big time. It is also true to say that I arrived in style. As a gesture of thanks for earning Luton a transfer fee that was like gold dust for a club like Luton, the directors arranged for a chauffeur-driven Rolls-Royce to take me from Kenilworth Road up to St James' Park. So I arrived at the ground for my medical in a Roller to be greeted by a crowd of media people bigger than I had ever seen in my life. There were television cameras, flashing bulbs, microphones and about 50 notebooks and pencils at the ready. It was all quite daunting for someone who had only ever been interviewed by two local football journalists at Luton.

When the Rolls-Royce stopped by the steps, the driver got out and came round to my side to open the door for me. As I stepped out, someone remarked, 'F*** me! This is the first time I've even seen a football player actually arrive *in* his signing-on fee!' It turned out to be Bob Cass, a great joker and one of the country's top football writers for many years, who was then *The Sun*'s man in the north-east. I would later do a deal with the newspaper that put me in a position of earning £250 a week for an exclusive column, at a time when I was earning only £100 a week with Newcastle United! All this at a time when I suppose the average national wage was about £25 a week.

Having passed my medical with flying colours, I was whisked into a press conference, where I explained that one of my reasons for wanting to come to Newcastle was the club's great tradition for centre-forwards, like Jackie Milburn and Hughie Gallacher. After the press conference, I found myself chatting to a mild-mannered, quietly spoken chap who talked in a very knowledgeable manner about football and Newcastle United in particular. Suddenly, it dawned on me who I was talking to – the great Jackie Milburn himself. It was a privilege to meet the man, who was then working as a journalist for the *News of the World*. We got on so well that

Jackie offered to give me a tour of Tyneside later that week, an opportunity I readily accepted as I knew I needed to find somewhere to live. We went to Tynemouth and Whitley Bay, up the coast, then across to Morpeth, Cramlington and Stannington, then on to Gosforth and Jesmond. He pointed out the shipyards at Wallsend and coal mines at Ashington and then took me along the Scotswood Road, where he told me of the armaments made at Armstrong Vickers.

'The lives of these people are humdrum,' he told me. 'They don't have much money in their pockets, but they like a pint and they like to talk football. So it's your job on a Saturday afternoon to give these hard-working people enough conversation for the whole week. It's your job to get on that field and have as many shots at goal as possible, to create as much excitement in the opposing penalty area as you possibly can. Don't let coaches talk you into anything other than what you've been bought for - that's to score goals. Remember, the opposing half is your stage. There are ten others in the team to look after everything in the other half. Eleven being there is not going to make that much difference. You are the match-winner. Let nobody talk you into being anything else.'

Jackie was great friends with my new gaffer, Joe Harvey, so it was music to my ears when the great man confirmed that goals were exactly what Joe was wanting from me.

I have to say I did not make the most thrilling of starts to my Newcastle United career. We lost 2-0 at Crystal Palace on my debut before fighting out a goalless draw away to Tottenham a few days later. For a player who had shocked the assembled media at my press conference by telling them that I aimed to score 30 goals, just as I had done in Division Two with Luton, it was a rather ignominious start. It goes without saying that an awful lot of questions were already being asked about my ability as a goalscorer at the highest level.

What changed everything was our next game, my home

debut, against Liverpool on August 21. Matchdays back then were very different to those at St James' nowadays. Fans would start arriving about two hours before kick-off to be sure of getting in. That day the place was absolutely jam-packed when I arrived. It was a 20-minute job just to park the car and I then had to fight my way through the crowds, including about 500 autograph-hunters. I firmly believe it's a player's duty to sign autographs when asked, but it was just impossible to sign so many if I wanted to be in the dressing room in time for kick-off. It was difficult to make myself heard as I shouted, as politely as I could, 'After the game, I'll sign all the autographs after the game.' Being a realist, I did wonder whether they would actually want my autograph any more after the match, but I need not have worried.

Under the shrewd, inspiring management of Bill Shankly, Liverpool were one of the best sides in the country, if not Europe. It was no surprise, therefore, when they quickly moved into a slick passing mode, taking the lead through an Emlyn Hughes penalty. But I grabbed a home debut goal from the spot to put the scores level. When I later accelerated passed Tommy Smith and smacked a left-footed shot into the roof of the net, the noise from the fans was quite the most incredible thing. It was beyond description.

The goal was a bit special but I wasn't prepared for what happened next. As we returned to our half for the restart, the Geordie fans began to sing a tribute to me to the tune of *Jesus Christ Superstar*, the hit musical in London at the time. 'Supermac, Supermac, how many goals have you scored so far?' They sang it over and over again – and my 'Supermac' tag was born.

When, in the second half, I fired a third past the left hand of Ray Clemence into the bottom corner, the cries of 'Supermac, superstar' filled the city of Newcastle. We were two goals to the good against one of the best teams in Europe and playing some wonderful football. I was dreaming of scoring a fourth and a fifth but there was still another twist in the tale of this particular game.

With less than a quarter of the game still to be played, Clemence duffed a goal-kick, the ball trundling towards me. It took a bobble as it reached me and hit my shin before looping back towards the Liverpool goal. I set off after it, with big Larry

Lloyd in pursuit and Clemence racing out of his goal to meet us. Having been first to the ball, I lobbed it over the advancing keeper before continuing my run, all the time watching the flight of the ball. To my disappointment, it landed on the roof of the net. At that exact moment, I spotted Clemence leap off the ground towards me as I ran full-pelt in the opposite direction. You can imagine the sort of impact there was when six studs, with the full weight of the Liverpool goalkeeper behind them, hit me smack in the face. The first thing that hit the floor was the back of my head. I remember thinking, 'Come on, get up!' But my limbs refused to respond to the signals my brain was sending out. Refusing a stretcher, I attempted to walk off the pitch but was in no fit state and had to be carried off unconscious by Newcastle's assistant-manager, Keith Burkinshaw, and our physio Alex Mutch.

When I came to, I was on the couch in the physio's room. I had absolutely no recollection of the game, though I was informed that we had won, despite Liverpool pulling a goal back after my departure. My lip was gashed and swollen, my cheekbone was the size of a cricket ball and my left eye was blackened. Oh, and I'd lost my four front teeth. Later, people told me that the loss of those teeth gave me a fearsome appearance on the pitch but I would prefer to have kept my teeth as I was forced to wear dentures from then on, taking them out before each game for the rest of my playing career. The worst discovery of all was that Ray Clemence got off scot-free for his actions. In fact, the referee did not even give us so much as a free-kick! Watching the incident again on Tyne-Tees TV the following day, I couldn't help but notice that Clemence didn't look to see where the ball had gone, keeping his eyes firmly fixed on me. No doubt he would argue that it was a complete accident, but I couldn't help thinking it might have been his way of exacting revenge for having a hat-trick put past him.

The third goal that day ensured I would remain forever in the hearts of the Newcastle supporters there to see that match. That game and my hat-trick are remembered as magical moments in the club's history. There is an affinity between the people of Tyneside and me that nothing whatsoever can break. The Newcastle supporters are something very special. They've won nothing since the Fairs Cup in 1969, yet they are still there, more eager than ever. It's just incredible that the club gets that level of support without winning anything. They are happy to see entertaining football but how they must wish for a major trophy. But, as Jackie Milburn said, give them plenty to talk about and they will keep turning up.

As the goals flowed for me at Newcastle, I was called upon to play for my country, first at Under-23 level and then for the full side. I'm proud to think that Sir Alf Ramsey, the manager who won the World Cup for England, was always a great supporter of mine and gave me my first five caps. In fact, I'd like to think my international career would have stretched beyond 14 caps had Sir Alf not been sacked in 1974. Unfortunately, his successor, Don Revie, was much less enthusiastic about what I could do, while the next man, Ron Greenwood, clearly did not rate me at all.

I made my full England debut against Wales in May 1972, though I failed to score in a 3-0 win in Cardiff. I then had an absolute stinker in a 1-0 home defeat to Northern Ireland, in what was my first appearance at Wembley, and was a substitute in the final game of that year's Home International Championship against Scotland at Hampden Park. I played an active role in the England side until Alf's sacking following England's failure to reach the 1974 World Cup finals.

Don Revie left me out of his initial squads, only calling me up to play the world champions, West Germany, in response to demands from the press. When I turned up for duty, his opening line to me was, 'You do realise that I don't want you here? I've been under immense pressure to bring you in and it's against my better judgement. You're playing on Wednesday, but if you don't score I'll never pick you again.'

It was hardly the welcome I'd hoped for, but I responded by scoring our second goal against the Germans, losing their great captain Franz Beckenbauer to head in at the far post from Alan Ball's cross. That 2-0 Wembley victory gave the whole country a huge boost ahead of our next game, a European Championship qualifier against little Cyprus.

I was flabbergasted when, before the game, Revie almost spat out his thoughts to me once again. 'I'm still not happy about you being in the squad,' he said. 'I feel you've been foisted on me by the press. The same rule applies as before -

if you don't score, I'll never pick you again.' I wondered what I had to do to win the guy over. Something told me that it wasn't just a football decision but something more personal.

When I told Alan Ball - my England team-mate and a World Cup winner from 1966 - what had been said, he made it his mission for me to become the first ever player to score six goals in one game for England. He checked the record books and discovered that such a feat had never been achieved. Then, as each of my goals went in on a night that was like living a boyhood dream, he kept encouraging me to get another and another. I eventually scored five, denied the all-time record by the post and having another disallowed for offside.

•CELEBRATION TIME: enjoying the moment after scoring against Manchester City.

As the crowd went daft at the end of the game, I looked across the pitch at Revie and thought, 'What are you going to say about that, you b*****d?' As it turned out, he said bugger all. In the dressing room, he made his way round, shaking hands with every player and congratulating them on their performance. But when he got to me, he blanked me, just like he'd done after the West Germany game. I'd just equalled the individual scoring record for England, but the manager never said a word!

My last game for Revie and for England was a European Championship qualifier against Portugal in Lisbon in November 1975. That night their keeper made three brilliant saves off me, but I was sure I would find the net sooner or later, only to be subbed about five minutes into the second half. I could only think that Revie was determined to stop me scoring again. As I walked off the pitch, I knew there and then that I'd never again pull on an England shirt as long as he was the manager. He walked out on England for the United Arab Emirates two years later, by which time I was playing the best football of my career with Arsenal, but the appointment of Ron Greenwood as Revie's successor was the worst thing possible for me personally. Unfortunately, I was the complete antithesis of his ideal centre-forward and I never won a single cap under his charge.

Given that the club has won nothing domestically since the 1950s, the city of Newcastle was absolutely buzzing when we reached the 1974 FA Cup final. If I'm brutally honest, though, our cup run was football bordering on farce, starting with replay victories over Southern League Hendon and Scunthorpe United, then of Division Four. After cruising to a good win over West Brom in the fifth round, we went three goals behind at home to Nottingham Forest in the quarter-final before a tremendous comeback gave us a 4-3 success, though only after the crowd had invaded the pitch, requiring a 15-minute delay that seriously affected Forest's concentration levels. The FA rightly decreed that the game should be played again, this time at Goodison Park. That game ended goalless, so a replay took place, again at Goodison, though I will never understand the reason why the FA insisted that the game should again take place at Goodison and not Forest's City Ground. This time we got the win, with me nicking the only goal to send us into the last four. There, at Hillsborough, we took an absolute battering off Burnley but I scored both goals as we came off 2-0 winners.

So, having made the final itself, where we would play Liverpool, we travelled to Wembley with our fans desperately praying we would match the previous season's achievement of our bitter north-east rivals, Sunderland, who had beaten the mighty Leeds United side of the era, despite being in Division Two themselves. Unfortunately, we got things wrong from the start. We made the mistake of preparing for the Wembley showdown by spending the entire week in a base in Surrey. We then inexplicably decided not to play Stewart Barrowclough, changing our usual tactics to incorporate Tommy Cassidy, with Terry McDermott asked to fulfil Barra's role on the right wing.

Though we went in goalless at half-time, we were terrible in the first half and were steamrollered by Liverpool in the second. It was all too easy for Bill Shankly's side as they ran out 3-0 winners. I had only one shot at goal in the entire 90 minutes, an effort from distance that missed by a mile. It was the worst game I had ever had personally and the worst team performance I'd ever been part of. We dreaded the open-top bus ride around the city centre the day after the final. There was a lot of anger in the players, not just because we'd been beaten but because of the manner in which we'd lost. We had

gone down without even a whimper. Bob Moncur, our captain, was so ashamed that, as we travelled across the high level bridge over the Tyne, he threw his runners-up medal out of the window and into the river. 'Why do I need a medal to be reminded I'm a loser?' he said bitterly.

I think we would have preferred to be ignored by everybody on our return to Newcastle. We would have deserved that. But it didn't happen. Instead, the fans packed the city, cheering us home as if we had won the final. At that moment, I saw Geordie support for what it was.

The season that followed our FA Cup final defeat, 1974-75, was very much a case of after the Lord Mayor's show. Something had gone out of the club and the Joe Harvey magic wasn't there any more. The big man, who used to swan up to the training ground and watch things going on, wasn't doing it with the boyish confidence he once did. As the season progressed he seemed to develop something of a stoop. Nothing much changed on the pitch, which hardly helped Joe. As always, we would slaughter some sides, then get slaughtered by others. We were brilliant, then awful. Unsurprisingly, we finished mid-table as usual.

Then, in the summer of 1975, came the final blow - Joe was sacked. Perhaps sacked is not quite the right word. According to the board, he was being moved to another position, though they were not prepared to expand far beyond the fact that he was no longer manager. It was a shabby way to treat a man who had served the club so well and so loyally as player, coach and manager for some 30 years.

Rather like Kevin Keegan when he was Newcastle manager many years later, Joe had a very simple philosophy. Basically, he looked to the team to score goals without worrying too much about the defence. If things started to go wrong, he'd just go and buy a bloody good player. That's how he came to sign Tony Green, for instance. There was no grand master plan or anything like that. He relied heavily on Bob Moncur, who played alongside Paddy Howard at the heart of our defence. Paddy was one hell of a customer to deal with, while Monc was a great reader of the game and a powerful leader, though he suffered from a serious lack of pace.

I had my criticisms of Joe but I liked him and he always looked after me as a player, so I was sad to see him lose his job. I would have been all the more disappointed with Joe's departure had I known then who they would appoint as his successor. In fact, I did not even know our new manager when I was told his name. I had simply never heard of him! His identity was revealed to me during a telephone conversation with John Gibson, a reporter on the Newcastle *Evening Chronicle*, while I was enjoying a six-week close season spell playing in South Africa with a club called Lusitano. John gave me three guesses as to the name of the new Newcastle manager.

'Brian Clough?' I tried.

'No, he was never even mentioned in the raffle,' came John's reply.

'Bobby Robson?'

'No, they weren't interested in him either. This is your last guess.'

'Please don't tell me they've appointed Jack Charlton!'

'No, not him either.'

'Well, go on then, John, tell me who it is.'

'Gordon Lee,' he replied.

'Gordon who?' I said instinctively, because I'd honestly never heard of the fella, even though he had been manager of Blackburn.

It was an unfortunate thing to have said, because the next day the back-page headline in the *Evening Chronicle* was 'Gordon Who? Says Supermac from South Africa.' So I was completely at odds with the new manager before he'd even set foot in Newcastle and before we'd even so much as exchanged a word. On my return to England, I was shown the headline and realised I had some bridges to build. I took a good look at the newspaper article to ensure I would recognise my new manager from the back-page picture, also noting the appointment as Gordon's assistant of Richard Dinnis, another man I'd never previously heard of.

I thought it might be a good idea to go to St James' Park, introduce myself to Gordon and explain what had happened. As I was making my way towards the doors at the stadium's main entrance, they swung open and out came the face I had

been looking at in the paper, our new assistant-manager. I stuck out my right arm to offer a handshake and uttered the immortal words, 'Hello, Dennis. I'm Malcolm Macdonald.' I'd only forgotten the poor bloke's name, thinking it was Dennis Richards. Not surprisingly, he blanked me. What a good start!

It got worse. When I introduced myself to Gordon Lee, he didn't say anything by way of a greeting. All he said was, 'Come into my office.' Once we were sitting down, instead of any small talk or even talking directly about my newspaper faux-pas, he opened the conversation with, 'Tell me about Terry Hibbitt. I hear he's a troublemaker.'

I couldn't believe it. I'd just rushed back from Johannesburg, only to be sat down in the manager's office and quizzed about one of my team-mates being a troublemaker! 'Let me tell you this,' I said, anger rising in me, 'Hibby's a great player – and that's all you need to know. Beyond that, this conversation is terminated. I'm off. I'll see you in training.' And away I went.

Soon afterwards, the manager was quoted in a newspaper article saying that he would not tolerate 'superstars', pointing out that one man did not make a team. As I read the article, I realised he had named me and only me. Our relationship went downhill from there, while Gordon created divisions within the dressing room by referring to any new signings as 'my players', whereas the others were just 'the players'. Soon afterwards, he told me, 'I've just signed a player who is going to score more goals than you!' I just looked at him with contempt and said, 'In your dreams! I don't think that bloke's been born yet.' The man Gordon was referring to was Alan Gowling. As it turned out, Alan scored more than me overall that season – 30 goals to my 24 – but I got more than him in the League – 19 to his 16 – and I felt that was where it really counted. Gordon and I agreed to differ.

On another occasion, he dramatically announced to the dressing room that he had just signed 'the new Bobby

•MAC MAGIC: In typically combative action for Newcastle United.

Moore'. The poor lad who never had a hope of living up to such an unenviable tag was Graham Oates, who had joined us from Blackburn. Oates made his debut for us against Leeds the following Saturday and I decided to see just how good he was. When Alan Gowling kicked off with a pass to me, I drove it straight at the feet of Oates. Not only did he fail to control the ball, but it looped up off the top of his foot, hit his chest, bounced on his shoulder and went behind him. In a bid to rescue the situation, he thrust out a foot and lobbed our goalkeeper to score an own goal. I couldn't resist having a go at Lee at half-time. 'Well, Gordon,' I said, in front of the whole team, 'I don't remember Bobby Moore doing anything like Graham has just done!' Not surprisingly perhaps, the rift between us became a chasm from there.

I was now well and truly established as a top-flight footballer and, at 25, was at the peak of my career. I was scoring between 20 and 30 goals every season, which meant I'd created a reputation as one of the danger men of the game. So it shouldn't really have mattered to me who became manager after Joe Harvey, because no self-respecting manager turns his back on goals. Unfortunately, instead of going with the flow and making the most of my scoring record, Gordon Lee decided to battle against it.

I have to say that first season under new management wasn't all bad. I was still enjoying my football, mainly because I found putting up with Lee a challenging lark. We also reached the 1976 League Cup final, though I'm not sure if we got to Wembley because of him or despite him. I rather fancy it was the latter. We played Manchester City in the final, with the two sides proving to be evenly matched. After going behind, we pulled level and thought we could go on and win the game. But a wonderful bicycle kick goal from City's Dennis Tueart knocked the stuffing out of us and it was an uphill battle from there. It was two final defeats out of two, but this time we could at least console ourselves that we had been involved in a damned good game of football, settled by a brilliant goal.

Events were pushing me towards the exit door at St James', with the friction between the manager and I undoubtedly the biggest influencing factor. One particular incident that convinced me I was no longer willing to put up with someone who was so small-minded in picking fights with players

happened after a battling 2-2 draw against Derby at the Baseball Ground. Down to ten men for most of the game after I think it was Micky Burns had been sent off after five minutes, we all produced superhuman efforts to take a point. One man in particular ran himself into the ground. A true hero on the night, Terry Hibbitt was absolutely knackered when he walked off the pitch on the final whistle. Gordon Lee, however, was about to give us another first class performance in man mismanagement.

Along with myself, Terry was the last to climb out of the communal bath. The dressing rooms were now empty apart from Richard Dinnis, the physios and two wicker skips in which they packed the kit and boots. On top of the skips was a brown paper parcel, clearly containing a pair of football boots. Terry, who never missed a trick, jokingly asked, 'Who's not travelling back to Newcastle, then?' Dinnis and the physios went scarlet as Gordon Lee came through the door, picked up the parcel, shoved it into Terry's chest and told him, 'You're not.'

He went on to tell a stunned Terry that Freddie Goodwin, the Birmingham manager, was outside waiting to talk to him. 'I've agreed a deal with him, so go out and talk to him,' said Lee, before marching back out of the room.

Never in my life had I witnessed anything so callous. 'I don't f***ing believe that!' growled Terry, a towel around his waist, dripping wet and exhausted from his night's efforts. After calming down, he agreed with me that he should go and talk to Goodwin but tell him he would go home and discuss any potential move with his wife before making any decisions. After getting dressed, I went to the players' bar for a beer, leaving Hibbitt and Goodwin to talk.

But no sooner had I arrived in the bar than Lee ordered all Newcastle players to board the bus immediately. Once we were on, he announced, 'Driver, let's go!'

I shouted, 'No, no. Hang on, Gordon, the wee fella is still inside talking to Freddie Goodwin.'

'Yes, fine, we can leave him,' he replied. 'He'll be in Birmingham tomorrow.'

'You what?' I questioned, telling him that Terry didn't plan to make any decision tonight and planned to travel back to

Tyneside with us to discuss his options with his wife. 'He's coming home with us tonight,' I said.

'No, he isn't,' Lee insisted. 'He'll be Birmingham's problem from now on. Driver, drive on! Get this bus moving.'

The driver, a lovely guy called Bob Green, was put in an awful position by all this. It was clear that, although he knew the right thing to do was to wait for Terry, he did not want to risk his job by disobeying the manager's orders. With catcalls ringing out from the players, he clunked the bus into gear and moved the coach slowly up the road. At that moment, Hibby came out of the doors to the ground, spotted the bus and started racing after us, his brown paper parcel under his arm. 'Bob, stop the bus!' we shouted. The wee fella's on his way!'

Still Lee was having none of it. 'Driver,' he said grimly, 'if you value your job, drive off now. We're leaving him here.'

I was so angry with Lee that I could have throttled him. 'Get this bus stopped now,' I demanded. But he absolutely refused, so leaving poor Hibby standing there in the middle of the road. All Hibby could do was go back into the Baseball Ground and order a taxi to the railway station. He eventually arrived back home at about nine the following morning, via several train connections. Not surprisingly, he did sign for Birmingham after talking it over with his wife. From my part, I was fuming with Lee and thought to myself, 'That is it. I've put up with this plonker long enough. He can go whistle now.'

My long-expected departure came that close season, during the summer of 1976, when I received a call out of the blue asking me to meet Gordon Lee at Newcastle airport. It didn't take much imagination for me to work out what was in the offing. Arsenal boss Bertie Mee had made it clear that he wanted to sign me before he had been sacked. But waiting for me at the airport with Lee was Mee's Highbury successor, Terry Neill.

Terry explained to me that his chairman had agreed a fee with the Newcastle chairman and he now wanted to get me down to London. What's more, he had a private jet there at the airport. 'We can talk on the way down,' he said.

Before joining Terry on the plane, I took great pleasure in saying to Gordon Lee, 'I hope this is the last time we'll meet as employees of the same club.'

I expected to quickly become an Arsenal player but it didn't happen like that. Instead, an apparent hitch at the Newcastle end meant Arsenal weren't yet in a position to talk contracts with me, so I spent the best part of a week hanging around first Terry Neill's house and then a London hotel waiting for some movement. I was eventually invited to the house of the Arsenal chairman, Sir Denis Hill-Wood, who met me in his garden that was about the size of Lord's. After a brief discussion, he waved over his butler, who brought out one of those old black Bakelite telephones on a lead that was about a hundred metres long. Sir Denis then made a phone call to his Newcastle counterpart, Lord Westwood. From the conversation it became clear that Newcastle had already reneged on two offers they had initially accepted of £275,000 and then £300,000.

'I'm getting a bit fed up with this, so here is my final offer,' said Sir Denis. 'If you accept it, I want from you an assurance that its acceptance is binding on the whole of Newcastle United Football Club and its board. I am making you an offer of exactly one third of a million pounds. Now, is that acceptable or not?'

Thankfully, the deal was finally agreed for £333,333 and I became an Arsenal player, so ending my stay at Newcastle United during which I formed a truly unbreakable bond with the club's wonderful supporters. I'm proud to say that I remain one of Newcastle's all-time top scorers, having found the net 138 times in 258 games during my five years on Tyneside. Knowing that I fulfilled my personal ambition by joining the likes of Jackie Milburn, Hughie Gallacher, Len White – and now, of course, Alan Shearer – in a long line of great Newcastle number 9s is a very special feeling.

Malcolm's Story:

HIGHBURY HIGHS AND LOWS

I HAD hoped that my move to Highbury would help me win some of the game's biggest honours but I was to be disappointed. I probably enjoyed the best goalscoring form of my life in my first year with Arsenal, but I was to add only another loser's medal to go with the two I already had.

My strike partner at Arsenal was a raw young talent called Frank Stapleton. I could see from the start that he was going to be a phenomenal player, though I had to first convince Terry Neill not to sell him to my old mentor Harry Haslam, the Luton manager, for £60,000. Frank, who would go on to become a wonderful centre-forward for Arsenal and Manchester United, was only 18 and still developing physically but I persuaded Neill to stick him in the team with me for three months. In that time, Frank grew from boy to man and became a major talking point in the game, though I was constantly on his back to improve in every quarter.

It had originally been the manager's idea to partner me up front with John Radford, a veteran of Arsenal's League and FA Cup double-winning side of 1970-71. But it was clear that our styles of play did not complement each other, so I was relieved when Neill saw sense and gave Frank his chance. It was clear that young Frank could become a great talent if he listened and learned – and he was only too willing to do both. Every day he would stay back with me for an hour's finishing practice, something that had become second nature to me, though Frank was the first player I recall joining me on a regular basis. I would give him tips on how to strike the ball, though one thing I didn't have to help him with was his heading. Although he would occasionally mistime his jump, he was good in the air from the very start and would go on to become one of the game's best headers of the ball.

Knowing what he could become, I constantly pushed and nagged Frank, in training and on the pitch, but all my chivvying paid off handsomely when I faced Newcastle United for the first time as an Arsenal player in December 1976.

Newcastle were doing well at the time and would eventually achieve a UEFA Cup spot thanks to a fifth-place finish, but I was determined to make an impact against them, especially to make a point to Gordon Lee. I was delighted to shut him right up with a hat-trick in one of the best games of football I can recall, the game ending in a 5-3 home win to Arsenal. That hat-trick represented just three of 25 League goals I scored in a wonderful first season at Highbury, making me Division One football's top scorer for a second time in three seasons.

The following season, the goals continued to come. Then came the beginning of the end. I tore the cartilage in my right knee after catching my studs in the grass as I walked across the pitch at Upton Park. Knowing that I had recovered from a similar injury in my left knee in just six weeks during my time at Newcastle, I wanted to have surgery immediately but I reluctantly agreed to Terry Neill's request to delay the operation as I would otherwise miss the sixth round and semi-finals of the FA Cup. We were well out of the title race but were going well in the cup so I understood why he was so keen to have me available. I scored one of the goals in our 3-2 quarter-final win over Wrexham and two in a 3-0 victory over Orient in the semi, but my knee was gradually getting worse. Despite my pleas, Neill insisted I played each game. As a result, the tear became so bad that a bit of cartilage was hanging loose and would get trapped in the joint, causing my knee to lock, with the result that I couldn't even straighten my leg.

Even so, I was picked to play against Ipswich in the FA Cup final, a match that saw Gatesy miss out even on the subs' bench. In the second half, my knee kept locking up so I'd have to stand like a stork on one leg waggling the other one just to free it up so I could get running again. To be fair to Ipswich, they were absolutely brilliant that day. They beat us 1-0 with a goal from Roger Osbourne, but we couldn't have had any complaints had it been 5-0. It was the first time that

•TOP GUNNER: in my new Arsenal strip after leaving Newcastle.

Ipswich boss Bobby Robson had won the FA Cup so, as gutted as I was at losing at Wembley yet again, I was really pleased for him.

From there, it was straight into hospital to have the cartilage sorted out. I spent the summer recuperating and got myself into peak condition for the start of the new season, only to go and suffer a similar injury in my other knee during an early season League Cup game against Rotherham. This time there was no messing about and I was taken straight into hospital to have the cartilage removed. But the problems really started when the plaster cast was removed. As the knee had been in the plaster slightly bent, the trick was to slowly work on getting it straight. That was where I had a problem, because I just couldn't do it. After three weeks of trying, I was sent back to a specialist, though X-rays revealed nothing untoward. I was eventually sent to a leading Harley Street consultant who, believe it or not, shared his name with Dracula creator Bram Stoker! When I rang the bell at his consulting rooms, I half expected to hear the howling of hounds.

What old Bram actually did was put an X-ray type camera on my knee to take pictures at every conceivable angle. Still he couldn't find anything and I wondered if the medical men would start to think I was making the whole problem up. Then, eureka! One of Bram's team spotted a tiny white speck on one of the images produced by the camera. The club surgeon Nigel Harris explained to me that, as I had already had two operations to remove cartilage in my knee, if a surgeon went in for a third time, it would almost certainly cause so much trauma to the joint that I would be unlikely ever to play again. It wasn't the news I wanted to hear, but I knew I couldn't carry on as I was. By then, I was struggling even to walk without limping, so I decided to have the operation.

When Nigel came to see me after I had come round from the anaesthetic, he could scarcely conceal his astonishment. 'You should see what we've taken out of your knee!' he said. 'How on earth it never showed itself on all the X-rays we shall never know, but here it is.' With that, he produced a sample bottle containing liquid and a piece of gristle growth about 14 inches long. 'I really had to rip open your knee joint to find it,' he told me. What Nigel discovered was that the problem had started when my interior cartilage had been removed while I was at

Newcastle. They had cut off the cartilage at the attachment where the blood flows and had not sealed it off, so the blood had continued to pump into the knee. The blood sort of calcified and turned into gristle, which just kept growing and growing wherever it could in the knee joint. In effect, it had zigzagged right through the inside of my knee joint.

As part of my rehabilitation from the operation, I grafted in the weights room and trained as hard as I could until the point that I was playing for the reserves two or three weeks before the end of the season. Arsenal had been struggling to score goals, so I even thought I had a chance of making the team for the FA Cup final when we faced Manchester United at Wembley. All week in practice matches I was in and out of the team and it was not until the day of the match that I was told I wouldn't start. I thought I'd be sub at least but I was to suffer the ignominy felt by Gatesy a year earlier by being left out altogether. Our two forwards, Frank Stapleton and Alan Sunderland, proved the manager's team selection to be right by scoring a goal apiece in a 3-2 victory, Alan getting the winner in the last minute of a dramatic Liam Brady-inspired finale.

My only thought then was to get myself right for the following season, so I spent the close-season playing in Sweden for a side called Djurgaarden. Unfortunately, I started to suffer a pain in my knee earlier and earlier in every game. A Swedish doctor fitted me with a wonderful metal knee brace that took all the strain off the joint and enabled me to play free of pain. But there was bad news on my return to England when the FA refused to give me the green light to wear the brace during matches. I was sure then that I was a goner, as I knew there was no way I would be able to play for 90 minutes without it.

The knee was in such a terrible state and the pain became so unbearable that I went to see Nigel Harris again. 'If I was allowed to wear this brace, it would be fine because it's a brilliant piece of kit,' I told him.

'Yes, it is,' he said. 'But you can't.' He went on to give me the news that I had dreaded. That my playing career was over at

•WEMBLEY WOE: shooting past Ipswich Town's Kevin Beattie for Arsenal in the 1978 FA Cup Final as I won a third loser's medal. At least I was on the pitch - unlike Gatesy!

MALCOLM'S STORY

•THE BOSS: during my spell as Fulham manager, presumably holding an invisible football! And what do you think of those funky glasses?

29. And that really was that.

Like a lot of footballers, I wasn't quite sure what to do with myself once I had retired from the game. Unlike the players of today, those of my era didn't earn enough to set themselves up for life, so I had to look for a new way to earn a living. A promising job with Thames Television fell through, before I was offered the opportunity to become Fulham's commercial manager. I spent a year in the job but found it difficult to get anyone interested in a club that was languishing in the old Division Three with average crowds of 3,000.

Thoroughly frustrated in my role, I often found myself thinking about how I could improve what was happening on the pitch as Fulham made a dreadful start to the 1980-81 campaign. However, I can put my hand on my heart and say that I played no part in the dismissal of either manager Bobby Campbell or his assistant, Mike Kelly, in October of that season. When they had gone, however, I contacted the Fulham chairman, Ernie Clay, and put myself forward for the role. He initially ducked and dived but I was eventually invited for an interview, after which they offered me the job. My appointment completed the circle. Whatever I did in life, I always seemed to do it first with Fulham. It was the club I always supported as a kid, it was my first club as a professional footballer and now it was my first club as a manager.

What I quickly realised following my appointment was that I had a big job to do just to lift team morale. I discovered that there had been a reign of terror under Campbell and Kelly during which players had been subjected to shouting, threats and punishment. I laugh when I hear about teacups being thrown across dressing rooms by managers. That's no way to be managing a football team, because you're not giving reasonable credit to the intelligence of people. Throwing teacups and raging all the time is not going to work with human beings. If you have to rant and rave, then you have to make it such a rare occurrence that when it happens everybody knows you mean it.

I constantly disagree with callers to the Century phone-in who demand that managers get into the technical area and scream at their players when things aren't going to plan. The truth is that it's the worst thing to do. Managers need to keep their cool. If players see bad temper coming from their

manager on the sidelines that might rub off on them, resulting in them getting bad-tempered too and getting booked. It's not a good message to send out. I had to just tunnel vision myself beyond all the noise and fervour that was going on around me. I would look straight ahead and analyse the game dispassionately. Even now when I watch a game, I am cold and analytical. It's not because I don't care. It's simply the way I've always been, because that's the only way to be when you are making decisions.

I quickly realised the gravity of Fulham's financial situation when I discovered that we had to draw an average attendance of 25,000 just to break even. I knew then that I would have to make some very difficult decisions in terms of cutting the size of the playing staff. While I did that, I also concentrated on improving some of the very good young players I had at the club. One of those was Tony Gale, the central defender who went on to play for West Ham and now makes a living as a media pundit. I also gave a first team debut, at 17, to a Welsh defender called Jeff Hopkins, who went on to win 16 caps for his country.

The game before Jeff's debut, I'd blooded another future international defender, Paul Parker. We were playing Reading, whose side included Kerry Dixon, a striker who would go on to make a big name for himself with Chelsea and England. I told Paul, all 4ft 13in of him, to mark Dixon. I tell you, he was brilliant. If he couldn't win the ball, he'd make sure Kerry didn't. Paul went on to play for Manchester United and England.

We were mid-table by the end of the season, well clear of relegation. We had so many good young players in the squad, with the likes of Gale, Hopkins, Parker and striker Dean Coney, that I felt very positive about the future. In charge of my youth team at that time was Ray Harford, a wonderful coach who later helped Kenny Dalglish win the Premiership title with Blackburn. He did a brilliant job with a fabulous group of youngsters to the extent that half the first team were able to represent the club in the FA Youth Cup. So obvious was his talent that I decided to make Ray my first team coach, making the difficult decision to sack George 'Geordie' Armstrong, my old mate from Arsenal.

Ray had played as a centre-half in the lower divisions because he didn't have the ability to take him higher as a player, but mentally he was international class. He had a phenomenal tactical brain, something I will readily admit I did not possess. Where Ray fell down was that he wasn't the best of communicators and would lose his cool easily. Fortunately that was one of my strengths. I was able to interpret the message Ray wanted to get over to the players and present it to them in a palatable form. Ray would be screaming at someone, but I would say, 'Ray, why are you doing that? Don't tell him what he is doing wrong, tell him what he should be doing.' As a manager, you have to take the passion out of it. You have to relax in the eye of the storm. Ray could never do that, but his tactical brain was something I didn't have, so we complemented each other perfectly as manager and coach.

Having won promotion from Division Three on the last day of the 1981-82 season, I really felt we had the makings of a side that could push on still further. And I couldn't believe my luck when I got wind of the fact that Ray Houghton, someone we'd been following very closely, was being given a free by West Ham. I quickly got a player signed up that would go on to enjoy a wonderful career with the likes of Oxford, Liverpool and Aston Villa, not to mention winning 73 caps for the Republic of Ireland. I now had the makings of a very good side. In goal, I had another Irish international in Gerry Peyton, while I had ex-West Ham player Kevin Lock partnering Jeff Hopkins at full-back. In between them were Tony Gale and big Roger Brown. In the centre of midfield, Robert Wilson had emerged from our youth scheme and created a fabulous partnership with the former Chelsea player Ray Lewington. Either side of them was Shaun O'Driscoll, a Republic of Ireland international, and Ray Houghton. Up front there was a nice blend of youth and experience in Dean Coney and Wales international striker Gordon Davies. On top of all that, we had the likes of Paul Parker and Dale Tempest in reserve.

My second full season with Fulham proved to be a remarkable one. Such was the self-belief in that team that during one notable spell we scored four goals away from home in each of our victories at Middlesbrough, Newcastle, Grimsby and Wolves. One of our outstanding early performances was that game at Ayresome Park, where we won 4-1 despite losing

Peyton, our goalkeeper, who was left with his scalp flapping on his skull after diving at the feet of David Shearer and being caught by the striker's studs. Substitute goalkeepers weren't allowed in those days, so we had to bring on Paul Parker at left-back and put Kevin Lock in goal. We won by keeping possession, by passing Boro into an hypnotic trance almost, then hitting them with our trademark quick breaks.

Our form was enough to make us real promotion contenders, but attempts at signing striker Tony Sealy from QPR fell through and I sensed that our chairman, Ernie Clay, didn't want promotion to the top flight. With nine games to go, we were 11 points clear in third place – the final automatic promotion spot – but then it all began to slip away. We went into the final game level on 69 points with Leicester, both of us hoping to take the third promotion spot behind QPR and Wolves.

We had a difficult last fixture, away to Derby, who were still in danger of relegation. It was 0-0 at half-time but Derby scored with about 20 minutes to play. That was the signal for the crowd, believing the goal would keep them up, to start filtering onto the pitch. First they were on the track around the pitch, then they started to encroach the playing area. I'm not talking about just a few people - there were hundreds and hundreds of them. It was so bad that I had to stand several yards inside the touchline myself to see what was happening in the Derby half! Yet, for some reason, the referee let the play go on. At one point, Robert Wilson went out towards the left wing to control the ball, only for some youth to come out of the crowd and kick him in the thigh. Down he went, Derby got the ball and the referee waved play on! That was how the final quarter of an hour of the game was played. We were trying to make shooting positions, but the players couldn't even see the Derby goal.

When the final whistle went, Derby the 1-0 winners, thousands of fans invaded the pitch, resulting in Jeff Hopkins being stripped of his shirt and shorts. By the time he managed to stumble into the tunnel, the poor lad was crying with anger, while his body was covered with a mass of welts and scratches. In a fury, I marched into the referee's dressing room. When he saw Jeff, the ref almost had a breakdown. He sort of collapsed in a heap and kept saying, 'It's not over, the game's not over yet.' When I asked him what he meant, he said the whistle we had heard had not been his. There were 90 seconds still to play.

I made it clear my players could not be expected to go out again and play for another minute and a half. It was out of the question for Hopkins, while most of the others had suffered assaults of one kind or another. A high-ranking police officer confirmed that there was no way he could get the pitch cleared for the game to continue. In the meantime, we heard that Leicester had drawn 0-0 with Barnsley, which put them a point ahead of us. What I really hoped for was that the referee would abandon the game and it would have to be played again, but a Football League commission later turned down our appeal without giving a reason why. I didn't feel that I got the support I had expected from Ernie Clay during that appeals process and it was the start of a swift deterioration in our relationship.

I knew I would have to rebuild the side the following season and didn't expect a lot from the campaign. By March we were sitting just below halfway in the table. Even so, we underlined my belief that we were well established in the division by thrashing Manchester City 5-1 at Craven Cottage. I remember that game vividly, not just because of our big win but because it was the day my first marriage broke up. I knew that a story like that involving – though not caused by – another woman would be food and drink to the tabloids. As I was no longer enjoying my work, mainly due to my worsening relationship with Clay, I offered the chairman my resignation to avoid any embarrassment to the football club. To my surprise, he urged me not to be hasty and assured me that Fulham did not want to lose me. Unfortunately, someone leaked the story of my marriage break-up to *The Sun* and Clay accepted my resignation on the second time it was offered. I believe that it was Clay himself who had tipped off the newspaper. To cut a long story short, it is my belief that he wanted me out of the club for his own personal reasons.

When I walked away from Fulham, I was confident I could get another managerial post in the game quite quickly. My record at Craven Cottage – promotion from Division Three in my first full season, then a narrow failure to go up into the First the following year – had surely marked me out as a young manager of promise. There were two jobs I felt I had a very good chance of getting. One was at my old club, Newcastle, and the other was at Aston Villa. There was also a vacancy at Sunderland, to replace Alan Durban, but I wasn't going to get a job there, not in a month of Sundays!

What I understand happened at Newcastle was that the six-man board were split evenly over who should succeed Arthur Cox as manager for the 1984-85 season, me or Lawrie McMenemy. Then the chairman, Stan Seymour Jr, decided to throw in a third candidate, Jack Charlton, as a compromise and got unanimous support for him. As for Aston Villa, their chairman Doug Ellis told me I would help him pick the team! 'Mr Ellis, let me stop you there,' I told him, during our brief telephone conversation. 'That is a condition I could never accept. I'd have to have total control over playing affairs, in particular over who plays and who doesn't. You either accept that or this conversation is ended.'

'All right,' he replied. 'We'll end the conversation, then. Thank you for your time. Goodbye!'

A couple of days later, Graham Turner was appointed to succeed Tony Barton, and I have often wondered whether Doug Ellis made the same outrageous demand of him and whether he was prepared to go along with it.

Unfortunately, it would be three years before I was eventually offered another manager's job. When the offer came, it was out of the blue. Unfortunately, it was not the most inviting of prospects either. It came from Roger Fielding, chairman of Huddersfield, who I'd met and hit it off with at a Football League meeting when I was commercial manager at Fulham. Having staved off relegation for about five years, Huddersfield were rooted to the bottom of the old Division Two with only five points and no wins from the first 11 games of the 1987-88 season. Despite my doubts, I thought I owed it to Roger to go up from my Sussex base and see what he had to say. Roger's infectious enthusiasm, combined with his realistic outlook on the club's immediate prospects, convinced me to take up the gauntlet of trying to galvanise the historic old club.

Alas, nothing seemed to go right from the start. Players I had looked forward to working with were either permanently on the treatment table or suffering nightmare form. Things went from bad to worse when we lost 10-1 to Manchester City at Maine Road. Our defence got caught out time and time again, with City's David White and Paul Stewart each enjoying a field day at our expense. Steve Walford, who I'd known from my playing days with Arsenal, had joined us on loan from West Ham in my misguided attempt to tighten up the defence, but he seemed to have lost all his old defensive nous. And yet the crazy thing about that game was that City had only 12 goal attempts to our 17!

That night I offered Roger my resignation, though he refused to accept it, telling me not to be so silly. With his words of encouragement, I decided to keep on trying. It came as a huge shock to me, therefore, when soon afterwards Roger called me to say he was no longer chairman of the club. He explained that he was planning to move to the tax haven of the Isle of Man but had discovered that he could only reap the tax benefits if he did not retain any directorships on the mainland. From the outset, Roger had warned me that his fellow directors would be against me, just as they were against him. Sure enough, he now warned me to watch my back. As a consequence, I was sure I would quickly be asked to follow Roger out of the club.

No sooner had I put the phone down than my office door opened and in walked the vice-chairman, Keith Longbottom, who announced he was now the chairman. I stood up, looked him straight in the eye and said, 'Congratulations, Mr Chairman. And when would you like my resignation?'

'We're not hirers and firers here,' he replied. 'Your job's safe, for the moment.'

I was undecided whether to make the first move and hand in my resignation, but knew I couldn't really afford to lose my salary in that way. But, oh, how I wish I had followed through with that initial thought. Instead, my relationship with my assistant, Eoin Hand, was to prove my downfall. I had appointed him to help out with first team duties, knowing that he had a wealth of experience and had coached the Republic of Ireland national side in the past. I thought it was an opportunity for him to use Huddersfield as a springboard back into Football League management. 'There are 92 League clubs,' I told him. 'You've got 91 to go for. Just leave my job alone!' Surprise, surprise, he would be my successor at Leeds Road.

I had got to know Eoin years earlier when he had spent the summer in South Africa with me when we had both played for Maritibo. But there been a sea change in Eoin's personality and he always remained distant in his demeanour towards me. He was negative towards anything and everything, bringing little to the party but moans and groans. In return, I felt I was nothing but generous to him. Indeed, it was through trying to cover for him that I was to eventually lose my job.

To cut a long story short, I asked Eoin to go out to Holland to watch a young English player I had my eye on called Mark Payne. I had promised to give a verbal report about the player to the board on Eoin's return to Huddersfield. To my astonishment, however, I discovered from the player that Eoin had never even attended the game. He reckoned he hadn't been able to find the ground where the match was played. He then pleaded with me, 'Please promise me you won't let anybody know that I never got there.' Foolishly, I agreed. When the chairman later asked me for Eoin's report on the player, I tried to cover for him, saying that he was planning to go out and watch him again the following week. But the chairman then revealed that he knew Eoin had not seen Payne play. Suddenly, it hit me that I had been stitched up.

Afterwards, I accused Eoin of betraying our friendship and costing me my job. In response, he said nothing. He simply looked at the ground and turned scarlet. I wrote a letter to the chairman, apologising for misleading the board and offering my resignation. The following day, he told me I could go. I walked away from Huddersfield's ground that May morning in 1988 knowing in my heart of hearts that I would never get another job in football.

Malcolm's Story:
MAN OF MANY TALENTS

SHUNNED BY football, I tried my hand at all manner of different jobs over the years following my departure from Fulham. Apart from my brief period back in the game with Huddersfield, I worked as a pub landlord, ran a hotel, enjoyed spells as a football commentator and a newspaper columnist and even spent four years in Italy trying to break into the premium rate telephone business. I have been bankrupt, seen two marriages break down and turned to alcohol in a bid to ease the pain suffered from my old knee injury.

Perhaps the most exciting episode, however, was the time I temporarily became a football agent, helping to bring the first ever top class Brazilian to English football. When I realised I would be waiting a long time for another job in football

management to come my way, I decided to get myself a pub. It was while working at the pub, The Far Post, in Worthing, Sussex, that I met a guy called Don Packham. He was a financial services rep who had a friend in Brazil called Umberto Silva. He showed me a letter from Umberto, who claimed he was very friendly with players at one of Brazil's top clubs, Palmeiras, and that many of them were keen on a move to Europe. There was one player in particular, a free-scoring striker by the name of Mirandinha, who was on the verge of breaking into the national team, who Silva thought might attract a lot of interest.

At first, I was completely sceptical about the whole thing. This guy had just wandered in and tried to convince me he had a brilliant Brazilian footballer for sale on the cheap. A likely story! Remember, this was long before the likes of Juninho were attracted to the English game. Don explained that he had approached me because the world of football was a closed book to him and I was the only person he knew who had access to it. I asked him to supply some proof of Mirandinha's ability by producing a video of the player in action, while I did some research myself. The story checked out and when I finally got to see the video it was clear the guy was quick and could score goals. He was a man after my own heart!

I first offered Mirandinha to Glasgow Rangers manager Graeme Souness. He was keen to sign him, but it didn't work out because the chairman, David Murray, suddenly put a block on Graeme's spending. I then approached Newcastle manager Willie McFaul, an old team-mate of mine, and got a favourable response. Newcastle became even keener to buy the Palmeiras striker when he scored for Brazil against England at Wembley in May 1987.

The next step was to arrange for the president of Palmeiras to come over to England to negotiate the transfer. I arranged and paid for his flight and agreed to meet him at Heathrow, from where we would travel up to Newcastle in a Rolls-Royce

•WHERE THE HEART IS: waving to Newcastle United's wonderful supporters on a visit to St James' Park.

owned by a good friend of mine, Bev Walker, a well-known sports agent who had agreed to give me some practical advice on the deal. But there was no sign of the president at Arrivals after his flight touched down and, smelling a rat, I came to the conclusion that Newcastle United must have made direct contact with him and arranged for him to fly straight on to Newcastle Airport. When I called United, they denied having any knowledge of the president's whereabouts, but I eventually tracked him down to the Fisherman's Lodge, one of Newcastle's best restaurants. There, he was in mid-meeting with most of the Newcastle board, manager Willie McFaul and club secretary Russell Cushing. They were clearly trying to cut me out of the proceedings.

'Good evening, everybody,' I announced. 'My associates and I are sitting downstairs and I think you need to talk to us before anything gets concluded. See you in a while!' With that, I walked back out of the room and rejoined Bev and a lawyer I had arranged to join us, given the nasty turn the situation had taken. When, some hours later and by now after midnight, the Newcastle party came out of their meeting, I let my lawyer ensure a deal was completed that kept me involved in the Mirandinha transfer. I certainly was not about to allow myself to be cut out of it, having already invested over £10,000 of my own money into flights, lawyers' fees and the like.

When Mirandinha arrived on Tyneside with his friend Umberto Silva in tow, I explained to them that I had negotiated a deal with Newcastle that would make the Brazilian the highest-paid footballer in the country. Newcastle had said they wanted the contracts signed at 10 o'clock the following morning, followed by a press conference at 11. Sadly, Bev and I were again double-crossed. We knew that we had to get Mirandinha to St James' Park for half past nine in the morning, but when we met down in the hotel lobby at about nine, there was no sign of the player, Umberto Silva nor Don Packham, the guy who had originally brought my attention to Mirandinha's availability. Don had turned up at the hotel the night before playing the big 'I am', so there could only be one explanation to their non-appearance in the hotel lobby - they had made their own way to the ground.

•SAMBA TIME: I'm proud of the part I played in making Mirandinha the first Brazilian to play in top level English football.

When Bev and I arrived at St James', it was too late. Don and Umberto had negotiated a new deal for Mirandinha, which they believed to be superior to the one I had agreed, but actually wasn't. In fact, the player would now be on £1,000 a week less than he would have been had he stuck with us. At the press conference, Bev and I had to just stand on the sidelines while Packham and Silva presented themselves to the public as the men who had masterminded the first transfer of a Brazilian footballer to an English top-flight club.

I'm glad to say Mirandinha did pretty well for a couple of seasons at Newcastle. At least the fact that he was one of United's top scorers supported my assessment of his ability. He did not stay for a third season, instead rejoining Palmeiras on loan. I think he felt he had made enough money by then to fulfil what I understood to be his real ambition of becoming a pig farmer back in Brazil!

Much later, after my brief spell with Huddersfield and a failed venture in the hotel business, I moved to Italy and spent much time and effort setting up a business in the developing industry of premium rate telephone calls. I got financial

•SUPERMAC MEETS SUPERMAC: talking football on a TV chat show with Ted MacDougall, who once scored nine goals for Bournemouth in an FA Cup tie with Margate.

backing from Birmingham City owner David Sullivan, the soft-porn mogul, who knew a thing or two about the premium rate phone business himself, while real backing came through a company of investors based in Hong Kong. People tend to raise their eyebrows when they here mention of premium rate phone lines, thinking of sex chat lines, but there is a massive part of the business that has no connection with that seedy side. We set ourselves up as service providers for customers to offer their information services in areas as varying as football, weather, travel, psychology and the Italian stock exchange.

We invested in a piece of equipment worth half a million pounds that could handle up to 200 calls at any one time. The whole business was set to mushroom in Italy, but then I started to hear whispers that something wasn't quite right. Sure enough, the Italian government shut the whole industry down over Christmas. I think they saw the profits that private investors were going to enjoy from this new growth industry and were determined to get a slice of the action. To ensure they did so, they closed the industry down and started all over again. I had returned home to England for Christmas but had fortunately had the foresight to move our expensive equipment out of our Milan-based business premises and into storage while I was away. It was a lucky escape because,

although we all lost out financially at seeing our whole industry closed down, our equipment was never seized, something my Hong Kong backers in particular were very grateful to me for.

To ensure any remaining ties with the business were cut, I returned home to England in 1996 with about £3,000 in my pocket and no obvious future prospects. I initially based myself at my mother's house and, after a brief settling in period, managed to get myself some work with Sky Sports. Then, while I was back in the north-east doing some work for John Gibson, my old friend at the Newcastle *Chronicle*, I was contacted by John Symons, programme controller for Century Radio, as it was then known. John invited me in to take part in a radio show with one of their presenters, Dave Roberts. I got there five minutes after the programme started, rushed in, sat down and got on with chatting to Dave. I had never met him before but, fortunately, we hit it off. Soon after, John Symons called me back in and offered me a season's contract to do a Monday to Friday phone-in with Dave. After some thought, I decided to take up the chance on offer and move back to Tyneside for the first time in 20 years to throw myself into this new radio show.

It would have been a great success but there was a dark cloud on the horizon. The injury to my left knee that had forced my playing career into a premature end was now causing me crippling pain. The pain was so intense that it affected my ability to drive a car or climb stairs, severely restricting my quality of life. I also made the mistake of turning to whisky to dull the ache. Worryingly, it reached the point where I would see off a bottle of Scotch a day just to allow me to get from A to B.

I reached crisis point the night two police cars stopped me on my way home from the Century studios. A breathalyser test revealed that I was over the drink-driving limit despite never having touched a drop since the night before. As a result, I was banned from driving for 18 months, while I also lost my job with Century as a result of the scandal around the press coverage. What I found particularly difficult to accept, given my reasons for drinking, was that everyone seemed to assume I was a raging alcoholic. The truth was that the left leg that had been responsible for my fame and fortune was now in danger of destroying my life.

My knight in shining armour turned out to be one of my old Newcastle United team-mates, Micky Burns. Calling me in his capacity with the Professional Footballers' Association, Micky told me the PFA wanted to help me with my problem – and I was delighted when he made it clear that he knew the real cause of all my anxiety was my knee and not my drinking. The PFA were fantastic to me, arranging for me to see an orthopaedic specialist, who replaced the existing knee joint. It wasn't the easiest thing to go through with, but I've never looked back since and getting a new knee joint certainly gave me a new lease of life.

I did have to do a certain amount of physical readjusting afterwards, mind. As any football fans who saw me play will know, I was famed for my bow legs, but it was necessary, as part of the operation, to straighten my left knee. It resulted in my left leg now being as straight as a snooker cue, while my right remains bowed – so I'm more of a D than an O nowadays! Best of all, I've not had a drop of alcohol since the day of the operation back in 1997. I will be forever grateful to the PFA for their help, especially as they paid the £12,000 cost of the operation.

Three years later came that phone call from Century fm that I talked about earlier in the book. It was the start of The Three Legends show and a wonderful new chapter in my life.

Bernie's Story:
STRIKINGLY DIFFERENT

BARRING CATASTROPHES, Teesside will remain my home for the rest of my life. I now consider myself an adopted Teessider, but I was a proud Glaswegian for the first part of my life. Although I was born in a hospital in Paisley, an area of Renfrewshire on the outskirts of Glasgow, I was brought up in Castlemilk, a huge Glasgow council estate about 10 minutes' drive from the city centre. An only child, I lived with my mother and father in one of countless high-rise tenement buildings that stood in the Castlemilk area, until I was 20, when my parents bought their own house in Fernhill, Rutherglen. By then I was a part-time professional with Morton but I still remember the thrill of realising that for the first time in my life we had a front and a back door!

We weren't exactly rolling in it, but then I was far from deprived either. My father, Hugh, was a delivery driver for the Co-op and my mother, Alice, was a tailoress. Though both Ma and Da are Glaswegian born and bred, having been brought up in the infamous Gorbals estate, their parents were Irish - my father's from the South and my mother's from the North. Though I never actually knew my grandparents, their Irish origins later played a major role in my football destiny.

Unlike some council estates of today, Castlemilk in the 1960s was the sort of place where everybody knew everybody, where by and large neighbours got on with each other, and people would check on the elderly residents. Strangers were relaxed enough to stand and chat while they waited at a bus stop. There was no need to worry about whether someone was about to pull a knife on you.

It was in Castlemilk that I took my first steps on the way to a professional football career when Da would take kids off the street on a Sunday and organise kick-abouts. Years earlier, one of the young regulars who Da now admits, with much embarrassment, he rarely picked was a young lad called Paddy Crerand, who went on to earn fame and honours with both Celtic and Manchester United. Because Da was the organiser, I'd be there too, from the age of probably only 10.

I hardly got a kick against lads in their late teens but I was there and that's what counted to me. Before that I remember Da trying to encourage me to play football, probably when I was as young as four or five, kicking the ball up and down the hallway in the tenement. From then on, football was all I was interested in.

My primary school, St Dominic's, was probably one of the smallest in Glasgow but I was still proud to be in the school team. Back then I was the regular left-back, though why that was my position is something I can't explain because even then I couldn't tackle a fish supper! I can only assume our manager, Mr Kelly, was struggling for left-footed players. The truth is that I was no different from the rest of the team - I wanted to be centre-forward, who would score the goals and get the glory. But I was not to get that honour until much later in my football development.

Half the boys in Glasgow dreamed of one day playing for Celtic. The other half had a similar dream, only theirs involved playing in the blue of Celtic's arch-rivals, Rangers. Da and I were two of Celtic's biggest fans. Kenny Dalglish was my boyhood hero and remained so even years later when I was playing for Middlesbrough. I only went off him when he joined Newcastle! King Kenny was pure class, making and taking goals. Bobby Murdoch, who later played for and briefly managed Boro, was Da's favourite – 'the greatest player of all-time' he would insist.

From a very young age, I accompanied Da on the weekly pilgrimage to Parkhead. Most weeks I was one of the many young lads who would get in free courtesy of what is known as a 'squeeze' on Teesside but what I always knew as a 'puntey'. The staff would turn a blind eye while my Da lifted me over the turnstiles. Once in the stadium, he would sit me down at the front, give me a bag of sweets and disappear back into the crowd to stand with his mates. 'Stay there and don't move!' he would tell me.

•IN SAFE HANDS: with my grandmother when I was a baby - and already working on that quiff!

77

I was only five years old when Celtic won the European Cup in 1967. I was too young to get to see the game but one abiding memory I do have is going to a packed Parkhead the night the team showed off the trophy. The place was heaving and there wasn't even a game played there that night. A few years later, I sat on my Da's shoulders as Celtic beat Leeds United in the European Cup semi-final in front of a crowd of about 140,000. Da kept an earlier promise and took me to Milan for the final against Feyenoord at the San Siro. We lost 2-1, though I have to admit I don't remember a dicky bird about the game.

I didn't enjoy my days at my secondary school, St Margaret Mary's, because football was all that I was interested in. By the time I was 14 I was playing left-half for Partick Thistle Amateurs. Our manager did his best for us, but quite honestly we were awful. We would be hammered 15-1 by the top sides like Ayr United Boys. Even so, I must have been doing something right because I was picked for a Glasgow select team when I was 16. Charlie Nicholas and Danny Cranie, who both became professionals with Celtic, were also selected,

but I felt nervous about the whole thing and decided not to go. Da didn't own a car and I wasn't happy about catching the bus and going on my own across Glasgow. The next day when I came home I couldn't believe my eyes. Da had wrecked my bedroom. My stereo was smashed and my prized records had been thrown around the room. I know those actions might seem extreme but I knew he was desperate for me to do well and hated seeing me blow what he felt was a great chance of being picked up by a professional club.

Before long I moved on to a club called Eastercraigs. After my experiences with Partick Thistle Amateurs, playing for a half-decent team like Eastercraigs was something of a luxury. Although I fancied myself as a striker, I was still playing at left-half. That was because Eastercraigs' centre-forward was a talented lad called Graeme Sharpe, later of Everton and Scotland fame.

I was 18 years old when I turned down the chance to join Scottish Division Two side East Stirling to sign for a junior league side called Johnstonburgh. My manager at Eastercraigs, Bill Livingstone, insisted that joining East Stirling would be a mistake because he felt I simply wasn't hard enough. He felt I needed an 'apprenticeship' in the local leagues to help toughen me up.

The following season, I joined Rutherglen Glencairn and I finally started to enjoy my football again. It was a hard league - similar to the Northern League in many ways - and boy, did it toughen me up! I was the youngest player in a side mainly comprising of ex-pros. One week I was carried off injured after one of my more dubious opponents had put me over the top of a pitchside barrier and onto concrete. That was the sort of treatment that the league's so-called hard men dished out. But, while it was often outside the rules of the game, it did the trick in helping me to toughen up.

After only a handful of games for Glens, my form attracted scouts from a number of league sides. Benny Rooney, manager of Premier League Morton, came along to watch me and liked what he saw. The first I knew of his interest was when I opened up the Glasgow *Evening Times* to see the headline, 'Slaven set for Morton'. Glencairn and Morton agreed a fee of £750 for my transfer - a drop in the ocean in

•A REAL LEGEND: that's me on the left with my friend Dennis as we meet Celtic superstar Jimmy Johnstone.

today's game of high finances but a huge fee for a club like Glens to receive back then. I officially became a Morton player on December 27 1980. It was a dream come true, but I was destined to remain a Glens player for another five months because the club refused to release me while they were still involved in the Scottish Junior Cup.

My first wage with Morton was £70 a week but it was like manna from heaven. I had been on the dole for a couple of years since losing my job as a van boy with the Co-op. That had involved travelling around the city delivering furniture. I couldn't say I enjoyed it, but it did give me a few pounds in my pocket. But when that job finished I struggled to find more work. I'd left school at 16 with football as my only career option. I sat exams in Art and English - though the latter was obviously with a Scottish twang! - but that didn't help me in my job search. I tended to spend long parts of the day in bed, only leaping out when I heard Ma come home from her work at the local nursery at two o'clock in the afternoon. Now my big chance with Morton would give me some direction in life.

Despite their place among Scotland's Premier League elite, Morton were a small-time club, who had developed a reputation as perennial relegation escapologists while existing on average crowds of only 4,000. My two years at 'Ton' both involved relegation battles, the first one successful and the second not. As a result of Morton's general lack of finances, their ground, Cappielow Park in Greenock, was in a dilapidated state, but it felt like Parkhead to me.

My first team debut came as a second half substitute in a 3-0 home win over Airdrie in October the season after I joined the club. I enjoyed further action as a sub a week later when we surpassed ourselves by achieving a 1-1 draw with Rangers at Ibrox. Then came my first start when Benny Rooney gave me the number nine shirt for a game I'll never forget. I couldn't have picked the opposition better myself. Incredibly, the visitors to Cappielow in front of a bumper crowd of over 12,000 were my heroes, Celtic. Only a few days earlier I had watched big name players like Charlie Nicholas, Roy Aitken and Frank McGarvey as a fan, but I was confident in my own ability, so I was far from overawed by the occasion. In fact, I went into the game determined to prove that Celtic's right-half, Dominic Sullivan, was the limited player I had often

insisted he was while watching Celtic from the stands at Parkhead. Packie Bonner - an Irish international team-mate of mine many years later - was in goal for Celtic that day and I still remember the fantastic feeling of beating a couple of defenders before scoring past him. Unfortunately, while I was racing up the field celebrating, the referee was blowing his whistle for an infringement. The game ended in a 1-1 draw and I felt I was starting to make my mark.

It was Airdrie who proved to be my lucky team again when I struck my first Morton goal in a 1-1 Premier League draw. Only 3,000 people were there to see my first half strike but it meant the world to me. I still remember it vividly. The ball came in from the right and I volleyed it into the top corner from just inside the box. On the crest of a wave, I could not have imagined that it would prove to be my only first team goal for Morton. I was in and out of the team for the remainder of that and the following season. Given the club's constant struggle for survival, I found it incredible that they weren't prepared to give a player like myself, fresh from junior football, a chance to prove myself with a longer run in the team. Playing for the reserves was incredibly frustrating because I knew I was better than some of the regular first team players. Some people may take that as a display of arrogance but I was simply confident in my own abilities - and desperate to prove it.

Eventually my patience snapped and I stormed into Benny Rooney's office. 'Why aren't I in the first team?' I demanded to know. 'There's nobody better than me at the club. You've just got your favourites and are playing them every week.'

Rooney was totally taken aback at the cheek of my outburst, sitting speechless in his chair. All the talking was left to the first team coach, Mike Jackson. 'What are you talking about?' he snapped back at me. 'You've been injured.'

I had been injured a few weeks earlier but he knew that I was now fit. 'That's garbage - I'm fit, I'm playing well and I'm scoring goals - and still I can't get in your team.'

Such a confrontational attitude probably did little for my chances at Cappielow, but it was just the first of many bust-ups I had with the manager. The longer I was ignored, the more I became unhappy at Morton. I would go into the dressing room before a match and check the teamsheet. If my name wasn't on it, I wouldn't hang about to watch the game. Rather than sit in the stands and watch my team-mates, I preferred to head across the city to watch Celtic play. One night, for a home game against Celtic, I had been named in Rooney's initial squad but my name was missing from the teamsheet when it was pinned up on the dressing room wall. I was more annoyed than disappointed, so I made a very public point of joining my fellow Celtic fans in the visitors' end of Cappielow, walking out of the players' tunnel and around the perimeter of the pitch, for all the supporters to see. With hindsight, it wasn't the greatest of ideas, but in the heat of the moment I really didn't give a damn what anyone thought.

Throughout my life, whenever I've felt I've not been given a fair crack of the whip, I have never been slow to say so, often in a very forceful fashion. It's a rebellious side of my nature but not one I am in any way embarrassed about.

Unfortunately, my outbursts slowly turned the club's coaching staff against me and there were one or two smug people on the day I was released by Morton.

I was called into the club's boardroom, where one of the directors told me, 'Well son, you've always wanted to be away from Morton. You've never really wanted to play here. Now you've got your way because the club is releasing you.'

I had half expected the news but it still came as a terrible blow. I still believed in myself, but it hurt to be cast aside. Even so, I was determined not to show it. I stood up, looked each of them in the eye and told them, 'I'll tell you what - I'll prove you wrong.' With my words echoing in their ears, I walked out. At that moment they were probably glad to see the back of the headstrong Bernie Slaven. But they must have rued they day they released me so willingly when they saw me banging in the goals for Middlesbrough just two years later. It hurt my pride to be given a free transfer but I was determined to bounce back. Just as importantly, I knew the decision to release me had been made by the stereotypical men in grey suits, who knew next to nothing about football. I left Cappielow with my head held high, confident that I could still make it as a professional footballer.

But there was no glamour comeback around the corner. My next game, only a couple of weeks after being released by Morton, came on an ash pitch at a place called Tory Glen, behind Hampden Park. As a favour for some friends, I played as a ringer under an assumed name in a Sunday League game. I actually scored a hat-trick, but things turned ugly when this big defender chopped me down from behind and then jumped on me. I instinctively had a go back at him. Within seconds, fists were flying from almost every player on the pitch. The referee desperately tried to restore order, before brandishing the red card in my direction. As I started the long walk off the pitch, I expected to see order reinstated and the game getting underway again. Instead, every member of my team followed me off the pitch, refusing to play in protest against my dismissal. That was the end of the match. The whole team got changed and left. Needless to say, that was my last game for the side. 'If that's Sunday League football,' I thought, 'I'll be giving it a wide berth from now on.'

If I had believed there would be a queue of clubs ready to offer me a way back into professional football, I was to be disappointed. In fact, Airdrie – then a Division One side - were the only club to come in for me. Even they were willing to offer me only a month-to-month contract. I played a few games for the club but, with my month's contract coming towards its end, I had the impression that the manager, Bill Munro, couldn't decide whether or not to sign me on a longer term basis. I made up my mind to act before Munro had the chance to tell me I could leave. I went in to see him and told him I wasn't interested in staying. The truth was that I hadn't really done myself justice, but I hadn't enjoyed my football there either and felt it was best to cut my losses and leave.

It was almost three months before my next Scottish League appearance. This time I found myself making another step down to play for Queen of the South in the Second Division. They were a far cry from the Celtics and even the Mortons of this world and were struggling to pull in crowds of 800. They were paying me pennies for travelling a couple of hours from Glasgow to Palmerston Park in Dumfries. In those days I still didn't drive a car and felt it was all a bit much. What's more, deep down I knew I was better than that. After just two games for Queen of the South, I moved on again, this time turning out for a side in the local Church League. Inside I was hurting that I hadn't found a new club, but I loved the game and took the chance to get in some practice with my mates.

As far as my faltering football career was concerned, I was in limbo. I was out of work and felt rejected by the game I loved. The future didn't look bright. But, in April 1984, a glimmer of light appeared in the form of the Wee Rovers. I will always owe a big debt of gratitude to Andy Ritchie, then manager of Albion Rovers. He was the man who converted me to the striker's role in which I enjoyed much of my success. He also turned around my career in the summer of 1984 at a time when it could so easily have been dealt yet another hammer blow. I had signed forms for Rovers for the final month of the 1983-84 season and played three games during their end-of-season run-in. Ironically, Benny Rooney, who I'd shared such a stormy relationship with during our time at Morton, was then manager of Albion and invited me to try my hand at Cliftonhill Stadium. The club were struggling at the foot of the table but I didn't take much persuading.

I thought things were looking up, but I should have known better than to count my chickens before they had hatched. Rooney left the club shortly after the season ended and I went on a fortnight's holiday to Spain wondering what the future had in store for me. On my return, Da told me Albion's new manager, Andy Ritchie, was coming round to speak to me. I had become good friends with Andy during our time together at Morton, but while I was never anything more than a fringe player he was hero-worshipped by Cappielow regulars in the same way as Charlie Nicholas was at Parkhead. 'Bernie, I want you to play in the role I played at Morton,' he explained. 'I want you to play in the free, roving role up front - and I want you to score goals.'

I needed no persuading. My immediate thoughts were, 'Great, no more chasing back to close down defenders!' The defensive side of the game had never interested me. Now I was actually being encouraged to forget about it and concentrate on what I did best - attacking the opposition goal. It was a dream. I happily agreed to sign another month's contract with a view to extending it if both parties were happy. My switch to the free role was a huge success and the goals flowed right from the start. Unfortunately, Ritchie didn't stay around to enjoy the success with me. He fell out with the

directors and walked out on the club only a few weeks into the new season.

The pitch at Cliftonhill was worse than a cow field, usually covered with gravel and pieces of stone. The ground itself was hardly any better, with just one dilapidated wooden stand. The club's training facilities also left a lot to be desired. On a Tuesday, we worked out on a concrete surface, moving on to gravel on Thursdays. You can imagine how many bumps we picked up in training. To make matters worse, Albion didn't even have a physiotherapist to look after the knocks so the players were left to take care of that side of things themselves. On the positive side, our average home attendance was around the 250 mark, so picking my father and friends out in the crowd was never a problem.

Small crowds or not, I thrived in my new role and was among the Scottish League's top scorers all season long in 1984-85. Unfortunately, Albion were not the best of sides. In fact, one newspaper report went as far as to suggest we were the worst team in Scotland. Certainly, we conceded goals faster than I could score them. But by the end of the season I had 31 goals, making me Scottish football's top scorer. At an end-of-season awards bash, I also picked up the Second Division Player of the Year award. It was an honour to be recognised by my fellow professionals, but I was given another even more satisfying moment that same evening. As I mingled with the other guests, I was greeted by the very directors who had chosen to release me from Morton two years earlier.

The fact that I had won the Player of the Year accolade was mainly due to the number of goals I had scored. But the award I had chased all season long was the Golden Shot award for the first Scottish striker to net 30 goals. As the Golden Shot winner, I was presented with a glittering trophy and a crate of champagne. Unfortunately, there was no point in hanging on to the bubbly myself because I have always been a teetotaller. I've never been one for alcohol, probably because of the example set by my father, who I have only ever seen drink the occasional pint of shandy. Unlike most young lads, I never gave booze a try, always preferring to stick to soft drinks like orange and lemonade, even when I was out socialising. Alcohol goes hand-in-hand with football for many players. I've had to put up with my fair share of leg-pulling from team-mates over the years about my teetotal ways. But I've never been one to follow the crowd. I decided at an early stage I would stay away from booze and cigarettes - just as my boyhood hero Kenny Dalglish had - to give myself the maximum chance of making it in the professional game. In fact, the occasional glass of champagne to celebrate football successes has been my only concession to my no-alcohol rule throughout my life.

I was proud to score 31 goals - 27 in the league - but at the back of my mind was the nagging belief that it was time to move on to bigger things. I wasn't on the best of wages at Cliftonhill. Thankfully, I had a part-time gardening job with Glasgow Corporation to boost my Rovers salary but now I was ready for a step up. I was linked with a number of clubs in the local press during the end-of-season run-in and scouts from several Scottish clubs came to take a look at me. Another scout reportedly came north of the border from Sunderland. That was the season that Sunderland reached the League Cup final but were relegated under Len Ashurst. Lawrie McMenemy took over that summer and one of the first things he did was sign Eric Gates. So if things had turned out differently I might have become a Roker Park hero and Eric would have had to be content with a move to Newcastle!

•FAN-TASTIC: watched by a single supporter at Albion Rovers. Maybe I really shouldn't moan about Boro fans after all!

Unfortunately, Albion chairman Tom Fagan was not so keen to see me go. Not, at least, unless the money was right. He went to great efforts to build me up in the press, insisting that he rated me in the £40,000 bracket. While that might be classed as peanuts in comparison to today's multi-million pound transfer deals, I knew that was the sort of money that could put clubs off. I was at the end of my year's contract but this was in the days before players could leave on a free when their contract had run out. Back then, the rules simply stated that Fagan had to offer me a better deal than I was on to retain the right to demand a fee. What they did was offer me an increase that could best be described as laughable. The whole thing was a sham. As a consequence, the relationship between me and the club quickly became extremely tense.

I was so incensed by their attitude that I told Fagan I would never play for Albion again. They responded by banning me from training with the rest of the team. Once again, it was Bernie Slaven keeping in shape on his own, hoping for a club to come in and rescue me from what had become a nightmare situation. I had refused to play for Rovers but the fact was that unless they agreed to sell me I could never play for any other club either. It was a terrible position to be in, especially as the club could legally refuse to pay my wages. It was a rule that meant some players were forced to quit the game at an early age. It was an archaic way of going on. Thankfully, the Bosman Ruling on transfers helped to change all that, though I tend to think the balance has now swung too far the other way. Average Premier League players now wield too much power, as they are able to hold clubs to ransom in demanding outrageous wages.

When Albion took the step of refusing to pay my wages I made up my mind to chuck the game in altogether if no club came in for me. To pack in the game that I loved in those circumstances would have left me a very sad and frustrated young man. I would have been left with a job with Glasgow Corporation's Parks Department. I was all too close to a life of cutting grass, trimming hedges and clearing up rubbish. I didn't have a trade, had no real education behind me and no prospects outside the game. Even so, I was determined that Rovers would not force me into a corner simply by refusing to pay me. I continued to train hard on my own, but I knew that some people would now have branded me a troublemaker.

The solution came out of the blue. A friendship I had hit up with Andrew Gold, a sports reporter with the Glasgow *Weekly News*, proved to be my saving grace. We took to each other when we met during my time out of the game. Without Andrew, I can say without doubt that I would have finished with professional football at the age of 24. Without Andrew, Middlesbrough fans would never have even heard of Bernie

Slaven. Nor would listeners to The Three Legends, so blame Andrew for your torment! Andrew understood my predicament - and he knew a good news story when he saw one. He realised there was a fantastic opportunity to kill two birds with one stone. His idea was to write to every club in the Scottish Premier Division and the top two divisions in England, informing them of my availability, while getting a good news story for himself.

He even went as far as to write the letters for me, leaving me to simply sign them. The letters said, 'Dear Sir, Last season I was the top scorer in Scottish senior football with 31 goals for Albion Rovers in the Second Division. At present, I am on 'Freedom of contract'. I have no intention of returning to Rovers. I am keen to sample full-time football at the highest level, and wonder if you might consider signing me. I would be willing to come to your club on a trial basis, as I am desperate to get back into the game. I honestly feel I have the ability to play for your club. Although I have not played since I took up 'Freedom of contract' at the end of last season, I have kept fit during the summer, training on my own every day. I am 24 years old, and hope that you will at least think over this approach. Yours sincerely, Bernie Slaven.'

Andrew sent off the letters on September 21 1985, but they didn't get the response you might have expected. Hearts were the only club in Scotland even to bother replying, while ten English clubs responded – all with an answer best summed up as thanks, but no thanks. There was no reply from my beloved Celtic and nothing from Newcastle. Neither was there anything from Sunderland, newly relegated into Division Two, possibly because they had seen me and ruled me out the previous season. Maybe they might have considered me if I'd written a couple of weeks sooner when they were still without a goal five games into the new season.

Another club that failed to reply were Middlesbrough. Where they differed from the others was that I received a telephone call from their chief scout, Barry Geldart. Having read my letter with interest, he invited me to Ayresome Park for a two-week trial. Bingo! On October 2 1985 - just 11 days after sending the letters - I arrived at Glasgow's Queen Street Station before catching the 7.30 morning train southbound. I was on my way to Middlesbrough. I could never have imagined that, 20 years

down the line, I would still be calling it home. Back then, I knew nothing about the town. I didn't even know where it was. I'd had to look it up on a map.

As the train approached Middlesbrough Railway Station, my heart sank. My first impressions of the place were terrible. Wherever I looked it seemed there were chemical plants bellowing out smoke and smog. Even what I initially took to be Ayresome Park's floodlights turned out to be lights from local industry. In truth, I was seeing only one side of the town. I now know Middlesbrough is a good town, while the surrounding area boasts countryside that should be the envy of other regions. But smoke and smog is what I saw first. It did not make me feel good about the place.

Blundell Park, Grimsby Town's ground, was where I took my first steps in a Boro shirt. It isn't the most hospitable of places at the best of times but on a cold October night with only a few ultra-keen supporters watching, I could have been back in Scotland with Albion Rovers. I had never heard of any my Boro reserves team-mates that night, but four of them would go on to switch clubs for fees in excess of a million pounds. Gary Pallister, Stuart Ripley and Colin Cooper would all win England caps, while Alan Kernaghan later made a big money move to Man City. But I knew I was only there on the strength of my 31 goals the previous season and got it in my mind that, no matter how I played, seeing me put the ball in the back of the net was the only thing that was going to persuade Boro manager Willie Maddren that I was his man. I was desperate to score and consequently shot at every opportunity. But it wasn't to be. The game ended in a 1-0 defeat. I felt I'd played reasonably well, but as I walked off the pitch I was convinced that I hadn't done enough to persuade the club to sign me.

The following morning I caught the train back home to Glasgow, believing the deal was off. The club wanted me to stay for a full month's trial so that they could have a better look at me. In fact, they wanted me to play for the first team against Carlisle United in the Full Members Cup. But the idea of a full month with the club gave me a huge dilemma. If I took up their offer only for nothing to come of it after the month was out, I ran the risk of losing my job with Glasgow Corporation too. That was a risk I wasn't willing to take.

Back home in Fernhill, I told Da of my decision. He couldn't

BERNIE'S STORY

•NEW KID ON THE BLOCK: The quiff in all its glory on my first day on Teesside as a Boro triallist.

believe it. 'You've blown chances in the past,' he warned me. 'If you blow this one you'll never make it as a pro.'

But I stuck to my decision until, a few days later, Geldart called me from his office at Ayresome Park. 'We understand the predicament you're in, Bernie,' he explained. 'Forget the month. We'd like you to come back for one more game.' I readily agreed to the suggestion. It was another bite at the cherry, without running the risk of losing my day job if things didn't work out.

This time it all went so much more smoothly. A few hundred people turned up to see Boro's reserves take on Bradford City at Ayresome Park on a Wednesday night - more than I was used to for first team games at Cliftonhill. I scored twice - a shot and a header - and made another two for my fellow forward, Archie Stephens, as we ran out 4-0 winners. Even so, I came off the pitch wondering if I had done enough. I wasn't to know then, but Willie Maddren was actually on the phone to Tom Fagan back at Albion at that very moment, haggling over a fee. He was totally convinced that I could do a good job for Middlesbrough Football Club. In fact, he had ordered the security guard to lock the ground's gates and ensure there were no scouts hanging around outside. Bradford City manager Trevor Cherry had been among the interested onlookers that night while Leeds United, Millwall and Carlisle

had all apparently made enquiries about me. Maddren was taking no chances.

The following morning I turned up at Ayresome Park and was invited into the manager's office. After some haggling, Maddren had persuaded Fagan to reduce his asking price to £25,000 - £15,000 down and another £10,000 to follow after I had made a set number of appearances. That was none of my concern. All I was interested in was whether the club was signing me. Maddren offered me a two-year deal with an option for the club to extend it if I did well. At £300 a week, the wages on offer were hardly a king's ransom, but they were massive compared to the £70 I had been on at Albion. Even taking into account the money I was earning with my parks job, it was a chance to more than double my income. I signed on the dotted line. I was a Middlesbrough player – and what a journey I was about to undertake.

Bernie's Story:

BORO BARMY

MIDDLESBROUGH SUPPORTERS will always owe a massive debt of gratitude to the individuals who helped pull Boro through its darkest hours during the summer of 1986. I'm proud to say I played my own small part, though others have never got the credit they deserved for all their spadework behind the scenes to pull the club back from the brink when it looked like debts would take Boro under. Modern day Boro supporters take the likes of Premier League football, cup finals and European travels for granted but Middlesbrough Football Club almost ceased to exist that summer. It might seem like ancient history to some of Boro's younger fans but it will always be very clear in my memory.

The summer of '86 wasn't only the turning point for Boro, but for Bernie Slaven too. Having suffered relegation to the old Division Three at the end of my first season on Teesside, the club's very existence was in doubt – and I was facing an embarrassing return back home to Scotland. Basically, it could all have gone either one of two ways. Thankfully, for me and the club, it all came together. Steve Gibson and local businesses saved the club's bacon and manager Bruce Rioch guided a very special group of players to back-to-back promotions. Most Boro fans have probably heard the story many times before but it was an incredible time.

As I walked off the pitch after a 2-1 make-or-break defeat at Shrewsbury on the last day of the 1985-86 season, I felt utterly dejected. It was a game we had to win to stay up, but our fellow relegation rivals were worthy winners, while Gatesy's Sunderland also achieved a last-day escape with a win over Stoke. But relegation was nothing compared to what the club - not to mention the players and the fans - was about to go through. The club had been struggling to make ends meet and attendances had dipped to little more than 4,000. Relegation was the straw that broke the camel's back. That summer, the club went into voluntary liquidation, the official receiver was called in and the gates of Ayresome Park were padlocked. What was left of the first team squad was forced to train in local parks and on playing fields. The situation hit rock bottom when our wages were stopped, though fortunately the Professional Footballers Association stepped in to help us out. For a few weeks, the likes of Gary Pallister, Colin Cooper, Tony Mowbray and myself actually had to collect our wages in envelopes from Middlesbrough Town Hall. There were times when I was in a panic and wondered what the future would hold for me. I just prayed everything would turn out all right and tried to concentrate on making sure I was fit.

My first year at Middlesbrough was not a happy time in my life. I was homesick for Glasgow, I was missing my family and things went from bad to worse on the pitch. Boro were a bad team, struggling against relegation from the very start. Their reason for signing me was very clear, because they were the League's lowest scorers. But I didn't have the best of times in front of goal. I scored in a 1-1 draw against Bradford City on my home debut but then I struggled to score on a regular basis after that. I was part of a team low on confidence that never seemed to get any sort of run going. Eventually Willie Maddren, who had given me my big break by signing me, was given the push. The club replaced him with Bruce Rioch, a strict disciplinarian. Although results improved slightly, it was a case of too little, too late.

Then came a summer of doubt that ended in a rescue package being pulled together with only hours to spare. The club survived by the skin of its teeth. Most people who cared about Boro were simply happy that the club still existed but Bruce Rioch was not so easily satisfied. Having originally feared that his appointment would mean the end of my short Boro career, Bruce went on to help me fulfil my potential as a player. His predecessor, Willie Maddren, was a nice guy, perhaps too nice. It's also a fact that he was given only very limited cash to spend on new players. Even my £25,000 fee was considered a big risk at the time. In the circumstances, he performed wonders to bring in players like Stephen Pears, Brian Laws, Archie Stephens and ex-Sunderland hero Gary Rowell, while he gave first team chances to youngsters like Pally - who he signed from Billingham Town for a set for training tops – Cooper, Peter Beagrie and Stuart Ripley. They all went on to prove they were good players and, given time, I'm sure Willie could have moulded us into a winning team. But time was something he didn't have and he was eventually given the bullet.

Any sadness I had for Willie was quickly forgotten amid a feeling of dread when Bruce Rioch was asked to take over team affairs. Rioch had a reputation as a midfield hard man during his playing days and he made it clear that he respected players who were in the same mould. He was a tough nut and he expected his players to be tough nuts too. So that ruled me out! I feared for my future, especially as I hadn't exactly set the world alight with my goalscoring since making the move south of the border.

But all my concerns were to prove unfounded. Bruce wasn't able to save us from the drop to Division Three, but I believe our rise over the next two seasons was down to two key reasons – the greet camaraderie forged among the players as a result of our ordeal of nearly losing our livelihoods, and Bruce Rioch's incredible motivational skills. That combination provided the club with a springboard to catapult us from near extinction to consecutive promotion successes. Rioch turned the liquidation saga into an opportunity to start to form a new team under his direction. There was no spare cash to bring in new players, so he was forced to rely on youngsters with little or no previous first team experience. Every last one of the players who remained at Ayresome Park truly had the club at heart. Every one of us considered it an honour to play for Boro.

It was clear that what was needed to get the team back on track was discipline - and it would have been hard to find a stricter disciplinarian than Rioch, the son of a sergeant major who had clearly learned a thing or two from his father. Rioch loved the game and rarely talked of anything else. His enthusiasm, combined with discipline, was a great influence on the players. Throughout the liquidation saga, he had

ensured that we had all prepared for the big kick-off as if it was just any normal season. With the club's future assured, he drummed into us why the previous summer's troubles could have a positive effect on us all.

In his team talks, he would stress why Division Three should hold no fears for us. 'The challenges ahead are nothing compared to what you have all come through,' he told us. 'What has happened to you in recent months will strengthen you as characters and make you better players in the long-run.' Whether he actually believed it or not, when any of us were around he always expressed confidence that we could bounce back from the previous season's relegation. He filled us with self-belief and ensured that any lingering feeling of failure was swept away.

A 2-2 opening day draw against Port Vale, at our temporary home of Hartepool's Victoria Ground, was the start of a great season for Boro and we were never out of the top three. A key factor in our consistency was that we avoided injuries and fielded the same starting 11 match after match. It reached the point where it was hardly worth checking the teamsheet because the line-up would always be Pears, Laws, Cooper, Mowbray, Parkinson, Pallister, Slaven, Stephens, Hamilton, Gill, Ripley. There was a tremendous team spirit and we were far too strong for the majority of teams.

I developed a great understanding with my strike partner, Archie Stephens. Although not the tallest of players, he was one of the best headers of a ball I ever saw and would get up to lay plenty of chances on for me, while scoring a fair few himself. While I was the more skilful side of our partnership, he was the tough nut and took the brunt of the physical challenges that defenders handed out to us. He was also a great character off the pitch. A chain-smoker, he had a broad Scouse accent and was never the quietest of blokes, which meant conversations between Archie and a broad Glaswegian like me had to be heard to be believed. I remember going through a stage of trying to claim goals when there was some dispute about who got the last touch, but I would never have dared argue the toss with Archie. If he said it was his goal, then it was his goal. If he said the sky was green, then the sky was green.

We eventually clinched promotion with a game to spare, thanks to a goalless draw at home to Wigan. Back in the dressing room, spontaneous hugging broke out among the players as we danced around trying to take in what we had achieved. In many ways, it was a miracle. Less than a year earlier the club had looked certain to die. Now we were going up! Even I broke my teetotal rule that night, enjoying a sip of champagne.

The following season brought similar success. Our rock solid defence was again our springboard. But the man who was the inspiration behind it all was Bruce Rioch. He was fully aware that we were a young side who were facing vastly more experienced teams but he used our naivety to good effect. In the dressing room before a match he would build us up. 'We are the best, there is no team to touch us in this division,' he would tell us, with total conviction. 'We are Middlesbrough.' The effect such passionate words had on young players was crucial to our success, eradicating any doubts any of us might have had about whether we were good enough. We would run onto the pitch feeling 10 feet tall, like we were Real Madrid! We were world-beaters and determined to prove it.

Another piece of Brucie psychology came after I'd had a bad game at Plymouth. He actually told me to apologise to my team-mates when we were back in the dressing rooms. Our next match was at home to Barnsley but despite my below-par performance I fully expected to retain my place. No player has a divine right to their place but I was the club's top scorer. But I was in for a shock! I couldn't believe my eyes when the team sheet was pinned onto the dressing room wall, as my usual number seven position was left blank. It read: 1. Pears 2. Glover 3. Cooper 4. Mowbray 5. Parkinson 6. Pallister 7.   8. Kernaghan 9. Hamilton 10. Kerr 11. Ripley. At the bottom of the teamsheet Bruce had written, 'Gentlemen, last week we managed to succeed at Plymouth with 10 men and I feel we might be able to succeed against Barnsley with the same number.' I was made to sweat over the possibility of being dropped until I was informed that I would be playing. I was annoyed and rattled at the time but, looking back, I know he had me totally sussed. Bruce knew what my reaction would be. 'I'll show you,' I said to myself. Sure enough, we won 2-0 that day and I scored the opening goal.

Another player Rioch took under his wing was defender Tony Mowbray. He made 'Mogga' club captain and, in many ways, his righthand man. Mowbray responded by setting the standards for the younger lads to follow. Such was his strength of character that everyone respected him but the younger players particularly looked up to him. Rioch's grit and determination rubbed off on Mogga and he often gave the impression that he was prepared to die for the club. Though he was never one for doing a lot of shouting, he also helped to organise the defence, with the effect that we conceded just 30 goals in 46 games during 1986-87. He was a born leader whose sheer bravery meant he would often put his head in where I wouldn't have put my feet. To me, Mogga will always be Mr Middlesbrough, such was his love for the club and the fans. I have always believed that one day he will return to the club as manager.

Alongside him in the centre of defence, Gary Pallister was already showing signs of the class that would bring him numerous England caps and a string of honours with Manchester United. Mogga and Pally were the perfect partnership. One was full of grit and the other was a more skilful, silky player. But it was fair to say that Pally was in no way as brave as Mogga. Few were. Pally and I would often shudder at some of the tackles Mogga threw himself into it.

We enjoyed another fantastic season in 1987-88 and thought we had automatic promotion sewn up by the time we went into the last game. Unfortunately, we fluffed our lines by losing to mid-table Leicester City at Ayresome Park in our final match. But we still had a second chance – and we took it. We beat Bradford City and then Chelsea. This was long before Roman Abramovich's multi-millions but Chelsea still thought they were too good to be playing the likes of Middlesbrough. Back then, the play-offs included the team who had finished third bottom of the top division, so they had been been forced into the play-offs after an awful season. Even so, they were still full of it before both games against us, telling the press what they were going to do to us. But we beat them 2-0 at our place, then held on to go down by a single goal at Stamford Bridge. Against all the odds, we had achieved our dream of another promotion.

But that was the day a hatred of Chelsea that has stayed with

BERNIE'S STORY

•GET IN! Enjoying the moment after scoring against Sunderland at Roker Park in 1989. Peter Davenport, later to join the Mackems, is pictured with Gary Parkinson.

least expected it. Our defence, which had played so well during the promotion years, simply couldn't cope with top-flight attackers week in and week out. So many times that season we scored three goals but conceded at least as many at the other end.

Worse still, for the first time since liquidation, there was real unrest among the players. That unrest followed the arrival of Peter Davenport from Manchester United on a far better deal than the rest of us. We thought it was a slap in the face for the lads who had helped the club win a double promotion. No one blamed Peter. He was a nice, quiet family man who never caused anyone any bother. There were always rumours that I didn't get on with him but they weren't true. We were never best buddies but I liked him, as a player and a character.

That unrest didn't help our cause, but we were never in the division's bottom three until the final whistle in our last game of the season, at Sheffield Wednesday. After all we had been through as a team - the uphill struggle from such desperate beginnings - relegation was hard to take. Our goal had always been Division One football. After just one year of it, we were down again.

me took root. On the final whistle, my immediate reaction was to run across to the 6,000 Boro supporters who had made the trip from Teesside. As I waved wildly at our fans, I turned round expecting to see my team-mates in celebration behind me. But there wasn't another player on the pitch. Chelsea's fans were rioting. They were storming the pitch to get at our supporters. I knew I was in trouble if I didn't get the hell out of there fast. I ran for the players' tunnel, guided by police who were desperately trying to form a wall to meet the rioting hooligans. As I reached the tunnel entrance, a bottle thrown from the crowd smashed onto the floor, inches from my feet. It was frightening. To rub salt into the wound, another so-called Chelsea supporter spat at me as I made my way down the tunnel. Unfortunately, our supporters endured some frightening moments outside, as Chelsea's rioting morons attempted to wage war with them. Thankfully, the police eventually restored order and we were able to go back onto the pitch to share the special moment with our fans.

Things didn't go to plan in Division One, despite the fact that we were one of the most attractive, entertaining sides in the top flight that season. Our Achilles heel proved to be the area in which we

While Boro had struggled as a team, I felt I had come out of it well and was delighted when local journalists chose me as the North East Player of the Year. I ended the season as the Division One's third top scorer, with my 18-goal tally bettered by only two other strikers - Arsenal's Alan Smith (23 goals) and Liverpool's John Aldridge (21). Arsenal and Liverpool had fought a season-long battle for the championship, culminating in a final day victory for the Gunners, while Boro had struggled all season. To finish third to those two in such circumstances gave me every reason to feel proud. How many goals I might have scored had I been in a successful side is pure conjecture, but I can't help but think I could have scored at least another five, maybe 10 more goals. Behind me in the goalscorers table were quality strikers like Manchester United's Mark Hughes and Brian McClair, Tony Cascarino and Teddy Sheringham of Millwall, Liverpool's Peter Beardsley, Wimbledon's John Fashanu, David Speedie of Coventry, Alan McInally of Aston Villa and Everton's Tony Cottee.

I enjoyed my best ever season for goalscoring the following year, 1989-90, but the season was a bit of a disaster for Boro.

We became the first Boro team ever to play at Wembley, losing narrowly to Chelsea in the Zenith Data Systems Cup final, but the league was our bread and butter – and that's where we struggled. Results became so bad that, less than three weeks before he was due to lead the team out at Wembley, Bruce Rioch was sacked. He had performed miracles in his first couple of years with the club. But now there was the real fear that we could repeat the journey in the opposite direction. There was no doubt in my mind that Bruce had done a fantastic job with limited resources. But it was equally the case that he no longer held the same influence over the players, a hold that had proved so effective in those first two or three successful years. The players just weren't responding to him in the way they once had. Things he said which might once have inspired them now seemed to leave them cold. The lads had grown up, they had their own ideas and were no longer willing to take everything Bruce said as gospel. Quite simply, they weren't listening to him - and that spelt trouble.

His successor as Boro manager was his former assistant, Colin Todd. But try as we might, we just couldn't pull ourselves away from the relegation zone. So we went into our final game of the season knowing that even a victory would not guarantee us survival. In true Roy of the Rovers fashion, the game was set up for a nerve-wracking finale. While we had to beat our north-east rivals, Newcastle United - themselves still in with an outside chance of automatic promotion - we were relying on fourth-bottom Bournemouth slipping up at home to the Geordies' fellow promotion chasers, Leeds United, at Dean Court.

The game was given a huge build-up in the local and national press. United strikers, Mick Quinn and Mark McGhee, had been scoring the goals all season and were full of boasts about how they were going to shoot us down, posing with six-shooters and cowboy hats to underline the point. Meanwhile, there was another story doing the rounds about how, if United won, the club planned to land a helicopter on the Ayresome Park pitch and fly the team back to St James' Park, where thousands of fans were watching the game on a big screen. My only thought to such over-confident hype was, 'Let's wait and see what happens.'

That match turned out to be one of the greatest games I ever had the fortune to take part in. I opened the scoring on the hour, turning in Paul Kerr's left-wing cross. The ball rolled towards the goal in what seemed like slow motion, hit the post and finally crossed the line after inching along it. I think the supporters in the Holgate must have sucked it in. During the ensuing celebrations on the fence, I was almost dragged into the Holgate end by over-exuberant supporters. In truth, United's goalkeeper John Burridge was at fault for the goal because he seemed to hesitate before deciding to try to get to Kerr's cross. But apart from the fact that I was elated to have put Boro ahead, there was no way I could feel any pity for Burridge. The previous season, in the First Division, he had played in goal for Southampton against Boro at The Dell in a game we had won 3-1. During the match, as a corner was swung into the box, he had intentionally stamped on my toe. In response, I lashed out at him, catching him on the ear with a wild punch. Fortunately, the incident had gone unseen by the match officials but I had not forgotten his unsporting tactics.

Just a few minutes after my opener against the Geordies, we went two-up. This time I intercepted a poor back-pass from United full-back John Anderson, rounded Burridge and squared the ball across the six-yard area for my strike partner Ian Baird to tap in. Barely had the game restarted than young Boro player Owen McGee deflected the ball into his own net to put United back in it. But Bairdy was on fire by now and put us 3-1 up to more or less sew up the win.

In the closing minutes, United defender Bjorn Kristensen elbowed me in the face. The two of us had always had scuffles whenever we'd been in opposition but I believe that sort of behaviour, showing a total disregard for a fellow professional, is completely unacceptable. I blew my top and

•KNEESY DOES IT: Further proof that jumping on a fence wasn't my only way of celebrating goals.

punched him in the face. He made a meal out of the incident and fell to the floor, presumably in a bid to get me sent off. Thankfully, the referee took no action. But while the ref may have missed the incident, the fans had not and they launched into a rendition of 'Bernie, Bernie Slaven...' Meanwhile, my unofficial minder, Bairdy, did his utmost to wind up Kristensen even further by flicking the back of his ears to insinuate the United defender's playing style resembled a donkey's! In the final minute, we wrapped up a fantastic day with a fourth goal, my 32nd of the season. The win was enough to keep us up – and force Newcastle into the play-offs, where they would lose to Sunderland, partly courtesy of a Mr Eric Gates.

Beating the Geordies in such circumstances was great. I had a knack of scoring against Newcastle, although the quickest ever derby goal I scored came against Sunderland a couple of seasons later. There were just 18 seconds on the clock when I opened the scoring at Ayresome Park, latching on to a badly misdirected back-pass from Kevin Ball, with keeper Tony Norman managing only to push the ball into my path. We went on to win 2-1, but I believe that goal is the fastest ever in a north-east derby.

The Newcastle win was the perfect end to a traumatic season for the club – and I then travelled to the Italia '90 World Cup with the Republic of Ireland. I didn't get a kick while I was

there, but I'm proud to say I made a World Cup squad. The reason I played my international football for Ireland and not Scotland needs to be explained. Back then, Scotland were much more of a force than they are nowadays. The Celtic duo of Mo Johnston and Charlie Nicholas, Manchester United's Brian McClair and Rangers star Ally McCoist were all household names. Nowadays I would struggle to tell you the name of even one Scotland striker, such has been their demise on the international scene. The players I've mentioned were all experienced international strikers who had done well for their country, so it was fair enough that I was behind them in the pecking order. But I became increasingly frustrated when Scotland boss Andy Roxburgh gave first caps to Chelsea's Gordon Durie and Aston Villa's Alan McInally before recalling David Speedie of Coventry. Not once did he even come to speak to me.

Fortunately, I had more than one option open to me. My grandparents were both from the Republic of Ireland - my late grandfather, Mickey Slaven, was from Knockastoller in Gweedore, Donegal, while my grandmother, Bridget, came from Ardoyne. Though both grandparents had died some years earlier, my great uncle, Jimmy Slaven, was still living on a farm in Knockastoller, as the last remaining member of the Slaven family in Ireland. Irish boss Jack Charlton had shown he was willing to take advantage of this international 'loophole' to call up top stars that had never so much as set foot in Ireland. Top quality players like John Aldridge, Ray Houghton and Kevin Sheedy - good players who felt they had little chance of winning caps for the country of their birth - qualified to represent Ireland through relatives and had become key members of the Irish side. That gave me some hope that he might consider me if I kept scoring the goals.

I still remember Big Jack calling me after training at Ayresome Park to discuss my international credentials. When he asked me how I qualified to play for the Republic of Ireland, I quipped, 'Well, I've got an Irish Setter!' I paused to wait for the resulting laugh. Instead, there was silence. I later came to realise that, despite being a former England international, Jack was fiercely patriotic about his adopted Ireland. That sort of joke did not go down well with him. At the time, I wasn't to know that, but I regretted my wisecrack as soon as I'd said it.

•BANG! A rare long-distance effort. My usual range was about two yards!

The fact is I was in awe of the man and felt very nervous just speaking to him.

Soon after, Jack called me into his squad, while Scotland continued to ignore me. I had been brought up as a true Scot, but my patriotism had been banged out of me by the constant knocks I'd suffered from my country throughout my football career. Scotland had never done me any favours. Where were the Scottish clubs when I was on the dole and in dispute with Albion Rovers? Where had Scotland been while I had been scoring 20 goals a season for Middlesbrough? No, I wasn't at all patriotic about Scotland any more; the country had never done anything for my football career.

The Republic of Ireland team for my first international, against Wales, included a man who Sunderland fans would now need no introduction to, Mick McCarthy, while future Boro players Andy Townsend and Chris Morris were also involved. It was a dream debut for me, because I scored a rebound from a penalty in the dying minutes to give us a 1-0 win. I played only once more for Ireland before Jack named his squad for the World Cup, so I was delighted to be included. I knew I had crept in by the back door and was out to enjoy every minute of the experience. Despite not getting a game in Italy, it was a real experience to be part of such an occasion, though I still maintain the highlight for me was meeting the Pope!

Back at the Boro, I never really hit it off with Colin Todd in the same way I did with Bruce Rioch. That's not to say I didn't like him. We simply didn't see eye-to-eye when it came to football and, in particular, my value to the team. Things came to a head when Boro took on struggling Charlton at Ayresome Park. We were 1-0 down at half-time and I knew I hadn't played well, but neither had anyone else. So I was staggered when Toddy told me I was coming off. My blood was boiling as I stormed into the shower while the rest of the lads returned to the pitch for the second half. As I showered, I made up my mind that there was no way I was going to watch the second half. I just thought, 'Why should I when I should be playing?' I felt like I was being victimised. Surely you don't take off your top scorer - a player who has proved on so many occasions that he can pop up to score a vital goal even when he isn't playing well - when you are a goal down?

With the game going on and the sound of the crowd reverberating around the ground, I walked out of the dressing rooms and out of the gates of Ayresome Park. I was going home. Just a handful of people saw me leave, though enough to ensure it was big news in the press the following week. But I had made up my mind that I didn't want to stay around, getting more frustrated and agitated. I needed to get away from it all. I drove home as Boro battled for vital league points. As I took my dogs for a walk on local wasteland, in the distance I could see Ayresome Park's floodlights. It was a strange feeling but I had no regrets about leaving. Ironically, it was a bad performance that, without me, didn't improve in the second half as Boro fell to a 2-1 defeat. We'll never know what might have happened if I'd stayed on but I'm confident a goal would have come my way.

We eventually lost to Notts County in the promotion play-offs that season, ending Toddy's short reign as Boro manager. On our day, we were a match for most teams, but we simply weren't consistent enough. The big name in our side was John Wark, but he didn't produce the predicted stream of goals from midfield. Gatesy always tells me what a great player Wark was when they were team-mates at Ipswich. He certainly enjoyed a great career. He had even appeared in the popular football film, *Escape to Victory*, alongside legends like Pele, Bobby Moore and Osvaldo Ardiles. During his barren run with Boro, however, some of the lads joked that maybe that performance had been the best of his career!

I was slowly being squeezed out of Middlesbrough Football Club by our new manager, Lennie Lawrence. It was clear from the start that Lennie didn't fancy me and we clashed time after time. Our relationship seemed to just hit a downward spiral. There was constant friction between the two of us. Ayresome Park just wasn't big enough for both of us. How I stayed on over the summer of 1992 I'll never know, but it wasn't long before Lawrence made it quite clear where I stood. If the right offer came in, I'd be on my way. We fell out so badly that he made me train with the youth team. It was the final insult, a way of belittling me and showing who was boss. After all I had been through with the club, it was very hard to take. Some of the other first team lads couldn't believe the way Lennie was treating me. As we changed into our training gear in the dressing room, they would tell me how

•CLOSING IN ON 147: John Hendrie joins me as I celebrate one of the last goals of my Boro career.

embarrassed they were about it all.

Press speculation suggested Sunderland could be interested in signing me but they never made a formal enquiry that I'm aware of. In fact, the only club to contact Boro at that point was Hartlepool United. I had a lot of time for their manager, Alan Murray, but I really didn't feel ready to drop down the divisions. It was Alan's idea to take me on loan and to put me in the 'shop window' with a view of attracting bigger clubs, but the idea was a non-starter because I made it clear I wanted a permanent move. There was some interest from Aston Villa and Nottingham Forest, but the most exciting prospect came with a telephone call from Stuart Ripley one evening. 'The King's been asking about you,' he told me, referring to his Blackburn manager Kenny Dalglish. 'Blackburn's secretary has asked me for your telephone number so I'm sure Kenny will be phoning you.'

I know many Newcastle fans reading this will have a very different view of Kenny, but just the prospect of Dalglish calling gave me an immense buzz. This was my boyhood hero, a guy I had worshipped from the Parkhead terraces, a player who had inspired me with his skills and professionalism. Now it seemed he was interested in signing me. Blackburn, who had come up through the play-offs behind Boro, were involved in the Premiership title race but their season was in danger of coming off the rails due to a long-term injury to Alan Shearer. Now, apparently, Dalglish saw me as an ideal replacement. It was an exciting prospect and I eagerly waited for the phone call...and waited...and waited. It never came. Could it be the negative influence of Mr Lawrence again? The answer was almost certainly yes.

I eventually left Boro for Port Vale but finally making the break was the hardest decision I have ever had to make. Despite the fact that I was not being made to feel welcome at the club, the place and the fans were special to me and it was hard to break those ties.

Over the years, I enjoyed something of a love-hate relationship with the Boro fans. I'd like to think that I was popular. But I was always aware that there was a sizeable faction that didn't rate me. One of their main criticisms was my tendency to be caught offside, particularly by negative sides like Oldham. I've often joked that my team-mates simply weren't releasing the ball early enough but I do have a serious answer to the criticism. I was never what I would call 'Ripley-quick'. By that I mean I didn't have the pace to give a defender a couple of yards start and still beat him to a ball. So I had to live on the edge, always trying to get that extra half-yard on the defence. Defenders are well practised in their tactics so I was always running the risk of straying offside - and I would do so nine times out of 10. But if, on the tenth occasion, the linesman's flag stayed down and I broke through to score a crucial goal, then those nine earlier offside decisions would be forgotten. The simple fact is that I scored that type of goal on many, many occasions. Even so, I have to admit I'd have probably scored 300 goals, not 200, if there'd been no such thing as offside.

So yes, I always had my critics. But I'm also proud to say I had my supporters, fans who loved me as a player. All I can say is they obviously knew the game better than my detractors. They were what Steve McClaren might call educated fans! After more than 380 games and 147 goals for the club, I almost felt like part of the furniture at Ayresome Park. I was proud of what I had achieved there. But I felt frustration, too, that I was being forced to leave. In my heart of hearts, I believed I could, and would, have been at the peak of my game had Lawrence not treated me with such disdain. Even now, with the benefit of hindsight, I am confident I would have scored goals if I had stayed. It remains one of my few regrets that I didn't play more top-flight football. It wasn't my fault that I didn't. I tried my utmost to keep us up. I can't help but wonder what more I might have achieved had I been fortunate enough to be in a better Boro side. If I'd had Juninho at his peak providing me with the chances, like Fabrizio Ravanelli later had, I'd have scored 35 goals.

Bernie's Story:

VALE OF TEARS

IT IS fair to say that things never went to plan for me at Port Vale. I joined the club believing we would win promotion and I'd be playing at a higher level the following season, probably facing my old Boro team-mates. Instead, we fluffed our lines, got beat in the play-offs and I ended up feeling terribly homesick. Quite simply, leaving Boro was the start of the end in terms of my playing career.

I couldn't have made a worse start to life after Boro. I was sent off on my Port Vale debut. Barring the Sunday game back in Tory Glen many years earlier, it was the first time in my career I'd been dismissed. I thoroughly deserved to go. I lashed out and kicked Leyton Orient centre-back Adrian Whitbread across the midriff in retaliation for one too many over-the-top tackles he'd inflicted on me. I didn't even wait for referee Paul Danson to show me the red card. I'd been so blatant, I knew I had to go and immediately started the long walk to the dressing room. Once there, I remember sitting thinking, 'What the hell am I doing here?' I was still trying to get my head around the fact that, for the first time in eight years, my life no longer revolved around Boro. Now I'd gone and let down my new team-mates and a club I knew had pushed the boat out to meet my personal terms.

The whole, awful situation felt completely surreal. My free transfer from Boro had all gone through a bit too quickly for my liking. Then, after just one day's training with my team-mates, I was asked to make my debut. There was no way I was mentally prepared for the game, but my new club needed me and this was what they were paying me to do. Despite my aberration, Vale actually won the match 1-0 to keep up their push for promotion but it was hardly the start I'd hoped for.

I'd have forgiven Port Vale players if they hadn't exactly taken to me after that awful start, but I got on well with them. Two of them I already knew very well, as I had played alongside Dean Glover and Paul Kerr at Middlesbrough. They were two of the side's most influential players, along with young midfielder Ian Taylor, who later made a big money move to Aston Villa. Defender Neil Aspin was also capable of playing at a higher level and I got on very well with him. I remember his pre-match meal was always pasta. 'Eat like an Italian, play like an Italian!' he joked. I didn't tell him about my love for a good Chinese!

Unlike most Division Three sides, Port Vale played a skilful, passing game, thanks to the football beliefs of manager John Rudge. We were in a five-way battle for two automatic promotion spots with West Brom, Stockport, Bruce Rioch's Bolton and our Potteries rivals, Stoke City. We were in the driving seat behind Stoke for much of the run-in, but a couple of slip-ups allowed Bolton to nudge ahead of us. Despite winning 4-2 at Blackpool in our final league match, having trailed at half-time, we came off the pitch to hear that Bolton had pipped us to second place by a single point, thanks to their own final day win at home to Preston.

But far from the season being over, what followed was the most exciting fortnight in Port Vale's long history. We beat Stockport over two legs in the play-off semi-final to ensure that Port Vale, a club that had never previously been to Wembley, would play there twice in eight days. Before the play-off final with West Brom came the Autoglass Trophy final against Stockport. Just as I had done for Boro, I had scored the goal that booked Port Vale their first Wembley date with a semi-final winner against Exeter. Now, just three days after beating them in the play-offs, we faced Stockport again beneath the famous twin towers. Having finished on the losing side on my first visit to Wembley with Boro, I desperately wanted to be a winner this time. The final was watched by a crowd of over 35,000, most of them Vale supporters but also two busloads from Middlesbrough. The game itself went like a dream, both for the team and myself. I had a hand in our opening goal early in the game, passing for Paul Kerr to score with a cool finish. I then fulfilled a personal ambition of scoring at Wembley before half-time. A second half goal from big Kevin Francis proved to be no more than a consolation for Stockport, with my strike proving to be the winner.

After a 117-year wait for the club's first Wembley appearance, Vale had to wait just eight days for a second. The opposition for our play-off final were Ossie Ardiles' West Brom, another of the clubs I could so easily have joined before plumping for Vale. We'd already achieved a league double over them earlier in the season, so we went into the game brimming with confidence. Unfortunately, we didn't perform on the day, had a man sent off early in the second half and fell to a 3-0 defeat to end our promotion hopes.

The following season was dominated by my desire to get away from Port Vale and back to the north-east. That was nothing against Port Vale, because they were a good little club, but my wife Karen was expecting our first child. When our first son, Dominic, arrived in January 1994, I was living in rented accommodation near Port Vale's ground in Burslem, while my wife and newborn son were 150 miles away on Teesside. It felt great to be a dad for the first time but I was only able to spend a few short days with Karen and Dominic before getting back to Vale for a big FA Cup tie.

I quickly realised it was a situation that couldn't be allowed to continue. Moving them over to Staffordshire wasn't an option. We were happily settled in Middlesbrough and had set our hearts on staying there. I was 33 years old and my contract had only five months to run. I knew I had to get back to the north-east as soon as I could.

Although things went reasonably well for me on the pitch, my mind really wasn't on football. I told John Rudge that I was desperate to get back to the north-east, though I accepted that, at 33, Hartlepool and Darlington were the most realistic options, especially as the salary was no longer important to me. Rudge was reluctant to release me, but he knew it was pointless hanging on to me when I wanted away. The press speculated that Sunderland and even Boro were interested in signing me but I don't think there was any truth in either story. I'd have walked back to Boro if I had thought I had a chance of re-joining them. But while Lennie Lawrence remained in charge, there seemed little hope of that.

Then John Rudge phoned me to say Alan Murray, by now in charge of Darlington, wanted to speak to me about a possible move to Feethams. I knew joining the Quakers, just half an hour up the road from Middlesbrough, would be perfect so agreed to meet Murray for talks. The money on offer was probably a lot for a small club like Darlington but it was peanuts in football terms. But money was of secondary importance. The key was a chance to be with my family while continuing to play professional football. I readily agreed terms with Alan and joined Darlington.

As far as the football went, the move was a big step backwards. Darlington were just a few points off the bottom of the Football League and in real danger of relegation to the Vauxhall Conference. But I had real respect for Alan and his assistant Eddie Kyle. I knew they would do their all to turn the tide. Returning to the north-east was like going back home and I couldn't wait to get cracking for my new club. I was delighted to see several hundred Middlesbrough fans swell the crowd for my home debut against Chesterfield. Unfortunately, I was unable to reward them with a goal. In fact, I would go seven games before netting for Darlington. I had been confident of scoring a few goals for the club, but I was shocked that chances were so few and far between.

From a very early stage, I realised I was never going to enjoy playing at that level. Without meaning to offend, Darlington made Port Vale look like Inter Milan. All of my new team-mates were good, honest pros who always gave 100 per cent but their up-and-under style was often lacking the skill I had previously taken for granted. It would be wrong of me to say Darlington were devoid of talent. Young defender Adam Reed, later to join Blackburn Rovers and now a physio at Boro, was as brave as a lion, centre-back Sean Gregan was a great stopper who read the game well, my strike partner Robbie Painter was big and fast, while midfielder Steve Gaughan was undoubtedly the fittest lad in the team. I also played a few games alongside a young Graham Kavanagh, who was on loan from Boro.

But the season went from bad to worse. When we lost a sixth successive match, it looked odds on Darlington would finish bottom of the table and suffer relegation from the Football League for the second time in just five years. We were staring disaster in the face. With just four games left to play, we were six points adrift of second-bottom Northampton. It was a case of do or die. We went into our final match, at home to Bury, still three points behind Northampton but I scored the game's only goal, while our rivals lost heavily to end all thoughts of relegation for us.

The following season my personal aim was to reach the 200 mark in career goals. I began the campaign just six short of my target but there were times when I might as well have been 106 short for the chances I was getting. I wasn't enjoying my football one bit and there was a point when I told myself enough was enough. There were critics who complained about my lack of goals and my poor form generally but I really believe Peter Beardsley would have struggled at Darlington. It was no fun playing on poor pitches with average players watched by poor crowds. Eventually, I took a few days off to think things over and decide whether this was really what I wanted to do. In my heart of hearts I still believed I was capable of playing at a higher level but this felt like death by football.

The only thing that convinced me to carry on was the thought of scoring my 200th goal - and the fact that I wasn't sure what else I would do if I packed in the game after all those years. Another boost was the manager's decision to move me onto the left wing. At my previous clubs, I'd hated being moved out of my favoured central role but things were different now. Down the middle at Darlington, I was just watching the ball fly way over my head. There were precious few good balls played to my feet. Out wide, however, I had a bit more time and space to play my natural game. The moment I'd been waiting for - goal number 200 - finally arrived on February 18 1995, after the best part of two months on 199. In terms of league points, the goal meant nothing, as we were 3-0 down with only four minutes remaining when I scored it, but it was still a proud moment.

My playing career was slowly but surely coming to an end. Between games, I was having daily physiotherapy treatment on a back injury that I believe I picked up when falling awkwardly on my Darlington debut. It was clear I was no longer as fit as I had once been. Apart from the problems with my back, I was constantly picking up calf and hamstring strains. I was 34 years old and was getting the impression my body was trying to tell me something. Even training became difficult because my back was in such a knot. When it got to the point when I couldn't even touch my toes, Feethams physio Nigel Carnell advised me to start swimming on a daily basis to help to ease the pain and keep myself fit. Finally, the time came when I couldn't train or play. With Alan Murray sacked, I was given a free transfer from Darlington in May 1995.

Having been sidelined for two months, being released was no real surprise. I didn't even have the consolation of a memorable last game. There was an attendance of just 1,500 at Spotland, home of Rochdale, for my last ever league match. In a way, my career had turned full circle. I was playing in front of the sort of crowds I had been used to when it all started back in Scotland 14 years earlier. All of this time it was believed my back problem was a muscle injury but I had eventually been sent to visit a consultant. I knew the results of a scan would determine any decision over whether to look for a new club. When the results came through, I knew my playing days were over. The scan revealed that discs at the base of my back had crumbled. The problem was probably due to wear and tear, combined with that heavy fall against Shrewsbury, and mild arthritis was even setting in.

'My advice to you would be to retire from the professional game,' the consultant said. 'Your back isn't going to get any better and you're likely to make it worse by training daily.'

Despite expecting the news, I was numb with shock. I had gone to the consultant expecting to be given a solution, only to be told to give up the game I loved. After some thought, I knew the only decision I could make was to follow the advice of the experts and retire from football. At the end of May I announced my retirement from the game. I stuck with the decision despite one or two appeals for a change of heart. Local non-league clubs, such as Bishop Auckland and Whitby, got in touch to offer me a regular game. I even had a chance to join Dalian, the Chinese champions, but I thanked them for their offers before turning them down, knowing my back simply wasn't up to it.

Bernie's Story:
RADIO GA-GA

I CONSIDER myself very fortunate to have had a great career in football. But unless they go into coaching or management, even lucky footballers have to find a new career once they give up playing in their mid-30s. Trying to adapt to life without football as the be all and end all came as a shock to my system. Quite honestly, it was no fun at all. But then along came Century Radio. Few former players can enjoy their lives after football as much as I do. And that's all down to my career with Century, not just on The Three Legends but also commentating on Boro games alongside Alastair Brownlee.

I was given my chance on Century when the station's bosses lost faith in Malcolm Allison. Big Mal, the former Boro manager, was well-known throughout the game, not only for his ups and downs as a coach and manager of numerous clubs, but for his reputation as a cigar-smoking, champagne-quaffing, larger-than-life character. He was renowned for his outspoken views, a style that proved to be his strength but was also his downfall as a radio pundit. During his commentaries, Malcolm committed radio's cardinal sin of saying a four-letter word on air not once, but twice. They gave him the push after giving him a second chance when he first swore on air. After the first occasion, Malcolm was temporarily taken off-air and replaced by Alan Murray. But, when Alan joined Graeme Souness at Benfica, Mal was given a second chance - and blew it again. During one of his Boro commentaries, he reacted to a poor refereeing decision by shouting out, 'Linesman, that's a f***ing joke!' That was the end of the road for Malcolm as far as radio work was concerned.

Malcolm's loss was my gain. His use of the f-word resulted in me receiving an emergency call from Century, and I duly stepped into his shoes for a trip to Arsenal on New Year's Eve 1996, a game which saw Bryan Robson, at 39, become the oldest player ever to appear for Boro's first team. It wasn't actually the first time Century had called on my services, as I had stepped in once or twice in the past when they had

tended to share the summarising role between various ex-Boro players, but that was the start of my long run as permanent summariser.

I initially worked with both Alastair and his fellow commentator, Dave Roberts, though having three of us on-air never really worked, so I wasn't surprised when the Century gaffers decided not to replace Dave when he left for pastures new. Ali and I quickly established our Laurel and Hardy-style double-act. Right from the start, we clicked on and off-air, probably because we're two completely different animals.

I know football fans who have heard our commentaries on Middlesbrough games have, shall we say, mixed views about Ali. That's mainly because his ultra-positive manner tends to irritate some people who want to hear an honest view of the game, not some one-sided whitewash, heavily biased in favour of everything Boro do right and conveniently forgetting anything they make a mess of. Fortunately, I sit alongside him to redress the balance. That's not to say that he sees the positive and I only see the negative. I'd like to think that I see the positives too. I'm not Mr Negative - I'm just a realist. If I praise the performance of the team or an individual player, then most listeners will know it must be because they have truly done well. If, on the other hand, Ali praises them, you're still left wondering what the truth is.

At times, it's ridiculous. If we get walloped by five, he will say we were unlucky. I can't imagine he really believes that, but he says it anyway. I know that he's talking absolute garbage and I sometimes think he knows it too. Never mind seeing things in a different light, Ali sees a light that nobody else in the stadium sees – and it's always a positive one for Middlesbrough. On the other hand, if I think something is wrong or someone isn't playing well, I say so.

Ali and I are a similar age and yet I regard him as my father figure. Without his advice and encouragement over the years, I doubt I would be where I am today. He has given me professional and personal advice on more occasions than I care to remember, always keeping me out of trouble when my headstrong personality might have led me down the wrong path. There have been times when I've been ready to explode, to chuck it all in, but he always calms me down and gets me to think about what I'm saying. For that, I will always be in his debt. He makes me laugh and he makes me angry. He has worked with me for so long that he is one of the few people in this world who knows what I'm all about. He is my psychologist. I would trust Ali with my life.

Ali has said some silly things on air during our Century commentaries over the years. He has always loved his clichés and I can only imagine that he must spend hours planning what cheesy phrase he could use if a certain player scores that day. One of his most famous – or maybe that should be infamous – statements was calling Boro's goalkeeper Mark Schwarzer 'the greatest Australian since Ned Kelly' when his last-minute penalty save at Manchester City clinched a UEFA Cup spot in the final seconds of the 2004-05 season. I understand that Kelly was actually a bandit, but it could have been so much worse, as Ali later admitted that the only other Australian he could think of was Rolf Harris! Then, on the night Boro reached the UEFA Cup final by completing an unforgettable comeback against Steaua Bucharest, he shouted out, 'Party! Party! Party! Everyone round my house for a Parmo!'. (Note to Geordies: a Parmo is a Teesside delicacy comprising a pork fillet smothered in bechamel sauce and cheese).

But, for sheer stupidity, nothing Ali has ever said even comes close to my regretful statement to thousands of listeners on Saturday December 12 1998. That afternoon a Brian Deane goal gave Boro a 1-0 win over West Ham, taking them to the heady heights of fourth in the table. Things were going great. There was every reason to feel optimistic about the future. Unfortunately, our next match was away to Premiership champions, Manchester United. As delighted as I was about our run of form, I was realistic enough to know that the chances of the unbeaten streak continuing the following Saturday were, at best, minimal. Ali, of course, thought we would win.

During the post-match phone-in, a caller asked me what I

•DOUBLE ACT: with my father figure and psychologist, Alastair Brownlee, before commentating on the UEFA Cup final.

would do if Boro actually won at Old Trafford. I knew we had not won there for nearly 70 years, so I felt I was on safe ground predicting that Boro's winless Old Trafford run would continue the following Saturday. Then came the fateful words I would live to regret.

'If Boro win at Old Trafford,' I smiled, 'I'll show my backside in Binns' window.'

I had been told that, in Middlesbrough, this was something the locals would say as a way of expressing their extreme doubt that an event would occur. In other words, I would show my backside in one of the poshest shops in town. To my understanding, it didn't usually mean you would actually do what you were saying – because that would be ridiculous. It was simply a way of emphasising how unlikely I felt the prospect of Boro winning at Old Trafford really was. But, little did I know, my fate had already been sealed.

News of my off-the-cuff promise swept through Teesside's football community like wild fire. As momentum started to gather, my comments became a major subject of discussion on the forerunner to Century fm's Three Legends show, The Bob Moncur Football Phone-In, with Ali – naturally – winding it up at every opportunity.

Then, incredibly, Boro went and won the game that I said they couldn't. They were three-up at one point but finally hung on for a 3-2 win. The Boro fans there celebrated by singing, 'Bernie, show us your arse! Bernie, Bernie, show us your arse!'

A couple of days later, with the agreement of the store manager at Binns, I turned up to show my backside in the shop window in Middlesbrough town centre. Ali and the fans had insisted I would have to go through with it, so I agreed, believing half a dozen shoppers were in for a shock when my rear faced them as they passed by. But I seriously underestimated the interest in the story. All manner of media people turned up – Sky, the BBC, newspapers, the lot – plus what looked like thousands of Boro fans. I couldn't believe my eyes. They were hanging on lampposts, they were leaning out of windows and there were kids on their father's shoulders. I had never seen anything like it since Boro had paraded through the town after winning promotion to the top flight years earlier.

To raucous cheers all round, I turned my back to them, bent over, lifted my kilt and revealed a pair of fetching red knickers designed to protect the innocent! On either cheek was written the scoreline, '3-2'. And first prize for call of the day had to go to the woman who took one look at my rear end before declaring, 'That reminds me, I've got to stuff the turkey!'

So have I learned my lesson? Well, I'm prepared to put my neck on the line and promise to go stark naked if Boro ever win the Premier League. I know I can safely say that until I'm 85 without fear of ever having to go through with the forfeit.

For all that Ali is the consummate professional, he is also the ultimate wind-up merchant, always plotting a new scheme. It was one of his barmy ideas that resulted in it being announced that I would stand as the first directly elected Mayor of Middlesbrough. With Ali as the instigator, it started as a joke, a bit of a laugh, but quickly got out of hand.

It all started in October 2002. During our usual Thursday night sauna at the Tall Trees health club – a weekly ritual we have pursued for as long as I can remember - one of our topics of conversation had been the recent decision by the people of Middlesbrough that they would like a directly elected Mayor. As we enjoyed a shower in adjacent cubicles, Ali's voice boomed over the sound of the running water. 'Bernie, the public of Middlesbrough want a Mayor,' he shouted. 'And I'm putting your name forward.'

I laughed and gave his humour the lip service it deserved.

'The first thing I'd do is pawn the chain!' I mocked. Joke over for the day, I thought no more of the subject.

But Alastair wasn't joking. His imagination had gone into overdrive. The next morning, he called me and said, 'Bernie, you are serious about this, aren't you?' He insisted on reading an article to me which he claimed was on Middlesbrough FC's official website. 'Boro legend Bernie Slaven today announced his intention to stand for the newly created position of elected Mayor of Middlesbrough,' he read. 'The town's residents last week voted to change its form of local government and the former Republic of Ireland striker is one of the first to throw his hat into the ring. Campaign manager Alastair Brownlee said he believed Slaven has all the attributes for the important role.'

To be honest, I doubted he had really put such a story on the club's website – but my confidence was misplaced. Within an hour of his call, my phone was red hot. I was taking calls from the media in Teesside, Glasgow, London, Dublin, everywhere. I decided to play along with the yarn. At this stage, potential contenders needed to only declare an interest in standing, so there was nothing binding, so I thought 'What the hell? I'll go for it!'

In the many media interviews that followed, I admitted that I didn't really know what the job of Mayor entailed. In fact, I was honest enough to tell them that I didn't know much about politics in general. The truth is that I have never had any interest in politics and have a very low opinion of politicians. But I told them, 'I love Teesside and I hate it when people from outside the area slate it.'

Meanwhile, other more serious candidates began to throw their hats into the ring. They included representatives of the local Labour and Liberal Democrat parties. But, myself apart, by far the most high-profile candidate was Detective Superintendent Ray Mallon, better known to all and sundry as Robocop. In his senior role with Cleveland Police, Mallon had gained national fame for his zero tolerance tactics, tackling criminals severely at all levels. His no-nonsense style had proved a success, with arrests up and serious crime down, but his abrasive manner had brought him into conflict with senior colleagues. Now he was ready for a career change.

I later discovered that he was seriously concerned when I

announced my interest in standing, but I simply continued to play along with the joke and enjoy the free publicity. During one memorable interview, I was bamboozled by the political jargon spoken by a pompous TV journalist. But when she asked me if I had a message for Mr Mallon, I was prepared.

'Yeah,' I said. With that, I produced a football, which I flipped into the air, caught on the back of my neck, flicked back up and brought back under control with my left foot. 'Can *you* do that, Ray?' I asked, staring into the camera. I would love to have been a fly on the wall in Ray Mallon's house when he saw that particular piece of news footage.

After several months of letting the public and the serious candidates believe that I would actually stand for Mayor, I announced that I was pulling out of the race.

I had reached a point in the campaign where I had to officially state my intention to stand. However, election law states that political candidates cannot run their own media shows within six weeks of an election. If I had not stood down at that point, I would have had to pull the plug on my Century fm work, and that was something I had no intention of doing.

Ali always insists that I would have won if I had stood for election, but I'm not so sure. I certainly had popularity and a high profile in the area, which probably would have enabled me to poll a respectable number of votes. After all, if the people of Hartlepool can vote in a guy who used to spend his Saturday afternoons dressed as a monkey, then anything can happen. But Ray Mallon was always the favourite to be Middlesbrough Mayor and I'm delighted he continues to do such a fine job for the town. I know I would not have made such a good Mayor. Until that whole episode, I had always found politics boring. But credit to Ali – it was great fun and fantastic publicity, for me personally but for Century too.

With the mayoral saga now history, we were free to concentrate once again on our role covering every Middlesbrough first team match for Century. I've learned over the years – whether on the phone-in or during match commentaries - that you have to be you. You have to say what you see. I know some things I say might upset or even offend players, but I am simply giving my view of what I am seeing on the pitch. I'm not saying that I'm always right – I'm

sure I'm not - but I say what I see. If the listeners or people at the club don't agree with me, that's fine. I believe it's the right policy, the only policy I can have when I have a job as an ex-professional footballer to give the listeners some insight and appraisal on Middlesbrough FC. Unfortunately, it's a policy that's meant I've had a few bust-ups with the club and individuals over the years.

On one occasion I said that Boro players Alen Boksic and Christian Karembeu should show us what they get paid for. I was entitled to do that. Both were international stars who had come to the club with big reputations, but neither was living up to it. Boksic wasn't playing often enough and Karembeu was playing too often, because he was rubbish. They were the big buck earners and they weren't doing the business. I've heard fans say that Karembeu wasn't trying. My opinion was that he was trying but he just wasn't good enough. He wasn't a good player. Those who said that the best thing about him was his missus - Wonderbra model Adriana Sklenarikova - probably had a point! There's no doubt that Boksic was a good player, but I'm not sure how good because I didn't see him play often enough. I was always one of his fiercest critics during his time with Middlesbrough. Guys who work at the club have told me that if he was 99 per cent fit, he wouldn't play. Meanwhile, Alan Shearer played for Newcastle when he was 45 per cent fit because he loved his club and wanted to play.

Normally my comments would have been forgotten by the following day but it must have been a slow news week because they were reported in the national press. As a consequence, they came to the attention of the players and senior staff at the football club, and I was hauled before Keith Lamb, Boro's chief executive. Maybe the players went to Keith first, I don't know. What I do know is that he contacted Century about my comments. As a result of his complaint to my employers, I went to see Keith. He had his say, telling me people within the club weren't happy about my comments, that he felt I was out of order, especially as I had always been made welcome at the training ground. His view was that we were all in it together, that my criticism was only going to make matters worse when Boro were already struggling at the wrong end of the league table.

But I felt Keith was missing the point. After all, I was only giving my opinion. He said there were many things that he might think but he wouldn't say them. I understood what he was saying because, in his role, Keith had to protect the club.

'But I'm employed to say it,' I said. 'If Middlesbrough want to employ me to say what they want me to say then I'll do that. I'm a Boro fan and I want the team to do well, but I'm employed by Century to give my honest views on what I see.'

I felt it was a case of players not liking negative comments aimed in their direction, even when it was the truth. When Boksic deemed to make himself available, there were times when he was outstanding, and I happily told the Century listeners how good he was. In fact, I well remember raving about him following his first game for the club, when he scored twice in a 3-1 win at Coventry. I pointed out that it was the best ever debut by a Boro player, better even than Ravanelli's hat-trick bow against Liverpool a few years earlier. But I hate it when I see guys cheating like he did in the weeks, months and years that followed – and I certainly wasn't going to pretend otherwise just to protect his or anyone else's feelings or ego. Too many people don't criticise individuals until they've gone, preferring to stab them in the back. Maybe more people should try saying what they really think while players are still there. Maybe it would make a difference and they might even see the error of their ways.

What really annoys me about the majority of modern players is that the hunger has gone. That's because they are getting the rewards even though they've not done it. Don't get me wrong. I don't begrudge the Alan Shearers of this world their salaries. Players like Alan thoroughly deserve a hundred grand a week. He scored the goals and played the games. People outside the game say, 'Come on, he doesn't deserve that.' But if he wasn't getting it, the club would be getting it or the chairman or directors would be getting it. Shearer certainly deserved it more than them. After all, it's the players that generate the crowds. Some of the greatest players ever have made nothing, but a lot of very average Premier League players are on £10,000 a week, and yet most of them couldn't trap a bag of Blue Circle cement. They've got the flash cars, the club house and a lifestyle beyond the imagination of most people. Within three or four years they've got the money in the bank and they are made. They don't have to work again. That's when the hunger goes.

While I've worked with Ali on Century throughout the last decade, I also spent several years working alongside him with Boro TV, the club's official television channel. Owned and run by the American cable giant NTL, the channel was hugely popular among Boro fans throughout a dramatic period in the club's history. It was actually the very first TV channel dedicated to one specific football club, launching a full year before Manchester United's much-vaunted MUTV. Sadly, the station is no longer in operation but I have good memories of Boro TV, despite the fact that my time there ended messily in the courts.

We were involved with Boro TV from its start back in 1998 when it was all done on a shoestring budget. Gradually, everything became more professional and we introduced more shows, including a Monday night live fans' phone-in and Bernie's Soccer Skills, which involved yours truly going out into the local community to teach kids about the beautiful game. There was even Bernie's tactics board, with Ali interrogating me on the likely formations and tactics the Boro manager and his opposite number would devise for the following game.

I enjoyed all of my work with the channel, though the show closest to my heart was a feature called Bernie's About. The long list of Boro players and personalities I interviewed for the feature reads like a who's who of Middlesbrough FC over the past 60 years. Among more than 100 names to feature were no fewer than nine members of the elite group to have had the honour of managing the club together with 18 of the club's full-time captains. They embraced Boro heroes such as Tony Mowbray, John Hickton, Juninho, Gareth Southgate, Fabrizio Ravanelli and, of course, Steve Gibson. They included legends of the game, like Brian Clough, Jack Charlton, Bryan Robson, Paul Gascoigne, Wilf Mannion, George Hardwick, Graeme Souness, Peter Shilton and Nobby Stiles. And they included such famed sons of Teesside as rock star Chris Rea, comedian Roy 'Chubby' Brown, Mayor Ray Mallon and boxer Cornelius Carr.

Just to show I wasn't totally biased towards Middlesbrough, I also gave the Bernie's About treatment to several famous football names who had no link to Teesside, including Newcastle United's Alan Shearer and Peter Beardsley, plus Sunderland's Niall Quinn.

One of my most memorable interviews was with the one and only Paul Gascoigne and his infamous best buddy, Jimmy "Five Bellies" Gardener. Gazza was his normal bubbly self, buzzing with the prospect of playing in the forthcoming 1998 World Cup finals. He talked as if his selection for the squad was a formality and told me about Boro psychologist Bill Beswick's England equivalent, faith healer Eileen Drury. A couple of weeks later his dream was over. Glenn Hoddle left him out of the England squad, allegedly resulting in Gazza smashing up the room in his hotel. To be fair, I was amazed Boro ever bought him. He had been a great player, but his best days were behind him. I told Steve Gibson that I wouldn't touch him. He had a heart of gold but everyone knew about his off-the-pitch problem. Was it wise to bring Gazza to the club when your star player, Paul Merson, was a recovering alcoholic?

I also interviewed Gazza's infamous best buddy, Five Bellies, who proved himself to be completely crackers. On meeting him, I noticed he had a nasty scar on his nose – it was about the size of a 10p coin and made him look like he had three nostrils – so I asked him what he had been doing. I was stunned to hear his explanation. It turned out that Gazza had offered him £300 if he could hold a burning cigarette lighter to his nose for 30 seconds. Jimmy was keen for the money so had carried out the forfeit and won the cash. A few weeks later, I bumped into Jimmy again, but noticed that his nose didn't seem to have improved. 'Yeah, that's because we had another bet and I did it again!' he admitted.

The five years I spent with Boro TV will always remain special to me. I loved it. I enjoyed meeting all the former players, working with Ali and the rest of the staff and chatting with the punters. But it all came to an abrupt and bitter end in December 2002 when I was sacked by NTL. It was a decision that would cost them dear in terms of bad publicity, as I have never been one to take things lying down.

Basically, they finished me when I deliberately failed to attend the recording of one of the shows I co-presented. I'd made the decision not to turn up in protest at their constant failure to pay me my monthly wages on time, despite numerous complaints I had made. Each month I would go to them and ask where my wages were. On one occasion, Ali and I went two or three months over Christmas without pay. Thank God, I had my Century income at such an expensive time. But it didn't seem to matter to NTL.

After my sacking, I was determined to take them to tribunal for unfair dismissal, but I lost out on a technicality. I was unable to prove I was an employee of NTL's, because I'd been paid by cheque each month. So I never got the opportunity to take them on regarding the real issue. It was a shame but I certainly don't regret taking them on. It cost me £5,000 in costs but I bet it cost them treble that. More importantly, I showed them I wasn't frightened just because they were a big, multinational company. All the media coverage of the case was embarrassing for NTL. It really didn't matter whether I had won or lost because my point was to highlight the treatment that thousands of employees suffer every year at the hands of these all-powerful companies.

Despite the fact that Ali stayed on at Boro TV after my departure, that whole sordid episode with NTL didn't affect my relationship with my Century sidekick. Our partnership as a commentary team is set to reach the 500 games mark during the 2006-07 season. So I have actually now commentated on more Boro games than I played in! That's some going – and I'd like to think we will carry on for many years yet. God knows how many thousands of miles we must have travelled to away games over the years, but I can say, with hand on heart, that I am as enthusiastic about the job today as I was a decade ago.

I've never once felt like not making the effort to be there. I see it as my duty to go. I like watching Middlesbrough, I'm a fan and I want to be there. I love everything about it. I enjoy the commentaries, I like the confrontation and I love chatting with the press I bump into and the former footballers I used to play against. I can't pretend it's as good as playing, because it isn't, but my enthusiasm never wanes. I've even had offers to leave Century but I couldn't do it. I don't want to commentate on just any team. For me, it's Boro or nothing.

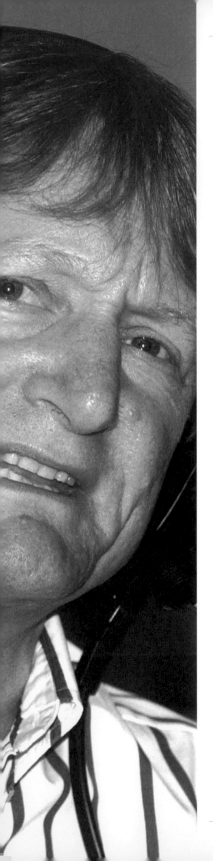

Eric's
LEGENDS 'n' LEG-ENDS

	Legends	Leg-ends
Sunderland players	Bobby Kerr	Milton Nunez (the
	Jimmy Montgomery	replacement for Niall Quinn!)
	Charlie Hurley	Nicolas Medina
	Kevin Phillips	(the new Maradona!)
	Marco Gabbiadini	Too many others to mention!
British football	George Best	Carlton Palmer
	Kevin Beattie	
	Peter Beardsley	
	Bill Gates	
	Roy of the Rovers	
World footballers	Pele	Marcelino
	Johan Cruyff	
	Maradona	
	Garrincha	
Football managers	Bobby Robson	Howard Wilkinson at Sunderland
	Bob Paisley	Lawrie McMenemy at Sunderland
	Bill Shankly	Graeme Souness at Newcastle
	Brian Clough	Ruud Gullit at Newcastle
		Kenny Dalglish at Newcastle

•LEGEND: Bobby Kerr

•LEGEND: Ozzy Osbourne

•LEGENDS: Herman's Hermits

	Legends	**Leg-ends**
Sports stars	Mohammed Ali	Malcolm on Super Stars!
	Lester Piggott	
	Tiger Woods	
	Steve Redgrave	
	Lance Armstrong	
	Roger Federer	
	Michael Johnson	
Musicians & Singers	The Beatles	All rap singers
	Herman's Hermits	
	Sweet	
	Bay City Rollers	
	Rolling Stones	
	Slade	
	The banjo player in the film, 'Deliverance'	
Songs	Little Arrows (Leepy Lee)	All rap songs
	Mr Tambourine Man (The Byrds)	Local Hero
	Two Little Boys (Rolf Harris)	Pigbag
	White Christmas (Bing Crosby)	
Film stars	John Wayne	John Wark
	Steve McQueen	
	Laurel & Hardy	
	George Formby	

	Legends	**Leg-ends**
Films	The Silence of the Lambs	Godzilla vs
	The Sound of Music	The Smog Monster
	The Great Escape	
	One Flew Over the Cuckoo's Nest	
	The Jungle Book	
	Kes	
TV personalities	Bill and Ben	Simon Cowell
	The Woodentops	
	Popeye	
	Ozzy Osbourne	
	Tom and Jerry	
	The Flintstones	
TV shows	Bilko	Question Time
	Who Wants to be a Millionaire?	What Not to Wear
	The Beverley Hillbillies	Big Brother
	The Waltons	
	Songs of Praise	
	All sports and wildlife programmes	
World figures	My Mam and Dad	Adolf Hitler

SUNDERLAND

Eric

THEY BLEW it. They blew it and I wasn't in the least bit surprised. Typical bloody Sunderland. They've been doing it for as long as I or just about anyone else can remember. I'm talking about that crippling lack of ambition that has ensured that what should be a great football club never gets anywhere near fulfilling its massive potential.

What an opportunity Sunderland had during the 2000-01 season. They were second behind Man United at Christmas, spent most of the season in the top four and were disappointed to finish seventh, even though it was the club's highest finish in nearly half a century. It galls me to think they never took the chance they had. But does it surprise me? Not in the slightest bit.

Back then, this club was shouting from the rooftops about how big it was going to be. So what happened? They threw it all away. We had 48,000 coming through the turnstiles every week, we had a fantastic new stadium and a good team. Everything about the club was good but what they had to do then was push on. That's not me being clever after the event. I said it constantly even then that the time to buy new players was when they were second in the table or even when they were seventh in the table. The money was there but they didn't do it, not in the way they needed to do it, bringing in the sort of quality that would take them to the next level.

This club should have been up there for the next 20 or 30 years. They should be up there with the Man Uniteds and Liverpools, challenging for the top positions. But the people involved blew it and the club went backwards yet again. The problem with Sunderland is that the club has always had what I call a corner shop mentality. They just don't think big.

Yes, they built the Stadium of Light. Great, but they had to.

Roker Park had a 22,000 capacity so building a new stadium wasn't as visionary as people imagine. Yes, the chairman Bob Murray and the board had the foresight to do it, but they got the land for nothing and most of the stadium was paid for with grants and the like. Then came the long-running saga over the Academy. I remember the club saying it would cost £9 million but don't worry. Three years down the line it was going to cost something like £24 million. Why?

As for thinking big on the pitch, do me a favour. People sometimes tell me to stop knocking the club all the time because things aren't as bad as I make out. I'm sorry but that's bull. This club should be one of the richest clubs going but the money's gone through the fingers. All we got for the last few years under Bob Murray was how the club was skint and they had to be careful. I get accused of knocking the club, but I've never taken a penny from Sunderland since my last pay cheque – and, with the club back in the top flight, I'd like to think I had earned that. And yet there are people who have come into the club, done little or nothing for it and walked away with millions. I'm talking about agents, managers, players and directors. I'm on the radio talking about the club and criticising them because I want them to do better and I get more stick than the people who have walked away with millions. There's something not right there.

I've been involved with the club in one way or another, as player, fan or commentator, for the last 20 years but they've never been ambitious. But that's always been the way, as long as anyone can remember. Gary Rowell, one of the club's all-time top scorers, tells me it was no different in his day. Bobby Kerr, skipper of the 1973 FA Cup winners, says the same. Even back in the '60s they were never ambitious. Charlie Hurley, a Sunderland legend, has told me that even in his day the club's directors were happy if the team stayed in the top flight and had a decent cup run. That's success? I just can't relate to that.

•PHENOMENAL: Eric was a big fan of Kevin Phillips.

And then our "golden era" under Bob Murray, complete with five relegations. Or was it six? Blimey, I've lost count, it happened that often. My first club, Ipswich Town, that little country bumpkin club, had 10 years on the trot in Europe. But the European experience of Sunderland, a club with 10 times the chances Ipswich will ever have, amounts to four games following the Cup win in '73. For the life of me, I cannot get my head round how a club the size of Sunderland hasn't been involved in Europe more than that. I tell you what, the people responsible should be ashamed of that. Newcastle have played about 120 games in Europe and even Middlesbrough, who we used to think of as the north-east's third club, have had two seasons in Europe and 20-odd games.

All those years under Murray, they never went for it. That's just wrong. It's soul-destroying for the true fans, the people who follow the club week in and week out, buy the season tickets, buy the shirts and live for the next match. It's disappointing for me too, but I'm not going to pretend it affects my life like it does the supporters. I don't pretend to be one of them but I want the club to do well because I'm proud to have played for Sunderland and I have an affinity for the city and its people. People say to me that I'm not a real fan because I used to watch the Boro as a kid. But we're not all clones. I have every admiration for passionate supporters who have only ever followed one club, but me and my parents followed Boro when I was young because my brother, Bill, was playing for them. I point out to those who criticise me that maybe if they had a son who played for Boro would they not go and watch him? So I do care about Sunderland and I do get annoyed that the club has always seemed happy to just muddle along.

To be fair to Murray, he backed Peter Reid with a lot of money and Reid wasted millions, but much of it was on players you

had never heard of – and have never heard of again since leaving the club. The likes of Carsten Fredgaard, Nicolas Medina and Milton Nunez come to mind. The fact that players like that were signed makes me think, 'Hang on, what's happening here?' I find it amazing. To this day, I wonder why they were signed. I have my doubts that they were signed for the benefit of the club. I don't want to go into that one too deeply because it will open up a whole can of worms, but I know every Sunderland supporter would like to know why millions were spent on players who were never seen in the first team.

When the club finally did spend big it was because they knew they had to be seen by the fans to be doing something. They had nearly got themselves relegated the previous season and couldn't score a goal to save their life at the start of 2002-03, so they panicked and let Peter Reid spend £10 million on Tore Andre Flo and Marcus Stewart. To do that and then sack him four weeks later was crazy.

When Sunderland got promoted back in 1996 I said Peter Reid deserved a medal as big as a bin lid. What Peter did was gel the players into a team. There was a good team ethic and no stars. I say they had no stars, but what they had was a lad called Kevin Phillips, who was brilliant. He was like a Johnny on the spot. 30 goals one season, 30 another. This fella used to get a goal out of the blue just when Sunderland needed it.

You can talk about coaching all you like, but managers have to be lucky. You can't buy that. Sometimes that luck comes in the shape of just one player who constantly gets you out of the sh**. That was Phillips. No matter how bad the team were playing, with Kevin on the pitch there was always hope that he would sneak a goal. People talk about Niall Quinn and the part he played. Quinny was a good player and he helped Kevin, but Phillips was phenomenal. I enjoyed watching him so much. For five or six years he was outstanding, he was the boy. Take Phillips out of the equation and we wouldn't have been up there even for those two seventh place finishes. It's a crying shame that in those two seasons when he banged in 30-odd goals and won the Golden Boot as Europe's top scorer he still wasn't given an automatic England squad. You would think that anyone who scores 30 goals would walk into the England side but he just didn't fit in. I don't think Kevin

Keegan, who was England manager at the time, fancied him.

There was some ill feeling towards him from a minority of fans when he left but I think that was very unfair. If a player does well, I'll shout it from the rooftops so for three or four years I did that about Kevin. He didn't have a great last season with the club and one or two fans were pointing the finger but he had stuck with it through the frustration of Sunderland's underachieving, so I thought good luck to him. Ten per cent of people will always criticise you, no matter what you do. And ten per cent of the fans will never forgive Kevin for leaving the club. They'll remind everyone that he was crap in his last season, but they'll conveniently forget about the five seasons when he was absolutely brilliant and, in my eyes, kept Sunderland going. But the majority thought Kevin Phillips was a great lad for coming on the show and many of them will say he was the best Sunderland player they've ever seen. We might not see a better player than him for the next 20 years.

I have to admit that I am surprised he hasn't done better since leaving Sunderland. He has held his own and he bagged a few goals at Southampton and Aston Villa but he's never got back to his best. I was a bit disappointed his proposed return never materialised at the start of 2006-07. From the club's point of view, it would have been a good move for Kevin to have come back, given the predicament Sunderland were in at the time. I wouldn't have expected him to come back and bang in 30 goals and be as good as he was at his peak but he would certainly have been better than what we had. At the same time, I don't blame him for not coming back because he no doubt felt settled in the West Midlands and could see the sense in making the switch from Villa to West Brom. And, let's be honest, at the time he might have looked at the start that Sunderland had made and wondered what was going to go on, especially because this was before the appointment of Roy Keane.

The first few seasons Peter Reid was at the club you could never have imagined his reign ending the way it did. He was hero-worshipped. All that bitterness was incredible after all he had done for the club but those last two years were just awful. I'm not totally sure what went wrong. Say what you want about his teams but one thing they had always had was a work ethic. That had gone out of the window by the time he

got the boot. In previous years, the team would fight like hell, no matter how well or poorly they were playing, but they went down with a whimper. I know Peter had gone long before relegation but the rot had set in while he was still in the hotseat.

He was even acting differently in his final months at the club. When things were going well he was always out there on the touchline. But when Sunderland were doing badly he didn't leave his dug-out. On one occasion I remember the kit man was the only guy stood on the touchline with the substitute. Peter was avoiding the bullets because he knew the fans would give him what for if he stood up and raised his head above the parapet. I felt he had to go.

One thing everyone always remembers from a TV programme on Sunderland was all that swearing he did. He maybe bullied or frightened players as a tactic. Flying off the handle can work if you do it occasionally but it has no affect on players if you keep doing it. Maybe, in time, that had a negative affect on players who knew him too well and contributed to his demise.

And knowing what I know now, I think Murray gave Peter free rein at the club. Reid thoroughly enjoyed it, pulling the strings and doing what he wanted. I go back to that meeting I had with Murray when he told me that black was white if Peter Reid said it was. The club's board gave him too much control and it all backfired.

Reid had to go for the benefit of the club. He had lost the respect of the fans and he wasn't having the same influence on the players. I just wish they hadn't given him £10 million to spend before sacking him. Having said, there is no way I would have wanted them to give even half of that to the man they replaced him with.

Shocked? I couldn't believe it when Sunderland announced that the man they felt could lead them out of trouble and back towards success was Howard Wilkinson. He had won the last ever top flight before the formation of the Premier League, with Leeds in 1992, but he had been out of the management game for a long time and was hardly an inspirational choice. I had my doubts from the off but I wanted to give him a chance and hoped he would do well.

But any lingering belief that that might prove to be the case was wiped from my mind during a half-hour meeting I had with Howard. I know this sounds horrible, but I was bored stiff. Soon after his appointment, I asked one of the staff at Century to drop him an email on my behalf, wishing him and his assistant, Steve Cotterill, good luck. I mentioned that it would be good if I could pop along and have a chat once he had settled in. Not long afterwards I got message back that Howard would like to meet me. I was delighted to have an opportunity to chat with him about football and the club, where I come from, what I do and to generally just say to him that if he had a problem with what I was saying on the radio then he could ring me any time.

But it's never that straightforward with Sunderland. When I got there, Lesley Callaghan met me at the stadium reception, took me up to the boardroom - and sat there with Howard were Bob Murray and John Fickling. I just thought it was strange that they were all there again. After a bit of small talk, Lesley said, 'Eric, you've called this meeting. Are you going to start?'

'I called a meeting?' I asked. 'I offered to have a meeting between me and Howard Wilkinson – and as far as I'm concerned that has f*** all to do with you three.'

Bob responded by saying, 'If that's the way Eric feels, we'll leave.' So the three of them walked out, leaving me alone with Howard, as it should have been in the first place.

The next half an hour was the most boring 30 minutes of my life. It was all about tactics and what he had achieved in his career. My mind went back to a time when he had wanted to buy me when he was manager of Sheffield Wednesday and I just thought, 'Dear me, I couldn't have played for this geezer.' The more I listened to him dourly giving his opinions about the game, the more I worried about the lack of impact he would have in the dressing room. For the sake of the football club and its fans, I wanted him to do well but I make no apologies for saying that I couldn't wait to get out of the room. I had watched Sunderland's last seven seasons but he never once tried to pick my brains or asked me my opinion about what had gone on at the club.

I know Howard didn't have a lot to work with because Peter Reid had left them in dire straits, but he was the last man to

bring in when they needed to turn things around. The team needed a manager with a bit of spirit about him to have a similar impact to Denis Smith and Viv Busby when they succeeded Lawrie McMenemy in my days. Within weeks of them arriving, the place was bubbling. With Howard, it was just boring. Not surprisingly, the team went down the pan. The club had to get rid of him and, after less than five months, they did.

Beyond a quick shake of the hand as we passed on the stadium stairs, I never got to meet Howard's second in command, Steve Cotterill, before the two of them got the sack. But I have met him since and have to say I was far more impressed with him than I was of Wilkinson. I used to see Cotterill down at the touchline on matchdays, always writing things down in a little notepad. It's my opinion that if you're a football person it's in your head. You don't have to write on a pad what you're going to say to the players at half-time or on the Monday morning. I certainly don't need to write anything down in preparation for The Three Legends. I know who played well and who didn't. So I used to see Cotterill scribbling down all these notes and I would be embarrassed for him.

But a few years after his departure from Sunderland, I was having a drink with my partner, Dorothy, at the bar in Ramside Hall Hotel and Steve was there with his Burnley team the night before a game with one of the north-east sides, probably Sunderland. He spotted me and joined us at the bar for the next two hours. He admitted that the Sunderland job hadn't been what he had thought it was going to be as he had expected Howard to take the backseat while he led, but it was the other way around. I have to say I liked him and couldn't help but want him to do well at Burnley.

But I couldn't believe it when, during our conversation, Dorothy asked him, 'Have you finished the book yet?'

'Book?' he asked, clearly puzzled. 'What book?'

'Well, I thought you were writing a book,' she smiled. 'Every game I saw you on the touchline, you were always writing something!'

When Mick McCarthy was brought in as Sunderland's third manager of the 2002-03 season I sent him an email wishing

him all the best, just as I had done with Howard Wilkinson. This time there was no pre-arranged meeting but I did end up chatting to him one night in Durham when I was out for a meal with Dorothy and some of our friends. I didn't really know Mick, though I had played against him in our playing days, but he spotted me from the other end of the bar, came over and introduced himself. He stood with me and my crowd and talked with us, and I couldn't help but warm to him. I thought, 'What a good lad'. From that day, I wanted Mick to do well more than I might otherwise have done if I had never got to spend any time with him. He had a positive influence on me just because he had been polite and taken an interest enough to come over and chat.

I never really got to speak to him again over the next three years but there's no doubting he had a real impact once that awful season was over. It was too late to do anything about relegation by the time Mick took over and I felt sorry for him losing game after game in the Premier League. There was a real worry that we could have been relegated again the

following year and just kept going downwards. I did wonder how far the club would spiral downwards before bouncing back up again.

But he sorted things out over the summer and they nearly won promotion at the first time of asking. For two years he did well with limited resources, taking them up as champions in his second full season. Obviously I was never in the Sunderland dressing room to see exactly what he was like but I heard a few very positive things and I bet he was a good fella to play for. Bernie, who knows Mick from his days with the Irish squad, tells me he was always straight as a die and I can imagine the players enjoyed playing for him. I'm sure he was great for the dressing room, in a similar way to Denis Smith when he took over from Lawrie McMenemy during my days at the club.

The truth is that anyone would be an improvement on Wilkinson, but Mick came in, stopped the rot and did a good job for the club. Let's face it, he over-achieved with what he

•WORRYING TIMES: Mick McCarthy always faced an uphill struggle at the Stadium of Light.

109

had at his disposal because he got no money and almost no support at all from the club. The fans were brilliant, turning up week in and week out, after all that they had gone through but it was disgrace that the club was in such a mess after the chances it had had.

Everyone knew it was going to be tough when Sunderland got back into the Premier League but I never dreamed it would be as bad as it was. You could see the squad wasn't really good enough but you hoped they could do enough to maybe finish fourth bottom and stay up by the skin of their teeth. There was reason to believe because I thought surely West Ham and Wigan, who had both come up with us but a long way behind, couldn't be any better than us.

So, like all the Sunderland fans, I hoped. Most of that hope had disappeared by the time the final whistle blew in our first game, against Charlton. We were so bad that we just looked doomed. Afterwards, I said that I knew there was a long, long way to go but on that showing we would not beat the 19 points we got in our last Premiership season. Sadly, I was right.

Mick dismantled the promotion team but I didn't blame him. That team would have been just as bad. Marcus Stewart wouldn't have been up to it so he had to let him go and get somebody else in. He chose Andy Gray, who had scored 20 goals for Sheffield United the previous season, and he bought Jonathan Stead, who most fans thought was worth a try.

But the truth is he spent something like £5 million, which was never going to be enough. I knew that, the supporters knew that and so did Mick McCarthy and Bob Murray. It was that corner shop mentality kicking in again. Mick had done brilliant to get them back up, the club was in debt but they had to have a go at staying up. For me, they never really did that.

I had a lot of sympathy for Mick but what disappointed me was the time he said the club had backed him. No, they didn't. I don't know why he said that. Maybe he was just trying to keep things right with the board but he was daft to say it because I don't believe he meant it. As soon as he said that I thought he had given the fans a noose to hang him with. Definitely it was the one thing that made the fans turn against him. Until then most of them blamed Bob Murray but they

started to point fingers at Mick once he came out with that crap. To this day, I honestly believe that maybe they missed out on a few players that might have made a difference. But I don't think for one minute that the 12 signings Mick made that summer would have been his first choice signings if the club had really backed him with the sort of money that was needed.

So it wasn't a lot of money but what he did spend wasn't money well spent. You have got to get better players than you already have but he didn't do that. I didn't see a good player out there all season. I know some people think I only ever knock the Sunderland players but I don't want to be critical. I want every player to do well and if they give me an opportunity to say something good about them I will take it. I don't want to go through the team saying, 'He's crap, he's crap and he's crap,' but they didn't show Eric Gates that any of them were good enough for the Premier League. I don't really blame the players for relegation because we didn't go down as a result of them having bad attitudes. They knew they weren't good enough and the fans accepted that as a group they weren't up to the task.

I'm sure Mick knew it too, but he couldn't say that. I think he was always as honest as he could be in press conferences but it's difficult when you are losing game after game. In my job, I can get away with saying the players were crap or they weren't good enough for the Premier League but Mick couldn't do that. He might have thought that privately but he knew he had to try and lift those players for the next game and try to give them hope. Sometimes managers sound like liars but there's only so much they can say if they want to retain a relationship with their players. But finally he knew the game was up and admitted he couldn't do any more with them. He was only saying what most of us had known for a long time.

Sunderland supporters certainly weren't backwards in telling the players they felt weren't up to scratch exactly what they thought of them. But that's always been the way with supporters up here, not just in Sunderland but around the whole of the north-east. This region often gets a lot of stick from people down south, some of it deserved and some of it not. If I could sell the north-east, I would say its biggest asset is the passion of its people. Certainly they are far more passionate than the people of Suffolk. In 15 years there, the Ipswich fans might have had the odd groan about what they were seeing on a Saturday afternoon, but ultimately they would clap us off the pitch whether we beat Barcelona or lost to Everton. Afterwards they'd walk down the stairs, get in their tractors and go home. For them, football is just a hobby, not a way of life.

In contrast, come to the north-east and do well and you'll be a hero to the people for the rest of life; everyone wants to know you and what you've had for breakfast. We all want money but if you want to be a hero, this is the place to be. Come here and do well and you can be a god. Money can't buy that. By the same token, by God, you'll get stick if you don't do it – more than anywhere else I can imagine. It didn't happen for me at Sunderland to start with and I had my work cut out to win the fans over. You have to have the balls to do it because they won't hold back in saying exactly what they think.

So those Sunderland players that didn't do it last season – and that was most of them – did get a lot of stick at times. Now it's up to them to show they have the balls to turn that around. But ultimately Mick McCarthy's signings just weren't up to scratch. I wouldn't say Kelvin Davis was any better than the 'keepers he replaced, Mart Poom and Thomas Myhre. But the season was always going to go one of two ways for Davis. It was obvious he was going to see plenty of the ball, so he was either going to be the hero or the mug. Unfortunately, he didn't have the best of starts and he became the fall guy. Having said that, he came back into the side and had the balls to get back on with it after that bad start. I have respect for the fella because of the way he did that. Whether he was a good 'keeper or not, I don't know. He has gone now but he might well bounce back at Southampton and good for him if he does.

Another McCarthy signing for the Premier League was Tommy Miller, signed from my old club, Ipswich. He was a local lad who had done all right at Ipswich, banged in the goals and held his own at that level. He must have been dying to do well but he didn't do it. He went missing too often. You would see him have a shot and then he'd disappear for the next 20 minutes. Bassila was a big, gangly lad brought in to strengthen the midfield but I watched him and thought, 'Well, what have you got?' I couldn't see what he was meant to be.

Up front they had Andy Gray, who had apparently played well for Sheffield United. Certainly he must be a better player than what he showed Sunderland fans last season because there was just nothing. Alongside him was Jon Stead, who I always thought didn't look a bad player at Huddersfield. But bloody hell! I hear people saying he worked hard and McCarthy would say things like, 'He has been excellent for me.' He was a centre-forward who didn't score a goal until the season was nearly over, so how could he have been excellent?

I heard people describing Dean Whitehead as the next Bryan Robson or Steven Gerrard, but I didn't go with all the hype around him. He was a good, honest lad, who did a lot of running around and had a brilliant attitude. I pat him on the back for playing all the games in a bad season for the club but he didn't show me anything to get excited about. People say he was Sunderland's best player last season. Let's be honest, that's not saying much. He might come back all the better for last season but he certainly hasn't proved himself yet.

The only member of last season's Sunderland squad who I know is Premier League standard is Julio Arca. I would scratch my head if a Premier League club had signed any other Sunderland player but I could understand Boro buying Arca. He had a poor season for us last year but he was certainly the best footballer at the club. Having watched the lad for four or five years, I always felt he wouldn't look out of place in a good Premier League side.

So there you have it. Definitely the worst ever Premier League team. There have been some bad teams in the Premiership over the years - Swindon, Barnsley and Watford spring to mind – but they were all better than last season's Sunderland team. The statistics told me that and my own eyes told me that. I don't think I'll find many Sunderland fans disagreeing with me either. In reality, they were down by Christmas and deserved to remain bottom all season. Despite my criticism, I honestly hope all the lads bounce back and prove me and others wrong.

As for what could or should have been done different last season, I guess hindsight is a wonderful thing. I couldn't help but look at Wigan and what they achieved. I think we all thought they would finish bottom but their attitude in going out to try to win games no matter what the opposition was refreshing to see. Well done to Paul Jewell for having the balls to do that right from the start. Of course, they might have got beat by four or five and their bottle could have gone but they got the results and their confidence just grew. Maybe Sunderland should have had a little bit more of that philosophy.

Right till the end, Murray kept trying to deflect the flack, even sacking McCarthy without having a Plan B in place or even any hope of Plan B making a difference. To say the time of McCarthy's sacking was strange is to say the very least. The club was going down any way and the people in charge had no-one lined up to replace him. McCarthy had taken them up in the first place and deserved another crack at doing it again. If they had someone better ready and waiting then maybe it would have been fair enough, but I can't help but think it was just a PR exercise. Kevin Ball was a good pro, a good character and had a great rapport with the fans so I think Murray thought it might appease the fans if he gave him the job. Thankfully, the supporters saw through it.

But the real problem goes back to that corner shop mentality. People have been saying it for 50 years, but Sunderland AFC could be and should be a top six club. Unfortunately, those in charge were arrogant towards the fans. They had heads as big as Gateshead. Once again, the club should have been more ambitious from the moment they got promoted. I know money doesn't guarantee success but without it you've got no chance. For too long all the talk from Sunderland has been that they are a big club. Well, it's time they started to act like one.

Bob Murray's departure and the take-over by Niall Quinn and his consortium during the summer of 2006 was hopefully the start of a bright new era for the club. Despite what I've said in this book about me and Bob, I had no personal axe to grind with him but everyone knew that the club couldn't keep just going on and on with him in charge because things had been left to fester for far too long. A lot of fans were saying they

wouldn't go back to support the team as long as Murray remained and they were voting with their feet, so something had to change. I genuinely believe that Bob had wanted to get out of Sunderland for a long time and was relieved to have finally cut his ties with the club. How history will view him will depend in many ways on what happens over the next few years. People will thank him for the stadium perhaps. If in 10 years time, Sunderland AFC has taken off – which I hope will be the case – people might say well done to Murray for putting the foundations in place with the stadium. But if it all goes wrong then people will say it was Murray's fault for leaving the club in such a dire position!

What no-one can deny is that the club was going nowhere under Murray. No matter who had taken over, the fans would probably have viewed it as a positive step but Niall Quinn's central involvement in the new consortium ensured the supporters were right behind the new regime from the start. Because of the affinity they have for him and all that he did for the club as a player, the fans want him to do well and trust him to do the right things for Sunderland. The take-over itself took months to happen but once complete I thought things would happen quickly, with a new manager appointed and signings brought in to strengthen the squad. Unfortunately, that didn't happen. Very little did. After a while I started to wonder what was happening because there had been such a lull and things were going flat. There was a danger that a lot of the initial good feeling would be lost.

The feelings of concern worsened with talk that Peter Reid might be on his way back. It was never officially confirmed but I believe they were seriously considering the idea of giving him a role until they realised how negative the public reaction was. In that situation you want a wow factor with any big appointment but half of the fans would have said, 'Never in this world.' It would have been a giant backwards step for the club. It was a bad idea.

When Quinny announced that he would be manager as well as chairman until he could bring in a top class manager my first thought was that maybe things weren't quite right with the consortium. Something didn't fit with a new consortium making all the right noises only to say they couldn't get a top class manager so the chairman would be the manager as well. There's no way you can do both the jobs. It's a hard job being a chairman and it's a hard job being a manager. Trying to do them both together is asking too much of anyone.

Even then I would never have guessed we'd make such an awful start to the season. Who would have guessed we'd lose the first four league games and get knocked out of the Carling Cup by a team bottom of the entire Football League? Without a shadow of doubt, I really believed we were facing the prospect of going down again if that had carried on. Watching those terrible early performances left me in no doubt that the players weren't as good as I thought they were – and I hadn't thought they were very good at all!

Thankfully, Quinny knew he couldn't go on when the results were so bad, so he went back for Roy Keane, who he originally approached months earlier. Quinny had always said his joint role was temporary, but if things had gone well in those first few games I have a feeling he might have stayed on as chairman-manager until the end of the season. Instead, he was left with no option but to stand down as manager.

The announcement that Roy Keane was Sunderland's new manager was greeted with glee by most fans. He might not have been the world class manager Niall was quoted as saying he wanted but my gut feeling was that he would get it right. Certainly Keane's appointment seemed like a great move to me because it had the effect of getting everyone talking about it and creating a buzz about the place. It was a coup for the club, no question. What's more, he acted immediately to bring in six new players on transfer deadline day. It was Niall and Roy's way of saying that they knew the players already there weren't good enough. They were out of their depth in the Premier League but I had hoped they would be good enough in the Championship. Results told you that wasn't the case. Who knows whether those six new players will prove to be money well spent. Personally, my initial thought was that they were good signings. I was surprised that the club was able to attract players like Graham Kavanagh and David Connolly from the Premier League, so well done to Sunderland for that. Some people argued that they weren't top class players or they were passed their best. That was true, but they were what Sunderland needed at that time. In my opinion, they were as good as what there was

anywhere else in the Championship.

While some fans thought everything would be okay and we would win the league once Roy took charge, I never saw it like that. Football's not like that. There's no magic wand. Roy was a winner on the pitch, but so was Bobby Moore, who failed completely when he tried his hand at management. We might end up saying that Roy Keane should have gone somewhere else and learned his trade before coming to manage a club like Sunderland. It made no difference to me whether the manager was experienced or not. Sunderland had one of them in Howard Wilkinson and look what he did, while I don't recall Lawrie McMenemy doing too well with all his years of management. On the other hand, Kevin Keegan hadn't managed before but went to Newcastle and the place took off. So whether Roy was a managerial novice or not really wasn't that important – though you can be sure that excuse will be used if things aren't going well six months down the line.

I wish Niall and Roy all the best and, like everyone else who cares about the club, I want them to do well. It could take the club a long time to bounce back because they've got no divine right to win promotion. I think it will be tough to do in 2006-07 after making such a bad start to the season but they should be good enough to do well in the Championship when you look at the likes of Southend and Colchester. Even if they get it only half-right they should be up there challenging and knocking on the door for the play-offs.

•NEW ERA: Niall Quinn's arrival heralded a new start for Sunderland.

The truth is, of course, that Sunderland are now the north-east's third team – and a distant third too. That's through no fault of the present regime but they've got their work cut out to catch up with Newcastle and Middlesbrough. Whether the big change at the top will be for the better or worse only time will tell but if Niall Quinn cracks it, phew, he will have hit the jackpot.

Malcolm

FOOTBALL IS all about hard work and doing all the basics well day in and day out. In time the blend will work if you keep doing the right thing. Eventually a golden opportunity will come along that gives you a chance to take it to the next level. Sunderland didn't just have that opportunity once; they actually had it twice. In successive seasons they were second or third in the league but missed both of those golden opportunities.

The first season they were third at Christmas, they did nothing and the season petered out. They eventually finished seventh, missing Europe by one place. Did they learn from that? No! The very next season they were second in mid-January and again did nothing and the opportunity slipped again. It takes years for those opportunities to come along and it was unforgivable to let it go twice. It was a nonsense. I can't work it out.

Whose fault is it? I blame Bob Murray and Peter Reid. When you have a chairman who says, 'If my manager says black is white I'm going to back him all the way', you've got a major problem because no-one is infallible. The club finished up failing not just miserably but embarrassingly.

Murray oversaw as many relegations as he did promotions in all those years there. I know he's a very intelligent man but I'm really not sure his heart was in the right place. The club's agenda doesn't appear to have been on aiming for success. They have shown a huge lack of ambition. They have this fantastic stadium but did it only ever get built because of the grants that were available?

I think Mick McCarthy performed a minor miracle to take Sunderland up after a couple of seasons at the club but I don't know where on earth he got the inclination that the players he brought in were going to do a job in the Premiership. Everybody was so kind to Mick. I've known him for many years and he is a terrific bloke. But Sunderland's Premier League record with him in charge was absolutely hopeless. His Premiership credentials are torn to shreds, if they ever existed in the first place.

To make matters worse, Mick insisted that the board had backed him when it was clear that they hadn't. The club said so many stupid things during that time – the chairman, the manager and the players – and none of it made sense. It was flying in the face of common sense but nobody shut them up, which neither Eric, Bernie nor I could understand. They were the worst team in Premier League history, beating their own abysmal record, but they didn't seem willing to accept that fact.

All those good supporters the club has have to now put their faith in a new regime. I have no doubt about the good intentions of Niall Quinn but it is his backers that will ultimately pull the strings. But I'm confident the Quinn-led takeover can only be good for the club – just as long as he is never tempted again to try being the club's manager as well!

I have actually known Niall since he was 13 or 14 years old. When I was manager of Fulham, I went over to Ireland to do some coaching work for the United College of Dublin. Niall was there and stood out a mile because he was just something else. I looked at the height of him - he was six feet two even then - and thought, 'If this lad can play a bit, he could be some player.' Boy, he could play! So I got him over to Fulham to take a really good look at him. In his autobiography, Niall recalls his spell with Fulham and suggests that I thought he couldn't play and got rid of him, but his memory deceives him. That wasn't the case at all, so I'd like to take this opportunity to put the story right.

When Niall came over, there were three of us – my youth scout Del Quigley, my coach Ray Harford and myself – all assessing him. It was the first time that I had actually discovered a player because usually others would discover them and bring them to me for a final decision. This time it was the other way around and I was asking Ray and Del for their thoughts. We put Niall straight into our youth side alongside 16 and 17-year-olds. We all knew he was a very good player, but the question was where we should play him. I was in no doubt that his best position would be centre-half. I thought he was David O'Leary reborn. Initially that was where we played him, but Del thought he would make a better midfield player, so Niall played the next couple of games in midfield. Then Ray said, 'I think you're both wrong. I think he's a centre-forward.' So he played the next couple of games up front. The truth is that our analysis was inconclusive because he was brilliant wherever he played! Our debate really didn't matter because this lad was going to be an outstanding player no matter what.

Sadly – and it frustrated me to death at the time – I wasn't able to hold on to Niall. He came to see me and explained that back in Ireland he played curling as well as football. As I recall, he played curling for the Irish Schoolboys team, but he explained his dilemma to me that if he signed the schoolboy forms I was offering him with Fulham that would preclude him from continuing to represent his country at curling. I told him it was his decision to make but asked him, 'What do you want to do with your life? Schoolboy curling is one thing, but we're talking about your career for the next 20 years.' He explained that he didn't want to break promises he had made to the people who ran the curling team back home. He eventually decided to go back to Ireland, play his curling and then come back to Fulham at a later date. I wanted to be fair to the lad but was very disappointed with his decision. I knew that back in Ireland he would not only be curling but playing football too – and that would mean other clubs would spot him and we would risk losing him. We actually got him back over to London after that, this time with his parents, but then Arsenal moved in and the rest is history.

It was no surprise to me in the slightest to see Niall enjoy such a wonderful career. And – as was so often the case – Ray Harford was proved right with his assessment, because it was at centre-forward that Niall thrived for so many years. I'm sure Niall will make a fine chairman for Sunderland. He is every bit the diplomat and very intelligent. When you are six feet four and have those wonderful, dazzling eyes of his on a really good-looking face, then you have a head start over most of us.

Niall, of course, got a good deal of stick for his short spell as Sunderland's chairman-manager, but I always had the feeling that he was just padding out time. I think that Roy Keane had already made his decision to become the next Sunderland manager and Niall was just treading water until Keane was able to start in the role. If Niall had tried to carry on the workload of a chairman and manager for much longer then he might have suffered a breakdown. It doesn't matter how intelligent you are, it's quite impossible to do both of those roles well. When the team lost all those early season games under Niall's charge, the alarm bells were ringing among Sunderland fans. But I believe Niall was calm throughout because he knew he was just keeping the manager's seat warm until Roy Keane was ready. All along, I'm sure Niall was thinking, 'Don't worry, it will all change when Roy comes in.'

If Niall was so confident, he certainly wasn't alone, because I felt the same way about Keane – and still do. In fact, I wouldn't be at all surprised if Sir Alex Ferguson is just keeping the Manchester United manager's seat warm for Roy, while he learns the ropes. There are no guarantees that will happen, of course. Roy needs to be a success as Sunderland manager first, but I have little doubt he will do that. His only potential downfall is his own self-destructive streak. I would certainly warn him against any more attacks on the so-called prawn sandwich brigade in the executive seats. Football thrives on the corporate fans so it's important he doesn't have a go at them just because they can afford better seats than most. People who have the character and spirit to survive as professional footballers and then go on to succeed as managers usually have a self-destructive button within their

•THE GAFFER: Malcolm is confident Roy Keane will be a success at Sunderland.

psyche. I have a feeling that Keane has a bigger button than most, but he is an exceptional individual, so as long as he avoids pressing it who knows what he can achieve as a manager? Sunderland are in for an enjoyable ride.

Bernie

IT WILL never happen, of course, but I would love to see all 20 top-flight managers given the same amount of money for team-building every season for maybe 10 years. That would be a fair league. We'd see who was a great manager and who had previously just had a lot of money to spend because the cream would come to the top. At the minute, in the main, money decides who finishes top.

That's why we don't really know who are the best managers about. For all we know, Mick McCarthy might be one the top three or four but he was never given the money to compete with the likes of Jose Mourinho, Alex Ferguson or Arsene Wenger. He certainly deserved a knighthood for getting Sunderland back in the Premier League.

Before Mick, Peter Reid did get money to spend but not on the scale managers at even a club like Middlesbrough have had. I had a lot of time for Reidy. I thought he did a great job for Sunderland until the latter stages of his spell there. Like Bryan Robson at Middlesbrough, he probably outstayed his welcome. When he let slip successive seventh place finishes to narrowly avoid relegation it was clear that his time was up. I was amazed when the club gave him £10 million in the transfer market – which he wasted on Tore Andre Flo and Marcus Stewart – only to sack him so soon afterwards. How could the chairman do that? If he was going to sack him surely the time to do was it before giving him the transfer kitty. It made no sense at all.

Bob Murray wasn't the most popular of guys. All Sunderland fans seemed to call the phone-in about last season was Bob Murray but they were picking on the easy target. It was the players who were to blame. Sure, Bob played his part in the club's failure but he wasn't on the pitch losing the games.

Players get off too lightly nowadays. There's too much talk of chairmen these days. Once upon a time, you wouldn't know the name of the chairmen. It's the managers, coaches and players that should carry the can.

As for who was to blame for last season's debacle, I think it was a combination of individuals. At the start of the season, I thought they might stay up, with the element of surprise and a bit of luck, but they had a nightmare. Bob Murray didn't give Mick McCarthy enough money, the players weren't good enough and you have to say that Mick was partly to blame because he bought the players.

I still don't know why Mick said the board had always supported him in the transfer market. He is a straight-talking guy and that was probably the only thing he said in his time at Sunderland that I can disagree with. I can only imagine he was under pressure to say it. When they were relegated a couple of years earlier, through no fault of Mick's, they sold all their big names so he was forced to turn to young lads and lower league players. He did an astonishing job.

I wasn't at all surprised to see him do so well. Having known Mick from our days as Ireland internationals, I have always felt he had the makings of a manager. He was a headstrong leader. If you crossed him, he would stab you in the heart, not in the back.

Maybe Sunderland Football Club didn't give him the same courtesy. They were crap last season but why sack him when it was clear they were heading back into the Championship? Mick was the boy who had brought them up, so why not leave him in the job, back him financially and give him another crack at it? I won't be surprised to see him do well for Wolves because he clearly knows what that level is all about.

The Kevin Ball appointment was farcical. It was just an attempt to appease the fans. The club appointed a guy who didn't have the credentials, just throwing him in to fill the gap. I've got nothing against Ball. He was a good professional who I played against a few times. He was a tough lad and kicked me a few times, while I just got on with scoring the goals!

Then, with Bob Murray finally gone after a long goodbye, in came the messiah, Niall Quinn. I know Niall from our Republic of Ireland days and he is a smashing guy, while his standing in the game is second to none. What he did in donating all his testimonial money to charity was a terrific gesture. In fact, I remember writing to him at the time to say that I took my hat off to him. I thought it was fair enough when Niall took over as the club's chairman following the takeover by the consortium he headed. But his decision to become manager as well was just outrageous. He was trying to do two difficult jobs that he was completely untried in. The fans initially went along with it but I don't think anyone was really surprised when it didn't work. Personally, I couldn't see why he ever put himself in that position when he knew the players he had weren't good enough. By all accounts, Sunderland were dreadful in those first few games of the season. Even Gatesy could have got a game, despite his 25-stone frame. Fortunately, Quinny is an honest guy and held his hands up to say, 'I can't do the job and I'm going to get someone in that can do it.'

As I recall, I think Niall said he was going to get a world class manager, but he then rephrased it to say world class name. Lo and behold, in came a man who had such special powers that he only had to sit in the stand and watch a game to get them their first win of the season. I doubt anyone would disagree that Roy Keane was one of the best midfielders in the world. Yeah, he had problems off the field as a result of his passionate attitude, but he was a winner. He is a winner. Forget the coaching badges, he has got the medals and top class experience. I know being a great footballer doesn't guarantee you'll be a good manager but I see something in Keane's eyes that isn't there with many others. He has a unique hunger and desire. He won't accept second best. If he gets the required backing, there's every reason to believe he'll be a success.

•REID ALL ABOUT IT: Bernie believes Peter Reid's time as Sunderland manager was up when he failed to capitalise on two seventh-place finishes.

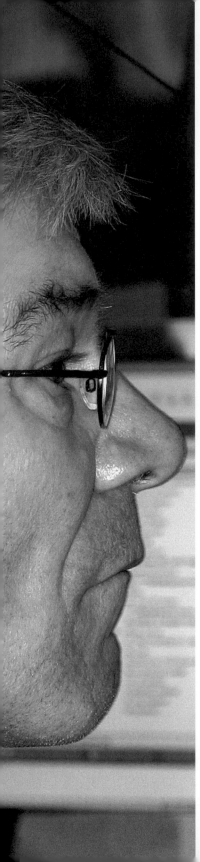

Malcolm's
LEGENDS 'n' LEG-ENDS

	Legends	Leg-ends
Newcastle players	Jackie Milburn Alan Shearer Hughie Gallacher Len Shackleton	Graham Oates Glenn Keeley
British football	George Best Bobby Moore Bobby Charlton Alan Ball Jimmy Greaves	Carlton Palmer
World footballers	Pele Maradona George Best	Carlton Palmer
Football managers	Sir Alf Ramsey Bobby Robson Alec Stock Joe Harvey	Gordon Lee Carlton Palmer
Sports stars	David Hemery Giacomo Agostini Stephen Miller	Carlton Palmer

•LEGEND: Tito

•LEG-END: Carlton Palmer

	Legends	Leg-ends
Musicians & Singers	Barbara Streisand	Heavy Rock
	Frank Sinatra	Punk
	Andrea Bocelli	Carlton Palmer
	Sarah Brightman	
	America	
	Eagles	
	Crosby Stills Nash Young	
Songs	Anything Sinatra sang	Everything like The Chicken Song
Film stars	Al Pacino	Tom Cruise
	Jack Lemmon	Woody Allen
	Sophia Loren	Carlton Palmer
	Cary Grant	
	Peter Sellers	
Films	Butch Cassidy & the Sundance Kid	Shadows and Fog
	Citizen Kane	
	Point Blank	
	All Pink Panther films	
TV personalities	Alan Coren	John Inman
	Bob Monkhouse	Carlton Palmer
	Eric Morecambe	
TV shows	Countdown	All soaps
		All reality programmes

	Legends	Leg-ends
Radio shows	I'm Sorry, I Haven't a Clue	
World figures	Josip Broz Tito	Robert Mugabe
	Winston Churchill	Pol Pot
		Joseph Stalin
		Adolf Hitler
		Napoleon Bonaparte
		Carlton Palmer

•LEGEND: Jackie Milburn

NEWCASTLE UNITED

Malcolm

GRAEME SOUNESS has a lot to answer for. That was my thought as Newcastle United kicked off the 2006-07 season with my expectations of the club about as low as they had been in a decade. I expected frustrating times ahead but you will not hear much criticism of Glenn Roeder from me over the next 12 months. What I do anticipate is that I will be mentioning the name of Graeme Souness rather more often than would be the norm with a former manager.

It is my view that under no circumstances must Roeder be judged as a success or failure for at least two years. It will take that length of time, or perhaps even longer, for him to put right the immense damage Souness wreaked on the club during his disastrous spell as manager at St James' Park. I don't think that the damage has even started to make itself evident yet, certainly not to the supporters and possibly not even to the chairman himself, Freddy Shepherd. The damage is so huge, so vast, that Roeder is going to do well just to keep the club ticking over for a couple of years while everything rebuilds.

I am not normally slow to criticise but I will be defending Newcastle a lot over the next 12 months as they recover from the full extent of the damage caused by Hurricane Souness. As Roeder rebuilds, Newcastle supporters must show great patience during what I expect to be a very difficult two years.

In April 2003, Newcastle United faced a home game knowing that a win would retain their hopes of nicking the Premier League championship. As it happened, they were beaten 6-2 by a rampant Manchester United side, with Paul Scholes scoring a hat-trick. That was Newcastle's chance gone and their visitors that day went on to pip Arsenal to the title. Even so, any team that has even the slightest chance of winning the

title four weeks before the end of the season has had a very good campaign. United eventually finished third, with Chelsea and Liverpool a country mile behind. There was such a gap that people talked about the top three. The club appeared to be established among the country's elite.

The following season they finished fifth, with Chelsea and Liverpool pipping them to a Champions League spot. Bobby Robson was sacked just a few games into 2004-05 and in his place came Graeme Souness. As a result, in February 2006 – less than three years after that big game with United – I watched Newcastle United produce the worst display of football I've ever seen from a top division side. After a £48 million spending spree, the club had gone from title contenders to a scrap to stave off relegation.

That game at the City of Manchester Stadium, a 3-0 defeat to Man City, was absolutely abysmal. That night I was unfortunate enough to be doing commentary for Century and, for the life of me, I couldn't work out what the Newcastle team's formation was supposed to be. In truth, this was nothing new but the performance that night was their nadir. I made no bones about announcing on air, 'Souness has got to be sacked.' I know the Newcastle supporters agreed. Thankfully, Freddy Shepherd also agreed and the chop duly fell the following day.

Fully 18 months earlier, on Souness's appointment, I had predicted that it would be a disaster, but even I did not envisage just how far backwards he would take us. Mercifully, Souness has gone but I will ensure he is not forgotten as the club begins to slowly pick up the pieces from the ruins he left behind.

Like every Newcastle supporter, deep down I am absolutely horrified that the club has now gone 51 years without winning a domestic trophy. That's a frightening statistic and one I must take my fair share of the blame for. Sadly, it is one I see being extended further yet. But it is my belief that Newcastle fans are different from most, in that they would rather see the return of entertaining football than break that silverware duck by winning the occasional minor trophy.

Knowledge and understanding of that philosophy is absolutely imperative in any man who takes on the role of Newcastle United manager. Of those fortunate enough to have held that role in recent history, Bobby Robson took it to heart, as did Kevin Keegan. Others were either ignorant of it or cast it aside. It is a risk the club's hierarchy takes every time it appoints a manager who does not know or share an affinity with the people, the place and the club.

Two men who never understood just what makes Newcastle United different from any other club were Keegan's successors in the St James' hot seat, Ruud Gullit and Kenny Dalglish. I have fond memories of Gullit as a wonderful AC Milan player alongside his fellow Dutchmen Frank Rijkard and Marco van Basten when I first lived in Milan. That team was a joy to behold. He came to Newcastle on the back of winning silverware with Chelsea but he joined the club at the wrong time. It seemed to me that he had too many problems in his personal life to give his all to the job. Managers need everything settled in their personal life to allow them to focus fully on the task in hand and achieve success. It was a great shame that that was not the case for Ruud during his time on Tyneside.

I held great store by what Ray Harford, my coach during my time as Fulham manager, had to say. Years after assisting me so well at Craven Cottage, he won the League championship with Blackburn Rovers as Kenny Dalglish's managerial sidekick. The impression Ray always gave me when talking about his time at Blackburn was that he did most of the coaching while Kenny spent much of his time on the golf course. It's always difficult to gauge how successful managers are when they take over a great side but Kenny did initially enjoy much success as manager of Liverpool before things started to go downhill. At Blackburn too, he won the title but again the club went downhill. The pattern repeated itself at Newcastle. In his first season with the club they finished runners-up but, yet again, they went rapidly downhill. It seemed to me that Dalglish's impact was even more short-term than Kevin Keegan's, the man he had replaced at

Newcastle, but the difference was that Kenny's side was nothing like as good to watch.

Keegan was a phenomenon but his impact was short-term too. He was a brilliant motivator and his players adored him but sooner or later they lost respect for him because his failings would always rise to the surface. All his strengths are there to be seen from day one, but as each day passes the strengths recede and his weaknesses poke their heads through.

I played in opposition to Kevin on my Newcastle debut when I scored three times against Liverpool. I also played with him for England Under-23s and the full side, travelling around Eastern Europe to play the national teams of countries like Czechoslovakia, East Germany, Poland, Russia and Bulgaria. I got to know Keegan well, though we never really got on.

I was in Italy when he took the reins at St James' Park and I followed the club's fortunes from afar. When he arrived, it was sh** or bust time for Newcastle United. They were struggling at the wrong end of the old Division Two table but Keegan came along and turned it around. With the like-minded spirit of Sir John Hall also influential, the next few years were brilliant for the club.

Kevin has great personality and is a good salesman, but I know from experience that there's not a lot of depth to back up those qualities. He needs the right people around him but he's never really had that. He could have had quality people around him with England but he always had this man Eric Winstanley, who I don't know too much about. What the country learned from his short spell as England manager was that Keegan was no coach, something every Newcastle fan already knew. As Keegan discovered to his cost, motivation alone simply isn't enough on the international stage.

When Keegan walked out on Newcastle for the last time, it heralded a bleak period that saw Dalglish and Gullit play a brand of football that was in no way comparable to the exciting play the Tyneside public had to come to expect and demand. But from mid-table mediocrity, they again established themselves as everyone's second favourite team, thanks to a man called Bobby Robson. The season that they finished third, I was exhilarated. Bernie is a very passionate watcher of the game, Eric is an impassionate studier of the game, while I am absolutely ice cold, so it takes a lot to get me so excited about football. But Bobby's side was fabulous to watch.

I saw Bobby formulate a side and bring youngsters through that augured well for many years to come. They finished fourth in 2001-02, his first full season as manager, while in his second I watched football as exhilarating as Keegan's side, though perhaps without the extremes. By that I mean the team that Bobby built still had defensive frailties of sorts but not as glaring as Kevin's side, while they were a little more cautious and less gung-ho than their Keegan era predecessors when it came to attacking. But more than that, they were successful. We were talking of Newcastle being part of the top three – and this was just three years ago.

From there, how I wish they had really gone for it. They had to go for signings who were of sufficient quality to help them challenge for the Premier League championship itself. The powers that be should have been asking themselves who they could see actually lifting the Premier League trophy. Sadly, they didn't do that. They brought in players that simply weren't of the quality to take them to the next level, the likes of James Milner, Celestine Babayaro and Stephen Carr. Spurs had decided that Carr was not going to be a prolific winner of trophies for them or anybody else, so they got rid of him as they began a new era. So why did Newcastle sign him? Nicky Butt's legs had gone. He had played in and looked quite good in a great Manchester United side with everybody making it happen around him, but he had to take on far greater responsibility at Newcastle and I knew he would never be up to it. Sir Alex Ferguson clearly felt they could do better without Butt, so why did Newcastle feel he was going to take them to the next level? They needed to bring in young players and forge them together as a team but chose to bring in players that other big clubs no longer wanted. It was no surprise to me, therefore, when the club started to go backwards.

Bobby's dismissal as Newcastle manager still rankles with many, though most people felt it coming at the time. His record suggested that he shouldn't have been sacked at all but I get the feeling that he was being undermined. I think he was being moved aside. A journalist friend of mine was stood talking with Bobby one day when another journalist came over and asked him about his new signing. Bobby asked, 'What new signing?' When the name of James Milner was spoken, he pronounced, 'What have they signed him for?' Incredibly, the club had signed Milner without Bobby's knowledge. For goodness sake, you don't have a dog and bark yourself.

Of course, Bobby's problems related far more to difficulties off the pitch than on it, as the club was attracting far too many unwanted headlines due to the activities of some of the players' personal lives. I think a lot of it was to do with the age gap between the young footballers and Bobby. They didn't know what he had achieved in the game and they probably didn't even really remember him as manager of England. Most of them just saw him as an old git, so there was no respect.

It wasn't the first time Bobby had suffered problems with big time Charlies, of course. It cost him his first job at Fulham and I learned from that never, ever to manage your old team-mates because it doesn't work. Then, when he first went into the Ipswich dressing room, players like Ray Crawford tried to dictate to him but he fist-fought them and got them out. He won the physical battle and kicked them out of the club. But by the end of his Newcastle reign I felt that his time had come and I was sorry for that because I had such great respect for him. Bobby was probably stuck in a bit of a time warp and it needed a new type of psychology. What it didn't need was Graeme Souness.

I was against the appointment of Souness from the very start and I said so on air. If the idea was to fight fire with fire then that was very unfair on Bobby. He had been dealing with a whole host of different problems, from the outrageous petulance of Craig Bellamy to a dressing room where half the players couldn't understand a word of English. I once asked Bobby what the major difference was between managing in the 1970s and managing in the modern game. He answered that when he had gone into a dressing room back in the

●CHOP SOUEY: That was Malcolm's demand long before Newcastle parted company with Graeme Souness.

1970s there was a whole group of players wanting to do it, but now it was about finding a way to motivate 11 millionaires. They didn't have the desire in-built. The manager had to create it.

Unlike Bobby's early days at Ipswich, the time had gone when you could fist fight people because the game had changed, as had society in general. Back then, if a manager had a scrap nobody would have said a word outside the club, but it doesn't stay quiet any longer. With Bellamy, he did it in public all the time. Bobby paid Bellamy the ultimate compliment by signing him, putting his reputation on the line and building the team around him - and yet Bellamy sh** on him time and time again. The truth is that I don't think Bellamy was a great player back then, though he became one at Blackburn under the influence of Mark Hughes, who he was able to respect because he had seen him play, had seen what he was capable of and what a nasty b*****d he could be. He related totally to Hughes, settled down and was brilliant, earning his big move to Liverpool. In contrast, he did it only in flashes for Bobby.

The suggestion was that Newcastle appointed Souness because he was a disciplinarian. If so, it was the greatest miscasting ever because Souness was never a disciplinarian. He was, and is, a confrontationalist. He went into a dressing room that was already heaving with confrontationalists, in the likes of Bellamy, Kieron Dyer and Lee Bowyer and – surprise, surprise – the result was confrontation after confrontation. Everything quickly went downhill.

Souness got rid of some of the troublemakers but he replaced good players with bad players. And he also made out some players to be trouble that really weren't. I don't think Laurent Robert was that difficult and yet Souness couldn't get rid of him quickly enough. Many people looked at the negatives - that he didn't work hard etcetera – but I'd have Robert in my side any day. Back in my playing days, I used to scream, 'Don't look at what I can't do, look at what I do do!' That was the case with Robert too. Each season he would score 10 to 12 goals - and that will do me from midfield - but he also probably made 36 with his crosses. Such was Robert's ability, forwards would receive his crosses as if the ball had been pulled back from the byline but it had usually come from 35 yards out. When Robert played, Alan Shearer seemed two feet taller and two feet wider. As soon as Robert wasn't doing it, Shearer was finished.

When Bobby Robson was sacked by Newcastle early in the 2004-05 season, I hoped they would think big and appoint somebody of the proven ability, like Ottmar Hitzfeld or Guus Hiddink. Instead, they appointed Graeme Souness, who had no track record whatsoever as a manager. I was just horrified. I couldn't see for the life of me any reason – not even a bad one – to appoint him. Don't get me wrong, Souness is a smashing bloke and was a great player who had my respect, but he was never a great manager. His only real successes were in Scotland with Rangers but can you take somebody's record seriously at Rangers or Celtic, where it's a two-horse race? He did quite well at Fenerbahce in Turkey too but that's a two-horse race with Galatasaray as well. Yes, he won the Carling Cup at Blackburn but Rovers were going right down the pan by the time he left Ewood Park. The Blackburn players were flapping like fish would if the water was running down the plughole. It's my belief that the only reason that he hadn't been sacked was that Blackburn couldn't afford to pay off his contract. You can imagine their delight, therefore, when they were put in a position where Newcastle were paying them compensation to take him!

I don't want this to sound like 'I told you so' but when Souness was first mentioned I said publicly that Newcastle shouldn't touch him with a bargepole. I remembered sitting on the same table as Souness at a North-West Football Writers' dinner and as we chatted I couldn't help but notice that he would ask the most naïve questions in response to the various points crossing the table. I was almost embarrassed for him. It was like chatting to a 16-year-old. I wondered if he was for real.

My concerns were further heightened when I considered how I had seen Brett Emerton playing for Feyenoord at right-back against Newcastle in the Champions League. He was like lightening from one corner flag to the other, had this fantastic muscular frame and could have been an Olympic sprinter. His ball skills weren't the subtlest but, by heavens, he was effective. And yet within 18 months of going to Blackburn he was so pale it was untrue and all of his power bulk was gone.

He could hardly raise a gallop. It was horrifying to think that the manager who had let that happen to a player who had once looked so promising was now in charge of Newcastle United.

To make matters much, much worse, Souness was bankrolled to the tune of £48 million – and they are a *worse* team for it. Absolutely frightening. The money was squandered on players like Jean-Alain Boumsong and Albert Luque. Boumsong took on a lot of criticism for a good footballer. But you don't want a good footballer at centre-half. Maybe he got away with it in France, but he was the wrong kind of player for the Premier League.

Of course, a massive chunk of that £48 million went on one player, Michael Owen. Some people insist Souness at least deserves some credit for pulling off a coup like bringing England's first choice striker to Tyneside but Owen was nothing to do with Souness. It is my understanding that the deal only came about because Real Madrid were so heavily in default to Newcastle in their payments for Jonathan Woodgate. That's why Liverpool were never really in the race for Owen. Liverpool could never have done the deal because Newcastle had such financial leverage over Real Madrid. Nevertheless, that's the kind of deal that as a manager you say, 'Phew! I can't believe my luck.'

Despite the injuries Michael suffered, it was a fabulous deal, but he looked like a fish out of water in his first season with the club. Owen is principally a great finisher in the mould of Jimmy Greaves, who comes alive only when the ball goes into the last third. Unfortunately, he hasn't developed his game since bursting onto the scene as a teenager. You rarely see him touch the ball on the halfway line and link up play with team-mates, like Mark Viduka does at Middlesbrough. He has got to be running at goal. But when you have a great goalscorer like that, you build a side around that one player because you know he will score a bucketful if you give him the right supply. The Newcastle team was not built for Owen and Souness never attempted to make it so.

Given all my reservations, I was not in the least bit surprised to see Souness quickly look like a man out of his depth as Newcastle manager. I don't think he had a clue. To make matters worse, he didn't have a great coach alongside him to cover his deficiencies. Sven Goran Erikkson became the highest paid manager in the world with England but I don't think he had a clue tactically. I wasn't the strongest tactically either, but I had Ray Harford sitting alongside me.

I took my hat off to Souness as a player and we got on well, but he wouldn't give me the time of day now. That's because not only did I insist he was the wrong man to appoint in the first place but, as things went from bad to worse, I publicly insisted the club had to sack him. For months, I found every polite way of expressing my belief that basically Souness seemed to be doing his utmost to get the sack. It seemed to me that he chucked money in any direction at whatever was available – no matter whether or not the target could play – and it pushed the situation to the limit. Having spent £48 million, Newcastle should have been a top side. Souness could have made himself a job for life. I have thought long and hard about why he didn't take the opportunity, why he was quite so bad, but I still have no answers.

There was so much that I saw that I just could not believe when I watched Newcastle under Souness. I started to leave games long before the final whistle blew, and that's not like me. But when it was so bad and I was watching players play in such a fashion that they could only look bad and they weren't doing anything about it, I could only come to the conclusion that they had been instructed to play that way. The only one who was truly playing his own way was Alan Shearer. I was witnessing players who were playing against their own natural instincts. That tells me they were being misdirected.

Newcastle had to sack Souness. They couldn't tolerate any longer the nonsense that was taking place on the pitch, otherwise they were in serious danger of getting hauled into the relegation area – and once you get caught, the black hole can suck you in. Newcastle were teetering on that brink so they had to make the change.

I thought the football club's decision to appoint Glenn Roeder and Alan Shearer on a temporary basis while all options were considered regarding what to do next was perfectly suitable and adequate. Shearer initially got most of the publicity and no doubt he had his say but it was clear that Roeder was the man in charge. Glenn acquitted himself absolutely brilliantly and surprised a lot of people. The terrific response from the players during the season's closing months tells you how well he was received in the dressing room, just as the lack of response told you what you needed to know about the players' feelings towards Souness. I don't want to take anything away from Glenn but it needed a breath of fresh air to lift the players out of the doldrums and get a response - and anything would have been an improvement on Souness. Having committed to letting Glenn be caretaker and seeing him get the results he did, the club was fully justified in giving him a chance over other higher-profile possibilities.

Now is the most difficult and important time for him. It's about how he goes about disbanding Souness' side and putting together his own. But the club has got to give him every opportunity. Are they going to give him the support that they gave Souness? No, they aren't. They can't - and that's why they've got to remain patient with him until they are in a position to give him the same support they gave Souness and Robson before him. Great patience now has to be shown because Roeder faces a very difficult two years as the full extent of the damage Souness caused starts to reveal itself.

Newcastle's playing structure was severely damaged by Souness. There are now an awful lot of players at the club who really aren't good enough for Newcastle to go out and achieve what they should be achieving. Senior people at the club have got to look at themselves and ask if they are going all out to try and win things. People ask if Roeder is up to the job. I don't know, so it's up to him to prove himself, to me and everybody else. What I would like his attitude to be is, 'Right, as the manager of Newcastle United, I am going to jump right into the pack of Mourinho, Wenger, Ferguson and Benitez and I'm going to shock the life out of them. And I'm going to take the players with me.' Over the last two or three years I have become sick and tired of watching Newcastle United fail to even make a game of it at the likes of Old Trafford, Highbury and Stamford Bridge. You've got to be going and competing but the team usually roll over and die.

Here's where Eric Gates and I fall out. Eric's philosophy on team strengthening is that if a player is better than what you've got then get him in. I say no, you don't. You only get him in if he's good enough to take you to the very highest level, to compete with the very best. One player alone can't

do it. You need to get a number of them. What I want to see Newcastle do is to start bringing in only that calibre of player. For heaven's sake, they've got the third biggest stadium in the country that they fill without an effort and they have one of the Premier League's top five wage bills, so they damn well ought to have one of the top five teams, otherwise they are getting robbed. If you're not in the top five then you've got to stop and ask, 'Who are the cheats?' Maybe cheats is too strong a word, maybe they are just not capable of performing at that level. But any question marks, get them out. There is no point in getting in, or retaining, substandard players.

What I expect of Newcastle over the next two seasons is mid-table mediocrity. I certainly hope for better but I'm not expecting it. If things go wrong we might even struggle to stay up. I am confident that Newcastle will not be relegated this season, but I do worry what will happen without Michael Owen to score 20 goals for them. That is a real area of concern because I think they are going to struggle for goals, even with the signing of Damien Duff. If you're not scoring the goals to give your defenders the breaks then you can expect your defence to under-perform. You need to go a goal ahead to relieve the pressure, so you can start to knock the ball about in a manner that you can't necessarily do at 0-0 or 1-0 down when you have to push and press. At 1-0 up, the whole game is different. Knocking it about gets the confidence of players built up. But recent history tells us that Newcastle don't hold onto a lead very long.

My chief concern is where the goals are going to come from. To avoid being relegated, you have to score a minimum of 50 goals. Where's 50 goals in the Newcastle squad? Michael Owen's injury is a disaster for him and the club. If Newcastle had signed Dirk Kuyt from Feyenoord during the summer then they might as well have packed up and gone home. He is simply not good enough. A year earlier the newspapers closely associated with Newcastle were linking the club with the young Spanish superstar, Fernando Torres. This was six months after I had first started to say on the Legends phone-in what a great acquisition he would be, but that is by the by. Torres, who was then only 21 years old, is six foot two, runs like the wind, has skills to die for, scores and makes goals. Luque, who they signed, was being touted as a great player

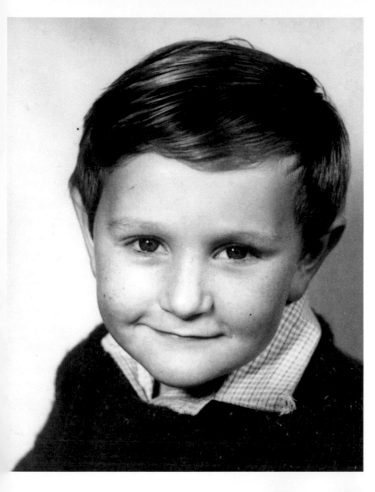

•BEFORE THEY WERE LEGENDS: Eric (above),
Malcolm (top right) and Bernie in their younger days.

•SKIP TO IT: State-of-the-art training, Gatesy style.

8 ARSENAL   25 PRESTON

LEADING COAL SCORER DIV
50/1 MALCOLM MCDONALD

14 HAWKEYE
15 ICY RETORT
17 JOZANDA
19 KISS-ME-HARDY
20 LAUREL BRANCH
22 MASTER PILOT
SUPER ALLOY
WALK ON
11

•DON'T BET ON IT: Despite the generous odds this bookie offered on Malcolm being Division One's top scorer in his first season at Newcastle, it would not have been money well spent.

•HORSE POWER: Eric hitches a lift.

•STYLE GURUS: Not a moodily-shot pop video, but Malcolm (right) with England team-mates Emlyn Hughes (left) and Larry Lloyd during a trip to Berlin.

FASHION SLAVE: Bernie kneels in front of Ayresome Park's Holgate end. But was he praying that his taste in jackets would improve?

•TOP GUNS: Malcolm and his Newcastle strike partner John Tudor are ready to shoot down the opposition.

•FIVE STAR: Malcolm scores a bullet header on the day he made history by scoring all five goals in England's victory over Luxembourg.

•IF THE CAP FITS: Boro chairman Colin Henderson congratulates Bernie on completing his conversion from Scot to Irishman!

•RED ALL OVER: Bernie celebrates after scoring past John Burridge in 1990, on a day Boro avoided relegation witha 4-1 home win over promotion hopefuls, Newcastle.

•TRACTOR BOY: Eric takes on Liverpool's Graeme Souness during his halcyon days with Ipswich Town.

•CROSSING PATHS: Gatesy in action for Ipswich against Boro's Willie Maddren and Terry Cooper.

•ROKER JOKER: Bernie in action against Sunderland, with Gary Bennett paying him close attention.

•GOING TO GROUND: Eric in action against future employers, Sunderland, including Roker keeper Chris Turner. Does this picture support Bernie's claims that Eric regularly dived?!

•LOCAL HEROES: The Three Legends during their Newcastle, Sunderland and Boro hey-days.

•CUP OF JOY: Gatesy shows off the UEFA Cup after helping Ipswich Town to Euro success in 1981.

•SO CLOSE: Bernie and Alastair Brownlee pose with the UEFA Cup. Unlike Eric, 25 years earlier, this was as close as they got to it as Boro were hammered by Sevilla in the 2006 final.

•RADIO STAR: Malcolm – or is it Marconi? - makes one of history's first radio broadcasts during his playing days. And what about the shirt?

•LEGEND, MY ARSE! Bernie pays off a debt in the window of Binns. So *that's* what a Scot-cum-Irishman wears under his kilt.

•THE BOTTOM LINE: Botty is a word that will be forever associated with Bernie!

•WHERE'S THE RED KNICKERS?
Eric almost reveals a little too much
about Bernie!

Bagpipes courtesy of Josef Collier.

•PLAYBOY LEGENDS: Phone-in contributor and Hartlepool fan, Bert, prefers to think of our heroes in a rather different way!

•FACES MADE FOR RADIO: The Legends in the Century fm studio.

•MAC'S MOTOR: Malcolm with his Mercedes.

•AT HOME: Malcolm in his secluded garden in Shotley Bridge.

•ANIMAL ATTRACTION: Bernie at home with his ponies and goat.

•PULLING BIRDS: Bernie shows how it's done with his pet ducks, Daffy and The Other One.

•HEN-PECKED? Eric's message to his feathered friends is clear - at least to those that can read?

•ANIMAL FARM: Eric at home with his horses.

too but Torres was leaps and bounds above him at six years his junior. But Newcastle had to go in for Torres before the World Cup, not after it. Atletico Madrid were desperate for money but they had a lot of potential buyers after the tournament. Even though the player has stayed in Spain for the time being, I reckon Newcastle could have got him and Luque as well. They could have had them both up front together.

I saw Luque play over in Spain and he was great for Deportivo La Coruna. But not ever has he shown anything like that form for Newcastle, though it has to be said that the club have often played him at outside-left, a position I never saw him play in during his time in Spain. I only ever saw him play there as a second striker, in a deep, Rooney-like fashion, joining attack with midfield. But he was playing at outside-left when he made such an ignominious start for the club, from which I don't think he has ever recovered. In that second game for Newcastle, at home to Fulham, he went down as if he had been shot as he raced for the ball beyond the opposing full-back. It was a hamstring injury and he was out for nearly three months. No matter what your quality, that sort of start knocks a player's confidence greatly because he feels so stupid. What you need in that first game is to create credibility. You might not have a great game but if you can create that credibility among your team-mates and the supporters, the rest can come later.

Sadly, Luque has completely failed to shine since. By the end of his first season with the club, I couldn't help but think that something along the way had happened at the club – something that will probably never make the light of the day – that had left Glenn Roeder convinced that no way would he ever trust Luque with a position in the first team. The reason behind those thoughts was because even when Owen was injured, Shearer was injured and Shola Ameobi was struggling, when Roeder really didn't have anything to lose, he still didn't put him in the team. I think Luque would have been finished at Newcastle in the summer but for the serious injury to Michael Owen but Roeder realised that with Owen injured and Shearer retired he might as well throw down the gauntlet and say, 'Right, you want a chance - you've got it.'

Newcastle supporters complained about the lack of big signings before the start of the 2006-07 season but I don't think the club had much money to spend. There was little left in the kitty because Souness had spent it all. During his spending spree, he probably used up some of the club's future transfer money as well as all the cash set aside to spend at the time. Given that predicament, perhaps it is time for Newcastle to have a rethink over their transfer policy. The players that Chelsea, Man United and Arsenal let go are not going to get you challenging with those teams because the reason they let them go is because they aren't good enough to do that. It is time to think it out afresh and start to look for the players on their way up rather than on their way down. By that I mean players like Dean Ashton, who was given his chance by Norwich City and West Ham. But for his unfortunate injury on the eve of what would have been his England debut I think he would have been perfect for Newcastle. Ashton has a genuine chance of being something between John Hartson and Alan Shearer. Whether he ends up closer to Hartson or closer to Shearer is up to him, but he is somebody that you can build a team around because he is genuine and will give you his all.

It is time for Newcastle United to take a leaf out of Arsenal's book. Keegan, Dalglish and Gullit were all known as huge spenders and Souness was worse than the lot. All left the club with huge transfer deficits, but Arsene Wenger's transfer record at Arsenal has left the Gunners £50 million in credit. He brings in raw players full of potential like Kolo Toure and Emmanuel Eboue for something like a million each and makes them Premier League stars. He paid a few quid for Nicolas Anelka and sold him for a fortune to Real Madrid a couple of years later. The man is magnificent at finding hidden gems.

•IN THE HOTSEAT: but Glenn Roeder will need to be given time to rebuild the club.

I occasionally talk to my old Highbury team-mate Pat Rice, who is now Arsenal's assistant manager, and have asked him what Wenger's real strength is. He has told me that you never see Wenger without a phone to his ear. He doesn't spend his time on the phone to other Premier League managers. Instead, he is constantly talking to scouts in Ghana, Nigeria, Rwanda, Korea or wherever the next superstar might be waiting to be discovered. Every day he contacts every one of them. He wants to know if they have seen anybody new and if they have been to see this or that player again. Apparently, he has a filing cabinet of a mind. He team-builds in the old-fashioned way and he is a master at it. Arsenal's current back four cost less than half of the £8 million or so that Newcastle paid Rangers for Jean-Alain Boumsong. To create a good defence, you don't need a fortune, but you do need good planning.

In the end, Newcastle ended up spending a fair few Bob, though they were pursuing the FA for compensation regarding Michael Owen's injury at the same time, so I do wonder if the plan all along was to cover themselves that way. The mistake Newcastle made was that they looked to get in quality stars without apparently realising that they needed to just bolster the squad with good cover players too. Deals like that could have been done in May before the World Cup. Even back then, it was clear that the goalkeeping area was fine, the midfield was OK, but the defence desperately needed strengthening and the forward line was virtually non-existent, even before the injury to Owen. Two players I would have gone for were Jason Roberts, who eventually left Wigan for Blackburn, and Carlton Cole, who joined West Ham from Chelsea. Roberts is a big, strong forward, who Newcastle could have signed for £3.5 million, while Cole is desperate to prove a point. Failing those two, Jimmy Floyd Hasselbaink was available on a free from the Boro. In fact, Glenn Roeder lived to regret his public statement that he was looking to sign players at the start of their careers rather than those, like Jimmy, getting towards the end. If that was the case, then why did he sign Antoine Sibierski on transfer deadline day?

Sibierski aside, why does it always have to be a headline-grabbing star name or big money with Newcastle? I had been impressed whenever I'd seen Obefemi Martins playing for Inter Milan over the previous couple of seasons, so I was all for him coming to St James' Park. My only concern was that he might be 32 and not 22! I know Bernie has had a laugh at my expense, stating that I didn't even know what foot Martins kicked with. The truth is that I knew what foot he kicked with but, to be brutally honest, I watched Martins in those early games and couldn't remember him kicking with his left or right foot! He made no impact whatsoever in his early games. In fact, he looked more like a starry-eyed kid. But then he shut up all the snipers – Bernie included - with a wonderful goal at West Ham in September. No duffer scores even one goal like that. It was an icebreaker and told me that Martins would go on to do well for the club. Having said all that, I really don't see him being a good striking foil for Michael Owen. I have a feeling it will be a case of either or. Of course, there are no guarantees that Owen will be even half the player he was when he finally returns from injury, so it was vital that Newcastle planned without him during his long absence.

I was very impressed with the capture of Damien Duff. At £5 million, I think his signing was an exceptional deal and yet I think it had been almost forgotten by transfer deadline day. For Duff, the challenge was never to prove to Newcastle fans that he was a good player but to prove to Chelsea what a big mistake they made in letting him go. I think their decision to sell him was their way of telling him, 'You ain't good enough, pal.' That should be his spur to prove them wrong. If he does do that, I can promise him that he will the greatest hero on Tyneside. He made a slow start at Newcastle and I couldn't help but think that I wanted him to be more direct and more positive, though I knew from what I had seen in the past that he had real quality about him.

Of course, where Newcastle really needed to strengthen was in defence. Instead, they signed not one single defender throughout the close season of 2006, while Boro stole in for both Jonathan Woodgate and Robert Huth, two central defenders Newcastle had been linked with all summer. My understanding of the situation is that while Roeder wanted to sign Huth, Freddy Shepherd thought they should go for Woodgate. If the manager and the player really were at loggerheads over who to sign, then it really raises the question about who is responsible for signings at the club. My belief is that if it had been Roeder, then Huth would now be a Newcastle player. Instead, we were left with a back four that everyone knew wasn't up to it.

Woodgate would have been a risk, especially as I don't believe that Real Madrid would have allowed Newcastle to get him under the circumstances they allowed with Boro, but he makes the game look so simple and, in turn, makes everyone around him look like better players than they really are. Just look at the effect he had on Titus Bramble when he was at Newcastle, similarly with Emanuel Pogatetz when he joined Boro on loan. In that way, he reminds me very much of Bobby Moore in his reading of the game. Woodgate isn't as brilliant as Moore was, but the pace he has makes him the only defender in Europe who can take liberties with players like Thierry Henry.

But it isn't all doom and gloom for Glenn Roeder. In fact, the current squad has a couple of gems of its own. I was hugely disappointed when Glenn made the decision to appoint Scott Parker as Shearer's successor as Newcastle captain in the summer of 2006, not so much because I think Parker is overrated but because there was another outstanding candidate for the job. That man – or, rather, that boy – is Steven Taylor. For far too long I've watched Newcastle letting in goal after goal but have seen nobody shake a fist at their team-mates. Taylor will do that and is the sort of player who would become better with the additional responsibility of being captain. I can pay him no higher tribute than to say he is of similar mould to Bobby Moore, who grew in stature with responsibility. I felt Roeder should have said to Taylor, 'Right son, you're in the team, you're the skipper, take no nonsense from him, him or him.' The lad has done it at every level and I have no doubt he'll do it at first team level too. One question that is asked about Taylor is his lack of speed. It would help if he had better players around him, but it doesn't really matter with him because he never causes you to think about it. He doesn't have to chase or reposition himself because his timing is immaculate and he reads the game so well.

United's other young gem is Charles N'Zogbia, a great player who I firmly believe will be a sensation in the next French World Cup squad. I've watched him over the last two years

and he is a phenomenon. He has lightening pace, wonderful ball skills, he'll go box to box and get inside each penalty area. He'll do the dirty defending jobs that need doing and then fly up to the other end. If Newcastle are struggling for a forward they could put him up front and he would score goals, thanks to his wonderful pace. He has come from a background of real hardship and I get the feeling that, no matter what, he will never let the lads down and will always succeed against the odds.

As anybody who listens even occasionally to The Three Legends phone-in will know, I am not Scott Parker's biggest fan. I can understand why the fans like him but he is not what I'm looking for in a central midfield player. One of the best central midfielders I was lucky enough to play alongside was Alan Ball, a brilliant player, who was my team-mate at Arsenal. The first time that I ever played with Alan was in an England shirt some years earlier when he said to me, 'Son, when the ball comes to me, if it doesn't come to you with my first touch, it will certainly come with my second. The one thing you'll never see me do is take a third touch.' Now wasn't that simple for me? When the ball was on its way to Alan Ball, I would make a run. If it didn't come, I would check and go the other way, knowing that I would get the ball seconds later. Just as he promised, I never saw Bally take a third touch, with England or Arsenal.

Not only does Parker not give the ball with his first touch, because he never gets his head up and looks, he doesn't even give it with his second. What he invariably does is get it and turn in a circle to make himself a bit of space, though never in a forward motion, always turning towards his own goal. The opposition know they don't have to dive in on the fella, that they can let him have it because he isn't a problem. While Parker goes around in circles, it allows all of his team-mates to get picked up. The opposition know that they've got three or four seconds to get themselves sorted and mark up. Parker then finally looks up and thinks, 'Where's the movement?' You didn't see it, pal! Ask yourself why Chelsea let him go.

People say that Parker is a ball-winner. Some of the time he is, but when he doesn't win it, he is inevitably on his arse. If any kid is reading this book, no matter what level you play at, do not go on your backside – always stay on your feet. There is no reason to go on your backside. The crowd love a good sliding tackle, crunching into a player and the ball flying into the air. That's all right when you win the ball but it's when you don't that you're out of the game and your team-mates have a problem because there's now an opponent running at the heart of the defence.

I think Parker is too slow, his touch isn't good enough and he doesn't get his head up. He is too long in the tooth now to change. He will do a lot of good things but he will do a lot of bloody awful things – and you can't have players doing that if you want to challenge at the top of the Premier League. You need players who get it right, right, right, time after time. To give him credit, Parker was much better at the start of the 2006-07 season. I even found myself praising him because he was finally getting into positions to create goal chances or score himself.

What people don't see in Parker are his failings - and what they don't see in Shola Ameobi are his strengths. They don't think his long-legged style and build is aesthetically pleasing but I find him quite graceful in a similar way to Peter Crouch. People take the p*** out of Crouch but he's got two good feet and is probably better on the deck than he is in the air. If you look at Ameobi's European scoring record, you will find that against top quality opposition he always scores goals. I believe that's because the players around him have a different attitude in those games and feed him in a different way.

Shola could become a very good player, but for a couple of years now I have felt he has needed working on. He needs a huge dose of goalscoring attitude and absolute greed. I don't think Roeder will be able to work with Ameobi, though I think he will work with a lot of players extremely well. Ameobi needs to work with somebody like myself, Pop Robson or even Bernie, someone that will teach him to be greedy. He needs to be shown the optimum moment to strike. But he has a lot going for him. He's big and strong. He went through a couple of challenges at Villa Park last season and you could see the utter panic in Villa's back line. None of the defenders wanted the responsibility of marking him. He murdered them and scored a good goal. But he then needed to go to St James' Park and follow on where he left off against Villa. He should

have been going all out to score in the first 15 minutes but he just didn't do it, I believe simply because he wasn't being told what to do. But I can see Ameobi and Michael Owen being brilliant together if they ever get the chance. Unfortunately, the worst player in the world for him to play with was Alan Shearer. The two of them just didn't gel.

Without doubt, Alan Shearer was one of the greatest players of all-time and certainly the best English centre-forward of the last decade and beyond. Shearer's goalscoring ability put him beyond the great Geoff Hurst, who was one of the most accomplished technical players I ever saw. Hurst's first touch was immaculate, he could hold off opposing defenders and oh, the runs he used to make. I was sent to watch him by my Luton manager Alex Stock. 'I wanna watch Jimmy Greaves,' I said, but Stock was insistent. 'No, go and watch Geoff Hurst.' He was right too. I learned so much off Hurst. His little checks and what have you, it would all be perfect timing to be in just the right position, thank you very much. In comes the ball, and then he would shield and control it. Everything would just open from there. Shearer was exactly like that - not as good a runner as Hurst when it came to making angles, but more directed towards goal and getting in a strike.

Whenever parents told me they had an 11-year old son who loved the game and asked what advice I could give to help him improve I would always say to take him to watch Shearer - not to watch the game but just to watch Shearer. I would tell them to ensure he watched how he worked hard to get himself set to control the ball. Watch Shearer's control and passing, the game's two most important basics. Everything else comes from those two things. I remember having this conversation in the press room prior to Newcastle's game at Sunderland in his final season as a pro. I told the guy I was speaking to that he should watch Shearer that day. The guy came back in at half-time and said, 'Do you know, Shearer's only lost the ball once in the first 45 minutes? I've watched players on both sides who cannot trap it, it's taking them four and fives touches before they get their heads up and see what's going on. But with Shearer it's control and up.'

Shearer was textbook in everything he did. He was as clean a striker of the ball that you could hope to see. It was only the last couple of seasons that he stopped being a textbook

•WAVING FAREWELL: but Malcolm believes Shearer will be back as manager.

contre-forward. That's when he started taking liberties, like leaning back when he was shooting. By his age, he had learned how to lean back and still keep his shot low. Opponents would come in and hit him just as he was shooting but he was so strong that they'd be bouncing off him as if they had never come into contact. Everything was so beautifully balanced and his goals record was phenomenal.

Delaying his retirement from playing for an extra season was, I felt, a mistake. It would have all been very well if he had been in a good side with lots of young legs about him who would have helped him in return for him helping them. But it was never going to work at Newcastle. There were times that season – all too often - when I saw him being played up front on his own. It was every bit as ridiculous as asking Wayne Rooney to play up front on his own in the World Cup, when two games before it had been a question of whether he would last 45 minutes. Oh come on! He's a kid and let's not forget the fact. And Shearer, whose legs had gone ages ago but was still doing it well on experience, being asked to play up front on his own, away from home? It was dreadful to watch and it was heartbreaking. He can't have enjoyed it because it's a thankless task. Asking a former England captain with records galore to play a labourer's role at the age of 36 when he was an artist? It was a crime against football and against a great player.

He brought a wonderful playing career to a close at the end of the 2005-06 season, finally leaving Newcastle as the Premier League's all-time top goalscorer. But he will be back, without a doubt. It is the most certain thing in football that Alan Shearer will manage Newcastle United. I don't know who will manage Man United, Arsenal, Liverpool or any other club in the future but I do know that sooner or later Alan will manage Newcastle. He has tremendous support from the board as it stands, so I think it's quite possible that he will succeed Glenn Roeder.

The truth is that I was worried the club might have even given him the job last summer. That would have been a disaster. Managing your old team-mates is always a disaster waiting to happen and sooner or later it all goes pear-shaped. The only exception to that rule was Kenny Dalglish when he took over at Liverpool. But 99 times out of a hundred it ends in tears. I witnessed it with Bobby Robson, who suffered utter nonsense in his first management job at Fulham. The players knew him too well and were too cosied-up. He stepped away but they kept coming ever closer. He couldn't get the distance. I remember him on a training field, trying to get this end-to-end movement working and an understanding about who was making a pass to where and who then needed to be making the movements, but the whole thing was just a shambles because the players were cocking it up and sniggering. Even with a tough guy like Shearer, what was he going to do - fist fight them? So I'm glad he didn't get the job then but I know full well that he will eventually get it, though thankfully by then the players he knows will have moved on. Shearer had to get away from Newcastle. He doesn't need the money so he needs to go away and manage a club like Hartlepool, learn the game, find out what works and what doesn't, how players react, and why they sometimes listen and sometimes don't.

I heard the suggestions that Shearer held too much sway and influence at Newcastle, especially during recent seasons. Bobby Robson wasn't going to let that happen and I believe that's why he and Freddy Shepherd were getting more distant by the day in his final months at St James'. Freddy was pro-Shearer but Bobby was saying, 'Look, Alan Shearer is a centre-forward. A very good centre-forward but that's all he is.' I don't really know what actual influence he had beyond his captain's role and personally I don't think the problem was Shearer. I felt the problem was how other people perceived Shearer. If some wanted to see his role as being more than it actually was then that's where the problem came in.

I am sure Alan will strive to become Newcastle manager - and if he sets his sights on something he will get there. I don't know that he'll be a good manager, though he has certainly got all the attributes to become one. He is very disciplined, he knows exactly what his capabilities are and how to get the best out of them. If he can apply that to all of his players then he will get the very best out of them and create a fine team. What often happens is that centre forwards who become managers don't understand how to manage forwards, former defenders can't get the best out of defenders and managers who were quick players tend to pick slow players. It's very strange how it works out. If Alan Shearer goes according to

•TAKING THE MICHAEL: Owen's long-term injury could prove costly for Newcastle.

that rule then he will do very well because he lacked pace and will therefore go for quick players - and that's what you need to succeed in the modern game. You need the quickest players, even if you have to sacrifice a little bit of ability.

Bernie

WHEN RUUD Gullit departed St James' Park nearly 10 years ago, he said Newcastle would never win a trophy while Alan Shearer was there. Shearer's retirement last summer after yet another season without a hint of silverware proved Gullit got it dead right.

Then, over the summer, I heard the Geordies saying they had established themselves as the north-east's top team again - all because they were in the Interjoke Cup. I think Roeder did extremely well getting that seventh spot from where Newcastle were when he took over, but let's not forget Boro reached the UEFA Cup final and FA Cup semi. Boro were undoubtedly the top side for a year but we never took our chance to establish ourselves in that position. But Newcastle have been heading backwards ever since they sacked Bobby Robson – and long may it continue. They've won nothing domestically for more than half a century and who knows when they'll stop the rot?

In my opinion they shouldn't have got rid of Bobby. It was wrong. The timing of his sacking was woeful. They should have made a clean break of it the previous summer instead of waiting to press the panic button when they made a bad start. They sacked Souness too, when I think they could have held on until the end of the season. In my opinion, Souness and Steve McClaren were as bad as each other at the time, but Souness got the sack, McClaren didn't. If I'd been in charge at Newcastle I'd have thought about sacking Souness but Steve Gibson wouldn't have. Who knows? Souness might

have turned it around, though maybe he had lost the dressing room. I know the Newcastle fans didn't want Souness in the first place, perhaps because he was Scottish. They wanted a Geordie, like Shearer, or at least an adopted one, like Keegan. I always wondered about the wisdom of putting Souness in charge but I don't think the fans gave him a fair crack. He kept putting out one fire and another would start. He had idiots in his team, who Bobby Robson, who I respect greatly, couldn't deal with. He had buggers like Craig Bellamy and Lee Bowyer, good players but trouble, and then the carry-on with Kieron Dyer. It was a comedy.

He replaced the trouble-causers with some bad players. He signed Boumsong, a French international? He was bad. Luque came with a big reputation but flopped. Michael Owen's injuries were a real kick in the knackers for the Geordies. When they signed Owen my confidence in Boro remaining the region's top team evaporated overnight, even though I knew Newcastle's defence was a nightmare. I immediately started to think Boro would soon be back playing second fiddle to Newcastle, though it was beyond me why Owen joined them. Someone should have questioned his sanity when he got off the plane at Newcastle Airport on his way to sign. He should have been put in a straightjacket and thrown in a padded cell. It made me laugh to think that Alan Shearer had apparently been instrumental in persuading him to move to Tyneside from Real Madrid. Imagine Shearer's sales pitch. 'Michael, I've been at Newcastle for eight years, I've scored 250 goals for the club … and I've won absolutely nothing!' The few games Owen played for Newcastle he looked the part because he was sharp and scored goals. Then bang, injury. He was a big loss. His injuries were the main reason for the downfall of Souness. There's no doubt his injury during the World Cup was a massive blow for Glenn Roeder as well.

But appointing Roeder was a weird decision. Putting him and Shearer in temporary charge when they sacked Souness was just plugging the gap, sweetening the fans until the end of the season so they could review it. Roeder did well and got a contract out of it but I still don't think it was the right choice. I'm not saying Shearer should have been considered either. It's not about big names, it's about getting someone who has the credentials. Guus Hiddink or Martin O'Neill would have been perfect. People came on the phone-in and told us that Roeder had had experience of management. Yes, he had, and he failed. I think it was brilliant what he did last season. He did well, there's no doubting it. But he couldn't lose. Even if Newcastle had carried on losing, the fans would have blamed it on Souness. Roeder picked up the pieces after Souness but I don't think he has some sort of magic wand. The players probably just liked him, so they played for him.

Oh yeah, that reminds me. The players! Let's start with the defence because that's the funniest! I found it astonishing that the Geordies never addressed the problems at the heart of their defence. For the last two years it's been obvious for all to see that they lack quality there. Boumsong was a nightmare. Roger Moore's brother hasn't cut the mustard. And then there's Titus Bramble! I remember a Newcastle fan coming on the phone-in and trying to convince us that Bramble was going to be the new Bobby Moore. I just told him, 'You're joking!' Bobby Moore? Roger Moore maybe. Or Dudley Moore. Actually, probably more like lawn mower!'

I have to say that it gave me great pleasure to see Jonathan Woodgate and Robert Huth sign for the Boro because, reading between the lines, it was clear Newcastle were after both of them. The Geordies knew all about Woodgate's quality but we nicked him. There was talk of Newcastle going for Huth as well, but again he came to Boro. That's when Newcastle fans hit the roof, especially when the club not only failed to add a quality defender to the squad but announced the capture of Antoine Sibierski as their transfer deadline coup! It was bizarre. Their fans were clearly disturbed and wondering what was going on, especially as it meant they weren't able to address the problem again until January, by which time it might be too late (fingers crossed!)

The one that there was no debate about was the signing of Damien Duff from Chelsea. I felt that was a very good signing, though God knows why he chose Newcastle over Liverpool. I can only think that maybe he couldn't get any more medals in his drawer. By my own admission, I didn't know a great deal about Obefemi Martins before he made the move from Inter Milan. I knew Dean Martin was a good singer, but Obefemi Martins? Time will tell if his £10 million transfer fee was money

well spent but I had to laugh when, after seeing Martins make his Newcastle debut, Malcolm admitted he still didn't know what foot he kicked with!

So that's my view on the Geordies. There was no pressure on Glenn Roeder when he was only caretaker but if it goes tits up now that he's the manager there's only one man who will get the blame. Knowing Newcastle, I wouldn't be surprised if he was one of the first casualties of the season if they have a few slip-ups. I certainly can't see them having a great season. Let's see how it goes but I don't think Roeder's initial impact will continue. I hope it doesn't.

Eric

CONVENTIONAL THINKING says that Newcastle are the north-east's top team. I want to argue with that view but I can't. In terms of outlook, spending, crowds and relative success on the pitch going back over the years they have usually left both Sunderland and Boro way behind. The counterargument – and I use it plenty - is that they've won nothing, but I know Sunderland would have swapped places with Newcastle and enjoyed Champions League and UEFA Cup football for the last 10 or 15 years. Even though Boro won the League Cup not so long ago, I still tend to think Newcastle have remained top dogs in terms of the overall picture.

The problem that some Sunderland supporters have with me is that I don't *hate* Newcastle. If that means I'm not a real fan in they're eyes then fine. I don't profess to be a true diehard Sunderland supporter. I admire fans like that but I'm not going to pretend to be one of them. For that reason, I don't really take the same joy that they do from Newcastle losing. My background is different from theirs. I followed Boro as a lad because my brother played for them, but when I moved to Ipswich I looked out for the results of all the north-east clubs. I was privileged to play for Sunderland and therefore they are the first result I look for nowadays. I don't have any great connection with Newcastle but I haven't really got anything against them either.

•OLD PALS' ACT: Gatesy gets some advice from Bobby Robson during their days together at Ipswich.

telly I would gladly sit and watch them and think to myself, 'Bloody hell, that is good football'. Malcolm argues that Geordies would rather have an entertaining team than a winning one, but I have a feeling they would much prefer a team that delivered both.

But, let's face it, Newcastle playing entertaining football has become no more than a distant memory. The last good team they had was Bobby Robson's side. Bobby knew how to play good football. He always has. No Bobby Robson side that I played for ever went out to defend in the hope of getting a 0-0 draw – and I don't remember seeing any of his other teams do that either. Looking back, you have to think it was daft of Newcastle to sack Bobby because they've done nothing since he left.

Bobby has always been a great man and was first class for me in my playing days, but I'm not going to pretend I was sad when he was sacked by Newcastle. Football is a rat race and it's tough at times. But, like me, Bobby is lucky to have been involved in football so long, so I can't have sympathy for him. That's just not me. So no, I didn't feel sad for him but that's not to say I think it was a good decision. I don't know for certain why Bobby was sacked but surely it couldn't have been for results on the pitch because they finished fifth in his final season at Newcastle. The suggestion was that he couldn't control the so-called troublemakers among the players. I knew Bobby 25 years ago and I had more arguments with him than anyone but he got respect. He was certainly able to sort out the dressing room back then, but it wouldn't be right for me to comment on what happened at Newcastle because only the people who were there to see it would really know. But if Bobby was sacked for losing the dressing room then it is a strange one. I bet Graeme Souness wishes he had lost the dressing room by finishing fifth.

If Newcastle were playing, say, Tottenham in the FA Cup final and you put a gun to my head to make me choose the one that I'd hope would win, I would say Newcastle. The truth is I wouldn't lose any sleep if they won or lost. But I can understand diehard Sunderland fans not respecting that opinion because I know a lot of them would say they would rather Spurs would win any time, preferably 5-0. The show wouldn't be the same if they didn't have that rivalry. It wouldn't have that edge. It's no different with Middlesbrough. When Boro beat Bolton in the League Cup final, I was happy for them. Would I have been bothered if they had lost? No, not really.

I enjoy winding Geordies up when they call the show – knowing that I'll get a mouthful back – but I don't really take any great delight in their misery that Newcastle United are a nearly club that has gone backwards big time in recent years. Newcastle were very good to watch during the Kevin Keegan and Bobby Robson eras. Back then, if Newcastle were on the

The appointment of Souness was a strange one. I rated him as a top class player, as a tough character who could play a bit too, but I was surprised when Newcastle turned to him. He was a disaster for them. Apparently he was taken there to sort out alleged troublemakers among the players but instead things just got worse and worse on the pitch, where it really matters. It was clear that the club wasn't going anywhere and there were rumblings among the fans. Just as with

Sunderland and Peter Reid and with Middlesbrough and Bryan Robson, the Newcastle fans knew there was a problem and were saying so long before the club acknowledged the fact.

Now it's Glenn Roeder's chance and I say good luck to him. I won't lose any sleep if he loses his job but I don't wish it on him either. What I did think was sad was that when the 2006-07 season got underway there was no real expectation of any of the north-east teams winning anything. I'm proud to be a north-east lad but the rest of the country just felt our sides were making up the numbers, Newcastle included. I agreed with them. Sunderland were in the Championship, Newcastle have gone backwards over the last couple of years and I didn't expect Boro to do anything either. There is always a chance that Newcastle might eventually get back to where they were a few years ago but they've slipped back badly and are a million miles away from catching the likes of Liverpool or Man United.

•GREAT SCOTT?: It's a big year for new Geordie skipper Scott Parker.

Bernie's
LEGENDS 'n' LEG-ENDS

	Legends	Leg-ends
Boro players	Wilf Mannion	Jon Gittens
	George Hardwick	Phil Whelan
	George Camsell	Michael Ricketts
	Tony Mowbray	
	Colin Cooper	
British football	Ryan Giggs	David James
	Dennis Bergkamp	All Rangers players
	Thierry Henry	
World footballers	Maradona	Jean-Alain Boumsong
	Kenny Dalglish	Stephane Guivarc'h
	Ronaldinho	
Football managers	Alex Ferguson	Graeme Souness
	Bill Shankly	Lennie Lawrence
	Jock Stein	
	Brian Clough	
	George Graham	
Sports stars	Ian Botham	Tim Henman
	Ilie Nastase	Eddie the Eagle
	John McEnroe	
	Bjorn Borg	
	Jimmy Connors	
	Alex Higgins	
	Mark Spitz	

•LEG-END: Eddie the Eagle

•LEGEND: Morrissey

•LEG-END: Jordan

	Legends	**Leg-ends**
Musicians & singers	Morrissey	Kiss
	David Bowie	G4
	U2	Black Lace
	Bruce Springsteen	Posh Spice
	The Beatles	Paris Hilton
	Rolling Stones	Jordan
	Frank Sinatra	Right Said Fred
	Sade	Timmy Mallett
	Luciano Pavarotti (Gatosy's brother!)	
Songs	With or Without You (U2)	Agadoo (Black Lace)
	Life on Mars (Bowie)	Shaddup You Face (Joe Dolce)
	Some Girls are Bigger than Others (The Smiths)	Love Me Love My Dog (Peter Schelly)
Film stars	Jack Nicholson	Ant & Dec
	Al Pacino	Madonna
	Meryl Streep	Austin Powers
	John Travolta	
	John Holmes	
Films	One Flew Over the Cuckoo's Nest	The Blair Witch Project
	Angela's Ashes	A Clockwork Orange
	Some Mother's Son	Moulin Rouge
	Saturday Night Fever	
	The Jungle Book (I'm the King of the Swingers!)	

	Legends	**Leg-ends**
TV personalities	Jonathan Ross	Bob Johnson
	Lorraine Kelly	
	Michael Parkinson	
	Des Lynam	
TV shows	Match of the Day	Love Island
	The Banana Splits	Big Brother
World figures	Pope John Paul II	Margaret Thatcher
	Nelson Mandela	The royal family
	Steve Biko	Myra Hindley
	Mother Theresa	President Bush
	Diana	Henry VIII

•LEGEND: Ronaldinho

137

MIDDLESBROUGH

Bernie

WHEN BORO kicked off the 2006-07 campaign with celebrations for the 20th anniversary of the club's rebirth, it struck me what a rollercoaster of a ride the past two decades had been. Since almost going out of business in the summer of '86, the club has seen all manners of ups and downs including promotions, relegations, silverware, cup final defeats, glamorous European football and plenty of games that have bored the pants off me. As Gareth Southgate took his first steps into management as Steve McClaren's successor, I couldn't help but wonder whether the Riverside rollercoaster was in for another enjoyable up or a nasty, stomach-churning downturn.

Boro chairman Steve Gibson surprised us all when he made Gareth the new manager and I'll readily admit he wouldn't have been my choice for the job. But I wish him well in the role - and he will certainly need plenty of luck if he is to emulate what McClaren achieved at the club. You can say what you want about McClaren – and I said plenty for his five years on Teesside – but it doesn't change the fact that without doubt he was Boro's most successful manager ever.

I thank Steve very much for bringing Boro the Carling Cup, while the European adventure was fantastic and getting to the final itself just amazing. In my wildest dreams, I never even considered that we might one day get to a European final. No chance. 20 years ago we were in liquidation, the gates of Ayresome Park were locked and I was on 300 quid a week. Now we've moved on to a UEFA Cup final and players on 60 grand a week. But thank you, Steve McClaren. No-one will forget those exciting cup runs in a hurry. As the only Boro manager ever to win major silverware, Steve has to be our most successful manager. Best manager? I don't think so. I'd have to give Bruce Rioch that accolade because what he

achieved for Boro, taking the club from the Third to the First Division with very little to spend, was far greater than what McClaren did with bags of money. To coin one of McClaren's most overused words, what Bruce did really was magnificent.

I don't want to take anything away from the achievement of winning the Carling Cup. Winning that elusive trophy after 128 years of waiting was brilliant. I'll never forget that feeling of elation as the Millennium Stadium's lights were dimmed and a spotlight picked out the gleaming trophy as it was carried onto the pitch for the post-match presentation. What a wonderful feeling it was to know the cup was coming back to Teesside. On the phone-in after the match, grown men of 80 who had been watching Boro all their life were breaking down in tears, trying to take in the fact that they had lived to see the day when 'typical Boro' threw off the shackles of history and won major silverware.

But I still can't see McClaren as a great manager. Millwall got to the FA Cup final a few years ago when they were outside the top flight. If they had won, would that have made their then manager Dennis Wise a great manager? Of course it wouldn't. Luck can play a major part in winning a cup. Home draws against lesser opposition, refereeing decisions and the lottery of penalty shoot-outs can all tilt the balance in favour of a club that might otherwise have struggled. For all that I enjoyed it, I have absolutely no doubt that Boro had a lot of luck on their way to winning the Carling Cup in 2004. You need luck in life, of course, and McClaren was definitely a lucky manager. That's not a bad thing to have in any walk of life and he will need plenty of it as England manager.

Luck was one thing Mac's predecessor, Bryan Robson, didn't have. Unfortunately, Boro lost three cup finals in a row under Robbo but I would much rather it had been him, not McClaren, who had broken the duck and won us our first trophy. Robbo deserved to win something for the football his team played. For the first four years he was in charge at the

Riverside, Robbo's team were entertainers. All credit to him, because he attracted some world-class players to Teesside and they played some great football without ever getting real consistency in the league. The likes of Juninho, Ravanelli, Emerson, Barmby, Merson and Ziege were all smashing players and I loved watching them when they were on fire. Boro fans still have great memories of that team with Juninho and Ravanelli and yet they were relegated because they were defensively garbage. You are meant to build a team from the back but Robbo built from the front and paid the consequences. Then he went the other way and became more defensive and it was mainly downhill from there.

Unlike McClaren, Robbo always had a good rapport with the punters – at least until the final year or two he was at the club. Three times in 12 months he came so close to winning us a first cup. The Coca-Cola Cup final against Leicester in 1997 is the one that still stands out as the time we should have put a cup in the Riverside trophy cabinet. Boro were one-up with extra-time more or less over and I could see the red and white ribbons on the trophy from where I was commentating for Century. But instead of being professional and closing the game off, we kept on passing the ball and trying to entertain. Then we got done, with Heskey scoring at the death. It was a major disappointment and heart-breaking, especially as we didn't really turn up for the replay. Martin O'Neill was Leicester manager at the time and I can't help but think that it was a case of him showing us what a good manager he is. He had nothing like the money or resources Boro had but he won the cup.

Then came two more finals. The FA Cup that same season, a week after being relegated when we failed to win our final league match at Leeds. We were relegated because we failed to turn up for a match at Blackburn and had three points taken off us as our punishment. But for that, we'd have stayed up. Unbelievable. So I don't think the players' minds were focused for the final against Chelsea. We were 1-0 down in 43 seconds when one of our glamour boys, Emerson, didn't do his job and gave Roberto di Matteo the freedom of the park.

Never having made it to a major final until '97, Boro unbelievably got to a third the following season, when they were playing in Division One. Who do we get? Only Chelsea

again! I've never liked Chelsea, not since their fans chased me off the Stamford Bridge pitch after our play-off success there 20 years ago. We've had our moments against them over the years – in the first ever game at the Riverside, the 3-0 drubbing in McClaren's final campaign with us and then the early-season win in 2006-07 – but they've had the Indian sign over us in cup finals. Sure enough, we lost to them again in the 1998 Coca-Cola Cup final, just as we had in 1997 and 1990.

Robbo was a popular figure with the Boro faithful but he overstayed his welcome. When results started to dip, he should have moved on – and he definitely should have walked away with his head held high the day Terry Venables was appointed to help him out. Venables saved the club from almost certain relegation, but his appointment was just embarrassing for Robson. It was clear that Terry was really in charge and Robbo's fate was sealed when the fans booed him during a lap of honour after the final game of the season. So it was exit Robson. The top job was offered to Venables but he turned it down – as he would do so again five years later – and in came Steve McClaren.

With all the money and backing he had from Gibson, Mac had more chance than most to do well as a manager – but he still never convinced me. He took the Carling Cup seriously in 2004 and won it, then got cocky the following season and virtually gave the cup away. The Euro run was great, but he neglected the league. He tried to explain our poor league position away by suggesting we weren't bothered about the Premiership, but even when we were taking it seriously we were crap. There was always a lot of what I would call kidology with Steve. Too often he would try to hoodwink the fans, but it didn't work.

It's my opinion that Premiership managers should be judged on the 38 league games when they are playing so-called top class opposition week in and week out. All the cup runs in the world can't hide the fact that Boro were majorly disappointing in the league for most of the five years under McClaren. Only once did his side beat his predecessor Robbo's best finishing position. That's terrible. Yes, he did great in the cups but far more should have been achieved in the league.

But there's another reason that, despite all his success, McClaren wasn't popular with the Teesside faithful. In fact, there's a lot of reasons. They go beyond the fact that everything was geared around the cups with the Premier League often forgotten about. I know it puzzles a lot of people who don't follow the club why the most successful manager in our history was so unpopular with the club's supporters. I think the pros just outweighed the cons.

There were plenty of positives with him, apart from the fact that he won us our only major silverware. I thought he was very professional, methodical, enthusiastic and ambitious in his approach to management and coaching. In five years I never read one bad thing in the press about Boro players - and I think that McClaren deserves much of the credit for that. I'm deliberately ignoring here the reports of Abel Xavier's worldwide ban for taking performance-enhancing drugs, which at least went some way to explaining his outrageous hairstyle and beard! But during a time when Newcastle and Sunderland seemed to attract plenty of bad press, it was to Mac's credit that Boro never did, especially after all the reports of Boro having been a boozing club in Robbo's days in charge.

So why did the fans never warm to Steve? It's a complex question but the answer has to involve some of the things he said. Suggesting entertainment didn't matter was a bad one, as was the thought that the fans needed 'educating'. One thing that annoyed me and most fans to death was his habit of describing Boro performances as 'magnificent' or 'breath-taking' when a blind man could see they were far from it. That was just insulting the intelligence of the paying public. Then he had the audacity to have a go at the supporters for not turning up. He was right, they weren't turning up, but you can't say things like that when you and the brand of football your team plays are part of the reason they are choosing to stay at home. Jose Mourinho can get away with saying controversial stuff because he is full of charisma but McClaren wasn't in such a fortunate position.

On top of that came the reality of low league positions and lack of entertainment. We saw some great one-off games at the Riverside, especially in his final season on Teesside, with the emphatic wins over Man United and Chelsea, plus two of

the greatest comebacks I've ever seen, against Basel and Steaua Bucharest. But the paying public buy season tickets for the league games and, in the main, they were boring. With all the big-name players at the club, Boro should have been playing more free-flowing football on a consistent basis. But too much of what McClaren was about involved negative tactics and an overly cautious approach to most games, even home matches against opposition we should have been putting on the back foot from the off. It's an understatement to say he was negative. He was geared towards not giving a goal away. He used to say the first goal was always the most important. I don't think Kevin Keegan ever had that attitude when he was Newcastle manager. Then there was this thing I saw England doing in the World Cup, defending corners with every player in their own box with no player left up front as an outlet. That was something Boro fans had put up with for a long time before England did it. For the life of me, I don't see the benefits in that. There was a lot of things he did that I, as a football fan and ex-professional footballer, didn't get and couldn't understand.

•WINNERS: Bernie's sons, Dominic (right) and Ryan with the Carling Cup in 2004.

I have heard people say that the team that got us to the UEFA Cup final was Boro's best ever group of players, but I can't agree. The team I watched 10 years earlier with Ravanelli and Juninho in it was far better. That side got relegated but it was much better to watch – and they got to three cup finals as well. People ask me, 'What do you want – a team that plays nice football or a team that wins?' I want an entertaining team that wins. Given the choice, I would prefer to watch the team of 1996-97 – and if you asked the 35,000 people that used to watch Robbo's team I think they would agree.

I can't say I ever really got to know Steve during his time with Boro. In fact, only once did I have a proper chat with him. When he first got the Boro job, he invited me to the club's training ground for a chat. I think he wanted to pick the little brains that I've got. He asked me about the team and we chatted about what he hoped to achieve. Then we talked about my role on The Three Legends show and I told him that I was honest and that I had strong opinions. He said he expected us to be at loggerheads throughout his reign as manager - and he was right, we were. Every now and then I got to hear that he was unhappy with my comments about the team, tactics or performances. He never confronted me but I'd rather he had. He certainly had plenty of opportunities but I guess he preferred to just ignore me.

Listening to Steve always got my back up. The truth is, I thought he was false – even before the introduction of his gleaming new teeth. I just thought he came across as unnatural and staged. I think he turned into a different animal in front of the TV cameras. Off the camera, he was more natural but he was groomed. He must have thought that was the right way to go but it was misguided. His tutor, who I believe was instrumental in everything McClaren said and did, was Bill Beswick. Boro's resident psychologist was the manager's crutch. I would regularly see them sitting in the stand before or after games, I guess discussing what they were going to say or do. I've heard that Beswick's advice included finding three positives in every negative. It was probably as a consequence of such guidance that Steve would say Boro were magnificent when it was plain to see we had been crap. It was ironic that one of the few times that he would have been justified in using his favourite word, the day of our Carling Cup victory, 'magnificent' never even touched his lips.

It's always been my opinion that birds and football don't mix, but McClaren and his sidekick obviously disagreed, if two tales I heard about their motivational tactics were anything to go by. In my days as a player we used to watch pornos to get motivated. I guess you could say it made us hard to beat! Under Beswick's guidance, the Boro players were still watching birds, but very much of the feathered kind.

This particular method came to light after Bolo Zenden scored a fine UEFA Cup goal in Austria against Grazer AK and then started flapping his arms. I wondered what this weird goal celebration was all about and was told by someone, whose name will remain anonymous to protect the guilty, that it was after watching 'the geese video'. The mind boggled. 'Geese?' I asked. Apparently, the video the players had been shown was all about how geese fly in formation and help each other. It was all about team spirit and morale, something McClaren and Beswick were obviously trying to instil more of in the Boro side. Thereafter, Jimmy Floyd Hasselbaink tried a similar wing-flapping celebration. I thought for a minute he was trying to get airborne but there was no way Jimmy could take off with that backside! The lads were obviously taking the Micky, as we were on the Legends show.

In fact, I think Steve's relationship with me was soured after the geese episode. I think our criticism ruffled his feathers! I can't see how watching a flock of geese could have motivated a team of professional footballers but why was Mac embarrassed about it? Someone from the club told me that he had a bee in his bonnet and that he might come and have a word with me. He never did do, though I wish he had. I certainly didn't hide – or take flight!

But Bill – or Buffalo as I took to calling him – was obviously something of a bird fancier if another tale I heard was anything to go by. This time, the story went that he had been telling the players about positive and negative parrots that apparently sit on everyone's shoulders. I understand that his advice was to listen to the positive parrot that would give you a 'can do' attitude, rather than the negative parrot. I'd had a chuckle about this but had put it to the back of my mind until one night at Century when the studio had been given a Caribbean theme for some reason. I looked up and there sat two plastic parrots. Not being knowledgeable enough on the subject to know my positive parrot from the negative variety, I decided to take no chances and took both of them, hanging them up behind our matchday commentary position at the back of the Riverside's West Stand. Incredibly, the birds were left hanging there all season, much to the amusement of those who spotted them. I never did work out which parrot was which. In fact, I'm even tempted to believe that there's no such thing as a positive or a negative parrot. Sorry, Bill.

For all the ups and downs of Mac's first four seasons on Teesside, none of them came close to the rollercoaster that was 2005-06, his final year at the helm. It will be remembered by many for the way he led us to the UEFA Cup final and FA Cup semi-final before he got the England job, but should also be remembered for awful league form and the fact that Steve Gibson kept faith in him when many chairmen would have sacked him.

The season was full of contradictions, so Boro fans never knew whether to laugh or cry. It frustrated me from the very start that McClaren insisted on playing Gaizka Mendieta on the right wing. Even before the season began, I said that there was no way that Mendi and Michael Reiziger could play together down the right. Reiziger had been a good player but was past it, while Mendi was never an outside right. Sure enough, it didn't work and Reiziger was shipped out, though McClaren persisted in playing Mendieta out of position until his injury. It was similar to the way Steve had played Bolo Zenden at outside left when Stewart Downing was clearly the man to play there. He held Stewy back. Only when Mendieta got injured did he move Zenden inside - and he was an absolute star, player of the season, while Downing showed us what he could do. That wasn't good management or ability by Mac. That was sheer luck.

The truth is we went backwards in McClaren's final season. Reaching a European final was a marvellous achievement but it papered over the cracks. Ultimately, we finished a lowly 14th in the league and had nothing to show for all our efforts in the cup competitions. Mac rested big name players ahead of the big games, only for us to perform poorly on the day. People have said to me that proof of the fact such a tactic worked was that we won the UEFA Cup semi-final against Bucharest. But I would remind them that we got beat by an average West Ham team in the FA Cup semi-final and didn't turn up for the UEFA Cup final. So despite all the chopping, changing and resting, we didn't win a thing.

And it's my opinion that Mac killed Yakubu with his squad system. I thought The Yak was quality in the first half of the season, he looked worth every penny of his £7.5 million fee. He looked like he was enjoying it, he was beating men, he was strong, quick and scoring goals. In the second half of the

season, when he was in and out of the side, no matter what, he was a totally different animal, but I don't blame him - I blame the manager. Yak was 24 and couldn't handle being left out. Why do you need a rest when you're a young player and on fire? 'Oh, you're doing well. Now I'm going to leave you out and give one of the other guys a chance to take your place.' It's like a punishment. He was on fire – and he wouldn't have gone out. He'd have carried on scoring and gone way passed the 20-goal mark. It was bonkers to leave him out. I'd never heard the likes of it.

Then, of course, Boro hammered the likes of Chelsea and Man United but lost at home to Sunderland, the Premier League's worst team ever. That tells me that when Boro played the big boys, the big players motivated themselves; the manager and psychologist didn't need to get involved. It was time for Steve and Bill to earn their corn when we were facing the lesser sides - that's when the players needed lifting and to focus, but they didn't do it. You've got all the motivation you need when you're playing the likes of Chelsea and Man U, but good players maybe need a wee lift against the lesser teams and we couldn't do it against the so-called smaller sides. Consistency? No chance. It was Jekyll and Hyde all the way. Out of 64 games, I probably saw 12 great performances and a hell of a lot more garbage.

In the guise of Mr Hyde, I couldn't believe it when Boro lost to Sunderland, the whipping boys of the Premier League. We got beat three and four by teams that could hardly play. Aston Villa were crap but they walloped us. As good as we gave the champions Chelsea, Villa gave us the same – and on our own patch.

But the other half of Boro's split personality, Dr Jekyll, came to the fore in the home legs of our UEFA Cup quarter-final and semi-final with Basel and Bucharest. Even Ali Brownlee, the ultimate optimist, had given up the ghost before we twice started comebacks that defied belief. The first one, Basel, we went three goals down and Ali looked at me and wrote on a piece of paper, 'That's it.' The look on his face told me he was thinking what I and most Boro fans were thinking - we were out. Unbelievably, we came back to win through to the semi-final. To do it again a couple of weeks later in such similar circumstances, and against better opposition in Steaua had me thinking that God must be a Boro fan. That night as we celebrated reaching a European final in the most dramatic way was the happiest I have been as a Boro fan. Everyone thought our name was on the cup, including me. But we were all wrong.

McClaren obviously played his part in those two great games. You have to give credit where it's due. He played all four centre-forwards to inspire the comebacks, which I have never seen a manager do in all my years of playing and watching the game. He threw caution to the wind, risking getting beat by six, but the strategy came off. Given his ultra-cautionary mentality, I think he showed a lot of balls to do that.

Apart from the flights, I thought the whole European experience was brilliant. There were some great trips and great performances. If we'd won the final, it would have been one hell of an achievement, but what a let-down the big game against Sevilla was. I really thought we had a great chance of winning the cup but we were way under par on the night. The guys who had been rested, like Southgate, Jimmy and Mark Viduka, were poor on the night but no matter how we played I think we'd have still got beat. I had heard reports that Sevilla were technically a very gifted side. That was misleading because they weren't just gifted, technically they were brilliant. They had such pace in the side. Five of their players were like Whippets. When McClaren switched to the four centre forwards by throwing on Maccarone and Yakubu, I didn't believe it would work again. I knew Sevilla would have had us watched and seen videos of our previous games, so they would have known that we might try that again. As it was, Viduka missed a great chance to equalise. We'll never know, but even if he had scored I don't think that would have really changed the game. I think Sevilla were far superior to Boro in every department and we just couldn't deal with them. They scored four and it could have been more. Boro were treading water towards the end. Maybe the occasion was too big for some of our players.

I have to say this about the Boro fans: I think they let themselves and the club down in the final. The Sevilla fans were in the stadium two hours before kick-off, generating a great atmosphere with flags, colour and songs. In a typical display of British mentality, Boro fans came in dribs and drabs, only really arriving in numbers about 35 minutes before the game got underway. I would have thought being there early to savour and create the atmosphere would have been worth missing another couple of pints for, but I heard some of our fans were asleep throughout the game because they were p****d. Don't get me wrong, i'm not saying that's why we got beat 4-0, but I think it needs saying that the Boro fans were poor on the big occasion.

While I'm on the subject, I've got to state that Boro have far too many fair-weather fans. There were apparently thousands of 'devoted' supporters who couldn't get tickets for the final in Eindhoven but I couldn't help but wonder where these fans were in the earlier rounds back on Teesside. We were crying out for European football for all those years and it finally came - admittedly some of it against pub teams I'd never heard of, like Litex Bras and Dnipro – only for the fans to not even bother turning up. I heard all the excuses under the sun for why they didn't turn up. It was too warm, it was too cold, it was too expensive and, on one occasion, that Ken Dodd was on at the town hall. Why they didn't just admit they couldn't be bothered, that they'd rather sit in the house or go down the pub to watch it, I don't know. The fans went on about McClaren not being honest, but many of them weren't either. These people that go down the pub to watch the games, I don't call them true fans. That's not support. If they can afford to have five pints, they can afford to go to the game.

One fan I will give credit to is the guy who threw his season ticket at McClaren during the 4-0 home defeat to Aston Villa. I think his actions woke up McClaren and the players. It let them know that the people of Teesside weren't going to accept crap displays like that. They'd had enough of it. In fact, that day most fans would have told you they'd had enough of McClaren, and I was one of them. The Villa defeat was the culmination of a terrible run of results and thoughts of relegation had started to enter my mind, because we really weren't playing well. The crowd was understandably full of groans and moans. That day, for the first time, I heard the Boro fans singing the name of McClaren. Unfortunately, for him, it was followed by another word – out!

Without a doubt, I thought Gibson would sack McClaren. In truth, he was probably a game away from giving him the chop, so that amazing result against Chelsea saved him. You have to say, 'Well done, Steve Gibson.' He didn't go with what the public were demanding. You have to take your hat off to Gibson, that guy has never let us down. He pulled off a masterstroke in keeping faith with Mac because everyone wanted him to pull the trigger, but he stuck with him and the guy ended up leading us to the UEFA Cup final.

Gibson has been accused of being too loyal to his managers and was criticised for allegedly being too close to Bryan Robson when he was in charge. But he couldn't be accused of that with McClaren. In fact, I bet Gibbo was glad to get rid of him. I can imagine he had a few sleepless nights when it looked like Phillipe Scolari was going to get the England job instead of Mac. If you're wondering why I would believe that, then ask yourself if you would be happy with your missus if she tried to go with three other men. Then think about what Steve Gibson must have felt when McClaren tried to leave Boro for Leeds, Newcastle United and Chelsea. A lot of fans have heard whispers suggesting he nearly moved to those clubs, but I can say that without fear of anyone suing me because I know it was true. He was always looking for a way out. There's nothing wrong with being ambitious and using the club as a stepping stone but it was the way he did it.

Gibson gave McClaren his big opportunity, gave him millions to spend and then stuck with him when many others would have given him the chop. If he had sacked him in February – and few would have blamed him if he had – then McClaren would not only have never got near the England job but I honestly believe it would have been years before he even got another Premier League club. His credibility would have been shot. But Gibbo stuck with him and the rest is history. He should give Gibson half his England wages!

As you might have guessed, I don't miss McClaren. At the airport after the cup final in Eindhoven, Ali spotted Mac and made a beeline for him, to wish him all the best and give him a kiss goodbye. I couldn't even bring myself to talk to him. It would have been two-faced of me because I was glad to see the back of him. He obviously ticked all the right boxes with the FA in a way that other contenders for the England job, like Sam Allardyce, didn't. Whether or not you like McClaren, it is a fact that he has done brilliantly to get the England job. That

is some achievement. But I think he'll be mullered by the national press. And I don't see the football changing. My prediction is that England fans will think Sven is still in charge and will realise that it has been McClaren's tactics they've been watching for the last few years.

As I'm not an England fan, I'm glad the FA went for McClaren. But if I'd been them, I'd have gone for Martin O'Neill. He was the best equipped for the job. He ticked all the boxes - he's smart, he has worked his way up the ladder and has sampled European football. For me, he was the top man. People associate him with long-ball football but he plays that style when it suits. Under his management, I once saw Celtic play 47 passes before scoring in a Champions League match. That isn't long-ball, is it? He simply uses it as an option. If you win with it, the fans will happily live with it. He won two cups in England, the treble in Scotland and got to the UEFA Cup final, just like McClaren. But, like Brian Clough and Jack Charlton before him, O'Neill isn't an FA man and wouldn't have been a puppet for them.

Ironically, Martin O'Neill would also have been my choice as McClaren's successor as Boro manager. He was the dream man, not because of his background with my boyhood heroes, Celtic, but simply because he was ideal. I know the club talked to O'Neill about the vacancy but I don't know why nothing came of it. I have heard suggestions that Gibson told him his dream was to bring the kids through, but that O'Neill told him he would do it his way. I can see why Gibson wants to build a team of local stars, but if you employ a manager, he has to have final say and you have to let him do it his way, no matter how you think it should be done. O'Neill has proved he can do it. I think we needed someone like him, someone who is charismatic, ruthless, talks the same language as the public and does it his way and no-one else's. I know he has certain circumstances regarding his wife, who has been seriously ill, and those issues are far more important than any job, but I would have been happy for him to have only worked three or four days a week, if that was what was needed to get him to accept the job. His mentor, Brian Clough, only turned up on the training ground a couple of days a week when he was Nottingham Forest manager. Anyway, there have been times when we've employed players on 60 grand a week who only

•THE RIGHT MAN: Martin O'Neill would have been Bernie's choice for the England and Boro jobs.

145

turned up three days a week. Boro's loss is undoubtedly Aston Villa's gain.

The other candidate Steve Gibson spoke to about taking the job was Terry Venables but I didn't fancy that idea at all. Terry did a great job in keeping us up a few years ago but he based his success on a sound defence and I don't recall seeing much attacking football that season. Sure, he had attacking teams when he was in charge of Spurs and England, but he had a nightmare at Leeds, admittedly at a difficult time for the club. I thought the idea that he was going to somehow groom Gareth Southgate and Colin Cooper as future managers was bizarre. I had my doubts he wanted to come into that environment. Although he joined up with McClaren for England, I don't think he'd have been committed enough to take on the Boro job. He has business interests going on in Spain and remains a Jack the lad. He still has the charm, but when I think of Venables, I imagine him opening his coat to reveal wads of mobile phones and watches, an Arthur Daley type character. He wasn't what we needed.

My next choice as Boro manager after O'Neill turned us down would have been Tony Mowbray, my old Middlesbrough captain, who has done so well in charge of Hibernian since moving to Scotland. Mogga plied his trade as a coach at Ipswich, has tasted European football with Hibs and has generally done very well north of the border. In fact, he even won the Scottish Manager of the Year Award ahead of O'Neill and Alex McLeish when they were in charge of Celtic and Rangers. To be fair, I thought Mowbray was a definite once Venables and O'Neill were non-starters. If it had been up to me, I'd certainly have loved to bring him back to Teesside – but only with his old Boro boss, Bruce Rioch as his sidekick. For me, as a Boro fan, that would have been the dream partnership. In fact, I suggested the idea to Boro's chief executive Keith Lamb.

I got the impression most Boro fans would have been happy with Tony too, though I was generally a lone voice when it came to shouting up Bruce's claims for a Teesside return. I think Bruce would be a fantastic assistant to Tony, having seen and done it all. I met Bruce at the time Boro were still looking for McClaren's replacement. I travelled over to Denmark, where he was managing Odense, to interview him

for my autobiographical DVD. It was clear that he still had the passion and love for the game, though he had clearly mellowed a bit from his spell in charge at Boro. In fact, he admitted that when he thinks back he regrets some of the things he did and said back then. When I talked up his claims at the time, some people said he would be out of touch with top-level English football, as his last job over here was with Wigan in 2000-01. Knowing Bruce as I do, I'm sure he won't be out of touch at all. Who's in touch or out of touch anyway? I don't go along with this line about football dinosaurs. It's nonsense. Pants. Bruce always knew the game inside out and still does, in my opinion.

Whether Mogga would have gone for a coaching partnership with Rioch, I don't know, though the two of them loved each other back in their Boro days and still keep in touch. What I do know is that Tony and Bruce would have been up for a Boro comeback. When I interviewed Mowbray for my DVD, I asked him if he would come back and he said that he would love to if everything was right. I asked Bruce the same question and he admitted he would love to have another go. The truth is that the two of them talk the same language, love football and love the Boro. Why Steve Gibson never offered Tony the job, I'll never know, especially as he ended up giving it to a managerial novice in Gareth Southgate.

When it was finally confirmed that McClaren was joining England, the bookies immediately offered odds on all of his potential successors. In there with the likes of Venables, O'Neill and Mowbray was one Bernie Slaven. Initially I thought it was funny that my odds were as short as 10-1. People I knew had a laugh about it and we all had a joke, but Boro later appointed someone else without managerial experience and there wasn't so much as a snigger. I've got every respect for Gareth but I believe I've got a far greater affinity with Boro than he has and, unlike him, I had already qualified for my UEFA B badge. On every count, I've got more than Southgate but he's the manager and I'm left to spend my working hours with Malcolm Macdonald, Eric Gates and Alastair Brownlee. There's no justice in the world!

Joking aside, I'd be lying if I said I wouldn't want the Boro job. I'd have snapped Steve Gibson's hand off if he had said to me, 'Look, Bernie, I still haven't got a manager I know you're

•MISSED OPPORTUNITY? Bernie would have gone for Tony Mowbray as Boro boss, as his second choice to Martin O'Neill.

a popular lad among the fans and you've got your B badge. I'd like you to be our new manager.' The first thing I'd have said would have been, 'Wait a minute, I ain't managed professionals. I need somebody to help me and tutor me along the way.' And Rioch is the man I'd have gone for. Like I say, he's been there, he's done it. He still has an aura and a presence about him, although he's more relaxed than he once was. He's still the immaculate Bruce that I remember so well – and he would make the perfect managerial mentor.

So what would I change at Boro if I was in charge? I'd certainly make every effort to get rid of some of the high earners who are no longer good enough, though I accept that's easier said than done. I'd tell the players to go forward more than we've become accustomed to Boro doing in recent years. Just as Gareth said he would do, I'd definitely set out to change the negative mentality and way of thinking instilled in the players by five years under Steve McClaren. The players inside would be under instruction to spoonfeed Stewart Downing and James Morrison, or whoever was playing on the right, at every opportunity. Downing is there on the left wing because he's got a left peg that nobody else in this country has got, so my message would be to give him the ball. Bolo Zenden was great at that when he was playing central midfield for Boro. If he got the ball, it was 'there you go', straight to Downing on the left wing. When Zenden left the club, Downing didn't see enough of the ball.

By the way, my views on Mowbray and Rioch weren't influenced by the fact that I might have got a coaching job if they had been in charge at Boro, though who knows what might have happened? When I interviewed Mogga, my final question was, 'By the way, if you do get the Middlesbrough job down the line, you will employ me as a striking coach, won't you?' I told him I was fed up with hearing Ali uttering the same old crap every week! He laughed, but his answer was serious. He told me that, if it helped the team even one per cent, then yes, he would employ me. On second thoughts, I don't think working with the strikers and continuing my radio work would work. Imagine the stick I'd get on the phone-in every time one of our forwards missed a sitter!

As we all now know, Steve Gibson decided to give Gareth Southgate the job of taking up the mantle from McClaren. I'm

honest enough to say that he wouldn't have been my choice, but if there was one player from Boro's UEFA Cup final squad that was a possibility for the role it had to be Southgate. That might seem like a flippant remark but it's not meant to be. From the playing squad, I'd have picked him, even ahead of my old team-mate and true Boro legend, Colin Cooper. I think Gareth is a bigger personality than Coops, more radiant. I've got massive respect for Coops but even in his younger days as a player he never struck me as exuberant or full of life. I think he has always been a little too deadpan, though I won't be surprised if he goes on to become an excellent coach.

I think Gareth talks very well, carries himself extremely well and, most important of all, he's an honest man. He has had to change in terms of his relationship with the players, but I will be interested to see how he speaks to the media. I hope he stays the same person because, as a player, he always impressed when he spoke. I usually found myself agreeing with what he had to say as he was always honest in his assessment of performances. Without hearing what I'd had to say, Gareth would usually back me up. He had seen the same game as me – unlike Steve McClaren. I was fed up with the tripe Steve was dishing out in his interviews. I would often stand at the back of his post-match press conferences and wonder what he was talking about. It was as if he had literally seen a different game. I'd hate to think Gareth would be anything like that as a manager. Early indications suggested he was going to be as honest as ever, even when the team had lost.

If I was a manager, I'm not sure I would say anything different to the press than I would to the players' faces in the dressing room. I'd maybe not pick out individuals when I was talking to the media. I wouldn't slag my players off in public because it would be stupid of any manager to start saying, 'Well, so and so was crap and whatshisname never held the ball up.' But I'd say that up front we hadn't held the ball up well and we didn't do it in midfield, without naming the culprits. I'd probably go through it in units, but the fans would know who I was talking about.

Managers can't be hypercritical – or they shouldn't be. Why managers do that, I don't know. When he was Boro manager, I know McClaren would often give it to the players straight, but he had a totally different message for the public. Why? If fans hear the manager picking out the positives from an awful game, they think, 'What game was he at?' You ain't kidding anyone by doing that, certainly not the fans. Sometimes I wonder if some managers think the public are thick and it's only players that understand the game. It's a difficult tightrope to walk, but you've got to be as honest as you can, otherwise all you're doing is embarrassing yourself and annoying the fans, the people that keep you in a job.

Not all managers are like that, of course. Gareth's old Crystal Palace team-mate, Fulham boss Chris Coleman, is the most honest manager around. I sometimes hear his post-match interviews and think, 'I tell you what, mate, you are dead honest.' It's wallop, no excuses. He practically says, 'We were crap,' without using those words. He is the most honest guy in the Premier League. Stuart Pearce and Sam Allardyce have always had similar reputations for saying it like it is, Jose Mourinho too. I take my hat off to the honest managers.

I don't really know Gareth, though I was delighted to get a chance to sit down and talk to him before the 2006-07 season got underway because I was keen to start up a better relationship with him than I had with McClaren. We had a good chat about our thoughts on the team and the players and I wished him well. One thing is for sure, I won't be as critical of any mistakes Gareth makes because I know he's a young manager, finding his feet in a difficult job. Whether Boro can continue progressing or have gone as far as we can go depends on what money Southgate gets to spend. Without the finance, I can't see there being much progress.

Robert Huth was the only big-money signing during the summer of 2006, though we nicked Julio Arca off the Mackems. But the big transfer story for Boro was the signing of Jonathan Woodgate on a year's loan from Real Madrid. There's no doubt that was a massive coup for Boro and for Gareth Southgate. I have always rated Woodgate as one of the best defenders around, and certainly better than his former Leeds team-mate Rio Ferdinand. I don't doubt Woodgate's quality for one second, but I still wondered if bringing him home to Teesside was the right thing to do.

First of all, I looked at his record of something like 13 games

in two years. That clearly left a big question mark over his fitness. I worried that if he was going to be in for three games and then out for five that would disrupt the defence and destabilise the whole team. Then there was a concern over Woodgate's troublesome past off the pitch. But the player insisted that he had matured and put all that behind him while, in Southgate, he has a perfect role model as a player and as a person. On top of all that, I was left wondering what would happen if Woodgate stayed fit and had a great season. Would he then stay with Boro on a permanent basis, as the Riverside faithful would hope, or would he head back to Real Madrid? And if, for whatever reason, Madrid still didn't want him back, wouldn't the likes of Man United and Liverpool be circling?

Thanks to the products of the club's fantastic academy, Boro have shown in recent times that there is more to squad building than dipping into the transfer market. Back in my Boro side of '86, we had a Teesside team and people said it would never be repeated, but in the final Premier League game of 2005-06 it happened again. All but one of the 11 starters and five subs against Fulham were homegrown players, each of them local lads. It was a nothing game with little to play for as Boro prepared for the UEFA Cup final, but when I saw the team I was delighted to be there to witness the occasion. They were all young boys, with an average age of about 20, but I thought they were great on the day. I know a lot of people think, or at least hope, that those players will become the core of the Middlesbrough team for years to come. Unfortunately, I can't see it. Five years down the line I think the majority of them will be long gone - some of them to Liverpool and some of them to The Dog & Gun.

One player The Dog & Gun should not plan on signing is Stewart Downing. I like Downing, big time. He is going to go far. Some clueless fans tell me that he doesn't tackle much or that he doesn't have a big heart. If that argument held any water then they should be saying that George Boateng doesn't score many goals, so he must be crap too. It's nonsense. Downing's not employed to tackle. He tracks back but, like me in my playing days, he doesn't really know what to do next. Downing has a left peg that no-one else in England has got. That's why he's in the England squad. I can only think that some people are green with envy to see the local lad who

•IN CHARGE: but Gareth Southgate will only take Boro forward with the right financial backing.

started with nothing doing well for himself and enjoying the good lifestyle he deserves. I'm sure the critics wouldn't be so hard on him if Boro had signed him for £10 million. Despite it all, he's not a big time Charlie. He's a great lad but I think some people resent his success.

On Boro's right wing, James Morrison can still do well, given a bit more belief. He's not in Downing's class but there's enough there to excite us. Lee Cattermole was fantastic in his first season but it will be a tall order for him to keep doing it. I've seen the likes of Steve Baker, Mark Summerbell and Anthony Ormerod come and go – lads who initially made a big impact but all too quickly disappeared without a trace. Lads like Morrison, Cattermole, Stuart Parnaby, Andrew Taylor, Tony McMahon, Andrew Davies and Adam Johnson have to make sure they don't go the same way. There are such high hopes for all of them, but history tells us that we'll be lucky if three of them really make it.

I went on record to say that the 2005-06 season was a big one for Boro, but 2006-07 is even bigger. The league form definitely has to improve because the odds of getting to another cup final are slim. But I saw nothing early season to alter my belief that we'd finish mid-table again. What gives me hope for the future is that Gibbo is still at the helm. He's no mug. He surprised us all with Southgate, as he did when he stuck with McClaren in February. Like me, many fans were stunned with Southgate's appointment, but my feeling was always that if that was who the chairman believed in then I and every other Boro fan should get behind him. Come the summer of 2007, we might look back on it as a nightmare decision or a masterstroke. I hope it's the latter.

Malcolm

AS A proud Englishman, I wish Steve McClaren all the very best with our national side but I don't give him too much hope. How he ever got English football's top job, I don't know, because it defies logic. Why was he even on the radar? He has got to where he is without the back-up of having achieved what you should before being bestowed such an honour.

Just look at our most successful England managers. Alf Ramsey, who led this country to its only World Cup success, won the Division One championship with little Ipswich. That's a qualification to get the England job. Bobby Robson, again with Ipswich, had them in the top six year after year for a decade, winning them a couple of major honours along the way, so he deserved the England job too. Now Steve McClaren comes along but based on what? Okay, he won the Carling Cup but that isn't enough. It's a one-off success in a competition that doesn't compare to winning either the Premier League title or even the FA Cup. Yes, he got Boro to the UEFA Cup final but he didn't win it.

Don't get me wrong, I would dearly love for him to succeed and to discover a whole crop of youngsters. If he can get England playing to their potential then he will turn the tide, but he has got an incredibly tough job. Steve has got to find a completely new and different style of play, something that will make Boro fans ask, 'Why didn't he do that when he was at the Riverside?'

But I feel sorry for him because in many ways he is p***ing against the wind. I hope he is able to distance himself from what happened under Sven Goran Eriksson but I think he has already been sussed by the London press. If you haven't got them on your side, you've got no chance because they will have you sooner or later. They had it in for Eriksson and eventually got their way. The fact that none of them appeared to be in support of Steve's appointment as Eriksson's successor wasn't the best of starts.

The FA thought Eriksson was a master tactician but he didn't have a clue. In Italy, he was known as 'the lucky loser' because he had a record of getting to finals but never winning anything. I won't say he is a con man but I think he has kidded his way through football, learning to put on that Swedish lack of expression and getting away with murder by speaking in such simplistic terms so that he actually never really said anything. Personally, I don't think he has a clue about the game and how it should be played. I believe Steve McClaren was doing it all for him. His complete lack of passion just made it all the worse. I wasn't expecting histrionics from him while he watched from the bench but I did expect to see someone who looked like they were in charge and knew what they wanted.

I have no doubt that Steve McClaren will give it everything. But there will always be a huge drawback for him, just as there was for Sven Goran Eriksson and Graham Taylor before him – and that is that he never played at international level. You can read all your coaching manuals you want but there's always going to be a credibility gap. So who would I have appointed, if not McClaren? How about Alan Ball? Yes, I can hear the cries now of, 'Alan Ball? You have to be joking!' But I most certainly am not.

When I first made the England squad, Bobby Moore was captain of the national team, an honour he had held with great distinction before and after leading the country to success in the 1966 World Cup. But by the time I was in the squad in 1972, I felt Bally should have been captain. That is no criticism of Bobby in any way, but Bally was already playing the captain's role, long before he eventually took the armband. He was brilliant at welcoming new boys like myself and taking us under his wing. He was always a terrific leader of good players and strong men. Wo betide you, however, if you weren't a good player or strong man. There, perhaps, was Bally's failing as a manager, as he was always in charge of lesser clubs, such as Portsmouth, Stoke City and Blackpool. But I always felt it was wrong to judge him on his success or otherwise in managing such clubs. Bally has been completely overlooked for consideration for the England job because of his deemed lack of success with lesser clubs. But what did Alan Ball know about players at that level? After all, he had only ever played at the very highest level!

I know that great players aren't necessarily great managers, but Alan was the manager even when he was only a player. I saw that man lift and carry the England team, often doing the manager's job, but there he was messing around with the likes of Portsmouth (long before their more recent elevated status). I have a sneaking feeling he would have found real success had he had the opportunity to manage a top club, perhaps one of his former sides, like Everton or Arsenal. Then, I think, we'd have seen the real Alan Ball as manager. He would have been the very best had he been England manager and had the opportunity to select from the country's top players. Now I know he will never get that chance. In my opinion, it is England's loss.

Steve McClaren shows a passion for the game that was beyond Eriksson and he is clearly a good coach. But a coach is exactly what he is. In my opinion, he is misrepresenting himself to football because he is not a manager, he's a coach. The most important part of being a manager is psychology and how to treat each player differently. Every player is totally different and you have to deal with them like that. The fact that McClaren needed a psychologist, Bill Beswick, as his assistant at Middlesbrough tells me that he isn't a manager. Taking Beswick with him to the FA is just embarrassing.

One thing I learned during my time in the game was that the great managers are also great psychologists. The great managers I played under – Bobby Robson, Alec Stock, Joe Harvey and Alf Ramsey – were all great psychologists. They didn't need to employ somebody else to do it. As a manager, you have to find a way. During my time at Arsenal, Don Howe was a great coach. I asked him how it had all gone so wrong for him as manager at West Brom when he was clearly such a wonderful coach. He told me that he had discovered that he wasn't a manager. It was something he didn't know until he had tried it but he knew he never wanted to manage again.

McClaren's belief in team rotation at Middlesbrough was a nonsense – and a tactic that I am sure annoyed his players even more than it did the club's supporters. It doesn't do anyone any good. Resting players to ensure they stay fresh? The last thing that players who are playing well want is a rest. The games can't come quick enough. I used to hate it when there wasn't a midweek game. There was nothing better than a game three or four days after scoring on a Saturday. If a manager had told me he was resting me when I was firing on all cylinders, I would have right-handed him – and I seriously do mean that. It would have been a total insult and I would have thought he was trying to do me damage. And I would have told anybody who tried to take me off when I had scored two goals to stick their subs board where the sun don't shine! It was quite bizarre that on such a frequent basis Steve used to take off Boro strikers who were on a hat-trick. It made no sense.

There is no question that McClaren was very good for Middlesbrough, but it was never going to last long. He was always going to be using Middlesbrough as a stepping stone to greater things. But rather than enjoy it and then panic when he left, Boro got organised for the day when McClaren would be gone. In fact, they got so well organised that it didn't matter a jot when he eventually left the club. More than that, his departure allowed the club to move on another phase.

That phase has begun with Gareth Southgate, an ideal captain of the ship. Gareth is a hugely intelligent man, not just in regards to society, but towards football in general. He knows the game implicitly, can talk about it with clarity and can get his ideas across. Just as importantly, he has the respect of all and sundry. Gareth has been promoted from within but I get the impression that it won't be the last time Boro do that if Steve Gibson's vision for a kind of coaching academy comes off. There are many in football who will watch Boro's progress with interest because what Gibson is doing is quite revolutionary. I think he is setting up a self-propagating system that allows each new manager to come from within the club, having learned the ropes as part of the organisation.

For the life of me, I don't understand the reason it hasn't been done before at other clubs. Many club chairmen will hope Gibson succeeds, but others will hope he fails, because they risk being embarrassed at never having shown the same kind of long-term planning at their own clubs. I have a feeling that other clubs have thought about doing something similar before, only to lose track as a result of the lack of longevity in football. Too many football people just don't have the patience to make such ideas work, but Steve Gibson seems to just poke his tongue out at the rest of football – and good for him. Too much in football is short-term. Lose a couple of games and suddenly the manager is under pressure and all too often sacked. If that sounds a little like Newcastle, then I will simply say that if the cap fits, where it.

There is a risk that Gibson's self-propagating idea could implode from within, but as long as players are being signed who bring with them new ideas then there should be no risk of the system going stale. Beneath Gareth, the club's coaches – among them, Boro's future managers – can learn and thrive. I can see it progressing to the point where, in a few years time, any good 29-year-old player with management ambitions will being saying, 'I want to go to Boro. I'll give them my everything for two years and then get on the coaching staff.'

Steve Gibson has transformed Middlesbrough over the last 20 years. To go from liquidation to the UEFA Cup final in that time frame takes great year-on-year strides. The club now is completely different from the Middlesbrough I knew back in the 1970s. They had a tremendous team back then, with the likes of Willie Maddren, Stuart Boam, Graeme Souness, David Mills and John Hickton, but it was a different club. Gibson ripped up the previous Boro and rebuilt it from scratch.

What has happened at Middlesbrough will not be lost on Niall Quinn. In fact, I think it will act as an inspiration to him. He will know that, while Sunderland have to have their own blueprint for success, Boro's long-term strategy is the way forward. It won't matter if they are accused of copying Boro, because it is so clearly the way to go. What is the alternative? Muddling through like some other clubs I could name?

Eric

MIDDLESBROUGH WERE traditionally the north-east's third team behind Sunderland and Newcastle but you can't say that anymore. Over the last few years Boro have caught up and, in some aspects, overtaken the other two. That is some achievement when I think back to the old Middlesbrough who my brother Bill was with for over 15 years. I'm sure Bill can't believe the difference in the club.

Some of the things Steve Gibson has done for the club have been brilliant. People forget just what has been achieved. They go on about the fact that Boro won the League Cup a couple of years back and reached the UEFA Cup final under Steve McClaren, but they've been in other cup finals as well over the past 10 years or so. That's brilliant. Newcastle might be a bigger club but Middlesbrough have actually overtaken them in recent years when it comes to what they have achieved on the pitch. They have put the likes of Newcastle and Sunderland to shame - and I put a lot of that down to Steve Gibson.

He's a football man. He knows the game and he has got it right more often than not. Just look at the way he handled all

151

the hysteria around Steve McClaren. Not only did Gibson stick with McClaren when many thought he should get the sack midway through the 2005-06 season, but he gave him a five-year contract. A lot of the fans called The Three Legends show to say they thought he was off his rocker, but that new contract earned the club a lot of money in compensation when the FA came calling and offered McClaren the England job. All the fans wanted to get rid of him, with the result that the club would have got nout, but he turned it on its head and got someone to pay the club money for him. So maybe Gibson is even cleverer than we think!

McClaren's appointment as England manager didn't surprise me because he had always been well in with the FA, having coached the side under Sven Goran Eriksson for all those years. Did I think he deserved it? No! Do I hope he fails? No! Good luck to him. He might prove to be a success. Personally, I would have appointed Alan Curbishley because I think he deserved a chance, but let's hope McClaren proves to be a good choice.

I'm not sure what the feeling was towards McClaren within Middlesbrough Football Club, but he was certainly under pressure from the fans during his final season. For a manager who won the club their first major honours and took them to the UEFA Cup final, he got an incredible amount of flak from the fans, much of it on the phone-in. He seemed to be so disliked by the fans. They'll all have their own reasons but I think he just came across as false. He came out with so much crap about the team being 'magnificent' when they clearly weren't. He was kidding people.

I used to sit and wonder why he would say a game was magnificent when all 32,000 fans there that day knew he was talking bollocks. But then, when you look at it a bit deeper, you think about the millions of people around the country, who hadn't seen the game but might hear him saying that they were magnificent and believe Middlesbrough must be playing great football. That is PR – not locally maybe, but certainly in terms of the image he projected to the country. And I have a feeling they were his target audience because he was always ambitious to get the top job with England. Imagine what people in high places would have thought if they'd heard McClaren giving an honest assessment of Boro games. 'We

played crap today.' Instead they heard him saying they were 'magnificent' or 'breath-taking'. Now he is the England manager. So who was daft?

The other crap he used to come out with that I could never get my head around was that his players were 'tired' and needed 'resting'. No, they didn't! I'm sorry but that is complete garbage. Bernie, Malcolm and me have said this time and time again on the phone-in. It's not because we're dinosaurs or out of touch with the modern game. It's simply that we're right. No psychologist or manager will convince me that players need resting. If you are playing a lot of games it means you are having a good season - and players that are doing well want to play more games. I always wanted to play as many games as I could and I would have been embarrassed to say I was tired. The whole stupid tiredness lark has crept into the modern game and, if managers keep saying it enough, people will start to believe it. But it's garbage.

As far as Middlesbrough are concerned, McClaren has gone now and the new man in charge is Gareth Southgate. Again, I'll say good luck to him. He knows the club and his heart is there. People say he has no experience as a manager, but I know plenty who had loads of experience but failed at more than one place. A case in point is Terry Venables, who some people thought should get the job ahead of Southgate. Gareth's early results were all over the place, so I don't know what kind of manager he will make, but I was impressed that he was able to sign Jonathan Woodgate and Robert Huth. Persuading them to turn down Newcastle to join Boro was a kick in the teeth for the Geordies. In the past you wouldn't have dreamed that top players would have chosen to join Boro instead of Newcastle but the times are changing.

It will be interesting to see if Middlesbrough kick on or fall back over the next few years. Well done to them for reaching the UEFA Cup final but if they don't build on it then it will mean nothing. Just as Sunderland shouldn't have gone shouting from the rooftops that they finished seventh in the Premier League, neither should Boro get too carried away because they still won nothing. Few people outside the north-east will now remember that Sunderland finished seventh for two successive seasons. Seventh was only great if the next year they had moved into the top four and then established themselves up there year on year.

Boro could go either way. I remember going to watch Boro when the Brazilians, Juninho and Emerson, were playing. This particular day they beat Hereford 7-0 and I thought, 'Hell, this place is buzzing.' It was brilliant. But, as time went by, the Boro fans started to say things weren't right and, sure enough, the club started falling away. To avoid a repeat of that, they've got to make sure they're not satisfied with saying they were runners-up in a European cup final. They don't want to look back in 20 years time and think that was the pinnacle and it was all downhill from there. They need to say, 'That's our standard and that's where we want to be every year.'

•ENGLAND'S MAN: but Eric questions if Steve McClaren was as good as he made out.

153

THE THREE GAFFERS

EVER WONDERED what Malcolm, Eric and Bernie would be like as managers? Here, straight from the horse's mouth, they tell us what they think.

Eric Gates –
Sunderland Manager

Eric

If you're asking me, 'Would I like to be manager of Sunderland?' I can honestly say it's not an ambition of mine. But, if things didn't work out with Roy Keane, Niall Quinn picked up the phone and asked me to be the new manager, I'd say, 'Yes', no doubt about it. Of course I would. It's pie in the sky, it'll never happen now, but who's to say I wouldn't have done a good job? I think I'd have done as well as anybody else has over the last few years, put it that way. I know what the club is all about and I've seen just about every Sunderland home game for the last ten years. That's got to be an advantage. How many of our games did Mick McCarthy, Howard Wilkinson or, for that matter, Roy Keane see before taking over at the club?

When my old Ipswich team-mate Terry Butcher was manager of Sunderland in the early '90s, his assistant was Bobby Ferguson, who had coached me throughout the levels at Ipswich. I was on the radio at the time and got a call from the club asking if I would be interested in maybe coaching the youths and reserves. For a while it looked like there might be an opening there for me, only for Terry to get the sack. I guess it just wasn't meant to be.

When David Hodgson first took over at Darlington, he enquired about the possibility of me joining him there. To be honest, though, it wasn't really worth my while and I decided against it. But I do think I would have something to offer. I don't think it will ever happen now, but I've got no regrets.

Malcolm

I honestly believe Gatesy would be all right as a manager. In fact, I think he would make a better manager than he would a coach. Because of his short attention span, he wouldn't want to laboriously drum a particular thing into a group of players, so he would need a decent coach alongside him. But Eric is a very, very shrewd man, who would give good advice. It wouldn't always sound it, but it would be good.

The one thing you must never do as a manager is say, 'This is how I did it.' That's the absolute no-no. Gatesy has the ability to get his point or instructions over without doing that. Yes, I could see him as a manager.

Bernie

The thing about Eric being Sunderland manager is that he would frighten the fans with his moaning and his looks. He won two caps for England at football, but he'd have had a hundred if there were caps for moaning. If his team won 10-0, he'd still moan.

In any case, I've never seen a manager with a haircut like Gatesy's. He'd have to have a haircut and buy some new gear to at least make him look like a manager!

Bernie Slaven –
Middlesbrough Manager

Bernie

I'd love to be Boro manager. But what sort of manager would I make? I know a lot of people think I'm bonkers, but I've worked under a few managers and I know that if I had the sort of money the likes of Bryan Robson and Steve McClaren had available to them, then I could do every bit as well as they did. I think I could be ruthless too. 'Fair but ruthless' would be my motto. As Bruce Rioch always said, I'd say to the players, 'I don't want you to like me, I want you to respect me. I don't want to be your pal, but if you've got a problem you can come to me.'

If I was going to drop a player who had played regularly, I'd go and explain to him that it was nothing personal, I'd put over my point and tell him why I was preferring someone else that day. I say that because I've experienced being left out of the team without being told why – and it's not nice. Some managers don't bother, they just say, 'That's my team.' I don't agree with that. I think players deserve to know why they are being left out.

Malcolm

Bernie wouldn't make a manager, but I think he would be a very good striker coach. I can imagine Bernie seeing a young talent and getting really wrapped up in helping him blossom and fulfil his potential. He'd get such satisfaction from it. But I think he would have tunnel vision, as opposed to looking at the bigger picture. As a manager, you have to look at the whole.

You might not be a tactical genius or know the ins and outs of defensive play – you have people around you who can look at that – but you have to look at the individuals and decide how they are all going to knit together. I'm not sure Bernie would look at the whole picture. He would love to be Boro's striking coach and I think he would do well at it. In fact, I think he'd be *great* at it.

Eric

If Bernie was Boro manager, he would be as passionate as anything. I think he would call a spade a spade and kick arse in the dressing room when it was needed. Yeah, he'd have no problem with that side of things.

The only trouble with Bernie is that you wouldn't get him there in time for a three o'clock kick-off! His time-keeping is atrocious and always has been. He would set a bad example for players and you can't have that.

Malcolm Macdonald –
Newcastle United Manager

Malcolm

As I've said earlier in the book, I understand I once came quite close to becoming the manager of Newcastle United. Arthur Cox had just gone. Apparently, the Newcastle board was split between choosing me or Lawrie McMenemy. Instead, the chairman, Stan Seymour Junior, threw in the name of Jack Charlton and he got the job.

It hadn't been much earlier that I had taken my Fulham side to St James' Park and demolished Newcastle 4-1, with Gordon Davies scoring the goal of the season. We absolutely murdered them. The season before that, we'd been in a different division, but we'd done the same to them then, winning 2-1 in a cup game. So I was the popular choice among the fans because they'd seen the side I'd put together at Fulham.

On reflection, however, none of it would have worked out. I think it would have been the wrong time for me and the wrong time for Newcastle. I don't think the board and I would have been of the same kind of thinking. I think they wanted a steady, safety-first policy. Jack was perfect for that. It was a time of plodding in the Second Division and they wanted nothing more, whereas I was somewhat more dynamic. My method, if you like, was more sh** or bust. Jack was anything but that. I was attack-minded and created more gung-ho type sides. I also wanted like-minded players who were prepared to have a go. I'm not sure it would have suited the directors at the time, though it might have suited the fans.

If the job had been offered to me I would have taken it but, in retrospect, I'm not so sure it would have worked out. I'm not sure there was *any* time it would have worked out. The club and the fans would have been right for me, but I think there would have been a real lack of compatibility with the board. Of course, it didn't work out with Jack either. I'm not sure it would have suited the board to have me as manager, because my affinity would have been not so much with them as with the crowd.

It's too late now ever to be involved in Newcastle. I wouldn't entertain it. It would create a contradiction in terms with what I do now in radio.

Eric

Malcolm would be too intense, for me. I would hate to think I was in the dressing room trying to get fired up and he was doing the team talk. Bobby Robson's team talks were slow, but he would also say something funny, albeit usually without meaning to.

I think Malcolm knows the game and thinks deeply about it, but he would send me to sleep. I'd rank him alongside Sven Goran Eriksson and Steve McClaren for his lack of passion.

Bernie

Malcolm has obviously sampled life as a manager, but I can't help but wonder what his half-time team talks were like. You'd be snoring if his performances on the Three Legends show are anything to go by! I don't know if Malcolm would be exactly inspirational. By the time he got to the second sentence the whistle would be going for the second half.

BERNIE BANGED UP

Bernie

ONE OF the fall-outs I had with Malcolm was over the quiz book he and Gatesy brought out, called *The Ten Grand Fan*. Having said my piece, not only did I put the incident behind me but I actually agreed to do a signing session for the bleedin' book – for which they thanked me with a wind-up that got me hook, line and sinker.

The three of us had been busily signing books for the long queues of punters for well over an hour in this big bookstore in the MetroCentre when my day started to take a turn for the worse. I looked up to see two police officers marching into the store on either side of a sergeant. Realising they were heading straight to the front of the queue, I joked, 'Hey, Gatesy, here's the boys in blue coming for you.' I carried on signing the books for the fans as the three coppers walked behind the table.

I thought nothing more of it until I felt a tug on my shoulder. I looked round to see the three of them staring down at me.

'Can I have a word with you, sir?' said the sergeant.

'Me?'

I was totally bemused. What the hell did they want to speak to me about? As I stood up, he produced what he said was a warrant for my arrest. He went on to tell me that they were responding to a complaint from a guy from Newcastle. They said he suffered from stress at the best of times but that my comments about Newcastle on the Century phone-in had caused him even greater stress. 'We are taking this matter seriously,' he explained, his straight face and deadpan tone backing up his words.

Gatesy and Malcolm played the part perfectly. 'Bernie, what have you done?' they asked, looking full of concern.

I was immediately suspicious but not of my Century

colleagues. This was soon after my sacking from NTL and I wondered if someone might be trying to stitch me.

The sergeant asked me firmly to walk with them out of the crowded store into the MetroCentre's packed mall. Heads turned and fingers pointed as puzzled passers-by recognised me and wondered why I was being led away by three coppers.

I was burning with a combination of embarrassment, anger and growing concern. 'Look, a joke's a joke,' I pleaded, grasping at straws. 'Jeremy Beadle, innit?'

'Just walk ahead, sir. We don't want to cause a scene,' came the reply, none of the three giving me eye contact or a glimmer of hope.

After my attempts to laugh it off had fallen flat I was now growing increasingly apprehensive. This was serious. And it was about to get much worse. We left the busy mall via a door that led into a car park deserted but for a big Volvo car. I remember thinking that this was getting serious, as I believed they were going to put me in the back of the Volvo and take me off to the police station. Instead, another turn brought me face to face with an imposing steel door. It was opened, to reveal a reception area behind which was a small, windowless cell. One of the coppers led me unceremoniously into the cell and shut the door behind me.

For a while I was left alone with my own thoughts, my mind racing to make sense of it all. I wondered what the hell to do. I'd never been in a police cell in my life. 'I'm meant to be on air for the phone-in in two hours,' I thought. Then another more serious question came to mind. 'What am I going to tell my kids?' At the same time I couldn't help think that the whole situation was crazy. I was in jail for nothing.

After a short while, a guy dressed in a suit and tie entered the cell and proceeded to read from a piece of paper details of the charge against me. After finishing, he held the sheet and a pen out to me. 'Just sign here, please,' he said.

'You can f*** off!' I told him. 'I ain't signing anything. I tell you what, you can get my solicitor.' So he took the name of my solicitor and left me alone in the claustrophobic cell once again, locking the door behind him. This time I was left for a

good 20 minutes. I'm not embarrassed to admit that I was sweating like a bull. I had gone. I was confused and angry.

Finally, after what seemed like a lifetime, the cell door opened again. All three coppers entered, but this time their expressions had changed. 'Smile!' shouted a female voice, as a woman jumped out and a camera flashed in my face to cheers and laughter. Behind them came a laughing Macdonald and Gatesy. I was the only person not laughing. I didn't see the funny side at all.

'You shower of b******s!' I shouted.

The whole bloody thing had been a stitch-up my Malcolm, who had arranged to set me up with the help of a copper friend of his, letting Gatesy in on the plan. But, in my opinion, it wasn't a wind-up. I love a good wind-up but this had overstepped the mark of any joke. They had taken me through the ringer and it took me a long time to calm down. I was half-expecting to be fed bread and water. I've never been in trouble with the law in my life but coppers aren't my favourite people. I rate them alongside referees. I would love to have returned the compliment and put in a complaint against those three coppers for wasting police time.

Revenge on Malcolm? I've thought about it. I have considered painting his black car with white paint - or there again I might just slash his tyres! Certainly somewhere down the line my chance will come to get my own back. Malcolm, beware…

THREE LEGENDS, THREE LIONS

Bernie

I WAS the victim of probably the funniest ever stitch-up on the show. It involved the three lions logo associated with England's national team. I was debating the subject on the phone-in with my two partners in crime and told them that I was sure the three lions each had names. Neither Malcolm nor Gatesy, two former England internationals, had ever heard about this but I was certain I had read it somewhere, though I had no idea what their names were. But when I got a text message during the ad break from Gordon Cox, a reporter on Boro's website and a lifelong friend of Alastair Brownlee's, I became more confident in my belief. Coxy's text read, 'Bernie, the names of the three lions are Sono, Acconsentire, Gaio (pronounced so-no a-con-sen-tee-ray gow)'.

I simply thought, 'Well, Coxy knows his stuff. I'm sure he would never give me duff info.' Ali wasn't around for me to check with, so I decided to go for it.

'I can assure you the three lions have all got names,' I proudly announced on air, revelling in the fact that I had information about England's national team that my two English friends had no idea of. 'They are Sono, Acconsentire and Gaio.'

What I didn't know, however, was that Malcolm and Gatesy had already been tipped off that I was the victim of big wind-up – and they were now part of the plot.

'Say those names again, Bernie,' said Malcolm. 'I didn't catch what you said there.'

'Sono, Acconsentire, Gaio,' I repeated, this time more slowly.

Malcolm and Gatesy raised their eyebrows and expressed their amazement that I had made such an announcement. We then carried on with callers before Gatesy asked me to remind him again on air.

'What were those three names again, Bernie?'

'Sono, Acconsentire, Gaio,' I repeated, blissfully unaware that I was setting myself up.

This carried on every 10 minutes or so through to the end of the show, during which time I must have repeated those three words six or seven times. The sucker punch came at the end of the show when we received a call from a lad called Paul Boanas, who worked on Boro's ProZone system and shared an office with Coxy at Boro's training ground. He explained that he was ringing about the three lions and the words that I had been saying for the past two hours.

'Do you know what those words really mean, lads?' he asked.

'No,' said Gatesy and Malcolm, huge grins spreading across their faces. 'Go on, tell us.'

Then came the punchline. Paul revealed that Coxy's tip-off hadn't been the names of the three lions at all. In fact, I had spent the entire evening announcing to the world, 'I'm a consenting homosexual!' I had been set up big time. Just for the record, let me state that I'm happily heterosexual, thank you very much.

BERNIE'S RANT

Bernie

I'VE GOT to recount the day that made me appreciate having a car – and just how awkward the police can be. I went to Whitby with Dom and Ryan one sunny Sunday afternoon. It was a scorching day and Whitby was jam-packed with visitors. We didn't arrive until about two o'clock, so parking spaces were limited. Then this guy told me it was all right to park here, that he parks here all the time. So I parked my car on the kerb and headed off down to the harbour with the boys.

After a good couple of hours, we headed back to the car, stopping to get fish and chips for the boys. But I couldn't see my car where I thought I had left it. Then this traffic warden comes over, asks me if I'm looking for my vehicle and informs me it has been towed away because I had left my handbrake off. I asked him to find out where my car was. A couple, who recognised me, told me that they had seen the traffic wardens and police towing my car away. We eventually walked a mile to Whitby police station.

I went in and said to the girl on reception, 'I'm here for my car.' She told me it would be in Scarborough.

'Scarborough?' I queried. 'This is Whitby.'

'Yes,' she nodded, 'But the compound is in Scarborough.'

I couldn't believe what I was hearing. 'How do I get there?'

'Not my problem. You can't go today anyway. It's shut.'

'What do you mean, it's shut? You've just told me they've put my car there.'

'Yes, but the guy puts your car in and then heads off.'

'OK then, I've got two boys here. How do I get back to Middlesbrough?'

'Again, that's your problem.'

'How do you know I've got money to get home?'

'I don't.'

By now, I was fuming. 'So hold on a minute,' I said. 'If I was a pregnant woman or an elderly person, how would I get back home?'

'Oh, under extreme circumstances we would help you,' she answered, unconvincingly.

I shook my head. 'You know what, I don't believe you.'

So that was it. I was stuck in Whitby with my two sons. Worse still, my mobile phone was dead and I had no idea what the numbers of any of my friends were, so I couldn't even ring anyone to ask them to come and get us. Thankfully, I had about ten quid left in my wallet, so we were able to get a bus back to Middlesbrough. I hadn't been on a bus for about 20 years! I had bought two lobsters that were built like Ali and Gatesy, so I could hardly carry them, but I had to carry them halfway across Middlesbrough once we got off the bus.

I had been told by the police woman I would be able to get my car the following day from Malton, which was where the guy was based who had taken my car on behalf of the wardens and police. So a friend gave me a lift to Malton on the Monday. Cue another unbelievable conversation.

'I'm here for my car,' I said.

'It's not here, it's still in Scarborough.'

So off I went to Scarborough to collect my car.

And then they demanded £120 on the spot, no prior warning, before adding that they don't take cheques.

I said, 'I tell you what, I don't know how you f***ers sleep at night. How can the guy in the street get his car towed away and then you demand £120 in cash before you'll return the car without having warned me in advance?' Fortunately, I'd taken enough cash, but it could easily have been a wasted journey.

The whole thing was farcical and reflected badly on the Whitby police and parking wardens. If I leave the handbrake off, I deserve the fine - no arguments. And the handbrake *was* off. But why do they have to make it so awkward by not allowing you to have your car back that day, taking it to Scarborough when you are in Whitby and not warning you that they don't take cheques? People need their cars for work but those involved seem to be making it deliberately difficult for people to get their car back. For that reason, I highlighted the whole stupid episode via the local papers. Hopefully, someone in a position of influence will have taken a bit of notice and will change things.

SCOTCHING THE ILLUSION

BERNIE DESCRIBES it as 'pure off-the-cuff banter'. It was the night The Three Legends phone-in sounded more like the Edinburgh Tattoo. It was pure theatre, Scottish-style. Bernie blasting out the unmistakeable sound of *The Flower of Scotland* as he revealed a talent, previously unknown to the public, as a master of the bagpipes.

All three Legends agree the show, early in the 2006-07 season, went down as one of the funniest in the phone-in's long run. Certainly it got a reaction from listeners quite unlike any other, as texts, emails and phone calls flooded into the Century studio from north-east football fans amazed and hugely impressed by Bernie's musical talent.

It was an occasion inspired by a six-goal victory for Scotland, an occasion almost as rare as are offers of modelling contracts for Gatesy. The fact that the win came against international midgets, the Faroe Islands, mattered little to Bernie, suddenly a reconverted Scot for the night. After all, Scotland had gone one better than England, who had scored only five against Andorra.

Bernie had been away from the show for the two previous nights, but was back for a rare display of Scottish patriotism. Converted to Irish following rejection by the country of his birth during his playing days, the former Boro star jumped ship again in unforgettable fashion. As Malcolm recalls, it came partly as a response to ribbing, in his absence, that he sounded uncannily like TV funny man Rab C Nesbitt.

'Eric and I told Bernie that we'd been playing soundbites of Rab C Nesbitt but telling our listeners that it was actually Bernie,' says Malcolm. They are actually quite similar, because you struggle to understand what either of them are saying! Everyone had had a good laugh over it, once again completely departing the subject of football for pure comedy. It's the kind of thing that highlights what our programme is really all about. Something really silly just took off and everyone wanted to get involved. It's the reason why a lot of

non-football people listen to the show. The reaction was huge - and that continued with Bernie and his bagpipes.'

The show began as normal, with Malcolm and Eric making the usual introductions and discussing the latest football headlines. But then came a change in direction. 'Malcolm,' Eric interrupted, 'I can hear bagpipes.'

With that came the sound of the doors bursting open as the unmistakeable sound of bagpipes filled the Three Legends studio. 'What on earth is going on here?' questioned a stunned Malcolm.

'I tell you what, Slaven, you are a barmpot!' added Gatesy, clearly in a state of hysterical laughter, as he tried to describe a scene of a kilt-wearing Bernie marching around the studio blowing the bagpipes. 'I didn't know you could play the bagpipes. I hope you've got something on under that kilt! I've never seen your face so red. That's the funniest thing I've seen for a long time.'

SCOTCHING THE ILLUSION

Finally, the tune – described by Gatesy as the music to the old *Scotch Porridge Oats* advert – came to an end. A breathless Slaven spluttered into the microphone, 'Those bagpipes are hard work, I tell you. Have a blow, Gatesy! Phew! I thought I was fairly fit.'

'We are very impressed, I have to say, Bernie,' announced Malcolm. He could well have been talking for thousands of listeners in their kitchens, dining rooms and cars.

Born-again Scot Bernie, apparently recovering slowly from his exertions, even went as far as to say he would try to play a 'wee tune' for any listeners with requests. From then on, the requests poured in. Malcolm recalls, 'By rights, it should have been finished by the first ad break at twenty past six, but the whole thing took on a life of its own. It captured the imagination of the listeners for the entire night.'

Sure enough, the requests came in – and listeners enjoyed more Scottish tunes as bagpipes filled the Century airwaves. So impressive was the music that it seemed Bernie's fan club, previously restricted to Teesside, appeared to be expanding to Wearside and Tyneside. The show – and Bernie's bagpipe playing – became the talk of the north-east, while the Scot-cum-Irishman-cum-Scot promised more of the same for Christmas.

But now, exclusively for readers of The Three Legends book, we can reveal the truth behind a unique show. It was all *a hoax!* Yes, the Legends listeners were had. 'I can't play the bagpipes at all,' admits Bernie. 'Despite my Scottish upbringing, the first time I ever held bagpipes was for the pictures for this book. Even then, I didn't even know how to hold them. The whole thing was done by playing CDs that happened to be in Century's catalogue.

'It was all just a bit of fun, so I couldn't believe the reaction from the listeners. So many people congratulated me on my ability. I even had a request to play at someone's wedding! I also promised to play the bagpipes at the Riverside if Boro won at Arsenal that weekend. I was confident I wouldn't have to worry, but Boro actually went ahead before eventually being pegged back to one each. For a while, I thought I was going to have to spill the beans that I can't even play the spoons, let alone the bagpipes.'

Incredibly, the whole idea came from a discussion between Bernie and Eric just 20 minutes before the show went on air. Gatesy laughs, 'Bernie had heard about the laugh we'd had calling him Rab C Nesbitt, so we agreed he'd pretend he was back to being Scottish again, to play on the fact that Scotland had actually won a game. I just said to Bernie, "As a wind-up, why don't you come in singing a Scottish song or something like that?" Then came the idea of the Scottish music. Kathryn, the show's producer, managed to find some bagpipes stuff in the Century archive and we were away.'

Bernie takes up the story from here. 'I stayed outside the studio until the right moment, then marched in, slamming the door as Rod Hardisty turned the sound up of the Scottish CD in the studio. I was acting as if people could see me, marching around and pretending to squeeze my bag and puff my cheeks. All the time, Gatesy and Malcolm were saying stuff and laughing.'

'Bernie played it well,' smiles Gatesy. 'Me and Malcolm had to do a bit of acting as well, pretending he was playing the bagpipes and wearing a kilt, with little or nothing underneath! The truth is that Bernie was marching around the studio in his usual dodgy gear, pretending to play the bagpipes. I was crying because it was so funny to see him.'

'It just took off from there. People had such a good laugh with it. It was a great thing that people didn't know whether it was true or not. Weeks later, people were still asking if he had really been playing them. I always told them, "Of course he was!" Only one person, who must have been a bagpipes player, saw through it. I think most others were convinced, despite their disbelief that Bernie could keep it quiet about having such a talent.'

Malcolm smiles, 'It was certainly one of the funniest shows. What I found incredible was that we actually had so many appropriate CDs available, because there isn't much call for bagpipes on Century usually! It was titillation for us, but the phenomenal response we got from the listeners was very funny. They just fell for it. It was a wonderful audio illusion.'

The final word must go to Bernie, who admits his musical talent does not stretch beyond his belief that Morrissey is the greatest ever rock star. 'The show was so funny. How do you beat that? It was pure off-the-cuff banter. To everyone we tricked into believing I was really playing the bagpipes, I'm sorry. But at least we've come clean about it now!'

The Best Of The Phone-In
WHO YOU GONNA CALL?

THE FINAL months of the 2005-06 season could hardly have been more dramatic for the north-east's 'big three' clubs.

This exclusive transcript featuring some of the show's best calls and text messages during that time reveals a unique insight into the thoughts of Sunderland, Newcastle and Middlesbrough fans during a period in which all three clubs lost their managers.

Sunderland fans suffered the worst season in Premier League history and could only pray that Niall Quinn's potential takeover at the Stadium of Light would reach fruition.

Members of the Toon Army feared they might even join their deadly rivals in the Championship until the dismissal of Graeme Souness, but Glenn Roeder's appointment as

caretaker manager brought about a dramatic change in fortunes, culminating in qualification for the Intertoto Cup.

And Boro supporters wondered whether to laugh or cry as Steve McClaren survived calls for his head before leading Boro on a two-pronged charge for cup glory.

Whether they were overjoyed at victory or dismayed at defeat, fans throughout the region called 0191 477 2000 more than ever before to express to The Three Legends their words of delight, sadness, hope, despair, happiness and anger – or simply to wind up their rival supporters!

Read on to relive a truly dramatic season through the words of Malcolm, Eric and Bernie – and the north-east's passionate football fans…

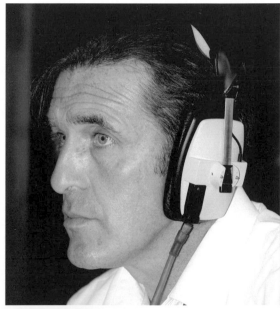

•ON AIR: Bernie, Eric and Malcolm during the phone-in.

In The News

FA Cup Round 3: Brentford 2 Sunderland 1

FA Cup Round 3: Coventry 1 Boro 1

FA Cup Round 3: Cheltenham 0 Newcastle 2

Tuesday January 31

Chris, Middlesbrough

Chris: Sunderland haven't been playing that bad and losing. Boro have been playing really poor and losing. They played Chelsea a couple of weeks ago and were beaten by an unfortunate goal.

Bernie: Sunderland battle for 90-odd minutes. They don't lie down. Technically they aren't great players, some of them aren't Premiership class. But if we go out thinking we'll pass it about with leisure, then we've got the wrong game.

Chris: Mick McCarthy is going to tell his players to go out and kick every player up the backside.

Malcolm: He has made it very clear that after the Brentford game that he is a very angry man. He will have transferred that anger over to the players, so watch out for the backlash tonight. They'll take it out on the Boro.

Chris: Absolutely.

Richie, Sunderland

Richie: I've never been so angry in my life, looking at this football team. How Mick McCarthy can look at himself in the morning, I do not know.

Eric: Mick knows the players better than us and if he honestly believes they are giving the best, well fair enough, but that's not good enough.

Richie: It's definitely not good enough. When he says he couldn't face the players on Sunday morning, he should be ashamed of himself.

Eric: Well, he just wanted to keep out of the way. Mick is clutching at straws for what to do and how to get the best

out of these players. He's got 18 games to go. He doesn't want a defeat in the cup, he doesn't want a defeat here tonight. He's clinging on to something. I think they'll go down, you think they'll go down, 90 per cent of the fans think they'll go down.

Richie: We know they'll go down. I've been up the bookies tonight and put a bet on with the bookies for the Boro to win 3-0.

Malcolm: It's amazing, isn't it, all the Boro fans are putting money on Sunderland, and all the Sunderland fans are putting money on the Boro!

Michael, Liverpool

Michael: Bernie, you nearly killed me on Friday with that drivel coming out of your mouth. I nearly choked on my lamb chops.

Bernie: What drivel was that?

Michael: You were speaking to some bird back in September and she said 'Oh we've got Boateng, we've got Mendieta, we're going to finish fourth. And you said 'yeah'.

Bernie: No, no, no. I never said that.

Eric: You did, Bernie!

Michael: You did, Bernie!

Bernie: If any of these guys can dig this tape out, I'll give you a grand because I never said.

Eric: You were talking about Champions League!

Bernie: I said 11th or 12th with what we've got.

Eric: You said Champions League!

Bernie: Pants!

Michael: You take a look at those tapes.

Bernie: What's your prediction for tonight?

Michael: 3-0 to Sunderland.

Bernie: You're off your head!

Pete, Middlesbrough

Pete: This game tonight, it's the big one for us. We've got to win tonight.

Bernie: It's a big game for both teams. A draw is no good to either team. I can't stand here and say 'Middlesbrough's going to win' because I don't know what team is going to turn up.

They've let us down too many times over the last couple of months.

Pete: Do you think it's time for a change at the top, Bernie?

Bernie: That's not going to happen because Steve McClaren has signed his new deal, but he's under as much pressure as McCarthy and Souness.

Pete: Say if we lost this game really heavily tonight, the pressure would be really on McClaren

Bernie: You are dead right. If we got walloped 3-0 tonight, when Sunderland's barely won a game, he would be under the cosh big time. Course he would. If we don't win this game we'll start wondering where we are going to get points from. We need to win about five games to say we are safe.

Pete: I'm going to go 2-1 tonight.

In The News

Sunderland 0 Boro 3

Premier League positions

	P	W	D	L	Pts
14 Newcastle United	22	7	5	10	26
16 Middlesbrough	23	6	7	10	25
20 Sunderland	23	2	3	18	9

Wednesday February 1

Alan, Sunderland

Alan: Eric, I've learned how to avoid the traffic at the Stadium of Light. You just stay till the end! It was embarrassing last night. We were looking forward to a good game. I have never before gone to a football match hoping it would be nils each. But we were dismal in the first half. On a positive note, we came out for the second half and for 15 or 20

minutes we had a real go. To highlight anybody, Arca - he's a cracking lad. He's full of skill and cracking to watch. I'm not a great fan of Kevin Kyle because I'm not a great fan of that style of football. But I'll tell you something, he's not as fit or sharp as them lads but he's hungry, he put himself about and he looked dangerous.

Eric: But effort and 'tried' isn't good enough for the Premier League.

John, Sunderland

John: I'm a season ticket holder for 50 consecutive years. My daughter in law from Darlington got in touch with the club to tell them and I got a letter back from Mr Murray, saying 'Thank you for your valid support, you're very special'. Eric, I don't know what's going on through there. I'm sick, sick to death. I get up on a Saturday morning, I used to get up with a bit of feeling, but I get up now and I just haven't got it.

Eric: It's easy for me because it's a job. It's been my life and I've been paid for doing something I love. I'm not putting myself in the bracket of the likes of you that have paid to see the team you love, but I never thought I'd feel this way – and I never thought I'd be like that with football - but I'm going to games and I'm not enjoying it. And that's sad. I love Thierry Henry and Alan Shearer, they are great players and there's still some good players about, so I'm not going along the lines of 'It was better in my day', but what I am seeing regular, week in and week out, is not good. I want to see good stuff, I want to be entertained. The reason they are on that pitch is because they are supposed to be able to do what the fans can't do.

John: Eric, we're not getting entertained whatsoever. I'm seriously thinking of not going to the game on Sunday and watching my grandsons playing instead.

Eric: It's like a Long Playing record, but what's got to change down there?

John: What's got to change for me is someone to come in and take the club over. Every year I say 'I'm finished' but then I get it every year.

Eric: Well, you've done your bit, lad.

What the Sunderland
board have done to
McCarthy, sending him
into the Premier League
ill-equipped, is like
sending a soldier to
Iraq with a pea-shooter
- Pete, Horden

Ray, Sunderland

Ray: I just wanted to say this because it's been building up in me the last few weeks. One week it's Middlesbrough supporters complaining, then it's Newcastle. This week it seems to be ours. Eric, you and 50,000 more know that the only way Sunderland are going to achieve anything is to get rid of Bob Murray and his merry men. Look at his record. Correct me if I'm wrong, but this is his 20th season. He took over in our blackest hour in the Third Division, but in the last 20 years we have only been in the top flight for seven seasons. Apart from that, we've had one FA Cup final appearance – and that's it. On the other hand, we've had relegations and the embarrassment of him taking us onto the Stock Exchange and having to come off that. I was one of the mugs that bought the shares. I let my heart rule my head because I love the club. We've got back in the top flight and had such an embarrassing season.

Eric: I know what you are saying and a lot of people are with you, but he can say 'Look, if anyone wants the club, come and get it'.

Ray: Nobody can convince me that there haven't been consortiums of businessmen wanting to take over Sunderland Football Club. If others can look at taking over the likes of Portsmouth and Aston Villa, you can't tell me that there haven't been a load of people looking at Sunderland, with a ground and a following like they've got. If he was a supporter of the club, he would have sold up years ago.

Eric: So you want him out?

Ray: It's the only way there's ever going to be success at Sunderland. I know that, you know that and 50,000 other people know that. But the only way you're going to get rid of him is voting with your feet and not turning up there. We've tried everything else, why don't we try that.

Dave, Newcastle

Dave: I think it's clear cut that Martin O'Neill and Otmar Hitzfeldt are the leading contenders with regards to Newcastle, while Sam Allardyce, who seems to be the insider's viewpoint, comes way, way down with regards to what Newcastle supporters are actually thinking about. Do you think that after Freddy Shepherd got it disastrously wrong with Souness he will listen to views other than his own?

Malcolm: He will listen to the football supporters of Newcastle United, of that I am sure. He will hold great store in what the Newcastle supporters are saying.

Dave: I would hope that would be the case, Malcolm.

Malcolm: I am sure of it.

John, Sunderland

John: I think Mick McCarthy has got to go now. If he has got to go – and I think he should have gone a few weeks ago – get him away as quickly as possible. The new manager can then assess the players he has, what he's going to do with them, who he needs, who he doesn't. The frightening thing for me is that McCarthy is trying to keep this squad together for next year. You've got to ask the question 'Why?'

Malcolm: But who are you going to get in at this time?

John: Haven't got a clue.

Malcolm: And probably your chairman would say the same thing.

Eric: John, I agree with what you said. If he got sacked tomorrow, it wouldn't surprise me. But in the climate of Sunderland Football Club, can you see them sacking someone, with the way the debt is and the penny-pinching that goes on? The club won't do it.

John: You've got to understand where I'm coming from.

Eric: But which way do you think the board will go? The argument will come back to you that the last time we were in the Championship he won it quite easily.

John: It's not going to happen next time, Eric.

Eric: I look more at the players. Mick has given Andy Gray an opportunity to prove he is good enough – he's not good enough. Time is running out on Jon Stead. He's been at Blackburn – hasn't done it. Come to Sunderland – hasn't done it. These lads have been given opportunities and haven't done it.

John: Bernie, you thoroughly deserved your victory last night. But don't get carried away. Everybody beats Sunderland.

Bernie: No, we're not getting carried away. We've got a long way to go. I felt sorry for the Sunderland fans. They just looked so down. I've been there and it's not a nice feeling.

John: There weren't enough people left in the ground to boo. Everyone was quiet. The apathy is awful.

John, Middlesbrough

John: I just want to say how good it was to see a bit of guile and guts last night. I know you can't get carried away by one performance and one result. I think last night showed why both teams are in the positions they are in, because it wasn't a great spectacle. It was quite scrappy but the important thing was to get a win. I think it was epitomised by Pogatetz. He was fantastic. He battled and scrapped, he controlled and calm. I was happy for him.

Bernie: He's had a bad time, Pogatetz. He's not looked the part and people have questioned why he's been in the team. He's been majorly disappointing. But he deserves to be in the team on Saturday because he was excellent. It wasn't a game for the purists but we never thought it was going to be. What would we have said tonight if we hadn't won the game? Where would we have gone from that?

John: I think we would definitely have been going down.

Bernie: At least we've got a base to build on now. We need to take all three points against Villa and get us on the way.

John: Definitely. I was disappointed with Sunderland in the first half. They didn't seem to have any fight. The first half, they just laid down.

Bernie: They were spineless, first half, Sunderland.

Eric: I'll tell you what I thought about the Boro side. It's been doom and gloom for you, you haven't been playing well, but there's something there for you to clutch at. You've got some good young lads coming through, you've got class players.

Bernie: No Boro fan comes on here and says we haven't got good players. It's the team. We've not got a good team.

Eric: You had a bit of fight in your side and if you keep that going you've got no problems. You've got a lot to play for.

Pat, Sunderland

Pat: I tell you what there's only one person in that team should be allowed his wages and that's Arca. The rest of that club, all them players are absolutely spineless and I will not go again this season.

Eric: No, no, no. I wouldn't say that. These lads are *not* spineless. They'll be good at a different level. Some will find their level next year in the Championship, some will

drop further, but they are not spineless. They are giving their best and it's not good enough.

Pat: Eric!

Eric: Yeah?

Pat: Can you stop butting in, I'm having my say. I'm telling you they are spineless. Will you listen? Danny Collins couldn't hit a barn door, as soon as he got the ball he tried to pass it straight away. As soon as Le Tallec got the ball he tried to pass it back to his defenders. Nobody wanted to do anything with that ball last night. They were all spineless apart from Arca. Every one of them should donate their wages this week to a charity.

Eric: Well, don't get me wrong, I'm not saying they are good. I'm saying they are poor, They've been found out at this level. But spineless is a hard word to use.

Bernie: Well, I think first half they were spineless.

Malcolm: They are not cowardly, are they?

Bernie: Well, Malcolm, I thought first half they were spineless, as a neutral.

Pat: I'll tell you another thing, most fans booed at half-time, but what do you expect them to do? We've got nine points, man. We're playing our hard-earned cash to watch crap.

Bernie: Pat, I want to know how you've got nine points!

Pat: I went on their website and McCarthy's saying they are playing well. Well for what? Has he got his head in the clouds? He's went and signed Rory Delap.

Bernie: I thought it was Roary the Lion.

Pat: I tell you it's a huge club and it's getting dragged right down.

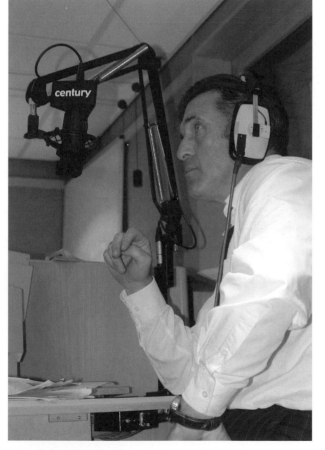

Brian, Newcastle

Brian: We are going to win tonight, Malcolm.

Eric: Ha, ha! Get him off now!

Brian: No, no - 2-1. Let's be honest, they're not that good, are they?

Eric: I tell you what it's an important game for you because if you get beat, you are in the mire.

Brian: The only good thing about it is we've got worse teams below us.

Eric: And who's worse than you?

Brian (laughing): Hoo-hoo! We've got two pretty close!

Gatesy: So Sunderland and Middlesbrough are much worse than you?

Brian: Definitely

Gatesy: Well I tell you what, I saw the Boro last night and they weren't good but I think they're a better team than Newcastle.

Brian: Do you?

Gatesy: Yeah, I do.

Malcolm: We're going to have to play an awful lot better than we did against Cheltenham on Saturday.

Brian: You're right. But I've got a sneaking feeling – and everyone will laugh – but I think we're going to win the FA Cup this season.

Laughter all round.

Gatesy: Get him off!

In The News

Man City 3 Newcastle 0

Newcastle sack Graeme Souness, with Glenn Roeder taking temporary charge.

Premier League positions

	P	W	D	L	Pts
Newcastle	23	7	5	11	26
Boro	23	6	7	10	25
Sunderland	23	2	3	18	9

Thursday February 2

Bernie: Welcome to the north-east's biggest football phone-in. Last night Newcastle got a 3-0 walloping and this morning Graeme Souness got sacked. Malcolm, you witnessed the game last night. You got a walloping, good and proper. This morning the manager departed. Was that a surprise?

Malcolm: No. There were enormous problems last night. I found myself saying the same things over and over again because the players were making the same mistakes over and over. We heard before the game that Newcastle United were going to play a diamond formation in the middle of the park. Emre behind the front two, understand that. N'Zogbia on the left, fair enough. That left Clark and Parker to play the right-side of the diamond and the base of the diamond in front of the centre-halves. The two of them spent the vast majority of the first half scrapping between each other who was going to play base position, hence nobody played right side and there was just a great channel in front of Peter Ramage, the youngster at right-back. It was like Genghis Khan and his hordes down that side attacking Ramage. And nobody helped him out.

Bernie: And Boumsong and company had a nightmare again. And Bramble. You could have driven a bus through them.

Malcolm: Freddy has bitten the bullet and given Souness the bullet. Souness has gone. I don't think he's offered the club anything at all. What concerns me is what's left. All of the money is gone and what we've got for it is rubbish.

Bernie: Are you being harsh there?

Malcolm: No, I'm not. I know what I'm seeing on the field of play. Nearly £50 million has been spent. Have we got a defence? No! Have we got a midfield? No! Have we got a forward line? No! What we have is a goalkeeper – and a centre-forward who was about to retire and has carried on for a season.

Bernie: If the players don't respond to Glenn Roeder, is there a chance you could be relegated?

Eric: Bernie, they could be relegated, no problem.

Bernie: At the minute, Malcolm, like it or lump your club is in turmoil.

Malcolm: That was the limits for me last night when I sensed around that people were going 'Heaven's above, Portsmouth and Birmingham have equalised, Aston Villa have got a late goal against Chelsea'. You're not looking at the Chelseas or the Manchester Uniteds or the Arsenals or the Liverpools. We're actually looking at the Portsmouths and Birminghams of this world. How worrying!

David, Newcastle

David: Bernie, what do you think about giving George Boateng a £10.5m contract?

Malcolm: Four years!

Bernie: What I can tell you instantly is there's not been a contract signed.

Malcolm: There hasn't? So there was nothing in the story? Because it's headlines in all the papers this morning.

Bernie: Well, Steve McClaren was quoted today saying it's nonsense and he doesn't know where the story has come from. Fabrication.

Eric: Yeah, but he said that about his own contract!

Malcolm: Yeah, he said that was signed and it wasn't.

Bernie: Why don't you keep your big nose out!

David: I'm a season ticket holder at St James' and have been for the last 10 years. I couldn't believe the atmosphere on Saturday, it was just like the old Keegan days again. It was absolutely fantastic.

Malcolm: It was such a change, wasn't it?

Eric: You win a game against Portsmouth, you think you've won the World Cup!

David: It was as if a cloud had been lifted from over the club. It was like a ray of sunshine.

Bernie: Who's your next game?

David: Villa, who beat you by four.

Bernie: Well, the sunshine will disappear then.

David: I don't think so like. I thought Boumsong played quite well on Saturday, the whole back four played well.

Bernie: Boumsong had a good game? The sun must have been shining!

Malcolm: Who really did impress me, for the first time, was Babayaro. But why such a complete change in the way they are playing? It was completely different attitude. I felt that an awful lot of things happened which told a story that it had been worse than we had actually realised.

David: I can't see the atmosphere changing. I think it's back to the good old days.

Bernie: I think you're getting carried away, David.

David: Well, we're not fourth bottom of the league, Bernie.

Bernie: Ha ha, but you're not far away from it.

Ray, Newcastle

Ray: It's a great day, great day.

Eric: A great day?

Ray: Eric, you don't know how good it is. Last time I was on here I said I would like to hear the words: 'I quit', but 'You're sacked' will do me.

Bernie: So where do you go from here now? You've employed Glenn Roeder as caretaker.

Ray: I know where we were going under Souness, so whoever comes in can't do a worse job. The tactics last night, I've never seen anything like it in my life.

Malcolm: It's a very extreme thing that you've just said. I wish that I could disagree with you and take you to task. Sadly, I see it exactly the same way as you and I can't argue with you.

Ray: I can't believe his tactics. It was the first time ever I've left the ground and been in my car before the game was ended. Someone said you might miss Shearer's record-breaking goal. I told them we would have to get over the halfway line before we could score.

David, Newcastle

David: I think it's a great day for Newcastle, because I could see us getting relegated under Souness. I couldn't see anything else but Newcastle being in the Championship next season under Souness. Scott Parker lacks vision. He's supposed to break the midfield up and get us going again. I don't see him doing that.

Malcolm: I'm told that there are 50,000 fans at St James' Park who all have a different opinion to me on Parker. I'm not so sure now. I think an awful lot of people are starting to see that maybe he isn't offering what the team needs. He's got a great attitude; I'm not knocking that. But you cannot play the game on the flat of your back.

David: David Batty would do that job, give it straight to an attacking midfielder and say 'Get on your bike, son'. Parker doesn't do that. He never passed forward.

Malcolm: I see Parker going round in circles.

David: I've never liked Souness. I never did think he had any tactical nouse about him at all. I mean, what's he done at any club?

Bernie: Well, he's won cups. He won things with Rangers, he won a cup at Benfica, he won a cup with Liverpool and he could have won the FA Cup for Newcastle.

David: He's won a Carling Cup, which for me is a Mickey Mouse cup, though I'll admit I'd love to win it.

Mick, Sunderland

Bernie: How are you doing?

Mick: I'm sick. Eric, what's happening at our club?

Malcolm: With all that's happening at St James' Park, you're just forgotten now.

Eric: Wait a bit, Malcolm, you think you're in a mess. I tell you what, there's a bigger mess down the road.

Mick: I've never been so sick, man. I went to Brentford on Saturday and had the realisation that we are going to be going to these grounds over the next few years. Then I missed the bloody last train back and didn't get back until Sunday afternoon, now our lass isn't talk to us. Then Tuesday night! It's dross.

Eric: What do you want to happen to your club?

Mick: Murray's got to start making the club a proposition so he can sell.

Eric: He won't. Nothing's going to change at Sunderland. Mick, you know as well as I do.

Mick: I'm just fuming, man.

Stuart, Newcastle

Stuart: My lottery number has come up today. I've never smiled as much for months. I've been depressed. I was going to jump off the roof at one stage. This is just fantastic news.

Eric: You got stuffed 3-0 and you're six points off relegation, and you're happy. There's something wrong.

Malcolm: I cannot argue with you that Newcastle have gone so far back, I find it frightening, to be honest.

Stuart: I think Freddy Shepherd has always tried to do his best for the managers he has brought in. My only problem is that he's given managers millions and they've wasted millions over the years. The next manager should be Martin O'Neill. Go out and say 'Martin, how much do you want?'.

Malcolm: I do understand your sentiments towards Martin O'Neill and I think he would do a fabulous job at Newcastle, I really do. But we have to be respectful of the reason why he left Celtic and took a sabbatical from football in the first place. It was because of a very serious illness to his wife and I've heard nothing to suggest that the situation has changed. I think it's very unfair to bring him into any equation with regards to Newcastle at the moment.

Eric: Why would Martin O'Neill come to a Championship side?

Johnny, Newcastle

Johnny: I think that things are going to change dramatically from the weekend. I hear that Graeme Souness was very unpopular with the players. That's why I think you'll find one player or another every week was saying 'We're all behind him' but they weren't. I think you'll find that now he's gone it will release a lot of the pressure.

Malcolm: So are you saying that Alan Shearer and Glenn Roeder will get a very good response then?

Johnny: I would like to hope the players will kick themselves back into gear because I think they've been terribly demotivated.

Andy, Middlesbrough

Andy: When you compare Souness's performance to McClaren's performance, McClaren must be thinking 'Phew, I got lucky there, didn't I?' Five-year contract, he's sorted, isn't he?

Bernie: I think it's what Steve's done in the past. If he hadn't achieved the Carling Cup, European football, he would have been under scrutiny and as much pressure as Graeme Souness, there's no doubting that. This season I think we're going to struggle. Because we've beaten Sunderland three I don't see all as bright and rosy or that we've turned the corner. We have to do it consistently and we've not did that.

Andy: I would love to get Martin O'Neill here. I think Newcastle are going to pinch him from under our noses, Bernie.

Bernie: I'm sure that Martin's got more sense than to go to Newcastle.

John, Newcastle

John: Bernie, you and Gatesy have been laughing your hats off at Newcastle. My hat's off to Freddy Shepherd because he's done something positive about the situation. But the situation is that you're below us and Sunderland have gone. I think Newcastle will win by three or four goals on Saturday.

Bernie: What gives you that confidence? You've just been walloped 3-0. I'm going to tape that and we'll replay it on Monday if you've got gubbed.

John: You can play it as much as you want. I think Newcastle will turn the corner and they'll stop up but unfortunately Middlesbrough and Sunderland will be relegated with Portsmouth.

Bernie: Middlesbrough?

John: Middlesbrough will be relegated this year because Gibson hasn't got the bottle to sack McClaren.

Malcolm: Now don't go poo-pooing that, Bernie. Because you're threatening Newcastle with relegation but you're nearer to it.

Bernie: I know that but you guys are blasé about it. There's a severe danger that Middlesbrough, Newcastle and Sunderland will get relegated.

In The News

Boro 0 Aston Villa 4

Newcastle 2 Portsmouth 0

West Ham 2 Sunderland 0

Premier League positions

	P	W	D	L	Pts
15 Newcastle	24	8	5	11	29
17 Boro	24	6	7	11	25
20 Sunderland	24	2	3	19	9

Monday February 6

Mark, Middlesbrough

Mark: Bernie, I'm ringing up and I just want to express how disgusted I was with what I saw on Saturday – and I'm sure I'm speaking for a lot of other Boro fans, probably most of them. It's just not acceptable.

Bernie: Mark, I agree with you. Something's got to be done because we hit rock bottom. I thought we were over our troubles, I'm sure most of the punters did, when we beat Sunderland, even though we know they are a bad, bad

WHO YOU GONNA CALL?

As an ex-pat and black and white through and through it was if a black cloud had been lifted from St James on Saturday. It was refreshing listening to the commentary to hear the crowd cheering again like the atmosphere from years past. It also seemed we played with the passion and excitement the Geordies expect. Congratulations to Glenn Roeder and Alan Shearer. We hope it continues for the rest of the season and that Freddy Shepherd gets it right this time when he appoints the new manager – Derek, North Carolina

team. But 4-0 against Aston Villa? We made them look like Real Madrid and, for me, they are not a good outfit.

Mark: Yeah, but Bernie, what is going to be done? Well, we all know, I think, what has to be done – McClaren has to go, doesn't he? I think he's lost the players and I know he has lost the fans, that much is obvious.

Bernie: The atmosphere was bad, there's no doubting it. I've never known it so bad and the punters were giving Steve McClaren a message, they were letting him know exactly how they felt long before the end.

Eric: Mark, I have to ask you what went wrong in your opinion? I saw you beat Sunderland – and yes, I know we're not a good side, we're poor, but you beat us comprehensively – but to then lose in that fashion by four goals…

Bernie: Eric, we were awful. Morale must be at an all-time low now and you've got to wonder where they go from here.

Mark: Well, Bernie, there's only one way we are going if McClaren stays and that's down. I just hope Steve Gibson knows that, I'm sure he does.

Bernie: The chairman has never let us down, he has always done the right thing for Middlesbrough and for the supporters. I know he'll be suffering as much as the rest of us, if not more. He'll know that was unacceptable and I'm sure he'll have had a couple of sleepless nights about what he saw. Steve McClaren has just signed a new contract for five more years and I'm sure a lot of the club's fans will be wondering why the club did that.

Mark: That's a joke really. I don't understand it, no-one does.

Bernie: Whatever happens, serious questions are going to be asked because Saturday was not a one-off, we all know that. It's been going on for a long time now and it's going from bad to worse.

Tony, Middlesbrough

Tony: Lads, I've only got one thing to say – and that's Steve McClaren, it's time to go, mate. Y'know, thank you for all the good times, all he has done for us – the Carling Cup, great, one of the best days ever, Europe I've enjoyed – but it can't go on. Saturday was goodnight as far as I'm concerned, Bernie.

Bernie: Yeah, it was a bad, bad performance all over the pitch. People will focus on the defence but no-one had a good game, no-one came out of it with any credit and

confidence has hit an all-time low. It was majorly disappointing.

Tony: Disappointing is an understatement, to be honest, Bernie.

Bernie: I agree, it was terrible, awful.

Malcolm: And I fear that things could get an awful lot worse before they improve, Bernie, because who have you got on Saturday but the champions!

Bernie: Malcolm, we know that and we face getting gubbed, we're all worried.

Tony: It could be six or seven, a repeat of the shocking game at Arsenal, but this time in front of our own fans. I'm dreading it, like. I fear for us.

Malcolm: Yes, I fear for what Chelsea might do to you if you don't show a dramatic improvement, because Chelsea really are an awesome side who take no prisoners.

Eric: The question has got to be, hasn't it, whether McClaren will be manager by then?

Tony: I hope he's not. He can't be. What does that state about our ambition if he stays? We could go down.

Malcolm: There is every possibility, make no mistake of that.

Tuesday February 7
Brian, Sunderland

Brian: I've been a season ticket holder since 1989, y'know. I've missed one home game since 1986 and I've missed three this season, believe it or not. I wouldn't miss for anything. I've written down some quotes from Mick McCarthy that he's said in the press in the last few days. One of his quotes was: 'If in the last two seasons we've not been a success then I'm a Dutchman.' Now for me success is winning championships, winning the FA Cup, Coca-Cola Cup, playing in the Champions League, playing in Europe. For a club like Sunderland that can get 48,000 fans, getting close one year and then getting promoted the next season is not success for me.

Eric: No, I agree with you.

Brian: Another statement is, 'It's been disappointing the last few results, but I'm hoping we can get back to playing how we were before the Brentford game.' I mean, is he watching a different team to me, Eric?

Eric: I've never gone along with the fact that they are playing well and what have you. I think Mick's got his manager's head on. He knows we're going down but he doesn't want to knock, knock, knock all the time. He is saying this because if a player is getting knocked week in and week out then the dressing room atmosphere will be terrible and gets the stuffing knocked out of it. I can understand the reason why he's doing it. If every game he's coming out with 'Well, he was terrible, he was rubbish and the game was terrible', it just gets you down.

Brian: I understand that, Eric. But on the other side of the coin, he's also saying next season we've got players that can be a force to be reckoned with next season in the Championship. I mean look at Southampton, Norwich and Palace, the teams that were relegated last season, they've got the likes of Andy Johnson and Dean Ashton.

Eric: It's hard to plan in football, it really is, but when it gives you the opportunity you've got to grab it by the cobblers and make the most of it. I tell you what, if you don't grab it you'll get left behind.

Bernie: Brian, thanks for your call. I think we need a break. You can't use the word 'cobblers'.

Eric: Why not? Your shoes have been to the cobblers a few times!

Peter, Middlesbrough

Bernie: Hi Peter. Come on then, Peter, did you go to the game on Saturday?

Peter: No, I won't go to games while he's there.

Malcolm: Who? While who is there?

Peter: You know who I mean – McClaren.

Malcolm: Oh, I thought you meant Bernie!

Peter: You look at the situation with Souness getting the sack. He's been the best manager out of the three north-eastern teams and he is the one that gets the sack.

Eric: You don't go and watch the Boro because of the manager?

Peter: I do not like the football he's playing. He cannot motivate the players. The proof is in the results.

Bernie: If the players aren't doing it themselves then the manager and coaching staff have to make sure they do it – and, at the minute, they're not doing it. That is the truth.

Peter: I want him to do well. I love this club, I really do.

Eric: Well, if you want them to do well, then why have you stopped going?

Peter: Why should I go there and spend my money?

Eric: But you've just said you want him to do well!

Peter: I *do* want him to do well.

Malcolm: Don't you feel that by being there you would help him to do better?

Peter: Alright then, Malcolm, what about Souness then? You've got 52,000 fans who wanted rid of him, but they were going week in and week out.

Malcolm: But they were getting their message across by being there.

Peter: Exactly!

Malcolm: But they weren't refusing to go. They were getting their message across though – and they did it in numbers.

Peter: Well, we do it the opposite way.

Malcolm: But does it really get the message across?

Peter: Well, it gets the message across that there's five or six thousand more fans that are really disgruntled by what they are seeing week in and week out. You know where I'm coming from, don't you, Eric? Look at your gates now.

Eric: I tell you, I watched Sunderland play Boro the other night. I think Middlesbrough have a lot going for them. You have young lads in the team from Teesside that might just do it. The young lad, Cattermole. Brilliant! At Sunderland, what have we got? Nothing! And you lot are doing more moaning than the Sunderland fans.

Paul, Sunderland

Paul: Where to start with Sunderland? I don't know why anyone is surprised about what Murray has said. He's got previous. I liken this season to the season we were gifted promotion when Denis Smith was the manager and then went out and signed two players, Peter Davenport and Kevin Ball.

Eric: They've always done the same, haven't they?

Paul: It's ridiculous what he's done. You've got to go out and take opportunities like we've had this season.

Eric: These are the same people that put us in the mire. It's being badly run the club.

I want the Boro to lose tomorrow and get rid of the Boro boss. He's been found out. He has to go now. When Boro get beat tomorrow he will be sent to Coventry, like the Boro fans
- Andy, Thornaby

175

Paul: The lad who writes for *The Echo* in Sunderland has written that Mick McCarthy and Bob Murray need to look at themselves because they are in denial. I think they both are. The players we've bought this season! It's a long time since I've been able to put two current players into my all-time worst eleven. One of them is the goalkeeper and the other is one of the forwards, Gray. He's one of the worst players I've ever seen in a Sunderland shirt.

Eric: Well, he hasn't done it, the lad.

Paul: I can remember going to see Sheffield United last season. We had been linked with Andy Gray and he didn't want to come at the time. I remember seeing him and being glad we didn't get him.

Eric: What can happen to put it right?

Paul: Well, I think the chairman deliberately keeps a lid on it. He turns up when we're doing well, gets all the plaudits, and then when it turns bad he goes into hiding.

Malcolm: This row between Mick McCarthy and the chairman…

Eric: It's not a row, Malcolm.

Malcolm: Well, it's very much a difference of opinion, to say the least. Are newspapers stirring that or is it a genuine difference of opinion within the club?

Paul: I think McCarthy has honestly spoken the truth. Where we are going to go with season ticket holders, I don't know. I'm thinking long and hard about whether I'm going to get one. All the time that bloke has been chairman the club have never once signed a player when I've thought 'God, I can't believe we've gone out and signed him.' Middlesbrough have done it with the likes of Ravanelli, Newcastle signed Shearer.

Eric: It's right. We've never signed a player that you thought 'Phew! What a player!'

Bernie: You weren't happy when you signed Flo. And you must have thought 'Whoah!' when you signed The Nose – Noseworthy!

Malcolm: What about Niall Quinn when you signed him from Manchester City?

Eric: Niall Quinn did a good job for Sunderland, but at the time we signed him we wondered if he was past it, will he be able to do it?

Paul: He was a tremendous player.

In The News

FA Cup Round 3 replay: Boro 1 Coventry 0

Boro 3 Chelsea 0

Aston Villa 1 Newcastle 2

Sunderland 1 Tottenham 1

Premier League positions

	P	W	D	L	Pts
14 Newcastle	25	9	5	11	32
16 Boro	25	7	7	11	28
20 Sunderland	25	2	4	19	10

Monday February 13

Tom, Middlesbrough

Tom: Bernie, I'm struggling to get over what happened on Saturday, I really am.

Bernie: Yeah, it was a special occasion, fantastic result.

Tom: I mean I went there thinking we were going to get hammered, I really did, Bernie. I was hoping it wouldn't get too embarrassing, that they wouldn't get five or six, but I feared the worse. I was there at Villa the week before and that was scandalous that game – and I blame McClaren for that.

Bernie: Tom, I'll ask you this question because I want to know how a team with one or two changes can go from the debacle against Aston Villa to the performance against Chelsea in one week. For once Steve McClaren would have been right to use the word 'magnificent', so it's typical of him that I don't think he did use the word this time. But it begs the question how that can happen.

Tom: I think it reflects on McClaren. I mean suddenly people are saying he's turned it around, that he's beaten Chelsea. But he didn't do it, the players did it.

Bernie: Yeah, but I see it the other way. Fair enough, Steve McClaren is the manager but he was also the manager when they were losing 4-0 to Aston Villa, 7-0 to Arsenal and struggling to beat mighty Nuneaton from the non-league when I felt we could have lost on the day.

Malcolm: Yes, where was Steve McClaren's influence then when it was all going so wrong for you?

Tom: What I wanted to say though, Bernie, is that Rochemback looked like a different player on Saturday, didn't he? That early goal seemed to give him confidence. I thought he had a great game. I've never been his biggest fan, I've criticised him plenty of times in the past but he was star man for me against Chelsea.

Bernie: Rochemback did well – and he kept his shot low instead of skying it like he usually does. They all did well. Yakubu, Downing, the whole defence excellent and strong. But these were the same players who let the fans down seven days earlier. It makes me wonder if they turned it on because it was the champions.

Tom: I just hope we can go on and do something now, Bernie. I mean relegation could still happen, though it obviously looks a bit better now. But we've got Europe coming again soon and I thought we'd have no chance. I'm looking forward to Stuttgart now instead of dreading it. I mean, we were going out, weren't we? If we played against Stuttgart like we did against Villa it would have been embarrassing out there.

Malcolm: Tom, don't you think it still might be? Stuttgart, I am sure, will be very difficult opposition. Yes, you've beaten Chelsea but you've also lost to a lot of very poor teams.

Tom: Well, I'm not too bothered what you think, Malcolm. Newcastle have got problems of their own and you're not out of the woods yet either. Bernie, I think we can do it on Thursday. A draw, 1-1 or something like that, would be great to give us a chance in the second leg here.

Bernie: Yeah, I agree. A draw over there and then bring them back to the Riverside. But right now Europe's not our priority. It's all about the league for me.

Pete, Middlesbrough

Pete: I've got two points I really want to make after Saturday and I'd like to know what you think. Firstly, brilliant result, brilliant game, loved it. I thought every player did his job, played their hearts out.

Bernie: No one had a bad game. Not one. It was a team performance.

Pete: Yeah, great stuff. I came away in a state of wondering what had happened, I couldn't believe it. I thought it would be the end for McClaren like, especially if we got walked on six or seven.

Bernie: Well, Steve Gibson was under pressure last week to make a decision and I know a lot of people felt there was only one decision, that McClaren would go. But credit to the chairman for keeping faith.

Pete: Aye, but he's not out of the woods yet though, Bernie. That's what I wanna say to you. Great, we beat Chelsea, scored three goals. But what about before that and what about next week? I watch Boro home and away as much as I can, I travel the country to watch them and what I saw against Arsenal was just rubbish. They weren't trying if you ask me. I don't mean the kids, I don't blame the kids, but the experienced players, that's not good enough.

Eric: Not like your manager then, Pete? Didn't he blame it on the young players?

Bernie: It was a shocking performance and it could have been ten. We were lucky not to concede more goals on the day. Henry was on fire but we were appalling, simply not good enough. I don't blame the younger players, the Taylors, the Morrisons, Bates and the young lad, Wheater. But there's a lot of questions not been answered as to what went wrong that day.

Pete: I know some people who were stood near me who said they wouldn't go again after the Arsenal game like. But we were good against Sunderland and then just rubbish against Villa.

Eric: Hang on, Sunderland made you look good. Yes, you did quite well, but you weren't world-beaters and I tell you what, you've still got some problems there.

Malcolm: Yes, don't let one result fool you into believing that everything in the garden is rosy because it's not, far from it.

Bernie: No, no, Malcolm, everybody knows that. The fans know that, Steve McClaren must know that, Keith Lamb and Steve Gibson must know that, I'm sure they do. Hopefully the players know that it's not been good enough.

Pete: We could go down still, Bernie. We could easily go down but then we go and beat Chelsea. I don't get that. I'm not complaining about us beating Chelsea, but hopefully things have gone on at the club that we don't know about because it looked like it. Because some players didn't look interested in the Villa game and then turned it on on Saturday.

Eric: Well, maybe they were tired against Aston Villa?

Bernie: Yes, that will be it. I tell you what, there better not be any of those excuses, because that's all they are.

Tuesday February 14
Mark, Middlesbrough

Mark: Right, I'm ringing up because I want to know what you think, Bernie, about McClaren. I still think he should get the sack personally. We beat Chelsea, one game and everyone thinks things are fine but I'm not having it.

Bernie: Well, Steve Gibson has made it clear that Steve McClaren still has his support and we've got to respect that. He has to see the bigger picture, what has been achieved since McClaren got here – the silverware, Europe.

Mark: Oh, come on, Bernie, you don't believe that.

Malcolm: Bernie, Newcastle United sacked their manager because he was under-performing and they are several points above Middlesbrough, who have retained their manager. So Steve McClaren must still be a worried man even with Steve Gibson in charge.

Mark: Alright, bigger picture – yes, Carling Cup, best moment of my life as a fan. Europe, brilliant, not that I've gone to many games. Well, I've been to two of them this season at home and I went over to Amsterdam for the Alkmaar game. But what about the league? What about the rubbish football? You've seen it, Bernie, it's been rubbish a lot of the time. I'm glad that fan ran on the pitch against Villa because I nearly joined him, I might have ran on if he hadn't because I'm just sick of watching negative football and we're not even winning usually.

Bernie: They've been some highs – Man United 4-1, we beat the Arsenal, Chelsea at the weekend. But there's been some big lows that have been majorly disappointing. No one can get away from that.

In The News

Blackburn 2 Sunderland 0

UEFA Cup Round of 32 1st leg: Stuttgart 1 Boro 2

Friday February 17
Mick, Middlesbrough

Mick: I just want to say how good that was last night. The lads were spot-on. I didn't think Stuttgart were as good as people expected but you can't ask for more than winning away in Europe.

Bernie: I thought they were very good. On the night, we deserved it. Stuttgart had their chances, missed them, we took ours. We should go through now and I will be surprised if we don't do it.

Mick: Bernie, I listened earlier in the week to the callers and I couldn't believe some of them. OK, Boro have been bad for the last few weeks, since Christmas probably, but some are just so negative. McClaren has done a great job for me.

Malcolm: What? You think he has done a great job this season, do you? 17th in the Premiership?

Mick: I think you'll find we're 16th, Malcolm.

Malcolm: Oh, well, that's all right then.

Mick: I think we can still have a good season. The league isn't good but we're looking like we'll go through to the last 16 in the UEFA Cup, we've got a hard game at Preston on Saturday but the players' confidence is back up now. Watching last night, it was clear the belief was coming back.

Bernie: It was a major improvement, there's no doubting that.

In The News

FA Cup Round 4: Newcastle 1 Southampton 0

FA Cup Round 4: Preston 0 Boro 2

Newcastle 0 Charlton 0

UEFA Cup Round of 32 2nd leg: Boro 0 Stuttgart 1

(Boro progress on away goals rule)

Friday February 24

Martin, Middlesbrough

Martin: Bernie, I'm a relieved man today after last night because it wasn't good, mate, was it?

Bernie: It wasn't good, you're dead right, but we won through. I felt in the first half we were far too negative, we didn't attack, we sat back and invited Stuttgart to attack us. It was asking for trouble and we got it.

Martin: But why we did that is beyond me because we were a goal up from the away leg. I went out to Germany and I thought we were excellent, to be honest. They had their chances but we took them and I thought we'd build on that last night, especially after winning a few games.

Bernie: Confidence should be high at the minute. We've had our problems this season but on the back of the Chelsea win, the display in the first leg and then even beating Preston, morale and confidence should be very good but it didn't look that way. We made life very hard for ourselves and it was a frustrating night for the supporters who paid good money for a poor night entertainment-wise, though I'm sure Steve McClaren will say it's job done.

Martin: I'll be honest enough to say this, I've never been a big fan of McClaren's and I'm still not, but the fans won't put up with negative stuff much longer. Yes, we qualified for the quarter-final but it was boring to watch and I don't give us any hope against a quality side like Roma playing like we did last night.

Eric: Aren't Roma on a long winning run or something? I think I heard that they had won quite a few games in Italy and they'll be no mugs so it could be goodnight.

Martin: Eric, I don't often say this but I agree with you.

Bernie: We will have to be a lot more positive against West Brom if we want to come away with anything. For me, that's a bigger match even than Stuttgart. The Premier League is our bread and butter and if we were to lose at West Brom - and Bryan Robson will have them ready against his old club - then we will be back in the thick of the relegation battle. We need at least a draw but I hope we go to try and win it.

Alan, Newcastle

Alan: How much better is the atmosphere at St James' since Souness packed his bags? Roeder and Shearer have been like a breath of fresh air running through the club.

Malcolm: Glenn Roeder has done very well, absolutely. It's still early in his time as caretaker manager, with Alan as his assistant, but it is certainly a giant step forward from what we were seeing under his predecessor. I don't think the players knew what they were supposed to be doing under Graeme Souness.

Alan: Malcolm, he was clueless.

Malcolm: He was, you have to say that. Certainly I could not make head nor tail of it, as much as I tried. But well done to Glenn Roeder and everyone else at the Newcastle United. There's still a long way to go yet, but we've made some steps in the right direction and I expect to see another one against Everton at the weekend.

Alan: I'm feeling confident, I have to say, mind. Everton are no great shakes and we're playing some decent stuff, we're getting there. It's nothing like what we saw under Bobby Robson but that will take time, I think.

Joe, Sunderland

Joe: I'm a Sunderland supporter, lifelong, always will be. I want to say all that before I make my point.

Eric: Go on, lad, we're listening.

Joe: I don't want to come on here and say, 'Murray out', because it's been said before. We can all say it until we're blue in the face and we all know the club won't move forward again while he's still here.

Eric: We all feel like that. It's just flat. There's nothing more to say. I don't enjoy the games, I don't enjoy coming on here

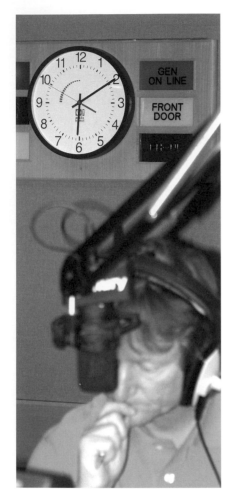

talking about it. It's just flat. The players are flat, the manager Mick McCarthy is flat, though he's battling on.

Joe: What I really wanted to say was that I hope things are going on behind the scenes beyond just Murray and whether he's leaving, to look at what has gone wrong and what can be done to stop it happening again.

Eric: Well, we've been saying that for a long, long time now.

Malcolm: You've been saying it for 50 years!

Eric: You're not wrong. We all know it's crap.

Joe: But everyone there needs to take a long, hard look at themselves and ask what they could have done differently or better, Eric. McCarthy, the players, Murray, John Fickling, everybody really. Right now, I know I'll be there next season. I love the club, I've had a lot of good times following the club, I never thought we would come up last season and well done to Mick McCarthy for getting us up, but I never imagined it would be this bad this season. It's been embarrassing.

Eric: It's embarrassing coming on here every night trying to think of new things to say on the back of defeat after defeat. But Joe, let's hope – because that's all we can do – that something happens, something that gives us some belief that things are going to improve. That's not going to come on the pitch now, because we're down, but off the pitch I'm sure they know things have got to change.

In The News

West Brom 0 Boro 2

Birmingham 1 Sunderland 0

Newcastle 2 Everton 0

Premier League positions

	P	W	D	L	Pts
11 Newcastle	27	10	6	11	36
16 Boro	26	8	7	11	31
20 Sunderland	27	2	4	21	10

Monday February 27
Andy, Middlesbrough

Bernie: Come on, Andy, what do you think of yesterday? Were you there?

Andy: No, I wasn't, I couldn't get there but I wish I had now because the buzz is coming back. I wondered if Chelsea might be a one-off but that's a great result, to go to West Brom and win at this stage when you are under the cosh a little bit.

Eric: A little bit? Come on! Yes, great, great result against Chelsea but you were still right in the thick of it at the wrong end of the table, still are really.

Malcolm: No, Middlesbrough most certainly are not out of the woods yet.

Bernie: And neither are you Geordies, Malcolm. If we are in it so are you.

Malcolm: Bernie, I agree wholeheartedly but the difference is that we have five more points on the board than you do at present and that can mean an awful lot even at this stage.

Andy: Lads, what I was wanting to say is about Hasselbaink.

Bernie: He scored two good goals yesterday. He was the difference between the two sides.

Andy: I'm just delighted that he is scoring goals like he has since the turn of the year really. It takes some of the pressure off Yak's shoulders if Jimmy is banging them in as well. I just think Jimmy's quality and it would have been a travesty if he had been allowed to leave in January because I think that might have happened.

Bernie: Jimmy's done it since Christmas. He's on fire but he needs to keep doing it if he wants to earn a new contract. I'm sure that's on his mind. Last season, first season on Teesside, he was quality but he was disappointing by his own standards early on this season. He still can't trap the ball but he's a terrific goalscorer and all teams need that.

Andy: He is, and I just hope they give him a new contract because he deserves it.

Micky, Newcastle

Micky: Malcolm, I'd just like to come on and praise some of the Newcastle players who have been done so well since Souness got the sack.

Malcolm: Well, several players have responded in a way that tells me that they were as relieved as we were to see Graeme Souness removed from his position in charge of the Newcastle United team. They look like different players and I think Glenn Roeder deserves great credit for that, Alan Shearer too, but you cannot underestimate the impact that the departure of Graeme Souness has had.

Micky: I'm just glad he's gone really because I was seriously worried we were going to join the Mackems in the Championship next season at the rate we were going. I never agreed with his appointment and I was proved right.

Malcolm: Not too many people, as I remember, did agree with his appointment and it remains beyond me why it was allowed to happen.

Micky: But do you think Roeder and Shearer are going to be the answer long-term, Malcolm? I don't. I can't see it. Shearer maybe but not Roeder.

Malcolm: I am certain that the long-term plan is for Alan Shearer to be manager of Newcastle United but right now he is Glenn Roeder's right-hand man and they are both making a good fist of managing the club after the problems we endured under Souness.

Micky: Shearer's the man for me. Got to be. After everything he has done for this football club, I love the man.

Wednesday, March 1

James, Sunderland

James: I've just come on to say or try to say something good or positive about Sunderland really.

Malcolm: This I do look forward to. You have got us all intrigued now, James.

Eric: I can't imagine what you are going to say, but go on.

James: Well, I know it's been bad, abysmal, rubbish results and everything. I've hated it at times. I never thought I would see a worse team than the one that got us relegated three years ago but this one is worse.

Eric: The facts tell you that. The league table tells you that.

James: Most of the players haven't been up to it but I think Dean Whitehead has looked quality at times.

Eric: Quality? Do you?

James: Eric, I know what you are going to say but Whitehead will go on to play for a top team in the Premier League. Well, that's my opinion anyway.

Eric: Yeah, fair enough, that's your opinion, but I don't see it. I don't see what other people see in Dean Whitehead. No, he hasn't been one of our worst players. Yes, he is full of effort and commitment, but a top player? Premier League class? Do me a favour, man! No chance.

James: Julio Arca hasn't had a good season by his standards but I think Whitehead has adapted well to the league and the step up to it, even in a terrible team.

Eric: I don't see it. I think they have all struggled. Arca is the best player, though you're right, he's not had a good season, no-one has. If Whitehead and Stead and the others bounce back and prove me wrong next season I'll say great. Well, they won't prove me wrong, but I hope they bounce back and show themselves to be better than what they have looked this season.

In The News

Sunderland 1 Man City 2

Sunderland sack Mick McCarthy, making Black Cats legend Kevin Ball caretaker-manager.

Boro 1 Birmingham 0

(Boro move 11 points clear of relegation positions)

Newcastle 3 Bolton 1

Premier League positions

	P	W	D	L	Pts
10 Newcastle	28	11	6	11	39
16 Boro	27	9	7	11	34
20 Sunderland	28	2	4	22	10

Monday March 6 2006

Bernie: Mick McCarthy has been sacked after three years in charge at Sunderland. I personally wish him all the best. Eric, is it a surprise?

Eric: It's not the biggest shock in the world, is it? Slightly surprising because I didn't think anything was going to happen until the end of the season.

Malcolm: What is the point? What is the benefit for Sunderland between now and end of the season?

Eric: The benefit would be if they had someone ready to come in now. It gives Kevin Ball a great opportunity. He can't do any worse, can he?

Malcolm: He can't, no. All he has to do is go and win a home game. If he does that he's done better than Mick McCarthy.

Eric: Everybody knows Kevin. He's a good character, he'll get his teeth into it and, boy, he will want that job, don't worry about that.

Ian, Sunderland

Ian: Totally the wrong timing. It's not going to improve anything. I cannot understand why Mr Fickling thinks him and rest of the board have the same aspirations as the fans. They never have. At the moment it's an embarrassment to be a Sunderland fan. Kevin Ball is a Sunderland legend, red and white through and through, but he hasn't got the experience. People are disillusioned now. Come season ticket renewal time, mine's going straight in the bin. How many more thousands of fans feel like me? It's sickening, it really is.

Eric: I heard a quote from Bob Murray today that, as chairman, he takes full responsibility for what has proved to be an unsuccessful and heartbreaking season. That's the first time I've heard him say that.

Ian: If he was a decent bloke he would say he is standing down, but he's made Mick McCarthy the scapegoat. I was never a fan of McCarthy, he was the wrong man for the job to start with.

Bernie: He got you promotion.

Ian: Bernie, we've had promotion that many times, we've been up and down. I mean, a monkey could get us promotion.

Bernie: Well, one did!

(Silence)

Bernie: Only a joke, Ian.

Ian: I've supported this club 30-odd years and I've known more disappointments than triumphs. While this guy is in charge this club is going nowhere. The board have waited until it's too late. They'll be lucky to get 10,000 in that stadium next season.

Eric: At least they've done something.

Malcolm: I'm afraid it smacks of cynicism.

Peter, Middlesbrough

Peter: I think it's absolutely disgraceful what they've done to McCarthy. They've tied his hands behind his back, then with 10 games to go they've decided to do something about this when they know they are down.

Malcolm: I agree with what you are saying but will Mick McCarthy regret the things he has said like, 'I was fully backed by the board'? I think he will regret those statements for a long time to come.

Peter: I feel for the guy, I really do. He has done the best he could do on limited resources.

Eric: The new manager will know he's going to be on limited resources.

Peter: What would you have changed?

Eric: What would I have changed? I couldn't have changed the attitude of the board. Something about Mick's body language at the weekend after the game told me that he'd had enough. I hear all this crap coming from the dressing room saying the spirit is brilliant. How can it be when you are getting beat every week? It can't be. Mick had to keep saying, 'We're doing okay, but we got beat'.

Peter: Six weeks ago I thought we were for the dreaded drop.

Bernie: There's better teams than us that have gone down over the years. But we're winning and now's the time to show that we've got quality.

Peter: This guy, the Yak, he's the man. He's top quality.

Bernie: He is quality. His holding up, his movement, his pace, his power, everything. He's not a big-time Charlie, he enjoys it.

Ray, Newcastle

Ray: Malcolm, I've got the greatest of respect for you, but I think you're playing devil's advocate or you are trying to provoke a discussion on the Ameobi situation. I've spoken to a lot of people and Ameobi is a lazy, idle footballer and he does not deserve the credit and the praise that you are giving him. He is letting the fans down every time he plays.

Malcolm: I can't believe you've come on after Saturday…

Ray: He missed a sitter!

Malcolm: Bernie, have you missed a sitter?

Bernie: Yeah.

Malcolm: Eric, have you missed sitters?

Eric: Oh, I can't remember.

Malcolm: Oh come, everybody misses sitters that is prepared to get in there and score a few goals. Everybody…from Jimmy Greaves, Denis Law, you name them, they've missed them. Pele, Ronaldo, Ronaldinho. Come on now!

Bernie: Yeah, but the thing you're missing here is that by the end of the season they still ended up with 25 or 30 goals. Has Ameobi?

Ray: I just don't think he's cutting the mustard.

Malcolm: Well, that's your opinion.

Eric: Well, let him have his say then!

Bernie: Go on, Ray, it's your call.

Malcolm: But I just don't think tonight is the time to say it after Saturday.

Ray: I think you're missing the point here. I know you talk to the grassroots fans. When it comes down to it, the guy's not pulling his weight. He's not showing the passion.

Malcolm: What do you call passion, for heaven's sake?

Ray: Passion for the team and the fans.

Malcolm: But everybody plays in a different style. You can't have 11 Scott Parkers making the team up. You have to have different kinds of players.

Ray: Of course, you have, I understand that. When the rest of the team was backs to the wall and the pressure was on, he wasn't back defending, but Shearer was.

Malcolm: As it so happens, Ameobi was back defending and made a mess for the Bolton goal.

Ray: This is what I'm getting at.

Malcolm: But you're saying he wasn't back there when he was.

Ray: And what did he do?

Malcolm: Well, he badly defended on the far post I have to admit.

Bernie: So where should he be?

Ray: He shouldn't be on the pitch. Send him to Sunderland!

John, Sunderland

John: You've got me the wrong time, I'm in the bath.

Eric: I can picture you now.

John: I bet you can! It came on the radio that McCarthy has got the sack, I thought, 'Brilliant'. I didn't want him there anyway. Then I heard that a Sunderland legend has got the job. I thought it was Gatesy, he had the job at last.

Eric: That would have been a shock!

John: You are the man they want in there, Eric. You talk like the fans.

Eric: They couldn't buy me out of this contract at Century!

Bernie: What do you want Eric for   the chairman, the manager, the coach?

John: The manager. He'd do the job.

Bernie: Have you been drinking the bathwater, John?

John: I said to you last year that promotion would be bad for the club and that McCarthy would get the sack.

Eric: Yes, you did say that it would be bad to come up and go down again and I tell you what, you're going to be proved right.

John: It's going to hit the fan base. If Murray walks away the club will be left in tatters. We need someone to come in, don't we? But not many people will touch it at the minute. Would we not be better declaring ourselves bankrupt and getting rid of all the debt? Then we can rebuild the club again, because at the end of the day we're going to go down.

Bernie: No, never!

John: You're kidding, aren't you?

Bernie: By, you Sunderland fans are clever lads!

Newcastle get beat off Manchester City and get rid of their manager the next day. Sunderland get beat by Man City and follow suit. Therefore, is Bernie worried about Boro's upcoming game on April 1, against Man City? If Boro lose may Boro make it a hat-trick of north-east clubs to sack their managers after defeats to City?
- Graeme

Next Manager at SAFC ? How's about Martin Allen along with Kevin Ball? The players wouldn't dare not give 100%. Keep the faith - Paul

Ameobi may not be world class striker but he has scored more Champions League goals than Boro and SAFC put together!
- Paul in Newcastle

Very sad 2 see Mick go. But now is the time for Bob to pull out all the stops and prove to the people that matter - the fans - that he does care, and get the right man in no matter what the cost
- Mackemjack. Forever loyal

I,d just like 2 say a
big thank you 2 Mick
McCarthy for getting the
club back 2 the Premier
League in the first
place. I wish him all
the best in the future.
I think he's a top bloke
who deserved better
- Mark in Durham

Eric, next Sunderland
manager is going 2 B
Chinese. His name is Win
One Soon
- Stevie, Sunderland

Gatesy, we all know it's
a lot deeper problem
than the manager but I
can't understand
Sunderland fans saying
they want 2 keep the
manager cos his Premier
record stinks. He should
have gone b4 Xmas
- Steve in Sacriston

Leave Bob Murray alone.
He has my full support.
Dinner's in the oven.
Good luck, darling
- Mrs Murray xx

Eileen, Sunderland

Eileen: I haven't been on for ages but I just felt so depressed. I always come on and am very optimistic but I had to come on tonight. Is it a good or bad move that Mick McCarthy's gone? I'm very sad because I think Mick is a very genuine bloke and he's good for football – and the timing is bizarre.

Bernie: Why do you think the club's did it now?

Eileen: I honestly don't know. If they were going to get rid of McCarthy I thought it would have been before Christmas, before the transfer window. I think there's no doubt even then we'd have still gone down but we could have built something to move on next season.

Eric: I think they've given it to Bally in the hope that he goes and wins five or six games before they send out season ticket forms. I think they are praying for that.

Eileen: I think that's a bit cynical.

Malcolm: But aren't they cynical though?

Eileen: No, I hope not, I really hope not. I think Bob Murray would love someone to come along with a load of money for the club. I don't like the way so many people are being critical of him. It is so easy for us to keep saying he should keep putting his hands in his pocket. You've got to say that it's a massive debt but we are still in a situation where I think it's a manageable debt.

Malcolm: How can it be a manageable debt when it has restricted McCarthy?

Eileen: The only positive thing I can say is that hopefully Kevin Ball can sort the defence out. There were such basic errors yesterday. You go two down in the first 10 minutes and you don't stand a chance, though I've got to say after that the team spirit was excellent and their heads didn't go down.

Les, Sunderland

Les: I'm phoning up about Kevin Ball being manager. I'm just over the moon, it's the best thing that's ever happened to this club. Everyone I have spoken to had been wanting Kevin Ball in for a long time.

Bernie: So what's Kevin going to bring you?

Les: I tell you what he's going to bring – and you can laugh all you want - but he's going to bring us 10 wins.

Bernie: Ten wins? You're off your head. Don't get me wrong I respected Kevin as a player but…

Les: I thought Mick McCarthy did a good job with the money he had but Ball's got something that McCarthy didn't have - he's Sunderland through and through.

Bernie: But how's Kevin going to lift morale in there?

Les: He loves the club.

Bernie: Yeah, but loving it isn't going to change it. I said months ago that Mourinho or Ferguson couldn't change Sunderland at the minute. So how is Kevin Ball, an inexperienced manager, going to change it?

Eric: That's not the answer at all. Jimmy Montgomery loves the club. Bobby Kerr loves the club. I love the club, believe it or not, despite the criticism. We were so proud to play for Sunderland. Of course Kevin loves the club, but he's not the only one.

Bernie: You need the players to love the club.

Les: After yesterday's match my head was down, I couldn't see a way out. I was sickened. I wasn't going to go to no more matches this season. I said, 'That's it'. Now I can't wait for the weekend.

Bernie: But you are still watching the same players. The way you are talking, is that not the way they got rid of McCarthy and put Ball in the job? Because they know guys like you will think like that. I think you're easily kidded.

Eric: Do you think in 10 games you think Kevin can turn around the team?

Les: Well, I might be exaggerating saying 10 games.

Bernie: OK, be serious, how many games do you think you are going to win between now and the end of the season.

Les: How many? I say we're going to win six.

Malcolm: What? What? What you are saying is that Kevin Ball, in the matter of three or four days, he's going to get a defence not making all the mistakes they've been making all season long and a midfield that's going to be bossing the game when they've been invisible all season and a forward line that's going to suddenly to start scoring goals. That, for me, is asking a miracle.

Les: Well, how do you explain how Newcastle have started playing?

Malcolm: Those players have done it before. The players in Sunderland haven't.

Les: All I want is someone managing the club who loves the club. I know you keep saying that's not enough.

Bernie: So if Martin O'Neill says I want to go to Sunderland, you'd say, 'No, I want Kevin Ball'?

Les: I would, yeah. I'd have no-one at that football club ahead of Kevin Ball.

Bernie: Brilliant, though I'm sure even Kevin will be scratching his head at that. Before you go, Les, can I just ask you're not related to Kevin, are you?

Dave, Sunderland

Dave: I'm just amazed and am quite embarrassed at some of the nonsense that some of the Sunderland supporters are coming out with. What's all the fuss about? I mean we knew we were going to go down before the season started.

Eric: No, you didn't know we were going down.

Dave: Oh, come on, everybody knew we were going down.

Eric: You had that hope, every Sunderland fan had. You didn't think it would be as bad as it is.

Dave: I didn't think it would be as bad, but would Sunderland supporters want to swap positions with fans from Forest, Derby, Leicester, people like that? Why are they feeling so sorry for themselves? Do you know we haven't finished below 23rd – that's third in the next tier – for the last 10 or 11 years?

Eric: Is that good enough?

Dave: Well, when you look at other teams that I've just named…

Bernie: Dave, I keep hearing that Sunderland is a big club but you sound like you're easily pleased.

Dave: Well, they are and they're not. People say Sunderland are fantastic supporters, but the reality is that we don't put the same kind of money into the club as Newcastle supporters do. We get the cheap school tickets. And in defence of Bob Murray, he hasn't raised the season ticket prices for the last five or six years.

Bernie: Well, how could he?

Dave: Well, when we got promotion he didn't raise them and when we had four seasons in the Premiership he pegged them at the same level.

Bernie: So what's he going to do after this season – is he going to give them all away for free?

Dave: Everybody's criticising him but he's trying to run Sunderland like a business. Everyone's slagging him off and saying how cynical but your last caller has just said Kevin Ball is the best thing since sliced bread. It's a masterstroke if he's right. Because he's about to send out season ticket forms and what he's trying to do is get the money in.

Malcolm: Isn't that cynical manoeuvring of Sunderland fans'?

Dave: Where do Sunderland fans think the money's going to come from?

Eric: How was this business being run when we were second in the table? Why wasn't he trying to run it as a business when we were going well?

Dave: Bob Murray will not go any further into debt because we haven't got the supporters that everyone thinks we have. The great proportion of the gate is cheap school tickets. I pay £500 for me and my son's season tickets. I wouldn't get one at Newcastle for that.

Eric: And you wouldn't want one either!

Tuesday March 7

Les, Sunderland

Bernie: Handsome Les, how are you?

Les: I'm absolutely fine, son.

Eric: You can't kid us, Les, we've seen you, man.

Bernie: You make Eric look like Richard Gere.

Les: Correct. At least I go after women instead of sheep.

Bernie: Hey, don't knock it until you've tried it!

Les: Eric, Murray and Fickling have got a chance to get the man that every Sunderland supporter wants.

Malcolm: Now I'm intrigued.

Les: Now Malcolm, I remember going on a radio programme 13 years ago and begging for them to get Brian Clough up here and they wouldn't do it.

Malcolm: There was a chance he was going to take the job at one stage, wasn't there?

Les: I'm led to believe he had a meeting with Keith Collins at the

So the Mackems sack the manager after being beaten by Man City ... as did the Mags ... then they put the Academy manager in charge, just as the Mags did ... I'm just wondering if they've changed their nickname from the Black Cats 2 the Copy Cats
– Eric, a Toon fan

McCarthy should have gone months ago. If you hound the chairman out after putting 7 million in God help the club. McCarthy is another failure – Keith

The Sunderland board should hang their heads in shame at their timing of McCarthy's sacking. We go from one crisis to another. We are an absolute embarrassment – Terry, Chester-le-Street

Thanks for your efforts, Mick. Much appreciated. I now just hope Bob Murray does the honourable thing and leaves his post. Martin O'Neill is my choice
– Phil from Preston

WHO YOU GONNA CALL?

I am sick to death of
pompous prats like
Slaven and Supermac
looking down their noses
at Sunderland
- Phil, SAFC and proud
of it

Bernie, shut your mouth
- Martin O'Neill is a
Sunderland fan, man -
you Scottish/Irish
puppet
- Alan, Sunderland fan

Malcolm, on Shearer's
replacement in May, why
not sign Van Nistelrooy
for £10m? Imagine Owen,
Nistelrooy, Solano,
N'Zogbia, Emre, Parker,
Milner with O'Neill as
boss
- Andy, Newcastle

186

time, but that all came out years later. I like Mick McCarthy, I trusted my club in his hands. He got us promotion and he bought players but it hasn't worked. But he's got integrity and he's a very honest and decent man. The players have given him their all, everything they could give.

Eric: Well, some of them have.

Bernie: Right, Les, give us this name.

Malcolm: I think I know who it is.

Bernie: I do as well.

Les: We all know who it is. The players have done their best for Mick. They've put Kevin in charge and the fans love Bally for his honesty and the kind of bloke he is, but he's not ready for the job. Somebody has to be put in a position to build a team at the top.

Malcolm: We're busily writing names down that we think you're going to say.

Bernie: And the names differ.

Les: Well, Sunderland haven't got a lot of money so they have to have a manager who players want to play for and who want to come here for him because he's a class manager. Everyone knows who it is - it's Martin O'Neill.

(Bernie plays *The Laughing Policeman*).

Eric: Bernie, behave, man! Bernie, he's being serious.

Bernie: Howay, Les, Martin O'Neill? You're joking, man. Tatum O'Neill or Jonjo O'Neill! You're as crackers as the guy that was on last night. There's no way on this earth you're going to get Martin O'Neill. You know that, Les.

Les: I tell you what, you can laugh all you like. This is what I would say to Bob Murray and the Sunderland board. If you got O'Neill you would get 40,000 season ticket holders.

Bernie: But it ain't going to happen.

Les: Well, it's up to the board.

Eric: Just because they got a new manager…40,000 season tickets? Are you being really serious?

Les: Eric, everyone believes in him. He talks like us, he thinks like us, he gets the best out of players. In my eyes, he's the best British manager around.

Eric: I know where you are coming from because it's an ideal situation for Sunderland, but where do you think they are going to get the money from to give him the contract or to buy the players?

Malcolm: And how are they going to persuade him to take a huge drop in money considering he's probably going to be offered something like £4 million a year to take the England job?

Eric: Are you going on the suggestion that he's been quoted as saying he's a Sunderland fan and that maybe he would like to come and do it here?

Les: Well, Newcastle would have him next week.

Malcolm: I think there is a fairly strong following for him among Newcastle supporters but I think the majority would say, "No" because they don't like the style of football he produces.

Les: Everyone's got their opinions but I can vouch for another 40,000 Sunderland supporters. That's who we all want. Murray and Fickling, who we all want to leave, have a chance to give every Sunderland supporter what they all want. How he does it is up to him. It's about time he got his finger out and gave Sunderland fans what they want.

Bernie: That would prove the club mean business but it would show a lack of ambition in O'Neill.

Malcolm: Sunderland's CV isn't very appealing, is it, to someone like Martin O'Neill?

Les: No-one's seen Sunderland win anything for years and years and years. He's got one last throw of the dice. It's a chance to give us a glimmer of hope, some pride. If he wants to fill that stadium he has to give us that man.

Malcolm: Well, I don't think he'll do it.

Eric: He's given you Kevin Ball and he hopes that he turns things around and then that will be Murray's magic wand. He's a favourite with the fans and that is his get-out.

Les: The chances of it happening are a million to one but he's got the one chance. With the greatest respect to Kevin Ball he won't attract international players.

Bernie: It's money that attracts players, Les.

Les: Not always. When Kevin Keegan went to Newcastle they were going to go down in the Third Division. He was a big name who had never managed before but he attracted players.

Malcolm: Yes, he did. But there was great change happening with the takeover by Sir John Hall.

Bernie: If the big players don't have the money to purchase the big names then they won't go there. The name is a start but then it's what's in the bank account.

Les: It will bring money in because the place will be full, then they'll have to extend again.

Bernie: What did you say, Les, you'll have to extend again? I tell you what, I used to think you were a sensible lad but you've lost the plot.

Malcolm: It's a very thought-provoking start to the calls. You both thought that Les was going to go for Martin O'Neill but I thought he was going to suggest Nigel Clough, who's non-league but seems to be putting together quite a CV.

Bernie: For me, that would be more realistic. Les is living in Cuckoo Land.

Reg, Sunderland

Reg: I'm going to have to agree with Malcolm, which I don't like too much.

Malcolm: Oh, that's breaking your heart, isn't it?

Reg: The name he said before is the name I've been thinking – Nigel Clough. And you've missed something out about him. He was actually born in Sunderland.

Malcolm: Was he? I didn't know that.

Bernie: No, he lived in the Boro, did he not?

Reg: No, when Cloughie lived up here, Nigel was born in Sunderland hospital.

Bernie: So that's why he should become Sunderland manager?

Reg: One reason.

Bernie: I think you Sunderland fans are crackpots. Yous are mad.

Reg: He's a Makem by birth.

Bernie: Oh, give him the job then!

Reg: I think he would build us up, he would get the attention of the media with the Cloughie connection, he's got experience in the lower leagues.

Eric: Why not? I can see your point.

Bernie: Nigel Clough has worked down there, gained experience…

Eric: He probably deserves a chance somewhere. If Bally got appointed tomorrow, I'd say, 'Good luck to you', if Nigel Clough got appointed tomorrow, I'd say, 'Good luck to you', if Martin O'Neill got appointed, I'd say, 'Good luck to you'. The only one that would be different would be Peter Reid, I'd say, 'Oh no, you're joking!'

Wednesday March 8

Colin, Middlesbrough

Colin: Only one thing to say about tomorrow night – COME ON!

Bernie: How do you see it going, Colin?

Colin: I want it to be better than Saturday because that was like being at the dentist's.

Malcolm: Do you think you should take the cavalier approach that you did against Chelsea?

Colin: Well I'd like to think we'd play like we did against Chelsea. We're playing the favourites. Let's have a real go.

Bernie: I agree, Colin, if we play cagey we'll get done. Let's go and have a real go.

Colin: I would like to see Steve McClaren, for once in his life, have a real go. I'd like to see Jimmy and Yakubu up front. But I tell you what, credit came out of the game against Birmingham on Saturday – young Cattermole.

Bernie: Oh, he was good, my man of the match. And Jimmy has been on fire in front of goal.

Colin: I tell you this, Bernie, when we win our lass generally doesn't have my tea ready. She expects a Chinese or an Indian.

Gatesy, how about getting behind the new manager instead of your negative comments week in and week out – you long-haired buffoon!
– Dave, angry Sunderland fan

How about Bob Murray coming on the show like Steve Gibson had the guts to do? No chance!
– John, Boro fan

Bernie, you may be the last British team tomorrow but most of the north-east will be wanting Roma to win so put that in your pipe
– Joe of Durham

Eric, what's happening down there? The fans are some of the best in the world, the stadium one of the best in Europe. Feel so sorry for you lot
– Wayne, Newcastle fan.

187

Gatesy, my list 4 next
SAFC boss would be 1.
Roy Keane 2. Alan
Curbishley 3. Sam
Allardyce. Forget
O'Neill, he will B
England boss. Such
ambitious appointments
will never ever happen
with Murray at the helm
- Anth

O'Neill 2 manage
Sunderland - in press
conference Jonjo said
he's sick of training
horses and wants 2 work
with donkeys
- Steve, Chester

Eric, tell Bernie he
won't be laughing
tomorrow night when
boring Boro get stuffed
- Tony from Seaham

Bernie: So if Boro win you treat her?

Colin: When I came in on Saturday I was full of hell. She said, 'I can't weigh you up, Colin. What am I having for my supper?' I said, 'I'll still give you it, my darling'. I'm not telling you what I had for afters, mind!

Bernie: Scoreline?

Colin: 2-0, Bernie.

In The News

UEFA Cup Round of 16 1st leg: Boro 1 Roma 0

Sunderland 0 Wigan 1

(Kevin Ball's first match as caretaker-manager)

Man United 2 Newcastle 0

Charlton 2 Boro 1

Tuesday March 14

Simon, Sunderland

Simon: For the first time in a very, very long time things are looking up.

Malcolm: In what way?

Bernie: He must be ringing up to talk about Newcastle losing, Malcolm.

Simon: No, no, lads. Well, yeah and no. I expected the Skunks to lose at Man United, to be honest, so I took that for granted. But I'm just feeling that a corner has turned slightly for us really.

Eric: Not on the pitch, not in terms of results, they haven't.

Malcolm: Are you going to tell us you might stay up now that Kevin Ball is in charge?

Simon: No, I'm not. Even the most optimistic Sunderland supporter wouldn't predict that now, I don't think, but I think Kevin Ball is a good man to have in charge right now. Loved him as a player, love him as a character.

Eric: Well, yeah, but what difference is he going to make? That's

what I keep asking and that's what a lot of Sunderland people are asking. Was it just a PR thing in the hope that they might sell a few season tickets in the summer or whatever? Because I can't see the point in it, not now.

Simon: I know what you mean but it's something to hold on to. It's been the a nightmare season, the worst in our history and I just think that Bally will put some fight into the players.

Eric: Well, they've had that all season but they're just not good enough.

Simon: And it's good that the Smoggies are going to go out tomorrow night because they are getting too big for their boots, saying their going to do this and that. Two weeks ago they were saying 'Sack the manager', and now he's the greatest thing, but Roma will stick three or four past them, I'm sure of it.

Eric: You might well be right, but that wouldn't make Sunderland's season any better.

In The News

UEFA Cup Round of 16 2nd leg: Roma 2 Boro 1

(Boro qualify for quarter-final on away goals rule)

Friday March 17

Graham, Middlesbrough

Graham: I'll make no bones why I'm coming on tonight, lads, and that's to wind up the jealous Geordies out there. They must be looking on with very envious eyes – I know they are – about Boro being in the quarter-final of Europe.

Malcolm: Jealous? Why would we be jealous, Graham?

Bernie: Well, aren't you, Malcolm? You've gone from Champions League to nowhere in about three years, Boro are in the last eight of the UEFA Cup and we have a great chance of going all the way to the final.

Graham: I really think we do. I think we can win it. I know we scraped through the other night but Roma are a top, top side but I was proud of the players on the night.

Schwarzer was brilliant, Cattermole was immense and Hasselbaink's goal was just quality. I think we can win it, I do. And the Geordies will still be watching *The Bill!* What's been happening in *The Bill* lately, Malcolm?

Malcolm: I think you had more than an element of luck, by all accounts, so I'm not sure where you get such confidence from.

Bernie: Malcolm, Roma were the favourites and we beat them fair and square over two legs.

Graham: It was a great night; I still can't believe it really - to go to a team on something like nine straight wins in their league and do that to them. It's got to be one of our best nights in our history, hasn't it? I thought we'd struggle after only winning by the one in the first game and it was backs-to-the-wall stuff at times but I think we deserved it on the night.

Bernie: Roma missed some gilt-edged chances on the night, there's no doubting that, and Schwarzer was magnificent – he was like the great Lev Yashin. World class cross from Downing for Hasselbaink's goal and then we were pinned back but we did it, that's what counts. Well done to Steve McClaren and the players.

In The News

Bolton 2 Sunderland 0

Newcastle 1 Liverpool 3

Blackburn 3 Boro 2

Premier League positions

	P	W	D	L	Pts
12 Newcastle	30	11	6	13	39
16 Boro	29	9	7	13	34
20 Sunderland	30	2	4	25	10

FA Cup quarter-final: Chelsea 1 Newcastle 0

FA Cup quarter-final: Charlton 0 Boro 0

Friday March 24

Jimmy, Newcastle

Jimmy: I watched the game the other night. I went down to Chelsea.

Bernie: Come on then, give us your views. What went wrong'?

Jimmy: Well, I'm not too interested in talking to you really, Bernie, because you'll be out soon enough as well. But Malcolm, I just feel sorry for Alan Shearer. I think he deserved to win something with Newcastle. All them goals! The man's a legend and it would have been a dream for him to play his last game for us in the FA Cup final.

Malcolm: Yes, it would, but Newcastle have flattered to deceive throughout. Alan Shearer's record in phenomenal in terms of his goals-to-games ratio and his service to Newcastle United. I just feel that it was asking an awful lot of him to inspire a cup final run at this stage in his career.

Jimmy: The man's a legend. You were a legend, Malcolm, though I never saw you play. I've heard how good you were, but I've seen Alan Shearer and he's given me some of the best days of my life. I just hope there is work going on now to replace him, if you can do such a thing, because that will take some doing. If we don't replace him we will be in big trouble.

Malcolm: He will take an awful lot of replacing and I just wonder if Newcastle United have the finances to do so. Not too many centre-forwards spring to mind when you try to think of people who could fill Alan's boots and they all would cost the sort of money that I'm not sure will be available after the money that was wasted under Graeme Souness.

Bernie: You've got Ameobi. He'll score you the goals!

Jimmy: I know you're joking, Bernie, but that's not even funny. I know Malcolm likes him, but Ameobi will never score enough goals. He's not a born goalscorer and that's what we need desperately next season.

It would be fantastic if Boumsong had a great World Cup. Then some foreign club might stump up the money to buy him!
- Matt in Newcastle

To the Geordie who asked how many Boro fans would be at Charlton! We're all skint after 4 thousand of us spent hundreds of pounds going to Rome! - Boro Kev

Hello Eric, I am in Fuerteventura spending money I had saved for next year's season ticket at SAFC. Enough is enough!
- Heartbroken, Fishburn

Well, we didn't quite make it again last nite. I feel sorry for Shearer. It wud have been gr8 if we had gone on to win the cup but it wasn't to be
- Alan, Stanley

Bob Murray shouldn't walk away from Sunderland...there's still 30,000 who would gladly give him a lift!
- Rainman

189

Malcolm, Michael Owen is the key man in the summer because I think he must be sold to finance the squad. There are far more problems than just replacing Shearer. Three defenders and three strikers
- **John in the Toon**

Is that all Malcolm and Eric can say in response to the Boro's recent run about how little supporters we had? They are jealous, plain and simple -
Rich, Billingham

Boro catchment area is 300,000, Barcode catchment area 1.5 million, so shut up, Macdonald
- **Dave in Boro**

Typical sad Boro! Catchment area, my backside! Your fans are fickle and cheap skates!
- **Andy, Toon fan**

Gatesy, u seem very interested in other people's attendances, especially Boro's. Well here's some for you - Crewe 4,000; Brighton 7,000; Millwall 9,000 cos that's where u and all the whinging Mackems are heading! - **Dan**

Well done Newcastle for getting yourselves big crowds. All you need now is some silverware and 3 cup quarter finals this season
- **Chris, Boro fan in York**

In The News

Boro 4 Bolton 3

Charlton 3 Newcastle 1

Sunderland 0 Blackburn 1

Premier League positions

	P	W	D	L	Pts
13 Newcastle	31	11	6	14	39
14 Boro	30	10	7	13	37
20 Sunderland	31	2	4	25	10

Monday March 27

Colin, Middlesbrough

Colin: What a game that was on Saturday.

Bernie: Great performance, good footballing performance from both teams. Both went to try to win the game, fortunately we got all three points. Our timing was perfection in the dying seconds of the game.

Colin: I tell you what, though, what the hell was Parnaby doing in the box in the 92nd minute?

Bernie: Well, what happened is we changed the formation - Parnaby had moved on to the right side of the four but then moved into midfield.

Colin: Do you think he thought he was still a full-back and was trying to get to the line and got it wrong?

Bernie: Parnaby has scored four or five this season and scored a tremendous goal in Europe.

Colin: Bernie, I'll be honest, I have criticised him but he's starting to look a better player. I always thought he was a Division One or Championship player but I don't know what the change is lately.

Bernie: Parnaby's done really well this season – and he's scored more than the Sunderland team. Look at Stead, for instance, he's not scored a goal yet but Parnaby's got four or five.

Colin: Come on, Bernie, you're better than that – but you are right.

Bernie: You're dead right!

Eric: I don't think anyone at Sunderland's got four yet.

Bernie: Yeah, he'd be top scorer at Sunderland and he's a full-back.

Colin: Just one other thing – I don't want to get too carried away at the moment but I'm 48 years old and I'm thinking this could be the season I've dreamed about all my life. Given the circumstances of 7-0 at Arsenal and 4-0 at home to Villa, I bet that guy who threw his season ticket at McClaren is glad they gave him it back!

Bernie: You're absolutely right.

Richard, Sunderland

Richard: I just want to talk about the events inside and outside the stadium on Saturday. I thought it was quite interesting that halfway through the second half the crowd were doing exactly what Mr Fickling had asked them to do, getting behind the team, and the lads were playing ever so well, trying to get back into the game. And then there was this incredible announcement about the gates would be locked after the game so fans would not be allowed to congregate and demonstrate. I felt sorry for the players because the whole atmosphere changed, and yet the club brought it on themselves. It was just an incredible own goal.

Eric: But have you heard that the club have distanced themselves from that announcement?

Richard: Well, they've got to take some responsibility. But it worked the opposite way to what they intended. I didn't stick around last time there was a post-match demonstration but this time me and my lads stayed back to observe what happened. I just think they are upping the ante and making life harder for themselves. People are genuinely trying to make a point. What happened to democracy and it being a free country?

Malcolm: I agree. The whole atmosphere of football has changed over the last decade or so. It is now much more a family game and what it seems happened after the game in terms of trying to stop a demonstration was far removed from what was necessary.

Richard: Someone has got take some accountability. People were having a shout and a whinge, that's all, so I was very surprised when the Police decided to break it up.

Eric: So it was a bad bit of PR, whoever's fault it was?

Richard: That's what I thought.

Tuesday March 28
Derek, Sunderland

Derek: I'm just so frustrated, like the majority of the fans. I go every week wondering how many we are going to get beat by. It's that bad. My son won't leave until the final whistle…

Eric: Some time it will change, you mark my words, and you'll have great days.

Derek: I'm not bothered if we go down to the Conference, I'll still support them. It's our club and I'll be there long after Bob Murray has gone.

Eric: We'll be around Sunderland a long time after these players. If they don't like a bit of stick, tough! This radio show has been going longer than most of them players have been at the club so we haven't anything to worry about. So I'm not going to be frightened about speaking my mind and giving my honest views about the players and the games.

Bernie: Some of the players don't like what we say but we don't like what we are watching, so it goes hand in hand.

Malcolm: Maybe it's because of this programme that Sunderland couldn't get any good players this season!

Bernie: Oh, yeah – it's our fault, Malcolm!

Derek: Bernie, Good luck for the two cups that you're in – I hope you win them both.

Bernie: That's very nice. Cheers, Derek. There's some fans like this, isn't there. We still want the Sunderland fans to come on. Eric, you've got three home games to play and, if you don't win one of them, it's going to be the worst record in the top flight since 1888. You've never won a game at home yet.

Eric: Well, we've got Fulham, Newcastle and Arsenal. They are the three homes games. Well, we'll beat Newcastle, surely?

Bernie: I'm going to put you down to beat them!

Malcolm (laughing): Oh, yeah!

Eric: I'm going to be positive. Fulham haven't won an away game all season. Newcastle, well, we're going to beat them. And Arsenal, last game of the season? They're not going to put a team out

Bernie: They won't have to put a team out!

We are the laughing stock of football. Murray doesn't realise what he's done to this once great club
- Paul, Sunderland

Macdonald, stick to slagging off NUFC instead of SAFC, you arrogant numpty!
- Phil, Sunderland

Dan, Sunderland

Dan: That record we're going to get is not a nice one to have.

Malcolm: I have the feeling that if you get that record, you'll have it for all-time.

Dan: Oh, forever.

Malcolm: It's an horrendous record to have around your necks. And you really don't need it.

Bernie: Do you think you can avoid it?

Dan: Well, of the games we've got, the only one is the Fulham game. Their away record is so bad but I just can't see us winning a game. Eric, you know how the fans are protesting and wanting Murray out? Well, I reckon you should go on a holiday to the Middle East and see if you can find us a sheikh, you know what I mean?

Eric: I've been trying to find a sheikh for ages.

Malcolm: His trouble is his shakes have always got milk in them!

Malcolm, Middlesbrough

Malcolm: Isn't it great to be a Boro fan?

Bernie: Oh, fantastic. Enjoying it.

Malcolm: Just something I want to get off my chest. This is admiration for Sunderland supporters, and I hate to say it, for loyalty to their club. In 1992, I was working and living in Jesmond, and as much as the Geordie fans wouldn't like to admit it, you could walk into any part of St James' Park on a Saturday afternoon because they were getting about 19,000 there.

Malcolm M: Yes, but what is the point you are making? When things are bad at Newcastle United, the supporters vote with their feet. They let the club know exactly what they are thinking by whether they or there or not.

Malcolm: I don't really want to get at you, Malcolm, because I used to admire you as a player. What I am saying is that the Sunderland fans are sticking with the club through very lean times. I don't think there's another set of supporters, other than possibly Man City, that do that in the country. And I include the Boro, even though I support them and I have done for 40-odd years.

Malcolm M: We have said time and time again that they are absolutely amazing and we can't believe such loyalty even exists on the planet.

Eric: On this show, you couldn't knock the Sunderland supporters, no chance.

Malcolm: Tomorrow morning I'm setting off early hours to get on Eurostar for Boro's game in Basel, but I've been struggling to get accommodation. I thought I was going to have to cadge a room with Bernie, but a lady called me this afternoon to offer me accommodation so, Bernie, you've been saved. But you won't believe what's going on in Switzerland.

Bernie: Yes, there's a clock convention or something.

Malcolm: You're spot on, it's a cuckoo clock convention.

Bernie: Yeah, I'm bringing a couple back for these two cuckoos!

Eric: I tell you what, there's a cuckoo going over but they might keep you, Slaven. And I bet there's more people at the cuckoo clock convention than there is at Boro!

Malcolm: Do you know where I'm staying? I'm staying in a place called Freiburg in Germany, wherever that is.

Bernie: It's just round the corner!

Malcolm: I'm travelling on the train with my wife and son. I've had to tell a little white lie to the school for the kiddie, because he's come down with this awful flu.

Bernie: Oh, that's understandable at this time of year.

Malcolm: It's going to be a great evening, I hope.

Eric: I've heard the Basel people hope it's going to be freezing so the Boro fans don't take their shirts off.

In The News

UEFA Cup quarter-final 1st leg: Basel 2 Boro 0

Friday March 31

Steve, Middlesbrough

Steve: I'm really looking forward to next Thursday night. I think it'll be a proper European night. I remember as a kid the two-legged European nights on TV, with the likes of Liverpool going to St Etienne a couple of goals down. It's not the same when you only play teams over one leg.

Eric: And what a night to remember if you can pull it back and go on to win.

Steve: Yeah, and I think we're capable of it. I've been to all the home games in Europe. This has the making of a great night when the crowd can get behind them. I think we can do it, I have a feeling this team Basel won't travel well. At least I hope they won't.

Bernie: I think we are well-equipped, we've got some smashing players, we've definitely got goalscorers who'll score in any company providing we give them the service, so it's important that we get the right players in the right positions.

Steve: I'd definitely play Morrison and Downing. If Downing isn't going to start going past people, I'd give Johnson a go.

Bernie: I watched with interest last night, even Stewy looked frustrated and was going inwards, like Mendi always does. When Downing played with Zenden, Bolo would get the ball and spoon-feed Downing. There you go Stewy – he'd keep giving him it and giving him it. That's an art in itself. Doriva and Parlour seldom gave Downing a ball last night.

Eric: But I also look at Downing and I think when you first came in the side lad, you were like a breath of fresh air. He had enthusiasm, he was like a kid playing in the park. He got the ball and he went at people and didn't worry about opponents. But I tell you what, now he seems more negative than he's ever been.

Bernie: Is that not about keep the ball, keep the possession?

Eric: Yeah, I think it's coaches coaching it out of him.

Steve: I think that happens but young Johnson, when he's come in, he's looked like how Downing looked a year-and-a-half ago.

Bernie: Yeah, but Johnson's not played 20 games on the bounce like Downing has. Downing done it for 20-odd games.

Steve: Johnson has that get-up-and-go like Downing had when he first came in the team to want to take people on. But as long as we get at them next week. But McClaren was coming out of the stairwells, he was up in the stands, he was up at the front. What's the story? I mean, I'm like that myself at the games but I've had quite a bit drink!

Bernie: But McClaren going up and down the stand is not why we conceded two bad goals. The timing of us conceding the goals was absolutely rank. We were looking to go in at half-time all square and come out all guns blazing for the second half, then we lose a goal – and then we lose another one when we got torn apart.

Steve: But look, an early goal next week, hopefully we fill the ground, and we can do it. Who do you think will be up front, Bernie?

Bernie: Viduka and Hasselbaink are the in-form strikers. The Yak looks off-colour. He looks as if he's annoyed that he's been left out when he was doing so well.

Steve: Viduka's the main man at the moment, for me, but I think I'd play Yak next to him.

Bernie: Steve McClaren is paid to make those decisions and let's hope he gets it right on the night.

Eric: You got beat but you haven't given up yet – and I think you're right, Bernie. It's not over by any means. Disappointing, yes, but it's not over.

Fred, Middlesbrough

Fred: Bernie, the Boro fans have nothing to worry about. It's 2-0 down at half-time and we had half a team out. I tell you, that banner that Basel had at the start of the game will rile the Boro fans. They'll have a flag night, they'll all be up for it. I'm quite confident but knowing the Boro, we never do anything simple. I can see us getting the two goals, them getting one back and then we're having to get another two – but we'll do it like.

Bernie: It's going to be a cracking game, it really is. We can play various formations but it doesn't matter about that. It's about the players on the night. If we've got the right players in the right positions, I reckon we can still do it.

Eric: Could you fit the three forwards in a team at home?

Bernie: Yes, but you're congested then and you've not got the width.

Eric: Yes, but I'm saying can you see them three playing together and forming a frontline or don't you think that would work? It would frighten the life out of the opposition, wouldn't it?

Bernie: Well, you would hope so but it's down to Steve McClaren. He's the manager, he's the tactician and he has to get it bang on. But it's another option.

Fred: I think you've got to guard against the counter-attack if we do that.

Bernie: We played into their hands last night. The big number five had his cigar out. He was about six foot three, every ball came his way and he was knocking it forward, knocking it to the full-backs and he was comfortable. They had about four or five players good players but I think we've got better individual players and collectively, we're better. We have to prove it. But if we can get through, get your money on that we will get to the final.

Fred: Parlour and Doriva were both off-form. If they were playing in my back garden I'd close my curtains. Eric, your season

has been so bad that it's not even fun to take the Micky out of Sunderland any more.

Eric: No, but I don't think you can take the Micky out of the Sunderland supporters. They've been brilliant, haven't they?

Fred: No, it's just the team. You've got one big game left and I hope you do well against Malcolm's lot.

Eric: You see, that's even flat for me. I don't want to say that if we beat Newcastle that makes everything okay. No, it doesn't. You look at the whole picture.

Arthur, Sunderland

Arthur: Eric, the thing I wanted to fetch up is what sort of a guy is this Alan Stubbs? When we played Everton, he was in the stand and he was still a Sunderland player. He says in tonight's paper that when Everton scored he had to hide his delight. What sort of a professional's he? I bet he wasn't hiding his delight when he was getting his thousands of pounds a week off Sunderland and they took him off the scrapheap.

Eric: Yeah, that's a point. Alan Stubbs was a good a player at Everton and I know it will annoy Sunderland fans to hear things like that. It's just another kick in the teeth for Sunderland fans in a miserable season.

Arthur: You don't go on like that, you know what I mean? I tell you what I would do tomorrow if I was Kevin Ball. I'd say if Stubbs is playing, take him out.

Eric: That is something that happened all my career. Say in the Ipswich Town team and the opposing centre-half had said something like that, I tell you what, it was up to our centre-forward to sort him out. And I really mean that – that was your comeuppance for things like that. But the way the game has changed now, there'll be players wanting to swap his shirt and kiss his backside.

Arthur: Eric, we're down and gone.

Eric: I can't believe they're going on about this could be the weekend Sunderland go down. It's just a mathematical thing. Hell, I haven't thought about staying up for about four months.

Arthur: I saw them the first game of the season against Charlton and we were crap then and I knew it was going to be a long, long, long struggle.

Eric: I said at the time on this show that on that performance we will not get 17 points this year. That's what I can't understand. The club must have known it. The manager, the staff, they all must have known it and it's come back to bite their backsides.

Arthur: They must think all Sunderland supporters are daft, saying we're trying this and we're trying that. They're not up to it. We're crap. I've never been back.

Eric: Yeah, it doesn't wash. The fans are fed up with hearing that the club and the players want the fans to get behind them. I want Sunderland to be a great club. What would make you go back?

Arthur: The players, if they show commitment, and if we've got a decent team that try. All right, you cannot win every week, but as long as they go and try and play proper football.

Eric: Is there anything that can happen over the close season that will make you say, 'Hey, I'm going to back the club'?

Arthur: Well, it's a big if, but if this Niall Quinn thing does come off and they invest and get a proper manager who gives you a little bit of hope, then you can decide on whether you go back.

In The News

Everton 2 Sunderland 2

Newcastle 3 Tottenham 1

Man City 0 Boro 1

Premier League positions

	P	W	D	L	Pts
12 Newcastle	32	12	6	14	42
14 Boro	31	11	7	13	40
20 Sunderland	32	2	5	25	11

April 4 2006

Kevin, Middlesbrough

Kevin: I hope Mendieta gets back as soon as he can. It might be next year now. I know he hasn't played well the last 10 games.

Bernie: I think that's him ruled out for the season. He hasn't played well but we don't want anyone injured.

Kevin: McClaren has got to play Morrison down that left-hand side now. He's got no option.

Bernie: It's a big decision but after hearing Steve do an interview on Sunday I thought he was going to put Mendi back in there.

Malcolm: Kevin, let me ask you if Steve McClaren has doubts about whether a youngster, Morrison, can cope with the tension that there will on Thursday night when you're having to chase the goals.

Kevin: Well, if he does it's only McClaren, because the fans don't. The fans are behind Morrison. What did he do when he went to Ostrava as a kid and scored the goal? McClaren loved him then.

Bernie: It's defies logic to me. The majority cannot be wrong. I've seen Maccarone, an £8 million striker, playing outside-right. I've seen Ray Parlour outside-right. I've seen Mendieta outside-right. There's only one outside-right in the club – and that's Morrison. It's nonsense that those three guys can be ahead of Morrison. I don't care who they are. Morrison showed more on Sunday than Mendieta has done in the last 10.

Eric: Bernie, do you think Morrison or Mendieta would have played on Thursday night if Mendieta hadn't been injured?

Bernie: I think Mendieta for definite.

Eric: You say that defies logic?

Bernie: I do, it's my opinion. There's nobody else. Surely, he wouldn't put Rochemback outside-right. Like Mendi, he gets dragged inside, like Mendi. It's as if there's a magnet. But we need pace at outside-right.

Kevin: It's not pace we need, it's attack, attack, attack, attack, attack. Bernie, they're on about Basel. Well, there's only one Basel and that's Basil Brush. So it's goodnight from me, goodnight to you, boom, boom!

Charles, Middlesbrough

Charles: I feel Boro have got to put the three forwards in on Thursday. Attack is the best form of attack.

Bernie: I think with two forwards on and with the young lads, Morrison and Downing, in the team, with the fitness, the power and the pace, I think we can do it.

Eric: I suggested you should play three forwards last week when you conceded two.

Charles: The young lads you're on about, they're all right but they're not strong enough. They get knocked off the ball too easily.

Bernie: Hold on, was Mendieta strong enough on the right wing?

Charles: No, I don't like Mendieta. His injury is not going to worry us at all. We needed that lad from Sporting Lisbon, Douala. The young lads we have are all right when it's going for them but they need some upper body strength.

Bernie: So how do you see it going Thursday?

Charles: I reckon three-nowt. We should get the three forwards on, get two goals first half and then tighten up in the second half and get a third for a 3-2 aggregate.

Rolf, Middlesbrough

Rolf: I'm up for the game tomorrow. Everybody should go there. It's the biggest game of our lives.

Malcolm: And I believe that you and every single Boro fan that attends has got a part to play in getting you to the semi-finals.

Rolf: We have. Bill Shankly used to say that the fans in the Kop would suck the ball in at Liverpool. Let's get out there on Thursday. None of his moaning and groaning, let's get in amongst it. We can have a moan and groan afterwards. We can make that bit of difference.

Eric: You've said something important there. You're not guaranteed to win, Rolf, and you might be disappointed. But if the Boro go on to win it, then it's a hell of a result.

Malcolm: If I was to give a teamtalk to the Boro fans, what I would say is don't be underneath at the bars getting beers and cups of tea and what have you. While Basel are on the pitch warming up, give them plenty of noise.

Rolf: Yep, get in there – tell all the lunatics to take their shirts off.

What if the Boro win the UEFA Cup and Steve McClaren gets the England job? Which will get the bigger street party on Teesside? Mind, I do wish the Boro luck tomorrow night
- Peter, Newcastle fan

Cuckoo clocks, neutrality, Basil Brush, Basil Fawlty, Basil Rathbone, sage and basil, your boys are going to take a hell of a beating, 3-0 Boro
- Swiss Dave

The Boro boys are Euro bound. 3-0 will do, 4-0 would be better. I do hope they win and stuff poor Basel and keep NE footy on a high for the minute. If they get beat a mist will descend and all will be doom at the Boro's home den
- John, Coxhoe, Newcastle fan

Hi Bernie, when the mighty Toon stuff Boro on Sunday will it be the same old excuse of your players being tired after a European game? Up the Toon - Lee

I have not missed a home game in Europe. But I bet you that the people who say they can't afford tomorrow's game will soon crawl out of the woodwork should we get to the final! Come on Boro fans, get behind the team in numbers
- Brian in Newton Aycliffe.

What about McClaren on Century earlier today, saying he expected nothing better than a titanic victory. Does the guy not know his history? It begs the question will there be enough fans to fill the lifeboats?
- Paul, Newcastle

Go on, Boro - don't be scared of Basel. 4-0. Go for the jugular. You can do it
- Kevin, Toon fan

McClaren for England, Mowbray for Boro and O'Neill for the Toon. That'll do nicely, thanks
- Toon fan

Hi lads, Niall Quinn has told the BBC that he hopes to buy Bob Murray out before the end of the season. Boro 4 Basel 1
- Phil, SAFC fan

Eric: Oh, no, you've gone too far now, Rolf. You've gone overboard. I've seen them and I don't want no shirts off!

Rolf: It will put the fear of God into them, Eric.

Eric: Oh, man alive! I saw them last time, I don't want to see them again.

Malcolm: Yeah, it was like looking in a mirror, wasn't it, Gatesy?

Rolf: Fantastic, tell everyone to be there. Keeping plugging it, Eric.

Eric: Well, it's not for me to plug. I just think it's a great opportunity for them. I tell you what, if it had been Sunderland, it wouldn't have needed plugging.

Rolf: No, that's correct. It's the biggest game of our lives. Could be the last time we're in Europe for years. Thursday – massive! Boro, get there.

Eric: Wait a bit, we want the chant, Rolf – let's hear it – attack, attack, attack!

Rolf (chanting): Attack, attack, give it to the Yak, attack, attack!

(laughter all round)

Malcolm: That's the kind of spirit that you need to put the fear of God into them.

Richie, Sunderland

Richie: Eric, you said that Sunderland supporters would be pleased to see the back of this season.

Eric: Yeah.

Richie: An honest supporter would say he wasn't getting carried away last season, because we knew we couldn't do it.

Malcolm: Even though you flew the Championship…

Richie: Yeah, but it was a very bad division we were in.

Eric: Come on, when the ball kicked off, we had a bit of hope, though we thought we might have a bad season. But nobody would have predicted the season we have had. I disagree if anyone comes on and says they knew we were going to have such a nightmare. It's the worst season in history, man.

Richie: Well, we tried to get a bet on the bookies in October that we would finish with less than 19 points but the bookies wouldn't take it.

Malcolm: Yeah, but that's in October when you had seen a number of games that gave you a very good idea. But at the very

beginning of the season, before you'd seen a ball kicked. Did you imagine that West Ham and Wigan could actually finish in the top half of the table and Sunderland be relegated in such horrifying fashion?

Richie: I've got to be honest, no.

Malcolm: Right, surely you thought you would finish above those two.

Eric: I thought all three would struggle and I just hoped that at least we would finish above those two and that one more would be bad enough for us to pip to the post.

Richie: What do we put it down to, Eric? Mick McCarthy wasn't that bad.

Eric: Well, I think the players haven't been good enough.

Richie: Mick McCarthy brought them in.

Eric: Of course he did. Mick took the blame. He got the sack. But the chairman and the board of directors have to take the blame too. But the players and the board haven't had the sack. There's only one man took the brunt.

Richie: And nothing's going to change, Eric.

Eric: The players and the board said they were all behind Mick McCarthy, but it's him that's taken the can and that's cruel.

Richie: Murray said that he had given him everything he wanted, but it's been the worst in history.

Eric: I tell you what, if they win the next six games and finish the season well, I'll be happy for them. But I'm not falling into the trap of getting carried away with them taking a point against Everton. Do me a favour.

April 6

David, Newcastle

David: Malcolm, Newcastle had a brilliant performance at home the other day. I think this is possibly our best chance to put about five wins together because we've got Middlesbrough away, Wigan at home, then away to Sunderland and then at home to West Brom. I'm just wondering what you thought?

Malcolm: Well, what's your point? It's a all bit late in the season, isn't it?

David: Well, we're still only six points off the UEFA Cup and you never know, do you? Football's football. Middlesbrough will be quite tough if they play well tonight but if they get beat they'll be thinking about West Ham in the FA Cup so they'll play the kids against us.

Malcolm: And you say that Newcastle United are good enough to go out and win all those games based on one good performance when in the previous four performances have been absolutely dire?

Bernie: Don't you mince your words, Malcolm!

David: Never mind the opposition, Newcastle United can beat themselves. When they prove themselves to us all then maybe we can start to think in those terms. I'm not being hyper-critical, but they don't give me any confidence.

Malcolm: I'd like to see a run put together.

David: Well, don't you think there's a chance to go on a run over the next four games and get in the habit of winning?

Malcolm: It's not up to me, it's up to the players. They have had an opportunity all last season and all this season to get a run going. Have they done it? No, they haven't. They don't need me to give them permission.

David: I'm not saying they do. I'm just asking what you think?

Bernie: It was a simple question, Malcolm.

Malcolm: I expect Newcastle United to do what they usually do. Win one, lose one.

Bernie: Hit and miss?

Malcolm: Absolutely, hit and miss. I certainly hope that Newcastle can go on that run, but I remain to be convinced.

In The News

UEFA Cup quarter-final 2nd leg: Boro 4 Basel 1

(Boro qualify for semi-final on 4-3 aggregate)

Friday April 7

Eric: Well done to the 24,000 Boro fans that went along there because we said it might be a night they will always remember – and I tell you what, it turned out like that.

Bernie: Yeah, it was a fantastic night, possibly the greatest night in the club's history. The game was full of incident, drama and goals, the players sweated blood for the cause. The fans were unbelievable. And for me, Steve McClaren cannot be praised enough. From the start of the second half, he changed it right away, went 4-3-3…

Eric: Well, hang on, don't go on about that - you said he had to do that right from the start.

Bernie: I know that, I know we said he had to throw caution to the wind, but we ended up 4-2-4 with four centre-forwards right in a line.

Eric: But you were 3-0 down!

Bernie: Oh, come on Eric. I've never seen it in the modern game. Four centre-forwards!

Eric: Oh give over, man!

Bernie: Well, come on then, Eric, give me a manager when their team has been struggling in Europe who has gone four strikers. I've not seen it. Well done, Steve McClaren…

Eric: Yes, well done…

Bernie: I thought it was absolute brilliant. Well done, the players. Well done, the fans. I thought it was the best night ever in Middlesbrough's history.

Eric: Don't go overboard about Steve McClaren's tactics because everyone knew what you had to do, that you had to go for it. Everyone was saying it beforehand.

Bernie: Yes, we had to, but we lost a goal and I thought that was goodnight, hand on my heart, I have to be honest. He was going to put Ehiogu on but at the last minute he switched it.

Eric: Oh, Bernie, come on!

Bernie: Eric, Eric, you can have a pop if you want.

Eric: Bernie! I'm not having a pop, I'm saying well done, but don't go overboard.

Bernie: Four centre-forwards! And we got the required result in the 90 minutes. That is one hell of an achievement. Steve McClaren, the coaching staff and all the players, brilliant.

Malcolm: I have to say well done. I hold my hands up. I thought the whole 90 minutes would go as the first 45 did. But that second 45 minutes, that was something that was quite out of this world. And I think totally unexpected. Did anybody in the ground at half-time say, 'Oh, we'll come back from this'?

Bernie, you've got more chance of the Pope playing for Rangers than going thru tonight. Get ya hankies ready for Sunday
- Elaine in Newcastle

Bernie, as you would say, I hope you get gubbed good and proper, as any self respecting Newcastle fan should. I, like you, could never wish a rival well - Jeff

I think it would be a really positive move if Quinny did take over the running of the club, I'm sure every single SAFC fan feels the same as me
- Philip, SAFC

197

Bernie: No, nobody, even my mate Ali Brownlee, Mr Positive, was thinking it's Everest to climb. Astonishingly, we turned it around.

Malcolm: Mind, to say four forwards, go the width of the pitch. The two midfield players must have been blowing their socks off.

Bernie: Rochemback was unbelievable.

(Bernie then plays The William Tell Overture)

Eric: What's that? Fox hunting?

Bernie: No, I'm against fox hunting.

Eric: William Tell? That's Austrian, isn't it?

Malcolm: No, he's the hero of Switzerland, William Tell.

Eric (shouting): Get him off!

Bernie: Hold on, I'm dictating tonight, not you! Tonight of all nights. I tell you what, how can a Sunderland fan try to dictate tonight? He's trying to say turn it off. Well, I'm going to dictate tonight. We're the Boro, we're in the UEFA Cup semi-final.

Eric: Put an apple on top of that quiff, see if I can knock it off.

Bernie: I tell you what, I'll knock you out!

Eric: He's Austrian, man!

Bernie: Eric, I can assure you he's Switzerland's national hero.

Eric: When I was at school he was Austrian.

Bernie: Yeah, but what school did you go to? You went to the barmy school!

Colin, Middlesbrough

Colin: Bernie, I want to dispel the myth, there was a lot of banners around the ground last night, a lot of singing and a lot of chanting, and we all know what they said – (singing) 'Geordies at home watching The Bill'.

Bernie: Oh, they were watching The Bill all right.

Colin: Bernie, they were NOT watching The Bill. They were watching the telly, they heard we were a goal down and they all turned over. They were ready to just cheer and jibe. But Dixons and Currys have had all the Geordies on today because tellies throughout Newcastle were destroyed with boots through them when Maccarone scored that goal to shoot us into the semi-final. Eric's saying don't go overboard…

Eric: No, no, Eric's saying well done, but he was going on about McClaren's tactics.

Colin: Well, I've never been the biggest fan of McClaren and some of the things he has done have left me bemused, but what he did last night was brave. And one word for those fans that didn't go to the Riverside last night – suckers!

Kevin, Middlesbrough

Kevin: What did I say to Malcolm? I said we'd get the goals and Malcolm, you said, 'You won't'. Malcolm, you know what you are? You're jealous!

Bernie: Oh Malcolm, are you jealous?

Malcolm: What? Oh for heaven's sake, Kevin, talk football but don't accuse me of something that just isn't true. Talk football!

Kevin: We played football and we attacked. Everyone sat round where we were believed we would get the three goals.

Malcolm: What, at half-time?

Kevin: Yes, we did believe it at half-time, of course I did. That was a bigger comeback than Liverpool's against Milan, wasn't it?

Eric: No, I don't think so.

Kevin: Liverpool had to get three goals to draw but we needed four in 45 minutes.

Malcolm: They actually did it in the final, come on now.

Kevin: There's plenty of time for us, isn't there?

Colin, Middlesbrough

Colin: I just had to come on to say that was absolutely unbelievable. I'm in awe of it. I've been a Boro fan for 48 years now, my father took me to my first match when I was five years old and he said that was the best game that he's ever seen. We went to the Carling Cup and that was a great day. But that was just unbelievable. When that first goal went in, I thought, 'Oh God, this is terrible, Malcolm's going to be right.

Bernie: Isn't it sad, you think of Malcolm? I thought the same!

Colin: But when the second goal went in, I just thought we were gonna do it.

Malcolm: But when you got two, even if you got a third it would have been enough for you.

Colin: I was willing to give the Boro a standing ovation for what they did even if they hadn't scored the late goal.

Malcolm: I understand that. I think it is an absolutely remarkable feat that they achieved last night.

Colin: I've knocked McClaren, but I've got to give him the plaudits for last night.

Bernie: You must, you must!

Colin: I just want to thank him for giving me the best night of my life.

Ray, Sunderland

Ray: The game last night was unreal. I was over the moon for them. I've been a Sunderland supporter all my life, but when the fourth goal went in I jumped off my seat shouting, 'Get in!' It was absolutely fantastic. I went to the Boro to watch the Man United game earlier in the season and that one and last night's game are the best I've seen this season. The game last night had everything.

Bernie: It did have everything – it had some great football, lots of pace, energy, tackles, penalty claims, goalscorers. It was just a great night.

Ray: Gibson's face at the end of it was a picture. It must have taken away all the disappointment of seeing only 24,000 supporters there. Bernie, that match was unbelievable.

In The News

Boro 1 Newcastle 2

Sunderland v Fulham abandoned due to snow

Premier League positions

	P	W	D	L	Pts
10 Newcastle	33	13	6	14	45
14 Boro	32	11	7	14	40
20 Sunderland	32	2	5	25	11

April 10

Dennis, Middlesbrough

Dennis: I went to the game yesterday and, you know, I half expected it. All of the lads I spoke to thought it was a non-event. I don't know what was missing. We started to wake up in the last 20 minutes but we still didn't really create anything.

Eric: I can't understand it. It was a local derby. In football, you can't switch it on and switch it off, I don't care what you say.

Dennis: Bernie, did you hear George Boateng's comments? He said they couldn't get motivated for the game. I never thought I would hear a player say he couldn't get motivated for a local derby.

Bernie: Yeah, George said it took them until the second half to get going. I thought they would be more fatigued during the final 45 minutes, but it was the other way around and it took them that long to get going.

Dennis: I can only put it down to the effort on Thursday. That was brilliant.

Bernie: The effort was phenonemol but…

Malcolm: The first time you had the ball was when you kicked off the second half.

Eric: Wait a bit. You say the effort on Thursday. They did nothing on Friday, they did nothing Saturday. They didn't care on Sunday.

199

```
Eric, you and Bernie
said the Toon wouldn't
get in top half of the
Premiership this
season. We're just
there. Wrong again, you
muppet!
- Paul, Toon fan


Bernie, see what
happens when you play a
proper side
- David, Newton
Aycliffe


Bernie, your season is
about to go up in smoke
big time. Mark my
words, Charlton will
turn u over on
Wednesday and u will go
out of Europe as well!
By the way, Macdonald,
keep your gob shut when
it comes to players.
You're clueless
- Jake, Toon fan


Bet the stench of sour
grapes on Teesside is
overpowering cos that's
all I've heard. Bad
losers + beaten by
better side, plain +
simple
- Vince, North Shields


Malcolm, Eric and
Elvis, there is only
one north east derby
game and it doesn't
involve Middlesboro'
- Neil in Hutton Henry
```

Dennis: The crowd didn't seem to be up for it either.

Bernie: It goes hand-in-hand. The fans need get behind the players and vice-versa. It never happened.

Dennis: I can't understand why he didn't start with two strikers.

Bernie: I looked at the starting team and I thought it would be good enough, but the players let McClaren down and the fans down on the day.

Dennis: Going back to Thursday's game, I thought Rochemback did great – and I didn't think he had a bad game yesterday, he worked.

Bernie: I thought he done well.

Malcolm: Rochemback had a nightmare yesterday.

Bernie: What do you mean a nightmare? What kind of nightmare? Rochemback did well. He played a couple of decent balls, put the ball through for Yakubu when he was brought down and it should have been a penalty.

Brian, Middlesbrough

Brian: I tell you what, these comments that McClaren has come out with have absolutely infuriated me. He is quoted today saying these last few months we have had priorities, which have been in the cups.

Malcolm: I thought your priority was to win matches.

Brian: Of course, it should be. This man is an absolute…he's hoodwinking the public of Teesside, a lot of people who go into debt to buy season tickets. And what are we getting?

Malcolm: I'm just thinking, should he become the England manager after the World Cup, what's he going to do – lose all the friendlies? But he'll win the European Nations Cup and World Cup games.

Brian: That's two derby matches at the Riverside, against Newcastle and Sunderland, we've been absolutely atrocious. The people of Teesside are just fed up with it. This man is putting out second rate teams.

Bernie: Ali put me on the spot yesterday. I know it's a daft question, but he said 'OK, we've had Basel, then Newcastle and then Charlton in the FA Cup on Wednesday. If you had to sacrifice one, which one would it be?' I told him that I would want to win all three of them, but which one would it be out of the three?

Brian: That's a hypothetical question.

Bernie: Yes, and you're not answering it, because you know which one it would be – it would be Newcastle.

Eric: A supporter would want the best team possible in all those three games and the best performance possible.

Bernie: Eric, I've got no complaints against McClaren about the team he picked. It should have been good enough to get all three points.

Brian: We should haul the manager over the coals about comments like this. Time and time again he comes out with gaffs and he is taking the Mick out of the public of Teesside.

Malcolm: And the major expenditure of any football supporter is the season ticket and what does that pay for? It's for the Premiership games. It's not for the cup games, is it?

Eric: Yeah, Brian, Bernie is saying that he didn't disagree with the team he picked, but it was his comments after the game that have annoyed him. If he'd been honest about the game…

Brian: I want him to be as honest as Stuart Pearce was last week.

Bernie: Is it not honest of him to say when he feels he has other priorities, Brian? You want honesty off him, but when he's given it, you don't like it.

Eric: If it's his opinion, he should have come out on the Friday and Saturday before the match and said that this game doesn't matter.

Bernie: Eric, I don't think you have to be a mind-reader to know what McClaren was thinking. He has proved it over the months, but I know where you are coming from.

Paul, Newcastle

Paul: I don't know where these Middlesbrough fans get their attitude from towards Newcastle. Someone came on here saying yesterday's game was our cup final. The truth is that our only derby is against Sunderland. Middlesbrough are no different from, say Leicester. I remember Middlesbrough playing us in the League Cup. At St James' Park there was only about 14,000. If it had been against Sunderland there'd have been 35,000. Middlesbrough will never, ever mean anything to us. It's just a one way thing. So it's their cup final, not our cup final.

Bernie: No, no, it was a nothing game.

Malcolm: Newcastle have mathematically an outside chance of getting into Europe and it's one that they must chase.

Bernie: But it was your cup final – and we have got bigger fish to fry!

Malcolm: I've never heard so much nonsense in all my life. I think you're all barmy on Teesside.

Paul: Bernie, if you can relate to when you were a kid, Newcastle against Middlesbrough is the same kind of thing as Celtic against Kilmarnock.

Bernie (laughing): Oh, yeah. I thought it was more than that.

Paul: It is from Middlesbrough's point of view because we're the north-east capital and we get all the spotlight.

Bernie: I tell you what, Paul, who you talking about? Man United? You're talking as if you're the biggest club in the country or the world. You've never won a blinking trophy for 50-odd years.

Paul: And our day will come.

Bernie: Oh, right, we've heard that for 50-odd years.

Malcolm: You're wrong, Bernie.

Bernie: Domestically, Malcolm. Sorry I forgot to say it was 50 years domestically since you won anything.

Kevin, Middlesbrough

Kevin: I've got a few views and I know you're not going to like them. I'm a Middlesbrough fan and I'm a realist. Football is a game of winners and losers, so you are going to lose some. I'm not interested in the Premiership at the moment and I'll you why. We're not going to get relegated, we're not going to qualify for Europe, so where's the interest? I want to go to Eindhoven or Cardiff.

Eric: Wait a bit! There's players getting 40 or 50 grand a week to perform to the best of their ability. Never mind where you are in the league.

Kevin: Here's my next view, Eric, and it's for you. I had the privilege of watching you play and I know you had some extended runs in Europe. But did you play well for 90 minutes of every game?

Malcolm: Do you think players can suddenly turn it on because it's a cup final?

Kevin: Let me put this way, if I go to athletics, I don't expect 100 metres runners break the record every time they run and I don't expect high-jumpers to do the same. You are going to get varying performances out of professional footballers as well.

Malcolm: So you're prepared to see 100 metres runners not even come out of the blocks – because that was the Boro on Sunday.

Eric: No, Kevin, I didn't play well every day. I had plenty of stinkers. But I never said I was too tired to play.

Kevin: I don't think the players say that. It's the sort of rubbish that it is being perpetuated.

Malcolm: It's being perpetuated by your manager.

Kevin: Every top manager says the same.

Malcolm: No, wrong! Not every manager.

Eric: And why do they say it? Because it's an excuse!

Kevin: If we had to pick one of the three games to lose it would have been Newcastle.

Eric: Let me ask you this then – what's better, going into the cup semi-final having won against Newcastle or having lost?

Bernie: Winning. I agree with that.

Eric: What's better – playing your centre-forward week in and week out when he's banging the goals, making him feel 10 feet tall?

Bernie: I agree with that one and all. Yakubu was on fire. Now he's lost form since he's been rested.

Eric: Yes, because he's been messed around.

Bob, Middlesbrough

Bob: I'm not Steve McClaren's greatest fan but I'm reluctant to criticise him tonight. Last week was one of the greatest matches I've ever seen at Middlesbrough. I put a lot of the credit down to McClaren.

Bernie: I agree.

Bob: But I look at what he did yesterday – and I'm not going to criticise him for resting players, because all the top teams, like Chelsea and Manchester United, do that. But what I do criticise is why we had to change the formation. Why couldn't Maccarone, full of confidence after what he did

How come McClaren can play 4 up front for UEFA Cup and then has 4-5-1 for Newcastle match? Why does he play too defensive with tactics instead of positive 4-3-3 all out attack? - Boro-Russ

Forget the cups for a minute. I'm a Boro season ticket holder and I've paid up front for my 19 home games and I'm so annoyed at the attitude from the Boro boss. Where is the loyalty to the fans who pay up front resting players?
- Mark in Redcar

I am sat here in fits of giggles at the whinging, jealous Smoggies. Keep up the funny rants from Yorkshire. Ha ha ha. PS Who sung Pigbag the most?
- Bill in Catterick

201

Steve McClaren has been
saying for weeks that
the cups are our
priority, not just after
the Newcastle game.
Doesn't Roeder or u 3
muppets listen?
- Steve, Boro

Bernie, I totally agree
with McClaren to play
weakened teams in
league. We have got the
biggest game in our
history coming up in
UEFA Cup. Can't believe
Boro fans moaning
- Mick, Guisborough

The reason the Boro
crowds have been poor is
due to the manager's
negative approach. Yes,
Thursday was great but
it was one game. When he
goes the crowds will
come back. Bring on
Mogga
- Steve, Billingham

the other night, have played up front with Yakubu?

Bernie: I thought we would play Maccarone.

Bob: Newcastle deserved to win but I don't think either side looked good. During the first 25 minutes, the game was there for the taking but we just didn't want it at all. I've got a view about Steve McClaren. I think that he is great when he has to attack when he has no other choice or when they've got nothing to lose against the likes of Chelsea or Manchester United. I think he struggles when he has to go out and attack in a bread and butter game. I don't think he knows how to do it.

Malcolm: Explain to me this – how does a football manager finish his most successful game with four forwards on the pitch, having got that success because of the four, and then start the next game with only one?

Bob: I don't know the answer to that. I wish I did. I felt very uplifted on Thursday after the Basel game. On Sunday, I felt like I'd been short-changed. I paid for my season ticket for all the home games, so we can't pick and choose which games we're going to go out and try and win. Success breeds more success.

Bernie: Yes, winning gives a team greater confidence. Now we've had a wee step back, losing to Newcastle.

Bob: I'm sad to say all this because I gave credit to McClaren for Thursday. That was out of this world.

Bernie: Best ever.

Bob: It really was magnificent. There is a strong chance McClaren will get the England job this summer. One of the reasons I will renew my season ticket is the fact that he will be going elsewhere. Whilst last week was magnificent, I've had to see a whole lot of dross this last year.

April 11
Mike, Newcastle

Mike: Just a quick word with Bernie – I rang up last week and said we'd beat you 3-1, but we only beat you 2-1, so sorry.

Bernie: It should have been three or four.

Mike: I tell you what, you had all sorts of problems with Ameobi.

He caused you hellish problems.

Bernie: Over the years big guys have always caused us problems.

Mike: You're a Morrissey fan, aren't you?

Bernie: Morrisey? Yeah.

Mike: So what were you listening to on the way home – Heaven Knows I'm Miserable Now?

Bernie: You're right in saying that. I had my window down. Could you hear it?

Mike: I could hear you crying, mate. I live on Teesside so listened to the commentary and you sounded so cheesed off.

Bernie: Well, I was. I can't hind behind it. I was majorly disappointed to get beat by what I regard as the enemy – in a nice way.

Mike: Malcolm, what are we gonna do about our next boss?

Malcolm: Well, you're not going to do anything. But Freddy Shepherd has got the dilemma, hasn't he?

Mike: My way of thinking is if we don't have somebody before the close of the season, whoever we get in isn't really going to have long to assess what's needed.

Malcolm: It's unfortunate for Newcastle that Sven Goran Eriksson decided to vacate the England job after the World Cup. So that job is up for grabs and people are holding out to see what the FA are going to do but aware of the Newcastle vacancy.

Mike: The problem for Newcastle, though, is that if the new boss doesn't come in until later in the summer, he's not going to have long to assess the squad and bring in who he wants to buy.

Malcolm: I think the chairman will have somebody in place before a week after the end of the season is over. I am sure of that.

Mike: I can see Glenn Roeder temporarily taking on the job into next season.

Malcolm: I don't think so.

Mike, Middlesbrough

Mike: Quick one about Sunday's game. The game on Sunday, we got beat, I'm disappointed, but I thought Newcastle's defence was the tightest I've ever known it. You actually marked both wingers out of the game. Roeder has done a tremendous job in organising your defence.

Bernie: Even Bramble looked a good player.

Malcolm: Yeah, and he had Yakubu in his pocket.

Mike: You're looking for a new manager and I don't think you're going to get much better than the man you've got. He proved at West Ham before his illness that he's a good manager.

Bernie: Yeah, he's doing a smashing job.

Mike: I want to have a go at what is now becoming a large section of Boro supporters, who I don't think have the ambition of the rest of us who attended on Thursday.

Bernie: Go on then, give it.

Mike: Every time we've had a European game, you've had fans coming on whinging about the ticket prices and using that as an excuse not to go. Steve Gibson has said he doesn't take a wage out of the club and that whatever comes into the club gets spent on it, whether it's players' wages, the Academy, improving facilities. If they are going to back Steve to the hilt, fans have got to realise that if it's 20 quid or 25 quid, it's for a good cause. It's for us. It's to make possible nights like last Thursday which will live in my memory forever. It was the best game I've seen at the Riverside. And that's down to Steve Gibson's ambition and ability to drive the club forward. I reckon we've got 50,000 or 60,000 Boro fans that have been to a game. Now you can make excuses for maybe 5,000 who had shift work, illness, can't afford to get to all the games, but that's so many who don't have an excuse. So where's their ambition for Middlesbrough? Because it's not matching Steve Gibson's or the rest of us that went along.

Eric: And you're not asking them to go to every game. It was a one-off game to go to even if they hadn't been all season. It is a lot of money to go to games week in and week out, we know that.

Mike: But you plugged it to the hilt. Steve Gibson is the most ambitious chairman in the league. The fans aren't backing him. I'm going to ask a hypothetical question. Say Gibson gets a half-empty stadium against Bucharest and decides that's it, I've had enough. The supporters of Middlesbrough are not backing me and there's a club up the road going cheap. I might buy them.

Malcolm: It's not going cheap though.

Eric: He won't do it.

Mike: I know, but it's hypothetical. So if he told Sunderland fans that he was going to buy their club and would do the same for their club as he has for Middlesbrough, but said, 'You've just got to prove to me you've got the same ambition. For the last game of the season, fill that stadium to the hilt.'

Eric: It would be full.

Malcolm: Without a shadow of doubt. If they really had hope in the situation they would fill the ground, I'm sure of that.

Mike: Yes. Steve Gibson has said every year on the radio, in the press, the programme and when he writes to season ticket holders, 'I want to drive Middlesbrough Football Club forward, I want to be the best we can be, I want to win a trophy every couple of years. Back me to the hilt, Middlesbrough supporters.' And what happens?

Eric: I'm with you, I know where you are coming from.

Mike: Newcastle fans would do it.

Bernie: It's comical, some of the excuses that come out. Eric was joking last week that Ken Dodd was on in the Town Hall. Maybe that was the reason why thousands hadn't turned up.

Eric: If Steve Gibson did decide enough's enough, I tell you what, you won't get a fella to replace him.

Bernie: No chance! The old saying is that you don't appreciate people when they are there. He is not one of the best chairmen, he is the best.

Mike: The good days like last Thursday will disappear because, if the fans don't come, he can't keep putting his hands in his pocket and enticing the best. I think 50 or 60 per cent of Boro fans are sitting on their bums at home, watching the Boro on the television and thinking how wonderful it is. It's going to disappear unless we get off our backsides and support the club.

Boro can beat anybody as
long as Malcolm keeps
predicting we will lose.
Bring on Chelsea in the
final!
- Phil, Stockton

Malcolm, that smug laugh
will choke U as well as
ur acid comments. Come
on, Mal, Newcastle would
swap places with the
Boro. All the tea in
China could not convince
me otherwise
- Chris, Boro fan

Bernie, I never thought
I'd hear the day when a
Geordie would come on
and call us arrogant.
How dare he? What have
they been for the last
50 years?
- Pinky, Boro fan

Bernie, I hope you're
right when you say Man
Utd might get 12 - but
how many will they get
in the 2nd half?!
- Christoon

April 12

Gary, Sunderland

Gary: It's been in the paper this week that Julio Arco doesn't want to play in the Championship next season. For me, he's the only one who's got the guts to stand up and say that, because every player should be saying exactly the same.

Malcolm: So you have sympathy for Arca?

Gary: Malcolm, that lad doesn't owe us nothing. He's stuck with us through thick and thin.

Malcolm: Well said, I thoroughly agree with you. I think he has shown as much loyalty as he possibly can.

Gary: I don't go to games as much as I should really, but if that lad was playing in a decent team – a Man United, Arsenal or a Chelsea, where they play football – he would be going to the World Cup with Argentina because he's got a footballer's brain.

Malcolm: Yeah, I see where you're coming from on that.

Gary: Eric, there's always speculation going on but I'm being told to stick my money, at 33-1, on Roy Keane being the next manager of Sunderland if this takeover happens.

Eric: I heard that ages ago but I don't think you'll get 33-1 on him.

Bernie: Would you agree with that, Eric – Roy Keane as your new manager?

Eric: Love it. Quinny there, Roy Keane, Mick McCarthy coming back as coach.

Bernie: Jack Charlton coming in too, maybe?

Gary: I'll be happy if it means Bob Murray is out.

Eric: Something's got to be done, Gary, but I don't know what's going to be for the better or for worse.

In The News

FA Cup quarter-final replay: Boro 4 Charlton 2

Thursday April 13

Michael, Middlesbrough

Michael: We were disappointed at the weekend but we've got bigger fish to catch.

Eric: Michael, that's a joke and you shouldn't be saying that.

Malcolm: Yeah, I'm staggered that someone can come on air and say that.

Michael: It's looking like McClaren is going to go out in style as the new England manager. He's going to be able to say, 'I won the Carling Cup, the UEFA Cup and the FA Cup.'

Bernie: If that's what it says on his CV, would it not be sad to see him go?

Michael: It would, but there must be other managers out there.

Eric: Wait a bit, let's talk about the performance last night, not about what might happen in the future.

Michael: The players were absolutely outstanding. They know what direction they want to go in now. Whether Bill Beswick has pointed them in the right direction or not…

Eric: What?! What's he got to do with it?

Michael: Well, he's the psychologist, isn't he?

Eric: What's he been doing in the league then? It's down to players, man. It's hype and it's bull. You are getting hoodwinked by people. The way they played last night wasn't down to a flamin' psychologist. Dear me!

Michael: It was down to the 11 men on the pitch.

Eric: Exactly!

Michael: Always is. I praise everyone. Even the staff selling the tickets, the cleaner, the guy who cuts the grass – not that there's a lot of it!

Kevin, Middlesbrough

Malcolm: Who do you want to praise?

Kevin: I'm gonna praise Steve Gibson and Steve McClaren. Without Steve Gibson, we know where we'd be. And Steve McClaren, love him or hate him, he's doing exactly what I'd do. He's resting players and what have you. He's putting younger players in for the league matches and putting the established stars in for the cup matches. That's the only area where we're going to have success this season. I'm talking as a man who has got four season tickets. I'm quite prepared to go and see juniors play.

Eric: I look at the Vidukas, he was brilliant. That's what I look at. I don't look at whether you won the game because you rested someone three days before. It doesn't even come into the equation.

Kevin: With so few games left, we're finding out how young players perform in the first team.

Bernie: We've got some massive games, Eric.

Eric: You play Portsmouth on Saturday. So you'd start playing the kids against Portsmouth, who are in a relegation battle. How do you think other teams around them will feel? Years ago, you'd have got fined for playing a weakened side.

Bernie: Other teams have done it, though. We are not setting the trend.

Eric: I'm not just blaming the Boro, but where does it all end?

Bernie: Portsmouth is a long way but I don't give a damn what side Steve McClaren picks, I really don't.

Kevin: I'm not sure if this is our seventh semi-final or ninth…

Bernie: And this season we could win two trophies.

Malcolm: You get there first, Bernie.

Briggsy, Middlesbrough

Briggsy: Everyone played well last night, it was a great performance.

Bernie: Everyone. There wasn't a weak link throughout the 90 minutes and the fans were great as well, so well done to all concerned.

Briggsy: The one player that stood out, for me, was Viduka. He was something special.

Bernie: I can't recall any fan ever criticizing Viduka's qualities as a player. The question has been about his mentality and is he fit or is he lazy? On the ball, when he is playing well, there's nobody better in that position.

Briggsy: If Henry or van Nistelrooy had scored the goal Viduka got last night, it would have been front-page news.

Bernie: For those that didn't see it, he's got his back to goal 12 yards out, he's got defenders on him, he turns, he drops his shoulder right and then left, there's about three or four

players surrounding him – and somehow he manages to put it in the net. It was a fantastic finish.

Briggsy: I couldn't believe the amount of people ringing in earlier in the week moaning about the team selection last Sunday.

Bernie: I think the fans wouldn't have been as harsh if it wasn't against Newcastle.

Eric: Wait a bit, why shouldn't they moan about the team selection on Sunday?

Briggsy: I think it proves…

Eric: No, no, no! Don't go down that line. It has proved nothing.

Briggsy: We're in two semi-finals.

Eric: You're not in two semi-finals because you rested players.

Briggsy: If you play your top team, are you guaranteed to win?

Eric: What? No, exactly right. If you rest players you're not guaranteed to win either. You've just answered my question.

Briggsy: It's been proved this season…

Eric: It hasn't proved a thing! Oh, nooo.

Briggsy: We're in two semi-finals. What more do you want?

Eric: Don't use resting players as the reason you won the game. It was because of them players on the pitch. They were brilliant.

Malcolm: What you're saying is that to have one good performance, you're prepared to tolerate a dreadful performance the game before?

Briggsy: At this stage of the season, yes, I am.

Even if Newcastle do beat us n send us down they won't have relegated us - we have dun it ourselves. This season has been indescribable. Very well dun 2 Boro tho. Hope they go all the way.
- Anth, Shotton, Sunderland fan

Bernie, I hope Viduka is here next season and also Julio Arca may sign for the Boro as rumour has it he was at the Riverside last night
- Khalid

In The News

Man United 0 Sunderland 0

(Sunderland relegated)

Newcastle 3 Wigan 1

Portsmouth 1 Boro 0

Sunderland 1 Newcastle 4

Boro 2 West Ham 0

Premier League positions

	P	W	D	L	Pts
7 Newcastle	35	15	6	14	51
13 Boro	34	12	7	15	43
20 Sunderland	34	2	6	26	12

Tuesday April 18

Jamie, Newcastle

Jamie: What do you reckon of the managerial situation at Newcastle at the minute?

Bernie: What do you think?

Jamie: I think they should give Roeder the job.

Malcolm: I think that's a fairly obvious thought to have at the moment. If Newcastle United qualify for Europe…

Jamie: I reckon they should give him it anyway.

Malcolm: If they qualify for Europe, I am absolutely convinced he will get. If they qualify for the Intertoto, he will get it anyway.

Jamie: I think he should just get it anyway. He's worked a miracle with us, like.

Malcolm: Where do you get a miracle from?

Jamie: Because of the situation we were in before he took over, the performances before he took over compared to what it's been like with him in charge.

Eric: Your performance wasn't too good at the weekend. I know you won and deserved to win…

Malcolm: I'm not in any way knocking Glenn Roeder. He has got to be a serious candidate for the job now, but I personally feel let's just leave it until the end of the season. I think what Glenn Roeder has done for Newcastle shows the horrors Graeme Souness brought to St James' Park.

Jamie: Even Albert Luque scored yesterday.

Mark, Newcastle

Mark: Is Eric there?

Eric: Of course I am.

Mark: Eric, I'm back!

Eric: What do you mean, you're back? I can't remember you.

Mark: Oooooh, ha, ha, ha, ha,ha, ha, ha, haaaaa! Oooooh, ha, ha, ha, ha, ha, ha, ha, ha, haaaaa!

Eric: Oh, it's not that clown on again, is it?

Mark: Oooooh, ha, ha, ha, ha,ha, ha, ha, haaaaa! Oooooh, ha, ha, ha, ha, ha, ha, ha, ha, haaaaa!

Eric: Bernie, get him off. Bernie, will you get him off!

Bernie switches on a recording of The Laughing Policeman.

Mark: Oooooh, ha, ha, ha, ha,ha, ha, ha, haaaaa! Oooooh, ha, ha, ha, ha, ha, ha, ha, ha, haaaaa!

Eric: Bernie, get the two buttons off! Which one's him? Get them both off.

Mark: Eric?

Eric: What?

Mark: Who's laughing now?

(Laughter all round)

Eric: Oh, give over.

Mark: Are you all right, Eric?

Eric: I'm all right, course I am.

Bernie: Mark, I think you're seventh in the league. You're not laughing now, are you?

Mark: Hey, that puts everything in perspective. We've had a terrible season and look where we are and where you are! Ha, ha, ha, ha, ha!

Eric: Mark, listen, seriously, even you can't believe you won 4-1 yesterday.

Mark: Oh, I can easily believe it. I was disappointed it was only four! Seriously, I couldn't believe how many empty seats in that stadium were yesterday for a derby game like that. Eight thousand empty seats. You could have given them to us and we'd have filled 'em.

Bernie: And the thing is, Eric, that could be your last derby match for a long time.

Mark: Precisely my point. It doesn't matter where you, whether you've been relegated. You couldn't even fill your own seats.

Bernie: And what do you reckon to that, Mark?

Mark: Oooooh, ha, ha, ha, ha,ha, ha, ha, haaaaa! Oooooh, ha, ha, ha, ha, ha, ha, ha, ha, haaaaa!

Malcolm: Get him off!

Eddie, Newcastle

Eddie: I'd just like to talk about yesterday's game. I agree with Eric about the first half being atrocious. I think it was as bad as in the first half of Souness' last game at Man City.

Eric: Wait a bit, no. I'm giving Sunderland a bit of praise.

Eddie: I am as well.

Eric: We weren't brilliant but that was a good fighting first-half performance. We got a goal and deserved to be in front, Eddie.

Eddie: I agree with that, but we were really rubbish and, to me, we should have been two or three goals down. But the second half, I don't know what Roeder said to them, but we were a different side.

Malcolm: No, I didn't get that impression, you know.

Eric: You got the breaks at the right time.

Malcolm: I thought it was as much Sunderland's poor play as anything else. Come on, that first goal, the lad's come out of the dug-out and continued his run straight through your back four. Bramble's knocked the ball from not far outside Newcastle's penalty area.

Eric: The penalty decision – a joke, shoved him over. The next one, two of them collided with each other and let Luque through.

Eddie: But you've got to take the chances still, you've still got to put them away. Roeder has really turned it around since he took over from Souness. I mean, you and Bernie laughed at us even thinking about sixth place and look it now.

Eric: I can't believe it. I still can't believe it.

Bernie: I can't believe it either.

Eric: By the way, Sunderland fans always slaughter Shearer, but Eric Gates is going to say this – what a brilliant penalty

Eddie: He hit it with venom. Even after the match, he said 'If I never get another goal, it's nice to get one here.'

Bernie: I can't believe you, Eric, saying he put a penalty away brilliantly. He's had plenty of practice. He's scored about 103 penalties!

Vince, Newcastle

Vince: Just a couple of points about Roeder being the next manager.

Bernie: Would you agree or disagree?

Vince: Well, I understand from the situation that he couldn't be the manager because he hasn't got the UEFA coaching certificate.

Bernie: He'll get it in the summer months, man.

Malcolm: He's one session away.

Vince: Let me finish. A team can appoint a manager temporary for a certain period. Now, believe it or not, Roeder's period finishes before the last game of the season so he cannot be in charge of the last game of the season.

Bernie: Isn't that embarrassing, Malcolm?

Malcolm: It's just the rules. But he is one session, one day away. It's not a pass or fail situation. He just has to do the session and that's it.

Bernie: I've said this before but Vialli, who was Chelsea manager, he won a host of trophies, then he left Chelsea, he did his badges, then went to Watford and he had a nightmare. He was brilliant without the badges.

Bernie: You know, the Sunderland supporters are saying 'That's it, I'm not going.' But a fan likes to see a winning team. If they get hold of the Championship like they did last season and start to win, I'm sure the supporters will go back again.

Eric: They'll go back, yes. But when Sunderland went down last time, I said that if they bounce straight back up the crowds will be 40,000, full houses there. There wasn't, you know. Sunderland Football Club have got to realise they've sickened off the die-hards who've been going for years.

Malcolm, keep your finger on the button and if any idiot comes on and tries a cheap shot at Shearer, a guy who has been a credit to the game for over 17 years, cut them off. Any attempts will more than likely come from Smogland, they are so sad! - Toon Terry

I have it from a very good authority that ex-Man U director John Magnier is definitely one of Niall Quinn's backers on consortium and Roy Keane is gonna B boss - Anth

The score yesterday should of been the other way round. We will beat the skunks when we return to the Premiership, watch out - Nathan

7th in the league, I can't believe it. 5th is as high as we can mathmatically get...can you imagine that! What an amazing turnaround. Well done, lads. Big Al, thanks for the memories - Gaz, Shields

Malcolm, one thing I will say is that if someone came in with a £15m bid for N'zogbia, I'd reject it. He and Milner on the wings next year - Paul, Newcastle

The cloth-cap brigade, if you like are saying, 'I've had enough.'

Malcolm: I've got to say that was the impression I got from all the anger from Sunderland fans that was around me. Some of them feel like, 'How dare you put me in a situation whereby, out of a point of principle, I'm not going to renew my season ticket?'

Eric: These are the fellas that have paid hard-earned money and that have watched the club for 40 years. They feel hurt by what has been done to their great club.

Vince: But you soon forget when the team start to win.

Eric: The difference is that the fans are not just going to walk back because it's Sunderland. They've got to do something before they go back.

Connie, Middlesbrough

Connie: I never thought I'd say this, but I can't wait for the Boro season to end.

Malcolm: Why?

Connie: It's doing my liver something rotten!

Bernie: Get off the drink, man.

Connie: I keep celebrating though. Then I get into trouble!

Malcolm: You could be a Sunderland fan and be driven to drink – and that's a lot worse.

Connie: I go to drink when Boro don't do so well, too, so that's even worse.

Bernie: I think you've got a problem, Connie.

Connie: I hope we do the business on Sunday. Then I'll have to celebrate again.

Pat, Sunderland

Bernie: Come on, Sunderland fan, Pat.

Pat: Bernie, shut up, you, because I'm about to say something to you that I don't think you'll like. This is my last word of the season. Obviously you know how we feel. Bernie, tell your little foot soldiers to shut their gobs, right, because you will never, ever have 40,000 fans in your stadium, not

even if you were first in the Premiership, mate. You will never, ever have support like Sunderland or Newcastle. Never, ever, in your history. So tell your foot soldiers to get off their high horses…

Bernie: Yep.

Pat: We've had it bad enough, we've had a terrible season, we've got 10 points and still got 30,000. End of story, end of season.

Bernie: Pat, I know you're a frustrated man, but…

Pat: Frustrated? You don't know what it's like.

Bernie: Pat, I do know what it's like. We've been relegated, we've been in liquidation. I know it's not nice.

Pat: Bernie, tell your fans to straighten their faces, right?

Bernie: They'll straighten them when we've got two cups in the cabinet.

Pat: Yous will never have two cups in the cabinet.

Bernie: Don't say never, Pat. We've got Bucharest and we've got West Ham, who we walloped at a canter at the weekend.

Pat: Eric?

Eric: Yes?

Pat: Wallop him!

Bernie: Why's he taking it out on me? I think he's a bit envious that we're in two semi-finals.

Malcolm: If you do end up with two trophies in your cabinet, will you still not fill your ground at the end of the season?

Bernie: I won't worry about that if we win the cups.

In The News

UEFA Cup semi-final 1st leg: Steaua Bucharest 1 Boro 0

Friday April 21

Peter, Newcastle

Peter: Malcolm, your co-presenters there were very, very disrespectful to me last time I came on.

Bernie: Oh, Peter, we only joke, man. We're not disrespectful.

Peter: It was just before the derby match between Middlesbrough and Newcastle. I predicted that Newcastle would win, which they did, and that they would beat them easily, which I think they did. It didn't reflect how much better we were on the day. You beat Bolton by four, you scored four against Basel and four against Charlton but you only got one against the really good team that you played – and we all know who that was.

Bernie: Oh, we put the kiddies out against Newcastle.

Peter: Never mind that. You're always making excuses. I had this with the Boro fan at work. I sat him down and gave him an analysis of what would to happen to you last night. I told him that Steaua were a good side and it would be a whole different ball game from the Basel match. You were very fortunate to get away with 1-0. I'm telling you this, I predicted that we would whack Sunderland. There's a Mackem at work and I told him that and he said I should be the fourth Legend. I explained to him that I wasn't quite as good a footballer as you three.

Eric: Yeah, but what have you been predicting all season to your mates? Winning the UEFA Cup, winning the League Cup, winning the FA Cup? Come on!

Peter: Eric! Eric!

Eric: Come on!

Bernie: He's gonna tell you in a minute.

Peter: Listen, Eric, I was on here months ago telling you that we could challenge for Europe. I also…

Eric: Yes, but you're the same fella…

Peter: Listen, Eric, listen! This is my call. Listen for a change!

Eric: Well, hurry up then.

Peter: Also the fact that Pederson cheated against us and that could be the difference between us or Blackburn getting into Europe.

Eric: Right, have you had your say now?

Peter: No, no! What I was going to say, Eric, is that another colleague at work, a Newcastle fan, reckons your team are going to be on for the record of the lowest ever points in a season.

Eric: Yeah, but you've just picked out the predictions you've got right but you're the sort that comes on at the start of the season…

Peter: Look, I'm not being wise after the event.

Eric: Oh, can I have my say now?

Bernie: Peter, I want to know how you think we're going to do on Sunday against West Ham and next Thursday because I'm going to tape this one.

Peter: I believe you're gonna get beat on Sunday though I think it will be close. And if you manage to beat Steaua then fair's fair but I don't think you will. I think Steaua will score and it will possibly be 2-1 to you but you'll be out.

Eric: But overall what I'm trying to get across, but you won't let me get a word in, I remember you coming on at the start of the season – you were going to win the league, you were going to win the cup but you've won nowt.

Peter: No, no.

Eric: You did! You did!

In The News

FA Cup semi-final: Boro 0 West Ham 1

Newcastle 3 West Brom 0

Portsmouth 2 Sunderland 1

209

```
Bubbles, they fly so
high they reach the sky,
then like the Boro they
fade and die! Your
season's over come
Thursday, Bernie
- The Tasty Turk, Toon
fan


Please play The Laughing
Policemen for Bernie and
the Boro fans - they're
gonna win nothing and
the Toon are marchin'
into Europe
- John, Toon


Bernie, 58 games is
taking its toll, let's
hope we can lift
ourselves for Thursday.
Come on Boro, do us
proud and let's lift the
UEFA Cup
- Tony from Redcar


Malcolm, we murdered
West Ham and should of
won. U are lovin' this
gloating to Bernie. Well
enjoy your cup final win
over the Boro the other
week cos u lot are
rubbish and when the
Boro get through on
Thursday night you will
be gutted like the rest
of the Geordies!
- Stoney of Ingleby
Barwick
```

Monday April 24

Mel, Newcastle

Mel: Bernie, hey, hard lines.

Bernie: Yeah, that's sport, it wasn't to be. Not good enough on the day and we're out.

Eric: What do you mean? They were hammered!

Mel: I would like to have seen you get there. Malcolm, with the season practically over now, do you think Glenn Roeder is the manager to take us into the future. I don't think he is. I would like to see Martin O'Neill come in.

Malcolm: From what I gather, he can't be the one to take us into the future because he hasn't got the necessary qualifications and would not be able to get those qualifications before the beginning of next season.

Mel: I didn't know that.

Malcolm: That's what I'm led to believe. I'm not saying that as absolute gospel.

Mel: Regardless of qualifications, do you think he is the one to bring top class players in and get a good squad together?

Malcolm: Immediately you bring up a point about buying top class players. I don't think Glenn Roeder has ever gone out and bought a top class player, has he? So I don't know what his selection process is like.

Mel: I think Freddy Shepherd said a couple of weeks ago that he would announce the new manager before the end of the season.

Malcolm: I think he said that though before the Football Association announced that Eriksson would go after the World Cup. That's confused everything, hasn't it?

Mel: Yeah. Any manager that comes in has got a mega job on. It doesn't matter who comes in, you've got to give him time. But as long as we see progress.

Malcolm: Do you think that Graeme Souness was a backward step so that you could go forward ten?

Mel: To tell the truth, I was disgusted. I never ever wanted him to come to Newcastle. Blackburn were in dire straights. Freddy Shepherd had insight to say, 'Hey, this fella's taking us down.' Because I think we might have went down.

Malcolm: Let me ask you this – certainly there have been some good results under Glenn Roeder, but have you seen the team play well?

Mel: I think last week in the first 45 minutes against Tottenham – and I think that was about it. Glenn Roeder has had some good teams to play who have been mid-table or lower. We met Liverpool, Chelsea and Man U and got beat every one.

Mark, Middlesbrough

Mark: Where do I start here? I've been at both games this week, I was in Bucharest and at Villa Park yesterday – and we blew it big style. We had a chance to take the club further than before and we probably won't get a better chance. Why I think that has happened is that the players lost their bottle

Malcolm: And I thought it was West Ham that were blowing it!

The sound of I'm Forever Blowing Bubbles rings out across the airwaves…

Bernie: Get that rubbish off. A joke's a joke.

Mark: Have you had enough, Malcolm?

Malcolm: I couldn't resist it!

Mark: Yeah, well, you should've waited until I'd finished, at least. They did lose their bottle for it – and they weren't tired. I travelled to Bucharest, went to work the rest day, I did two double shifts, went to Villa Park, so don't tell me they're tired.

Bernie: My beloved Boro, your beloved Boro go on about being tired but we've worked it out that it's a myth. We've played 57 games as a club but the top player has only played 41 – and that's Mark Schwarzer, the goalkeeper. I bet you I played 40-odd games a season and I got nowhere near semi-finals. That puts it into perspective.

Malcolm: Shall I tell you what the frightening thing is? It's excuses that you are going to get beat before you play the game.

Eric: Mind you, it's not just the Boro. We hear a lot from the Boro because we're in the north-east, but it is throughout the country.

Bernie: I have never heard a Gareth Southgate or a Yakubu saying they are tired. Never.

Mark: What we've seen too often this season is them not closing down.

Bernie: First half, we were comfortable, they didn't trouble us. Schwarzer was redundant, defensively we were sound. Taylor and Downing did well on the left in the first half, disintegrated second half. Up front I thought Hasselbaink and Yakubu, just like against Bucharest, it was like coming up against a wall. We played the ball up and it came straight back.

Malcolm: Yep, they were dreadful. Absolutely dreadful.

Mark: Can I highlight one who always seems to get let off in these situations. I thought Stewart Downing was OK in the first half…

Bernie: Yeah, he was.

Mark: But Sven was at some of these matches and I'm afraid that lad won't be going to Germany. He lacks a bit of heart, a bit of bottle and a bit of commitment.

Bernie: This is the thing, Mark. We had a few furious callers on after the game, obviously upset that we'd been knocked out of the competition. They were having a go at the manager and then they were having a go at Stewy. OK, second half he wasn't at his best, but first half I thought him and Taylor formed a good partnership on the left. Isn't it a case of the local lads, born on the doorstep, being easy targets? Mendieta has had stinkers and I've not heard people coming on saying he was rubbish or lacks heart. I've never heard it about Rochemback, it's always the local lads that get it.

Mark: Last time I was on I was calling Schwarzer and Rochemback.

Bernie: Well, I always feel that those that come on here always have a go at lads like Downing – and I think there's a wee bit of envy there. He's a local lad who's done well, got a nice car, nice house. I just think they resent that and I don't like that.

Mark: We just want to see a little bit of heart and bottle. I mean how many times did he back out of tackles yesterday?

Bernie: But he's not that type of player. He's a guy who gets the ball, switches play, hits it 60 yards. He's probably one of the only players who can do it. Yesterday he's nutmegged a lad and he's put a couple of crosses in. On the ball – smashing. Off the ball – yeah, he couldn't tackle a dinner.

Mark: The whole team were gutless. They didn't work for each other, they were awful. That's why the fans have stopped going to the football games this season. I don't know whether I'll go next season. I probably will, because that's what good fans do.

Eric: I'm not just having a jibe at you, but was it 2,500 tickets left over? You couldn't sell them for a semi-final!

Mark: These fans could have missed a great game. They missed a great night in Europe the other week. Tough on them if they do. But I don't care about them, I just care about me and those who were there yesterday. We sung our hearts out and deserve more than what we got.

Bernie: You did – and well done to the Boro supporters that went. So how do we lift morale for the big game on Thursday? Can we do it?

Mark: Let me get in that dressing room and I'll lift them. I'll lift them off the end of my flamin' toe – that's what I'll do!

Eric: Yeah, they talk about players being tired. But maybe some players need a kick up the backside and to be told 'You are the luckiest lads alive'.

Bernie: To have a chance on Thursday, the biggest guy we need in the team is Mark Viduka. We need him.

Paul, Newcastle

Paul: Bernie, unlike the first Newcastle fan, I've got no sympathy for you.

Bernie: That's all right, Paul. I understand.

Paul: Malcolm, something you said on Saturday disgusted me. You criticised the Newcastle fans for singing Alan Shearer's name, saying it would have an adverse affect on Michael Chopra. How dare you? You think they should be singing about the lads that were on?

Malcolm: No, I didn't say that. Do not put words into my mouth. Come on and criticise me by all means. But do not put words into my mouth.

Paul: Well, what did you say?

Malcolm: What I said was it will not help young lads like Michael Chopra and Shola Ameobi if they are hearing the name being chanted of someone who's not even on the field.

Paul: They should take the positives from that then and be thinking 'I want that to be me.'

Malcolm: But what positives are there from that for Michael Chopra?

Paul: Ten years ago or more Alan Shearer was in their shoes.

Malcolm: And four years younger than Chopra is now, Shearer had scored a hat-trick in his first game against Arsenal. So they are worlds apart. Come on, face reality. Chopra is desperately trying to carve out a career at St James' Park.

I'm gutted, Bernie, all we need now is to be beat on Thursday and McClaren NOT to get the England and the season will of been a disaster – John, a worried Boro fan

Full credit 2 Sunderland fans who sold out allocation at Pompey after atrocious season and longest trip of season. Top, top support – Matt, Jarrow

Malcolm, we will always sing Shearer's name from now till the day we die. If players r affected by this then tell them to get out of Toon. Get a grip man. Man Utd players seem to play ok when they hear Eric Cantona sang every game – Hutch, South Shields

Congratulations Bernie, you have made most Geordies hate Boro more than our arch enemies Sunderland through your rash comments – Darren from the Toon

Bernie, your last caller Colin was an idiot saying you always have a dig at the Boro. We all know you're a top Boro fan. Downing 4 England – Neil from Stockton

Oh Malcolm, u shot ur self in the foot. The Gallowgate End sang Shola's name for both goals. Get a grip & sit with the real fans – Paul

211

If Bill Beswick goes with McClaren if picked 4 the England job will he change the 3 lions to 3 geese? - **Christoon**

I would just like 2 apologise to all the Geordies with the Boro on ITV1 their normal lifestyle will b altered but don't worry, The Bill will b rescheduled - **John, Thornaby**

Anyone who knows Glenn Roeder will know he's a born leader. Give him the job and a bit of money and we'll be in the Champions League next season - **Lee**

Bernie, Colin Cooper to play and captain Boro last game of season? Fitting tribute - **Kev of Brotton**

Gatesy, Quinny must be wondering what the hell he's letting himself in for. I feel Murray has damaged the club so much that it could take years to repair it. Good luck Niall, you're going to need it - **Philip, SAFC**

How can McClaren even be considered for the England job? Tactics, what tactics? His team are 14th in the league and when they go behind in the cup he just throws on all his strikers and prays! - **Pete, Newcastle**

216

Ronnie: We have, we have – and I can hold my hands up.

Bernie: And you're seventh, Ron, not sixth.

Ronnie: We're joint sixth, Bernie, joint sixth! But good luck for Thursday – and I take 4-1.

Eric: Is there any hope for Sunderland?

Ronnie: I don't think you'll come straight back up, mind. I hope that things get sorted out because there's nothing like playing the Mackems. That's a proper derby game – none of these small towns in Yorkshire.

Wednesday April 26
John, Middlesbrough

John: I just want to say to Malcolm, who was moaning about how we didn't score against West Ham the other day, questioning how many chances we had. But how many chances did Newcastle have in the FA Cup semi-final?

Malcolm: What's that got to do with anything? What has that got to do with anything?

John: And who are you playing in the semi-final of the UEFA Cup tomorrow?

Bernie: He'll be watching The Bill!

Jan, Middlesbrough

Jan: What I'd like to say is we've got a fish shop for sale here in Middlesbrough – and if Malcolm would like to buy it, he'd probably do a decent job because he doesn't know much about football.

Malcolm: Oh, right! And you're the expert, of course, that knows how bad I am.

Jan: When I was in Thailand two years ago, watching the Carling Cup final, we went into a bar. The first two shirts I saw were black and white, and from the minute that first ball got kicked the two Newcastle fans were slagging us off. But the more they slagged us off, the better we played and obviously we won.

Malcolm: Oh, so they had a real affect on you, didn't they, from over in Thailand.

Jan: There was another two guys with Sunderland shirts on who were absolutely rooting for Middlesbrough.

Malcolm: Jan, what do you expect opposing football supporters to do?

Jan: If you are a true north-east person, you should be glad a north-east team is doing so good at the moment.

Malcolm: Newcastle are doing marvellously in the Premiership, thank you.

Jan: Whereabouts? You explain to me whereabouts?

Malcolm: A long, long way higher than Middlesbrough, in a different half of the table in fact.

Jan: All you've done is talk about your own club or slag the other clubs off.

Bernie (laughing): Jan, Malcolm's just given me a nudge, he wants to buy the fish and chip shop.

Malcolm: I think it would be a relief to answering calls like this, Jan, I have to say.

Jan: I tell you what, Bernie, being a north-east person, he should just be glad that Middlesbrough are doing good. All he does, he never lets anybody finish, he just slags Middlesbrough Football Club off.

Bernie: Jan, give us a score for tomorrow.

Jan: I just hope we walk away with a place in the final.

Thursday April 27
Tim, Middlesbrough

Tim: Is Ireland's number one there please? I'm a little bit excited, can't wait for it tonight. I was devastated on Sunday. It was serious, gut-wrenching. That was the game to win to get into Europe. Tonight is massively important, without a shadow of doubt. But we've had a cracking season - win, lose or draw tonight. I will be devastated if we get beat, but we can do it. Timmy the optimist. We can blitz them with the team we've got. I'm not sure what happened on Sunday, we lost the plot. It's beyond me. We need a better performance tonight. But that bloke beside you, Bernie, I have listened to the tripe he has come out with this week.

Eric: Who are you talking about? Ali?

Tim: There's only one bloke I mean – the bloke with a black and white top on.

Eric: Oh, you must mean Malcolm!

Tim: Honestly, people like Woodentops, Bill and Ben…I watch them with the kids and I understand that. I listen to him and it's like watching grass grow!

Malcolm: How come you've just said exactly what I said earlier in the week?

Tim: Every single person this week has had a go at you.

Malcolm: You've just had a go at me and started calling me all sorts and you've agreed with me.

Tim: Every night this week I've listened and giggled as one person each night has had a go at you.

Bernie: I don't know if you were listening earlier in the week, but Malcolm will be leaving in the summer months. He's going to open a fish 'n' chips shop.

Tim: I would put a health and safety guy in with him because he'll probably kill himself.

Eric: What a great start to the show! We've got thousands of callers waiting so just give us the score for tonight.

Tim: No problem. Bernie, let's get it done. Up the Boro. Let's get Viduka on and let's get at them. Hey, what about Cattermole?

Eric: Give us the score!

Bernie: Cattermole's still injured.

Tim: It's gonna be – I am confident – it's gonna be…

Bernie: He could be on the bench tonight.

Tim: Sunday morning I took the kids out along the riverside in Stockton and we bumped into Ali. We talked and talked and talked.

Eric: What score did you give us?

Tim: I will take 3-0 tonight. And can I take Malcolm's place?

Malcolm: With a score like 3-0, you are welcome to it!

Jamie, Newcastle

Jamie: Although I'm a Newcastle supporter, I'd like to talk about Steve McClaren. I hope Steaua Bucharest win tonight because I'd like to wipe McClaren's smile completely off his face.

Malcolm: You've caught him smiling, have you, Jamie?

Bernie: What, do you think a defeat tonight for Middlesbrough would mean the end of the road for Steve McClaren and England?

Jamie: He's been out of the FA Cup and hopefully he'll be out of the UEFA Cup, because I don't want him to be the England manager.

Bernie: I thought the appointment was going to be an Englishman? And all of a sudden they've switched it.

Jamie: According to Sky Sports News this morning, Scolari has been offered the job.

Malcolm: He's been offered it and they are awaiting an answer from him. Surely they cannot go back to Steve McClaren after this?

Jamie: No, I wouldn't want him as England manager, he's not had enough experience.

Bernie: Is that not an insult to English managers?

Malcolm: They have been dragged through the papers in every single direction. And for what? I really am quite disgusted by all that's gone on.

Eric: Jamie, what about the score tonight?

Jamie: I think Steaua Bucharest will win 2-1.

Dave, Middlesbrough

Dave: Hey, this is absolutely magic.

Eric: What is?

Dave: We don't need to win that Mickey Mouse cup – the FA Cup. This is the real thing. 4-0 to the boys tonight.

Eric: 4-0?

Dave: 4-0, there we go! Who's up front?

Malcolm: You predict 4-0 and you don't know who's playing up front?

Bernie: The team sheet has just been handed to me. Hasselbaink and Viduka.

Dave: That'll do me. I tell you, Eindhoven here we come! You've got to be confident, haven't you?

Eric: Dave, give us a song.

Dave: Give us a song? Geordies at home, watching The Bill! Geordies at home, watching The Bill!

Bernie: Keep it going!

Dave: Geordies at home, watching The Bill! Geordies at home, watching The Bill! Hey, I'm on Century!

I would welcome Peter Reid back as under him we played the bet football I have witnessed in all my years as a Sunderland fan - Phil, SAFC fan

England managers - we have had a turnip, a Swede and now a carrot head. God help England - Dave, Newcastle and England fan

To all sad Boro fans who are glad McClaren has went - pathetic! He's the most successful manager you've had! He'll do much better with better players at England - Pete, SAFC 4ever

O'Neill hasnt had anything expected of him at the highest level. Newcastle and Boro expect the best. O'Neill will go 2 Sunderland as he can not lose. Average manager, average club - Andy, Bishop Auckland

Bernie, I can't surely be the only Boro fan horrified over the prospect of Tony Mowbray being our next manager? - David, Stockton

Malcolm, you need to remember that we are playing with Mr Souness's team. He always said they would come good. You just can't let him alone can you? - Madelaine, NUFC

Thank you Glenn Roeder for bringing European football back to Newcastle. Bring in the right players, get rid of Boumsong and become a legend on Tyneside!
- Pete, Newcastle

Although I'm a Sunderland season ticket holder my sis is a Boro fan and I'll be backing them all the way. 3-1 Boro - Mel, Spennymoor

Good luck Boro. McClaren will do a good job for England. Just a shame it's after the World Cup. C'mon the Boro
- from Gary, Newcastle fan.

4-1 to Seville, Saviola hat-trick
- Keith, Sunderland

Sudden improvement in wealth in the Boro then. Everyone going to Holland but couldn't afford to go to home games. Ficklest fans in world
- Tom, Northumberland

Bernie, I am a Newcastle fan. I hope and pray along with the rest of the country that you win the cup. I mean that sincerely
- Mark in St Peter's

Bernie (laughing): *You're doing great. Keep it going!*

Dave: Geordies at home, watching The Bill! Geordies at home, watching The Bill!

In The News

UEFA Cup semi-final 2nd leg: Boro 4 Steaua Bucharest 2

(Boro qualify for UEFA Cup final on 4-3 aggregate)

Richard, Middlesbrough

Richard: Bernie, there is a God!

Bernie: I've always believed in God but that result last night confirmed it.

Malcolm: And I wonder what Steaua have done to offend him.

Richard: We were two-down and I prayed. That Roman god, Maccarone, came on and he got us going.

Malcolm: So is he a big occasion player then? Is that what he's limited to?

Bernie: No, he came on on Saturday and I thought he was disappointing but he came on again last night and two goals – hey, come on! I thought he worked his socks off, he really did. Every one of them did.

Richard: I thought that if we played Steaua 10 times they'd beat us every time.

Bernie: After last night I don't know the game. At 2-0 down I said we would never, ever come back from this. They were a well-drilled, organised outfit. I could not for the life of me see us coming back.

Eric: I think everyone in the country thought that.

Bernie: I have to say a big, big well done to the supporters because at 2-0 down they stayed behind the team and stuck in there. They got what they deserved.

Eric: Do you know what? These fans will be talking about the two games for a lifetime. They will be talking about the Basel game and that game last night for as long as they are alive.

Malcolm: But how do you go out in the final? Do you go with Plan B

and then switch to Plan A, because your Plan B always seems to work better?

Bernie: It doesn't matter, Malcolm, because we always seem to come up smelling of roses. I have to say, Viduka was immense, he was brilliant up front. Downing created three of the goals, the work rate of Boateng and company was phenomenal. First half we were sixes and sevens but the second half was as good as you'll see. Technically they were very good in the first 20 minutes. But the second half they couldn't get out of their half. They must have thought we had three extra men, they were petrified.

Eric: I've got to say well done to the crowd. We're always first to have a pop but full house, well done to them.

Bernie: I've got to praise the fans because at 2-0 down and 20 minutes gone they stayed behind the team and believed. I don't know where they got that belief from.

Keith Lamb, Boro chief executive

Malcolm: Was last night the best you've ever had in your time at the club?

Keith: Yes – and the most up and down. I have to admit that at 2-0 down I thought it was all over. Lightening doesn't strike twice, we ain't going to pull back three goals. But the team never seemed to lie down. It was very similar to the Basel game if you look at the goal pattern and when we scored. And Steaua did exactly what Basel did. After an hour of high-tempo football, they just folded. It's a testimony to how demanding the Premier League is because these continental teams aren't able to keep going for 90 minutes at that pace, while our lads just kept going and going and going.

Eric: I saw you on TV with Steve Gibson, giving him a cuddle and what have you. But the question I've got to ask you is, at 2-0 down, what were you actually saying to each other.

Keith: Nothing! When they scored the first goal one of the Steaua supporters ran on to the pitch and collapsed. He was carried off on a stretcher and I went downstairs to see what was happening. I was just coming back up the stairs to the directors' box and they scored the second goal. I just couldn't handle it. I never went back into my seat. I went back into my office, put the tele on, turned the lights off and just sat there watching the rest of the first half on television. At half-time I went back into the boardroom and had a chat with Steve Gibson and Sven-Goran Eriksson. To be fair to Sven, he said 'If you score early, you've still got a game on here. It's not over yet.' And, sure enough, he was right.

Eric: Yeah, but I can imagine you thinking, 'You're just being polite there, Sven, aren't you?'

Keith: Absolutely!

Bernie: But can you believe the turnaround? The last time you were in here you were facing the flak, Boro were struggling and nothing was going right. Now we're in the final of a major European competition. It's a dream, isn't it?

Keith: Of course it's a dream. But it's the same manager, it's the same coaching staff and the same players. It just shows you that all the ingredients were right but weren't functioning properly.

Bernie: And talking about Steve McClaren, Scolari has just had a press conference to say he is pulling out of the England job. Keith, there's been a lot of talk about McClaren and the England job. What is the situation there?

Keith: Just the same as it was two or three hours ago. Steve has handled the process. We gave permission for the FA to talk to Steve, as other clubs did, but we can complain about how long it's dragged on. Steve McClaren has handled the situation magnificently, to use a word of his! He's pushed it to the back of his mind and kept his focus on Middlesbrough Football Club.

Eric: But there must be a real threat of you losing him now?

Keith: We don't see it as a threat, it's a possibility. If you're English and your country asks you to be their next manager, you don't turn it down. If your country calls then it's an honour. Clearly we don't want him to leave but if they want Steve and Steve wants the job then fine.

Alastair Brownlee, Century fm's Boro commentator

Alastair: How many parmos does Macdonald's fish shop want? Fifty parmos? There's been a queue of people at my house all day! The wife is going mad. Everyone round my house for a parmo!

Eric: Ali, there's only one person missing from this studio now that we've got Keith Lamb here – and that's you. The only reason we couldn't get you is you're too big to get in here!

Bernie: He knows you're kidding, Eric, because you're in! Ali, seriously, you've done over a thousand commentaries of Middlesbrough games, you're a diehard. Was that the greatest occasion you've done a commentary for?

Alastair: The answer simply is yes, it was. To be 2-0 down against a very good Steaua team and all hope draining out of everybody and then for the side for the second consecutive UEFA Cup tie to produce a performance like that, it was the greatest Riverside night. And probably going right the way back to 1967 when I first walked through the gates of Ayresome Park, the greatest Boro game I've ever seen.

Good luck the Boro, it makes a change from the Big Head Mags!
- SAFC fan!

I hope Boro win 4 the team and Gibson but I also hope they lose because those fans don't deserve that team
- Darrin, a Mag

Match prediction for tomorrow: Sevilla 3 Middlesbrough 0, regards
- Senor Dane Hamza, Chairman, Treasurer, and sole member of the recently formed Benton Branch of the Sevilla Supporters Club. Howay the Vill!

Just like to say gud luck to Boro and thanks to Steve McClaren 4 putting north east footy back on the international map
- Nick, a Mackem fan

Legends! I don't know why everybody's getting excited. By the end of the night we'll only be let down again and drinking ourselves stupid! Same old story in the north east of England - destined to win nothing!
- Pete, Newcastle

Typical Boro fans - your 1st European cup final and you sing about Geordies! Such a chip on your shoulders
- Paul in Newcastle

Good luck to the boys. Wonderful scenes here this morning, seeing all children arriving at school dressed in Boro kits. Tension building
- Carole, Boro fan

Wars have come and gone, natural disasters have occurred but in Marske Workingmen's Club one thing has remained constant - bingo on a Wednesday night. Except tonight. Big screen in the concert room. Best of luck
- from a Newcastle fan

Eric: Ali, did you sleep last night?

Alastair: No! I got home and had a little read of the programme – and people then kept waking me up shouting, 'It's my turn for a parmo!' What did bring a little bit of a lump to my throat is that the boss, Steve McClaren, went into the press conference after the match last night and, unprompted, told everybody that the players watched a DVD before the game of the highlights of our UEFA Cup run to remind them what they were capable of – and he said that they played Alastair Brownlee's commentary from the Basel game. So I felt I'd played my part last night. But at the end of the game I was trying to think of famous Romanians and it was either Dracula or the Cheeky Girls, so I decided to go for the line about a stake through the heart of Dracula!

Eric: Anything to say to Keith Lamb, Ali?

Alastair: Big congratulations to everybody at the club. We're all looking forward to going to Eindhoven – and does he want chips with his parmo?

Vince, Middlesbrough

Vince: I cried tears of joy last night?

Malcolm: Did you really?

Vince: I was thinking of back to 1966 when we won the World Cup but I tell you what, last night was just unbelievable. Unless you're a Boro supporter, it's impossible to know how we feel.

Bernie: I bet a few boots went through televisions in Newcastle last night!

Vince: Well, imagine what Sunderland fans must be feeling like.

Bernie: To be fair, there's been a lot of Newcastle and Sunderland fans coming on and wishing us all the best. There's been a few saying they hope we get gubbed as well.

Daryl, Middlesbrough

Daryl: Fantastic! Wow! I am absolutely amazed. Seriously last night I couldn't sleep. When I eventually got back from the Riverside last night, it was like Rio Carnival on the streets of Middlesbrough.

Eric: Rio Carnival! Come on! Who are you kidding? You mean there was four or five outside a fish shop or something?

Daryl: I'm not kidding you it was absolutely phenomenal, the atmosphere in Middlesbrough last night. And long may it continue right up to the final.

Eric: The Boro should be buzzing now.

Daryl: I've had a bit of a ding-dong with Eric and Malcolm in the past. To be fair, it's all a bit of fun and a big up to the two of you because you've seen the light now.

Eric: What do you mean – seen the light?

Daryl: You know what I mean, Eric. You've been converted!

Eric: I've given credit where credit is due, that's all.

In The News

Birmingham 0 Newcastle 0

Boro 0 Everton 1

Premier League positions

	P	W	D	L	Pts
7 Newcastle	37	16	7	14	55
15 Boro	35	12	7	17	43
20 Sunderland	35	2	6	27	12

Man United 1 Boro 1

Sunderland 0 Arsenal 3

Tuesday May 2

Colin, Middlesbrough

Colin: I didn't think that anybody could possibly have won any money on that game on Thursday night. But I've just been talking to my mate and he was telling me that a guy he used to work with, who is actually a Newcastle fan, tried to put a grand on it at half-time because got offered odds of 25-1 for Middlesbrough to go through. They wouldn't take the bet at the stadium because they couldn't cover it. But they allowed him to put a hundred quid on and he got his 25-1. What possessed him to do that, I don't know.

Bernie: What about last night – did you see any of the Manchester United game?

Colin: I think it was an excellent result, to be honest with you. I heard Alex Ferguson afterwards and, from the clips I saw and the commentary, I don't know what game he watched.

Bernie: I like to think I'm honest in my assessment. We out-played Manchester United in that first half performance. We passed it better, our movement was better, we had better chances. They changed it in the second half, Ronaldo perked things up and Brad Jones made a couple of good saves, plus the penalty save. Cattermole was fantastic. He had a rush of blood to handle the ball and give away the penalty, but don't let that tarnish his performance.

Colin: We don't want any rushes of blood in the final, but I think it's 'Clattermole' he is being referred to now, Bernie.

Bernie: Clattermole? There was one challenge he wiped a lad out totally. I mean, legally. He got the ball, wiped the lad out. He put in a great performance, but so did Downing and company. There was so many good performances, it was hard to separate them.

Colin: Finally – and this is going to sound extraordinary coming from me, because I've never been the greatest fan of McClaren – but I think we all realise that he's gonna be the next England manager, and what a way to bow out that would be next Thursday night, to win that. And I hope the Middlesbrough fans get a chance to thank him. I think there'll be more that want to thank him than don't, Bernie – win, lose or draw – because he's taken us a step further than Bryan Robson or any other manager. He's got the silverware in the trophy.

Bernie: I agree with you, Colin.

Anastasia, Newcastle

Anastasia: I want to ask you a question. You know how Manchester United play Manchester City in the derby and Everton play Liverpool in the derby? How far is Liverpool from Manchester compared to Sunderland or Newcastle from Middlesbrough?

Malcolm: Well, not dissimilar, I would have thought.

Anastasia: That's my point. I'm not being funny and I've got nothing against Middlesbrough. I think they've done fantastic, the way they are. But I've never felt Middlesbrough should be classed as a derby.

Malcolm: Well, in effect the north-east can't have a derby. You can only have a derby with a two-club city or town. That is the true meaning of a derby.

Anastasia: What I'm saying is that we can stretch the borders a little bit in that people in Sunderland might say, 'Oh, we'll go to the Metro Centre' or people in Newcastle might say, 'Oh, we'll go to the Empire Theatre', but how many people in Newcastle or Sunderland ever say, 'Oh, come on, we'll go to Middlesbrough and while we're there, we'll go past the ICI plant'?

Malcolm: I know a couple of people that said they were going swimming at Redcar. They never came back! I josh, I josh!

Anastasia: Sunderland and Newcastle are close so that's a derby, but why do they say Middlesbrough is a derby?

Bernie: Oh, it doesn't really matter, does it? You should be proud to play against the Boro.

Anastasia: Excuse me. Why? Give me one good reason why. At the end of the day, the likes of Sunderland get 26,000 fans there though they've never won a home game. Newcastle's had 52,000 and we've had a rubbish season up until the last couple of games. Middlesbrough have had the glory – FA Cup and UEFA Cup – and their gates are still sub-standard.

Bernie: We've nothing against Newcastle or Sunderland, Anastasia. If we win the trophy, the next time we play you I will bring it up to St James'.

Anastasia: Don't bother, pet.

Eric: You haven't seen it!

Anastasia: I don't care!

Eric: You don't know what a trophy is!

Anastasia: I might go to see it if Sunderland win it but I'm not going to see it if Middlesbrough do. I've nout against them but I don't think geographically Middlesbrough is a derby.

Bernie: OK, no one is arguing. I tell you what, I'll sleep better tonight for knowing that.

Richie, Sunderland

Richie: After watching that shower of crap yesterday, the first thing Niall Quinn wants to do when he comes in is get rid of the vast majority of them.

Eric: It was shocking. We are talking two Premiership sides.

Geordies at home watching Seville. Geordies at home watching Seville. He he he he he ha ha ha ha
– Robbo, NUFC

No goals, no Europe, no manager, seventh bottom. What a great season. We sacked our manager, yours got the england job. Come on Glenn, keep it going
– from Steve, top dog Mag

A quite lousy effort, totally outplayed + outclassed. I'm a very, very upset bloke. However it's been a truly fantastic journey lads, thoroughly enjoyable for this Norwich City supporter in exile! C'mon the Boro! – H from Otley

Ha ha ha Bernie, never mind, tape The Bill 4 me next season please, cheers – John, Newcastle

I'm still so proud of the Boro and proud to be from the small town in Europe. Well done lads, thanks for the great memories. You're all heroes – Paul, the Boro

It won't be the last time in the final. Steve Gibson won't let it be. I think this is just the start. Look at how far we have come – Graeme

The Geordies at home couldn't watch watch The Bill, so the Geordies at home all watched Seville, no Europe next year so what's all the fuss, if it's Europe you want then you can watch us
- Ed, Toon fan from the Gill

The lads done brilliant. Never forget that. Upset for Steve Gibson more than anything but well done lads! We'll be back
- Vince in the Boro

Who is the small town in Europe now Bernie?
- Davey, Toon fan, Birtley

Bernie, hold your head up high mate. Boro had an amazing adventure in Europe, the envy of many a club
- Terry, Chester-le-Street

Bernie, unlucky mate. You were totally outplayed, your ridiculous absurd jammyness deserted you. We may be ONLY in the Intertoto but at least we're in Europe! - Col

Roy Chubby Brown, Bob Mortimer, Chris Rea, Rory Underwood, Don Revie, Paul Daniels, Kirsty O'Brien, Journey South - can u hear me Journey south? your boys took one hell of a beating! Ya just a small town in Yorkshire!
- Kingy

Malcolm: I thought you were on a three-second delay to Arsenal.

Eric: Arsenal were half-cock and I tell you what, they murdered us.

Richie: And Mick McCarthy must take the blame for this, y'know. That's his team. He bought the rubbish.

Malcolm: You see, the one thing McCarthy had never done before he arrived at Sunderland was pick a side in the Premiership.

Richie: Everybody's got to start somewhere, Malcolm. But that first half was absolute rubbish. I watched the first half, refused to watch any more.

Eric: I look at the set-up of the side. These are all strikers – he played Stead wide on one side, Murphy wide on the other, and two lads up front.

Richie: The one lad who did all right was The Nose – Noseworthy. He tracked back. But the rest of them were absolutely dire.

Eric: All right Richie, I've got to agree with you.

In The News

Bolton 1 Boro 1

Sunderland 2 Fulham 1

(Sunderland's first home win of the season – in their last home match)

Newcastle 1 Chelsea 0

Aston Villa 2 Sunderland 1

Fulham 1 Boro 0

Sunderland relegated, breaking their own record for fewest Premier League points in a season
Boro field the youngest ever Premier League team, average age 20.
United finish the season with six wins from the last seven games with victory over the champions to qualify for an Intertoto Cup spot.

Premier League positions

	P	W	D	L	Pts
7 Newcastle	38	17	7	14	58
14 Boro	38	12	9	17	45
20 Sunderland	38	3	6	27	15

Tuesday, May 9

Matt, Middlesbrough

Matt: What do you reckon to the score for tomorrow night?

Bernie: We can only guess and summise. If I was a betting man, I'd probably say it will go into extra-time. It will be a tough old game. They've all been tough games.

Malcolm: Talk about sitting on the fence.

Eric: Yeah, Bernie, he's asked you for a score. What's the score going to be tomorrow night?

Bernie: If you're gonna stick my neck on the line, I'll say 1-0 to the Boro after extra-time. I don't see a lot of goals in it. I've got a wee feeling Ray Parlour could play in the midfield, with a four-four-two formation.

Eric: Ray Parlour? Where's he come from?

Bernie: I do hear that Parlour could be playing on the right.

Malcolm: Is Morrison injured?

Bernie: No, Morrison is training.

Eric: Matt, what do you reckon to that?

Matt: I reckon it'll be 3-1 to Middlesbrough and Maccarone will score.

Cliff, Middlesbrough

Cliff: I'm just ringing to wish the Boro good luck tomorrow night. I hope we can lift that cup.

Bernie: I'm speculating that Parlour will play on the right. Would you be happy with that, Cliff?

Cliff: No, I wouldn't, to be honest. I think we should go with Morrison and if not, Maccarone. I just think we've got to give them something to think about. I'm not saying it's negative to play Parlour but it's not as attack-minded.

Malcolm: Do you think that Steve McClaren might be playing a little too much respect to Sevilla?

Cliff: I don't think we should be giving them respect. It's a final. You've got to go out there and win the game. It's a one-off. You're not gonna get a second chance. Let's go out and win the game, that's my feeling like.

Malcolm: The thing that I find with Steve McClaren is that usually his Plan A is nowhere near as good as his Plan B.

Cliff: You can't say that, Malcolm, because…

Malcolm: I can and I have.

Cliff: We've got to the final, what more do you want?

Malcolm: Yeah, but you've got there in the last two games on the strength of Plan B in each game.

Cliff: Yeah, well, it's worked, hannit?

Malcolm: But that's what I'm saying – his Plan B is a lot stronger than his Plan A. Bernie is speculating that you're gonna start not with Morrison wide right, but with Ray Parlour.

Cliff: I wouldn't start with Parlour.

Brian, Sunderland

Eric: Brian, would you like to see another season like we've just had?

Brian: How does nay chance sound like? The less said about last season the better. To be honest, I've phoned up about Boro. I've got no love for the Boro but I remember watching the game against Bucharest in the semi-final, and I tell you what, I wish they win for one man only – Steve Gibson. If Sunderland had a chairman like him, we'd be laughing. I only hope that Niall Quinn can do that.

Bernie: Steve Gibson was on the flight coming over and he's a bit pensive, obviously. He knows it's a massive game. We're all hoping and praying that it doesn't go begging and that we win the thing.

Brian: I really fancy them to win it and I hope they do for him. But don't get us wrong, I've got no love for the Boro.

Eric: Give us a score for tomorrow.

Brian: I think it'll be 2-1.

Eric: I'm gonna ask you about Sunderland. You know this takeover thing – something's got to happen fairly quickly, I would have thought, so people can get moving in the summer.

Brian: Well, they've got to. They've got to get the season tickets sorted. Last year we got them in April. I'm a season ticket holder and I'm renewing it next year, no matter what happens, but I would like to see something happen at least before the end of the May.

Eric: Yes, the quicker the better. Getting the new board in, getting the new manager in. I would hate to think it's gonna drag on all summer, wouldn't you?

Brian: Oh God, no. That's the worse case scenario. We can't possibly have that. If Niall Quinn going to be the chairman, we need him in, we need a new manager and we need to see players coming and going.

Eric: I would hate to think it's gonna drag on all summer, the season starts and we still don't know who's coming in, who's gonna be the manager.

Brian: I hope not. But I want to ask another question about this European coaching badge. I want to know when these guys are taking these tests, which football genius marks them? I mean is it Brian Clough or Bill Shankly from heaven?

Bernie: It's ex-school teachers or frustrated footballers that take their coaching sessions.

Brian: Who are these guys to say that these footballers…

Bernie: A lot of these guys are frustrated footballers that never made the grade at the top level, they've got a wee chip on their shoulder some of them. I went to York to do my badge years ago. There was about 20-odd guys and I think 16 or 17 failed out of 20 pros. It was unbelievable.

In The News

UEFA Cup final: Boro 0 Sevilla 4

Andy, Newcastle

Andy: Hello, Eric. Hello, Malcolm. And I was gonna say hello Bernie as well. Where is he?

Eric: Oh, he was frightened to come in man.

Andy: Ha, ha. I thought he wore a red shirt, not a yellow shirt!

Eric: It's yellow tonight.

Andy: I had a little song for him as well.

Eric: What's the song – come on, you can tell us.

Andy (singing): The Geordies at home, we weren't watching The Bill, we were watching the Boro getting stuffed off Seville. Everybody round mine for a ham and peas pudding stottie!

Laughter all round

I fell off my bike, missed my bus, lost a tenner, burnt my tea and watched the match last night. Life is great
- Derek, Toon fan

Alan Shearer, a Geordie, a legend, a gentleman, but just like me a Toon fan. Good luck mate and thank you for 10 top years of memories and 206 gr8 goals
- Gazza, NE1

Alan Shearer's testimonial last night was brilliant. The noise and sight of 52,000 Geordies waving black and white scarves was truly awesome. A night I will NEVER forget
- Andrew

What a night. Seeing Big Al, Sir Les and Rob Lee in the team again brought back some great memories. Scarf waving was a wonderful sight to see. You had to be there. Just a marvellous night to end a marvellous career
- Nik in the Toon

How many finals or semi-finals have Newcastle been in this season? Top team in the north-east, I don't think so!
- Angela, Boro fan

Eric: Oh, my!

Andy: What a night, what a night!

Eric: What do you mean, 'What a night'? You must have been disappointed for them. I was disappointed for them.

Andy: I wasn't. I was in my element. I cracked open about seven cans. It was great, man. After all the stick they've been giving us for the last few weeks.

Malcolm: And the irony is that with all that stick that they have been giving us Boro will not be in Europe next season. They'll be watching The Bill while Newcastle have got one Intertoto tie of two matches to play against lesser opposition and that'll put Newcastle into the UEFA Cup.

Andy: Well, will Bernie be able to record The Bill for us while we're out there, Malcolm?

Malcolm: I think so, yes.

Eric: A sad season for north-east football this year, wasn't it?

Andy: It wasn't that bad.

Eric: What do you mean?

Andy: Newcastle got rid of Graeme Souness, then we got ourselves into Europe. Sunderland got relegated with the least amount of points ever.

Eric: Oh, you're not gloating on Sunderland's demise and Boro's failure last night, are you?

Andy (laughing): Oh, you'd better believe it, Eric.

Malcolm: Does that make it a good season for you then, Andy?

Andy: The season's been fantastic, Malcolm – would you not agree?

Malcolm: I can't agree because I have to say through the season from the very beginning up until the beginning of February I was having a nightmare. I hated it. I dreaded going to St James' Park for fear of the horrors I was going to see.

Andy: The way we were going, we were gonna be down there in the relegation battle as well.

Malcolm: Yeah, I thought so.

Andy: Thank God we got rid of him in the end. And Roeder has done such a fantastic job.

Paul, Middlesbrough

Paul: Hi Eric, hi Malcolm.

Malcolm: Hi Paul, are you still crying?

Paul: I'm not crying at all, Malcolm.

Malcolm: It's just a frog in your throat, is it?

Paul: I tell you what, I've been proud to be a Boro fan all season and I'm still proud to be a Boro fan.

Malcolm: Absolutely. Jolly good.

Paul: Whatever any Newcastle fans come on and says, what they can't do is take away the memory of the quarter-final, semi-final and experience of yesterday that I've got. And I think that every Boro fan should hold their heads up high. We were beaten by a very, very good side last night. They are fifth in the Spanish in the league and have some real quality players. Having said that, I don't think we really turned up on the night.

Eric: You've just mentioned those other two games. I think everyone believed afterwards that Boro's name was on the cup. It wasn't to be, was it?

Paul: No, it was just one game too far. If we'd gone out last night and got beaten by a mediocre side then I would have been very disappointed.

Malcolm: They weren't a mediocre side. They were a very good side. I thought their football was tremendous. They looked so organised, they looked compact, they moved the ball all over the field. I thought they were absolutely brilliant.

Paul: The day itself was fantastic. The Dutch people and their hospitality, the way it was organised. By God, the fans that went there were treated well. We never saw any trouble whatsoever. Good luck to Newcastle next season. If you get past the first stages, your fans might have a chance to enjoy it, Malcolm.

Alan, Newcastle

Alan: I really wanted to have a go at Bernie, y'know.

Malcolm: He's in hiding.

Alan: I think he is in hiding. What it was, do you remember back when Newcastle played Boro and I came on the phone because Boro had said, 'We have bigger fish to fry than Newcastle'? It didn't go down very well. If they had said it before the match it wouldn't have been so bad but they said it after the match. I suppose now they'll have to settle for stickleback and chips.

Malcolm: Well, they've been well and truly fried, haven't they? Battered.

Alan: Outclassed, I thought.

Brian, Newcastle

Brian: Me and me mates are just walking up to the Alan Shearer testimonial game here, Gatesy, and we've just got a little song for you.

Brian & mates (singing): Geordie boys, watching The Bill, Geordies boys watching Seville!

Brian: We love it, son, we love it. It's the only reason I rang up – just to gloat!

Malcolm: It's become funny now but it wasn't though, a bit earlier in the season, was it?

Brian: Oh, it was. We always knew they would fall flat on their faces, Malcolm. They've got no fans. Even at nil-nil we couldn't hear them last night. The Seville fans made all the noise. It was absolutely great. Anyway, what I wanted to say was that this man Alan Shearer is an absolute god. I heard your statistics earlier, Gatesy, about all the goals he knocked in at Blackburn – 30-odd a season. What you forget is that he had career-threatening injuries in both the seasons that he got 30 goals. This kid would have been record goalscorer for England and had he stayed fit at the Toon he would have had 300 goals, never mind 200.

Eric: No, no, I'm not forgetting that. I was praising him for what he did at Blackburn.

Brian: He is an absolute god. He has played in a mediocre, average, rubbish Newcastle side for at least for or five seasons that he has been at the Toon. This man has

carried us season after season. They want to build statues to him. He's an absolute colossus.

Eric: There you go. Give us that song again before you go.

Brian & mates (singing): *Geordies at home watching Seville.*

Simon, Middlesbrough

Simon: I've just about recovered from last night. Little bit gutted, but you know how it is. To be honest with you, Seville were by far the better side, the best team won. They did deserve to win, though 4-0 was probably a little bit harsh but they took their chances. I let the Geordies have their gloating now because we've had good fun and if you're gonna give it, you've got to take it too. Let them have their fun and I hope they have a similar sort of run next year.

Eric: Let's be honest, it's good to have a bit of banter, isn't it? We're not falling out, that's what football's all about. We're not fighting anyone.

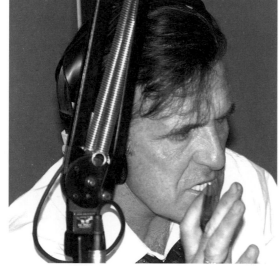

Simon: I was listening to the radio last night and the reaction from the press in the southern part of the country was just ridiculous. They were saying they were an embarrassment to England, it was disgraceful and they should never be allowed in the UEFA Cup again.

Eric: Absolute bull.

Simon: The fact of the matter was we got there. We deserved to get there because we beat Roma, Stuttgart, Bucharest, teams that were pushing for the Champions League at the start of the season. They were good sides. We used our luck up in the previous two games and we didn't get any in the final.

Malcolm: But Sevilla were the best side you met.

Simon: They had pace all over the park. There was only really Rochemback, Downing and Morrison who could keep up with them. Southgate, as fantastic as he is - and he's been a marvellous player at every club he's been at - his legs just weren't quick enough. We're disappointed but as long as the 14 that played come off and say we gave 100 per cent, you can't ask for any more than that.

THE SECRET LIVES OF THE THREE LEGENDS

Ever wondered what Eric, Bernie and Malcolm get up to away from The Three Legends show? Read on to find out...

Eric

My partner Dorothy was left a farm by her dad when he passed away a couple of years back. He ran it until he was 90, having lived there all his life. It was a full working farm with animals, wheat and barley. There's about 300 acres of land in all, plus a farmhouse that is hundreds of years old. Dorothy had picked up a fair bit about farming from her father, but I knew nothing about the business, so we really didn't know what to do at first, whether to keep the farm or sell it. We eventually decided to give it a bash and I think Dorothy's dad would have been proud of her.

I take an interest in the running of it, in a fashion. I'm not a farmer by any means but I'm getting into it. You could say I'm a pretend farmer. Fortunately, we get a lot of help and advice from local farmers. There'll be half a dozen of them meet in the living room of our farmhouse each Sunday morning to talk about football and farming. It's something they always did when Dorothy's dad was alive and they've continued the tradition despite his passing. The place has really come alive since Dorothy's cousin, Martin, his wife Joan and children Michael and Jonathan came to live in the cottage on the farm.

In addition to the help and advice we get from the local farmers, we have contractors who come in to work the fields. At present, it's mainly arable land growing wheat, barley and rape. We got rid of all the machinery – tractors, combined harvester and the like – plus the cattle. There were about 40 cows at one point. The cattle have gone now, but for a bit of fun we got some pigs last year and they then had piglets. Within no time we had 17 piglets running around.

It's a business but we're doing it for fun as well. Pottering around the farm keeps me busy and gives me something to do when I'm not at Century. I'm a lazy b*****d by nature, happy doing nothing, but I'm enjoying picking up bits and bobs, seeing the corn coming in and feeding the livestock. Groups of school kids have been to visit, while all friends and visitors get shown around.

The pigs are pets as well as farm animals but eventually the piglets had to go to the butcher. We'll breed some more now and the process starts over again. Bernie was shocked when I told him about the pigs going to the butcher. I think he had this distorted, idealistic belief that we'd somehow keep them all as pets without a call to the butcher ever being made. Then the next year we'd have 180 pet pigs! He just can't understand that we can't do that, we've got to get rid of them. Whether it's pigs, cats, sheep or cows, we can't just keep them, no matter how many there are. It's a business, when all is said and done.

I know Bernie is an animal lover but he's a hypocrite too, because I've seen him eat chicken and pork. I don't tell anybody what they should eat or drink, and I don't want anyone telling me what I should do either. I offered Bernie the chance to save the pigs' bacon and he liked the idea of having some little piglets running round his land, but he was soon put off when he saw how big they grew. But if anyone wants a pig, Eric will give them a pig!

Every first-time visitor leaves with a couple of dozen eggs. We have 40-odd hens, sheep plus a dog, five cats, ducks and a fishpond with about a hundred Koi carp. I class myself as an animal lover, but not in the way that Bernie does. I will have no qualms about eating one of my former pet pigs for my Sunday roast – just as long as the butcher does what has to be done. So get yourself to McMurchies in Haswell for the best pork in the north-east!

•HEN-PECKED: Looking like the Pied Piper with my hens.

•HAVING A MARE: And no jokes about what I get up to with our sheep!

Seeing the piglets being born was great, something I had never seen before. It's my responsibility to feed the pigs, though they're fed when I'm ready. You won't get me getting up at the crack of dawn to go and feed the animals. So I feed them and clean them out. Sometimes I go to the Century studios in my wellies stinking of the farm. It's a good job you can't smell over the radio or we'd get some complaints!

I never imagined living a life anything like this. I was a footballer for 21 years, now I'm trying to run a farm! It's fair to say it's a different way of life, but I'm very content. We're out of the way and nobody bothers us. My wife, Ruth, was a north-east girl. It didn't work out for us but I've got nothing but praise for her. How she put up with me for 20 years, I'll never know. I still class her as a friend now. We have two grown up kids, Martyn and Lauren, and I'm proud as punch of both of them, as well as Martyn's son, my grandson, Alexander. Martyn is a computer genius, while Lauren studied law.

Despite doing a lot of after-dinner speeches and charity work, it's all a far cry from my former career as a player. But this is my life now. Down on the farm during the day, talking football for two hours every night. It's not a bad life, that's for sure.

Bernie

Eric is what I would call a farmer, not an animal lover. He's the sort that sees a pound sign when they look at cows and sheep. He recently said to me, 'Bernie, why don't we buy 2,000 ducks at whatever a head? We feed them for x amount of time and we'd probably get a fiver profit on each one.' I asked him, 'And what happens then? Do they get murdered?' When he answered yes, I told him, 'No, you can leave me out of that.' I couldn't do it, no way. You can call me a hypocrite but I could not kill my own animals to eat them.

I remember being away in Singapore with a group of ex-Boro players on one of the annual football trips that Steve Gibson organises. This particular night, I was starving, so I was

delighted when I heard we were going to a top fish restaurant that night. But I found myself declining to eat at all when I saw a huge tank in the centre of this incredible floating restaurant, teeming with fish and lobsters so that diners could make their own choice which one they wanted to eat. Call it double standards if you like but, while I'm happy to eat all manner of seafood, I couldn't possibly pick out a living creature and order it to be served to me on a plate. I just don't like the idea that I would have personally put an animal to the sword. I'm soft like that – if there's a fly in the house, I always give it an option of getting out rather than just kill it.

While it was hard enough realising that I would have to sit and watch the rest of the lads enjoying their meal, my attention soon turned to a beautiful giant turtle swimming around the tank with the fish, just waiting for a customer who fancied turtle soup. Turning to my fellow animal lover, Gary Gill, I said, 'Gilly, I think we should buy that turtle, put it in a taxi with us and release it in the sea.' You may laugh, but I was serious. What's more, Gilly was all for the rescue act. Our minds were only put at rest when the restaurant manager explained that the turtle was purely decorative.

I've now got my only little animal sanctuary on three acres of land I bought at auction. I've had my house built there and it's perfect for me. I hope to stay there for good, along with my animals. It was always my dream to get somewhere in the country. I was brought up in Glasgow, a big city, but I always liked the countryside. After the hustle and bustle of the Legends show, I love to retreat to my house in the country where there's only me and the animals.

I love animals, always have done. When I was a kid, I was never allowed a dog, but I had gerbils and budgies, things like that. Then, when I moved to Middlesbrough, I got myself a couple of dogs. I've got two dogs now, an Irish Setter and a Dalmation that I got from a rescue centre. I hate animal cruelty, so I always had a positive view of the RSPCA but I've changed my mind about them now. A few years ago I had a nice place near Osmotherly in North Yorkshire with a great garden surrounded by a high fence. I went to the RSPCA to purchase a dog. It was just a mongrel that I knew might eventually get put down. They explained that they would have to do a house-check to ensure the dog was coming to an appropriate home. That was fine. But when they came out, they told me my fence wasn't big enough. This fence must have been about four feet six. I told them, 'It's a dog I'm getting, not a kangaroo.' The guy insisted the dog would get over it. So what if it had? If the dog had jumped the fence it was only into the countryside, not a busy road or somewhere that might endanger it. It was nonsense. I could not understand it. I've kept dogs for years and I've never mistreated any of them. I gave up and went elsewhere to get a dog.

But since moving to my land, I've slowly got more and more animals. Even when I was living in a caravan while the house was getting built, I had them. There's Sean and Mac, my dogs. There's Patrick the peacock and Patricia, his bird. I've got ponies called Ginger and Blacky, because of their colours, plus a young foal, Little Blacky. I was looking at the ponies one day and I could see these legs sticking out the bottom of Blacky! I didn't even know she was pregnant. I watched the foal being born and then called the vet. It was perfectly fine.

Then there's the ducks, Daffy and The Other One - I've never thought of a proper name for him, nor my two cats. And the goat is just The Goat. There's Big Cock - that's the cockerel, not me! - and His Bird. Not forgetting several chickens that I've never bothered naming.

The ducks have a tendency to just wander everywhere, but the dogs have got an instinct and tend to chase the birds. The young duck, Daffy, was sitting on about 10 eggs and one of the dogs bit her, clipping her wing. I came home one day and saw her wing was dangling. It has recovered well now, but I try to keep the dogs away from her.

One thing people can't call me is a sheep-shagger, because sheep are one of the few animals I don't have! I have to say, I'd like Highland Cattle, even one of them. But my latest 'pets' are bees. I've got a beehive where the cats are meant to sleep. They're not really pets, they just set up home there, so I moved the cats' blankets. I know you are supposed to get them out with fire but I wouldn't do that. I'm happy to let them do their stuff. I just want to let them bee!

I got Big Cock and the cats off Gatesy, though he gave me no choice but to have them. We were in the Century studio one

night when Eric asked me, 'Bernie, do you want a cockerel?' I told him I had enough animals so no, I didn't. But at the end of the show he went out to his car and then came back into the building carrying a bag with a old piece of string around it. He walked in the studio with a big grin on his face, put the bag on the desk and ran back out laughing. Me, Malcolm and Rod Hardisty just looked at each other. I opened up the bag and there was this old cockerel, dripping with condensation or sweat. I couldn't believe it. The poor thing had been in the back of Gatesy's car for the duration of the show and there was clearly very little air getting into the bag. I said I would take it because it was pure cruelty that he had put it through. So that's how I got a cockerel. He now struts about my garden as if he owns the place. He wakes me up at four in the morning, especially in the mating season. But we all make a noise when we're mating, don't we?

Why Gatesy didn't want it, I don't know, though it was probably because he's just another poor farmer. I fall out with him regularly over his attitude towards animals. I find him very amusing until it comes to animals. All I can say is that he'll be dealt with later down the line. As for the cats, Gatesy phones me this time and says, 'Look, I've got two kittens. Do you want them?' I told him, 'No, I don't really like cats.' 'Fair enough,' he replied. 'I'm just gonna drown them.' And he put the phone down. I was pretty sure he meant it, so I rang him back and ended up agreeing to take them both. I had a few rats at the time so I thought they would come in useful. They are quality, I love them.

Unlike Eric's farm animals, there is no chance any of mine will ever end up on the dinner table. I hate fox hunting as well. I tell you what, I'd love a fox to run onto my land and the hunters to follow it in. They would never touch the fox on my land, I promise you that. I've never taken part in protests against them, but I've spoken to farmers and told them I don't know how they can do it. Unfortunately, it's probably nothing they haven't heard a thousand times before.

I'm proud to say my love of animals has rubbed off on my two boys, Dominic and Ryan. I'd like to stop eating meat, but I'm not a vegetarian. In the main I only eat chicken but I do try other meats. Dominic doesn't eat meat, not since one day in the car when the two of them were in the back and I was

•BLASTS FROM THE PAST: With mementos from my playing career.

singing along to a song called *Meat is Murder* by The Smiths. The boy asks, 'What's that about, Dad?' I explained that Morrissey, The Smiths' legendary lead singer, was singing about the fact that he was against killing animals for food. That was the end of the conversation and I never gave it any more thought.

Then, a couple of weeks later, my missus, Karen, called me and asked me if I had lifted the bacon from the kitchen. I didn't know what she was on about, so she told me that she had left some bacon slices next to some tomatoes ready to cook breakfast. I assured her that I hadn't touched the bacon. A couple of days later sausages went missing and I was accused again! I thought she was winding me up, but she told me that she had asked the boys and they insisted they hadn't touched them.

There was clearly something amiss, so I got the boys on their own and said, 'Look, bacon and sausages don't just disappear on their own, so where are they? If they are in the house, they will stink the place out, so you'd better tell me.'

Eventually Dominic admitted, 'I lifted the sausages and bacon.' I asked him, 'What have you done with them?' He said 'I've hidden them in the field.'

I wondered where this was going. 'Why have you done that?' I asked.

He answered, 'Well, that's meat, isn't it?'

He was making his protest a bit too late to save the pigs! I had to tell him that he couldn't stop people who wanted to from eating meat, but if he wanted to give it up that was up to him. To be fair to him, he has stopped eating all meat. My youngest, Ryan, was on the crusade with him for about six weeks, then he gave in when he got to McDonald's. Dom's only 12, so I've tried to tell him that he needs to eat meat to make him strong while he's still growing up, but he's not having it. In all honesty, I'm proud of him for sticking to his principles. Good on him.

My boys live with their mother, while I live in my house, which has taken a long time to get how I want it. When I first saw the land, it was just a flat field with a rotten, old wooden hut that the wind could have blown down. It was like an old cricket pavilion. An elderly man who used to live in the nearby village

had used it as a retreat. He had built it himself, complete with living room, bedroom and a wee bathroom. No doubt it was smart in its day, but it just needed demolishing by the time I saw it.

My idea was to get the land and build on it. I got other people to go to the auction and do the bidding on my behalf. Their names will remain anonymous to protect the guilty, because I ended up paying way over the odds for it. When they came back, I said, 'Go on then, tell me what happened.'

'The good news is we've got it,' came the reply.

'What's the bad news?'

They then told me how much they had agreed I would pay. Let's just say I was shocked.

I paid money to get plans drawn up for the house I wanted to build. The architect assured me that he knew exactly what I would be allowed to build there, insisting that I should leave it all to him in terms of getting the planning permission. But the plans were rejected by the local council. So he got his money, the council got their money and I had nothing to show for it. I was not impressed.

I then had to get new plans drawn up. The main problem had been that the council were insisting they would only give planning permission for a building big enough to have one bedroom. It was ridiculous. I faced having a house on three acres of land that didn't have enough room to put up my parents when they visited from Glasgow. So I hit upon the idea of building a basement because that wouldn't cause the council any problems. So my house looks like a bungalow but in fact it's upstairs and downstairs, it's just that the lower level is underground. My bedroom is downstairs, so it's pitch black at night. It's like Bin Laden's cave! I love it. It's unique and different.

All the time while I was battling over plans and then having the house built, I lived in a caravan on the site. The caravan of love, as I called it. I was in there so long that friends started calling my Gypsy Rose Lee and asked me to read their palms! I can joke about it now, but in all honestly it was hard going to live in a caravan for more than a year with two dogs. It was dreadful. Unfortunately, I already had the ponies and stuff I needed to keep my eye on, so I felt I had to be there. It was like a fridge during the winter months. I got in from the Legends show one night and it was ice cold, I could see my breath. I had gas cylinders so there'd been no heating on all day. No joking, I slept in my shirt that night. Mind you, living in a caravan definitely made me appreciate living in a house a whole lot more!

Malcolm

I have spent more than 20 years of my life, in three spells, living in London, but the north-east is my home. I loathe London now. There's no way I would ever go back to live there. Only when my family moved to Sussex when I was 17 did I realise that you could get places in 20 minutes that would take an hour-and-a-half in London. When I was manager of Fulham, I used to spend six hours-plus getting to and from work every day. That's no life. I was leaving my home at quarter to six in the morning to give myself a remote possibility of being at my desk by nine. Now I set off from my home in the countryside, far away from the city, and I'm in the Century studio in Gateshead half an hour later.

I love the people of the north-east and I love the countryside. There are times when I cringe, but in the main the people here have huge hearts, and such a generous spirit about them. In some parts of the country, you might as well be in China because the people seem so different. In the north-east, I have always felt so accepted, right from my first move here when I joined Newcastle. I know it makes things a lot easier if you're the local team's new centre-forward, but I've always thought that people have a genuine interest in you and warmth about them.

I lived in Morpeth throughout my spell as a Newcastle player. I then bought some land in a tiny hamlet alongside a river in the centre of a beautiful conservation area just outside Morpeth, intending to build a house on it. Just as I was about to give the go-ahead for the build, Gordon Lee stepped in and I moved out. I sold the land after the move to Arsenal, though I really wish I hadn't. Someone else has now built exactly what I had planned on the site.

•FEATHERED FRIENDS: Feeding Patrick and Patricia, my peacocks.

•HOME SWEET HOME: A quiet moment on the doorstep of the house I had built in the North Yorkshire countryside.

231

•CROSSWORD TIME: 3 across - former football stars, now hosts of a popular radio phone-in...

When I came back to the north-east to do some work with Century, I thought I was only going to be back for about nine months so I rented an apartment in Jesmond. Then I met Carole, who is now my wife, changed my plans and decided to settle down in the north-east. From Jesmond I went to Carole's rented flat in Heaton. We then bought a lovely house on the Quayside in Newcastle. I remember being woken up by a band playing as HMS Newcastle went past our bedroom. The yacht had royalty on board so I gave them a wave! But the quayside got a little bit on the rowdy side for us. We wanted something quieter.

When I was a player, I used to lunch at a place called the Milk Maid, under license from the Milk Marketing Board. It was owned by Mike Quadrini, who later opened all the Tuxedo floating nightclubs. I used to go for lunch there every week with Frank Clark and John Tudor, together with a few local businessmen. I remember Frank telling me about a beautiful place called Shotley Bridge that was ripe for buying brilliant property at rock bottom prices. All these years later, I told Carole we should have a look there, but she he was horrified. 'We can't go there,' she said. 'That's where people go to die - and it's hours away' Carole knew Shotley Bridge only as a place that had once had a hospice for cancer victims who had gone beyond the pale.

Of course, when we went there it was anything but what she expected. Not only did it take us just 25 minutes to drive from the Quayside, but it's a beautiful, quiet village surrounded by wonderful Durham countryside. We don't have a farm, like Gatesy, nor a virtual animal sanctuary, as Bernie does. But, like Bernie, I'm soft about animals. In fact, the main hobby for Carole and I is walking our dog. To give you a clue how much of our life revolves around our dog, I can tell you that there's a cushion in our house that reads, 'The dog and its housekeeping staff live here!'

I am very happy to talk football in those paid hours that I'm with Century, but living with Carole is a release from football. My wife has no interest in football at all and I have to admit I'm happy to get home and be away from that focus. People talk to Carole expecting her to be a football nut, but she tells them that she's not interested. The usual reaction is, 'You live with Malcolm and you're not interested?'

I wish I had a pound for every time I've heard someone say, 'I bet you wish you were still playing.' My God, I'm in my mid-fifties and I've got an artificial knee. Do me a favour! But they are probably struggling to think of something to say, so I would never poo-poo them for it. I see it as my responsibility to talk to supporters and recall the memories we share. As I leave the press room at St James' Park, I have noticed there are those teams that will come out of the players' area *en masse*, rush down the steps onto the bus, close the doors and they're away. They cannot get through the throng of autograph-hunters quickly enough. In contrast, Chelsea stars come out and sign autographs for everyone that wants them. Man United and Arsenal are the same. And yet all three of them are top of the table. I think the clubs make them aware of the importance of the fans to the players, as opposed to the other way around. They give them the right outlook of the job in hand.

As a result of my playing career and my ongoing media work, I suppose my profile is second only to the current Newcastle players on Tyneside. Yes, I do like to escape the attention, but – like Eric and Bernie – I never forget my roots. We all know what it's like to be supporters. We all know we are just the same as the man on the street. The only difference is that we had that ability to fulfil our ambitions and dreams. So I think it's up to us to take the memories back and share them with people. It's a very significant moment in someone's life when they approach a former footballer and say to them, 'Do you know you were my boyhood hero?' We were part of people's dreams and imagination. I wanted to be Johnny Haynes, others wanted to be Bobby Charlton or Alan Shearer. It means so much to me that maybe some people had a fight in the schoolyard over who was going to be Malcolm Macdonald.

QUESTION TIME

The Three Legends answer questions sent in by north-east football fans

ON THE RADIO

If you could have any non-football guest on the show, who would it be and why?
- *Jonathan, Middlesbrough.*

Malcolm: Can they be dead?

Bernie: How are you gonna have a dead person on your show, Malcolm?

Eric: Malcolm would still have a conversation with them - and he'd even be too slow for them!

Malcolm: On the radio show I had during my playing days at Newcastle, I once did an interview with Eric Morecambe, an old director of mine at Luton. It was the best radio. Just talking about being a director, he was hilarious.

Bernie: I'd get Morrissey in. He's a superstar. He probably wouldn't turn up - or would walk out on the show, but it would be great if he did me a song as well.

Eric: Jesus Christ.

Bernie: Yeah, Eric, you could ask him, 'How did I ever end up looking like this?!'

Have you ever peed yourself laughing on the show? I have, while listening!
- *Peter, Jarrow.*

Eric: I wouldn't go that far, but there have been times when we just couldn't stop laughing.

Malcolm: Metaphorically, we have.

Eric: I've fallen off my chair a couple of times, while Bernie has had to leave the studio because he hasn't been able to stop laughing.

Have any of you ever taken a night off from the programme and lied about why you stayed off? - *Mark in Sunderland.*

Bernie: I lied to the public - or the lads lied for me. I went to see Celtic play Blackburn Rovers in the UEFA Cup. Newcastle had won in Europe the night before, so Malcolm and Eric accused me of being a yellow belly, but they knew where I was.

Malcolm: None of us have ever bottled coming on the show because of results over the weekend or the night before. If we had, the other two would never let them get away with it.

Eric: To be honest, it's the opposite, if anything. If your team has had a bad result, then you know it's gonna be a right good one - and you want to be there.

•HILLMAN MINX:
Malcolm's first car.

What are your highlights of the Ten Grand Fan over the years. Mine is the lad who got the Joe Payne questions two years in a row and got it wrong both times - because it was me! - *Jon Coburn, Middlesbrough.*

Bernie: The highlight for me is I get six weeks off!

Eric: And the highlight for me and Malcolm is that Bernie gets six weeks off!

Who would you pick to take your place on The Three Legends and why? - *Nick, Newcastle.*

Bernie: There's nobody could do it. They've not got the personality. There might be some good footballers among my ex-Boro team-mates, but they don't have my charm, charisma and panache! Seriously, I don't think it could happen. I look at Malcolm as the school teacher, who is very important for us two lunatics. That's what makes it work. If Malcolm was a loony like me and Eric, it wouldn't work.

Malcolm: The show needs that blend of humour, but for all the madcap goings on there is also discipline. So many comedy shows on TV and radio have failed when they've tried to change the personnel.

Eric: I don't think it would ever change. We have an agreement that no-one stands in for us. If one of us left, I think that would be the end of the show.

Bernie: Let's face it, I would prefer not to have Malcolm or anyone else from Newcastle on the show!

How much money do you get for doing this show? - *Dave, Boro.*

Bernie: Not enough!

Eric: I get twice as much as Bernie - but don't tell him!

Malcolm: Put it this way, I get more doing this than I did playing football!

PLAYING DAYS

Just to compare with modern day players, what was the highest weekly wage you were paid in your career? - *Steve, Newbottle, Sunderland fan.*

Eric: My highest was £750 basic. I think I earned 81 grand one year, that was my highest annual earnings.

Bernie: Mine was £1,200 a week - and I only got that because Pally was on it already.

Malcolm: I was on £500 a week when I signed for Arsenal in 1976 - and that was the highest wage in the country, by far. I had to keep it quiet, because Alan Ball and the like were on £200 a week.

Eric: It's frightening to think that players now are earning one-and-a-half times a week my best ever annual income - and they can't even play!

What was the first car you bought as a footballer? - *Rich in the Boro.*

Bernie: I didn't drive until I came to England when I was 24. My first car was an Astra. My first sponsors' car was a red Fiesta with big yellow writing down the side of it. The other lads called me Postman Pat! I never drove it again.

Eric: Mine was a green Ford Capri 1600. I was 18 and had just passed my test.

Bernie: Are you sure you've passed your test, Gatesy, because I've seen your driving?!

Malcolm: The first car I bought as a footballer was an Austin 1100. Before that, when I was a part-time pro at Tonbridge, my mother gave me a couple of hundred quid and I bought a Hillman Minx.

At your peak, how much do you think you would be worth in today's transfer market? - *Tony Benson from Sunderland, SAFC fan.*

If you were playing today, what do you think your transfer value would be? - *Alan, Redcar.*

Bernie: 50 grand - double what Boro paid for me in 1985!

Eric: £10 million.

Malcolm: Well, if Bernie would be worth £50,000, I would surely be worth £50 million!

Do you think you three would have formed a good strike force? - *Michael, Boro.*

Eric: Yeah, why not?

Malcolm: Yeah, we would have done. Eric would have played in the hole behind us, because he was the best in that role that I've ever seen, while Bernie and I would have been well suited. I was happy to get the ball on the halfway line. Others would play Bernie in and I would get there with my pace. It would have worked.

Eric: I'd have loved it, putting balls through to Malcolm. I wouldn't have bothered with Bernie - he'd have been offside!

Were you ever part of or witness to team-mates having a punch-up in the dressing room? - *Dave Henderson, Whitley Bay.*

Malcolm: Newcastle were playing at Molineux. Terry Hibbitt knocked a cross-field ball that I just failed to stop from going into touch, despite running my arse off to get there. In response, Hibbitt held his hands out, palms up, to the crowd, as if to say, 'What can you do?' Johnny Haynes had done the same thing to me some years before when Fulham played Middlesbrough. I swore nobody else would ever get away with doing that to me again. So when we got back into the dressing room, I got hold of Hibbitt by the scruff of the neck and hung him up on a peg. Just as I pulled my fist back, John Tudor got hold of my arm to try to stop me, so that when I threw my punch he went flying over my shoulder and the top of his head hit Hibbitt right on the chin. The two of them were spark out!

Bernie: We were training on Redcar beach when Bruce Rioch was Boro manager. I did something to upset Stuart Ripley. In response, he kicked me right across the waist. Another time, during training at Port Vale, Peter Swan punched me with his hammer-sized fist. I told him he was gonna be knee-capped for it - and, for a while, he believed me. He thought it was something I could arrange via my Irish connections!

Eric: There was a lot of stuff like that happened in training, so it doesn't really stick out in your memory.

If you could go back and change anything about your career, what would it be? - *Jonathan Hyde, the Boro.*

Bernie: I'd take Lennie Lawrence never to have been Boro manager, in which case I'd have played more games and scored many more goals for the club.

Eric: I would love for Ipswich to have beaten Man City in the semi-final of the FA Cup in the 1980-81 season. We should have p***ed all over them, but we got beat. It just didn't happen. If we'd won, we'd have played Tottenham in the centenary cup final.

Malcolm: I still look back to Newcastle United's game against Leeds United in 1972. I was about 30 yards out when the ball came over my shoulder and I went for what was probably the impossible by shooting for goal. I was about to volley it when Trevor Cherry struck the side of my knee. I watched my leg bend around almost to my shoulder. I was in plaster for a fortnight and it was the start of all my knee troubles.

If you could change the result of one game you played, which would it be and why?- *Gary Bullock, Heaton, Newcastle.*

Bernie: If Middlesbrough had won at Sheffield Wednesday on the last day of the 1988-89 season, we'd have stayed up and I'd have had at least more season in the top division. That was a bad a day. We lost, went down and I never got another chance at that level. If we'd won, I might even have been invited up for a post-match drink with Bruce and the rest of the team. Instead, I was the only one not invited.

Eric: Well, apart from the cup semi-final I've just mentioned, I'd say Ipswich getting beat by Middlesbrough when Bosco Jankovic scored two goals against us and we lost the championship. I'd have loved to have won the title and the FA Cup, but those two games cost me both.

Malcolm: Probably the 1974 FA Cup final. Getting beat 3-0 by Liverpool was the disaster of disasters.

What goal gave you the most satisfaction? - *Ray from Hetton.*

Eric: Every goal gives you great satisfaction. Your worst goal gives you the same feeling as your best goal.

Malcolm: I remember seeing Gary Player on television explaining how to use a driver. He said, 'I have swung this club about 10,000 times, I've hit a lot of good ones, but I've probably only ever hit one perfectly.' I understood what he was saying, because that was exactly the same for me when I scored against Leicester. It was a breakaway, Irving Nattrass crossed the halfway line, sh** himself and knocked the ball square. I ran onto it and hit it like a missile. It was the best ball I ever struck in my life. It hit the net at head height from 40 yards out.

Bernie: For me, I would say a goal I scored against Aston

Villa that got Middlesbrough to Wembley for the first time in the ZDS Cup. Bruce Rioch described it as a world class goal. Also scoring against Sunderland in 17 seconds!

Eric: My last Sunderland goal, against Newcastle, and a great goal I got at Liverpool in front of the *Match of the Day* cameras. The Kop just went silent and then gave me a round of applause. Great memories.

Who were the best and worst players you played with? And who is the best player you played against? - *Jonathan Fisher, Redcar.*

Eric: I was privileged to play against the likes of Platini and Cruyff, the best players of my era. Of those I played with, Kevin Beattie. The worst was Steve Hetzke.

Malcolm: Of those I played with, I would say the best were Liam Brady and Alan Ball. At the other end of the scale, Graham Oates.

Bernie: At the Boro, I would say the best was Gary Pallister. With Ireland, probably big Paul McGrath, because he was one of the greatest. As for the worst, Jon Gittens.

What's the strangest pre-match ritual you ever saw? - *Martin Wheeler, Hartlepool Fan.*

Bernie: Tony Mowbray would never touch the ball before kick-off. Coops used to bang the door with his fists before every game.

Eric: This has just come back to me, but Alan Brazil used to like a hot bath before the game. He used to say, 'F*** the warm-up - I'm warming up in here!' I

remember one day he was in the bath and he shouted to Kevin O'Callaghan, 'Cally, pass the f***ing soap.' Sure enough, Cally threw him the soap, just as Alan turned round. The soap hit him right in the eye! It half-blinded him. He honestly couldn't see. It was touch and go whether or not he played in the game. He eventually started but he couldn't see out of one eye for the first 45 minutes!

Malcolm: I often used to go to sleep in the dressing room or treatment room before a match.

Eric and Bernie, would either of you played for Newcastle? - *Paul in Newcastle.*

Bernie: Yeah. When I was up in Scotland, it wouldn't have mattered to me about playing for Newcastle. And I'd have gone to Sunderland or Newcastle when I was pushed out of Boro by Lennie Lawrence.

Eric: Yes, I would have done - but thank f*** I didn't!

Bernie: Yeah, I agree with Eric there!

Malcolm, if you were a bad player, would you have considered playing for Ireland? - *Linsa, High Howdon.*

Bernie: That is f***ing outrageous!

Eric: That's a good one that!

Bernie: There are some bad players playing for England now.

•JON GITTENS: the worst player Bernie played with.

239

Which referee did you least look forward to being in charge of your game? - *Phil Brown, Port Moody, British Columbia, Canada (born and raised in Middlesbrough).*

Bernie: The referee I would have chosen I actually never had for a competitive match because he was a Middlesbrough fan - Jeff Winter. He always appeared to me to want to be the centre of attention.

Malcolm: Similarly, a fella in the '70s called Roger Kirkpatrick.

Eric: I remember him. Big side bangers and a big, fat, round belly.

Malcolm: That's him. When an incident happened in a game, he would blow his whistle and then run to the furthest point on the pitch, stop, turn round and make the player he wanted to speak to walk over to him. Why he did it, I don't know, but it put him right in the spotlight. The players just wanted to get on with the game, but he was arsing around like that.

Eric: No-one really knew the referees. I'd be struggling to name six referees from my era. I had my arguments with them, got booked by them and got sent off, but afterwards I would forget about them.

Bernie: That's a good point. I was there to play football, so never really noticed them.

Was there ever a point in your career that was so bad that you just wanted to chuck it? - *Paul McArdle, Lobley Hill, Gateshead.*

Eric: Believe it or not, in football you have more bad times than good times, but the good times make up for the bad times.

Bernie: During Boro's 1986 liquidation, I could quite easily have gone home, especially as I wasn't settled in the area at the time. The other time was when I was at Darlington at the end of my career. I only went there because my first son had just been born and I needed to be back in the area.

Eric: Under Lawrie McMenemy at Sunderland, I didn't enjoy training for the first time in my career. It was a chore. But the only time I wanted to chuck it was when I went to Carlisle at the end of my career.

Malcolm: The only time I really got down with the game was my last couple of seasons as a Newcastle player. The manager didn't help, but it was really the fact that the club never gave me an extended contract.

Who was the most feared player in your eras? - *Mally and Sarah, Middlesbrough, long-time listeners.*

Malcolm: The one from my era was the Italian left-back, Giacinto Faccetti. He was wicked and a hundred times worse than anyone in this country. He was always so late with his tackles.

Eric: Graham Roberts and Paul Miller at Tottenham. There was always a scrap on with them two. For some reason, they hated playing against us. They were hard lads and dirty b******s. I always thought that they would break your leg if they could.

Malcolm: I once saw Graham Roberts absolutely frighten Leroy Rosenior.

Did you or your respective teams play any dirty tricks, just to have the edge in a match? - *Richard Ives, Hebburn.*

Bernie: Eric dived all the time, he was full of dirty tricks! I used to watch him on my black and white telly in Glasgow and he was forever diving.

Eric: I never dived in my life.

Malcolm: I remember the opposition playing a mind game. When I took Fulham to QPR to play on their artificial surface, we were going into the unknown. Ten minutes before kick-off, someone opened our dressing room door, shouted. 'You'll be needing this!' and slid a bucket of gel across our floor. The players didn't know what to think or what it meant.

What was the worst league ground you played at and what was the best? - *Iain, Sunderland fan, but exiled in Newcastle.*

Malcolm: Leicester City's old ground, Filbert Street. It was a sh**hole of a ground. I hated it. I hated playing on it. It was tight, enclosed and I couldn't guage space on it.

Eric: I used to hate Chelsea, Stamford Bridge, before they built the new stand. It was derelict and, as a player, it felt like you were miles away from anywhere. But it was another experience again when I went into the Third Division with Sunderland. I saw some right sh**holes then, the sort of places I didn't think existed. I remember we played Bristol Rovers at Bath. Gordon Armstrong broke Kenny Hibbitt's leg with a bad tackle, there was hell on and they beat us 4-0. It was an awful place. The dressing rooms were like a dog kennel. I was having a shower and there was only Reuben Agboola left in the bath. Suddenly, the roof fell in, the ceiling came down and one of those long fluorescent lights was left dangling down, inches off the water. Reuben was frightened to move because that lad would have been dead if the light had touched the water. After all that, their officials accused us of smashing the dressing room up!

Malcolm: The Stamford Bridge pitch was crap as well. I also remember playing at Carlisle's Brunton Park and the sheep behind the stand were making more noise than the supporters. And Halifax, that was another bad one.

Bernie: The Shay! We went there in fog once and could hardly see each other on the pitch.

Eric: Liverpool was always a great ground - and Newcastle, because I always scored there!

Bernie: Everyone scored there, Eric! I would say Old Trafford was the best.

Malcolm: Hillsborough.

Bernie, if you'd had the chance, would you have joined Rangers from Albion Rovers? - *Peter, Boro fan.*

Bernie: Would I f***!

Eric: You lying b*****d! I don't believe you!

Bernie: All right, it would have been impossible, because they didn't sign Catholics at that time.

Malcolm: Yeah, but if they'd been prepared to make you the first exception?

Bernie: I'd have had to get past my Da first! Back then in Scotland, Catholics didn't marry Protestants and they didn't play for Rangers.

Bernie, bearing in mind that there are no fences to jump on at the Riverside, how would you celebrate a goal if you were playing now? - *Simon, Harrogate.*

Bernie: I might not score these days, because I'd get no service!

Malcolm, who was the last Newcastle player to kick the ball in the 1974 FA Cup final? I'll give you a clue - it was in the first half! - *Stevie, Sunderland.*

Eric: That is a good one!

Malcolm: And he's not far wrong!

LIFESTYLE

Have any of you been to a fancy dress party? If so, what did you go as? - *Phily G, Sunderland.*

Bernie: Gatesy went to a Halloween fancy dress party, didn't bother dressing up and still won top prize!

Malcolm: When Alan Kennedy was playing for Newcastle United at left-back, he went to a fancy dress party with his number three shirt on his back. When asked what he had come as, he just answered, 'Newcastle's left-back'.

Bernie: When I was with Boro, we all dressed up in fancy dress and went round Middlesbrough town centre. I went as medallion man, blew my hair back, sprayed it, wore a false moustache and put on

these big glasses. I went right round town but no-one knew me.

Eric: I always had my long hair even at Ipswich. For a bet with the lads, I once ran out for a game at Portman Road with a long-haired mop of a wig on. I wore it for the first ten minutes and no fan even noticed I had one on!

Have you ever had a lap dance?
- *Mark in the Boro.*

Bernie: They weren't lap dancers but I once arranged some dancing girls for Alastair Brownlee when we worked at Boro TV. It was Ali's birthday, so once the cameras were rolling for our weekly show, I said to him, 'Happy birthday, I've got a surprise for you. On you come, girls!' Out came these girls dressed in leotards. I thought it was brilliant. Ali's face was bright red. The next day, the station's gaffer called me and went crazy with me.

Eric: Lap dancers once came to my table - but they f***ed off and paid me!

Malcolm: Lap dancers weren't around in my day!

I would like to know what your favourite meal is - *Jeff from Hartlepool.*

Eric: I love steak - or just about anything else.

Bernie: Yeah, because you're a murdering b*****d!

Eric: I love all meat and can eat as much as you want - but medium to rare steak is my favourite. And ice cream!

Malcolm: Rare rib-eye steak for me.

Bernie: Lobster thermidore.

Eric: You cruel b*****d! Living creatures and you get them killed by boiling them in a pan!

Now that players have famous wives, which celebrity did you wish was your other half? - *Michael Laverton, Consett.*

Bernie: You mean which celebrity do you see on TV and think, 'I'd love to do her?'

Eric: Betty Boop and Cat Woman.

Bernie: Popeye's missus, she was a darlin'!

Which player's wife did you fancy the most? - *Andy, Boro.*

Bernie: I'll answer that - Karembeu's wife, Adriana, the Wonderbra model. That was the only press conference I ever went to - and it was only to see her! I'm sure that Robson signed him because of her, because it can't have been down to his football ability.

If each of you could pick three famous people, living or deceased, to have dinner with, who would you choose?
- *Alan Potts, Westerhope.*

Bernie: I'd invite Jack Nicholson. Morrissey would be there - and Mandela.

Eric: I'd want skinny gits, who would leave most of the food for me! So Lester Piggott, Kylie Minogue and Ghandi! Then I'd have some dinner.

Malcolm: The former leader of Yugoslavia, Tito, who for me was one of the most fascinating men, the only national leader who held off the Russians. Winston Churchill and a manager, Giovanni Trapattoni.

We found out about Bernie's hidden talent with his bagpipes. Have either Eric or Malcolm any talents we don't know about? - *Jim Rooney Gates*

Eric: I've starred in a few porn movies! As a kid, I was good at all sport - cricket, rugby, tennis, the lot.

Malcolm: I suppose I could have been a sprinter.

If you had not chosen professional football as a career, what would you like to have done? - *Ian, a Boro-mad fan in Eston.*

What do you think you would be doing now if you weren't lucky enough to have had a career in football?
- *Paul Stoneman, Stockton-on-Tees.*

Malcolm: I had a really good job offer in the insurance business when I was a young lad at Fulham, so I'd probably be doing that.

Bernie: I'd probably be in a council flat in Glasgow with four kids and no money.

Eric: I'd probably be a gypsy living in a caravan!

Eric, do you think it would have hampered your career if you had come out of the closet while you were still playing? - *Stuart, Durham.*

Eric: Nah! I did, but my team-mates didn't believe me.

•ERIC'S FANCY WOMAN! Betty Boop.

243

FOOTY ISSUES

Do you think the atmosphere would be better if all women were banned from football grounds? - *Boroboy.*

Malcolm: Well, chains aren't long enough to stretch from the sink to the football stadium, are they?! Seriously, no, I don't think banning women would improve the atmosphere. It's the people that Roy Keane has said he gets sick of, the so-called prawn sandwich brigade, who don't pay any attention to the football.

Bernie: Women don't really understand football, though I don't mind them coming along to watch the games, especially the good-looking ones. At least if the game is crap we can look at them! The best ground is Upton Park because they've got their cheerleaders, The Hammerettes. It still rankles with me that Boro waited 129 years for European football, then came the big night against Lazio. Lo and behold, I looked to the far side and the linesman was a lineswoman. She should have been doing the dishes around that time! When I complained about her on the phone-in, Gatesy and Malcolm encouraged women listening to call the show and give me what for. This woman comes on and says, 'I want to talk to Slaven. You are nothing but a male chauvinist pig.' I said, 'Hey, I don't like being called a pig!' She started telling me how this woman had worked hard to get to the point of working the line. I said 'I'm not doubting she has worked hard and well done to her, but she shouldn't be in a man's game.' She hammered me. At the end, I said, 'Are you married?' 'No.' 'That's not a surprise.' And we cut her off!

Another night, a guy had sent Malcolm an old book, The Housewife's Guide from the 1950s, and it included advice about how a woman should look after her husband. There was a list of bullet points advising them to make themselves look pretty for their husband getting home from a hard day at work with nice make-up and doing their hair, give him a kiss, get him a hot or cold drink, have his tea ready, always smell nice. Plus, of course, don't do any noisy hoovering around him and, if he comes in late from work, never question him. If he stays out all night, he must have a lot on his mind. I said it was the sort of philosophy I agreed with and that women should turn back the clock. This female caller came on and started making out that I was encouraging domestic violence. It was ridiculous. How can you fight with a duster? I did get a lot of support. A barrister came on and agreed her fellow female had got the wrong end of the stick. I got a text from one woman who said, 'Bernie, if you ever get to heaven and meet God, she's going to be furious with you!' I assured her that I was very confident God was a man. It's my philosophy that if women want equality and there's a fridge to be moved, why do they still ask a man to do it?

Eric: Have you finished, Bernie? Because I think the poor atmosphere is to do with the club officials not allowing people to shout and swear.

Bernie: Yeah, I'll go along with that.

If you were a management team, who would be manager, who would be assistant manager and who would be head coach? - *Steven Cook, Sunderland.*

Eric: That's a hard one

Bernie: Gatesy couldn't be the coach, because that would mean he'd train the lads - and he'd be a bad example to them! You need someone who looks the biz, so that's me or Malcolm. Give Malcolm the manager's job because he's experienced in management.

Eric: No, I wouldn't give it to Malcolm. He'd put the players to sleep with his team talk!

Bernie: Malcolm would be the manager, Eric the psychologist and I'd be the coach.

Eric: Yeah, I can do all that Bill Beswick psychology - all the 'look into my eyes' bit.

Bernie: That's a hypnotist, Gatesy, not a psychologist!

Why do you think women's football isn't popular, because I think most of the games shown on TV are very good? - *Helen, Whitley Bay.*

Bernie: Because they've got big t*** and can't run!

Eric: It is popular. There's more and more women playing every year. I don't know why more don't watch it, because I enjoy watching it.

Bernie: If you picked 11 models, the stands would be full! But have you ever seen a darling on the football park? I've not! Seriously, I just don't associate women with football, they're not physically built for it.

Malcolm: I think they are a hundred years too late, because they are always going to be compared with what is long-established as a male sport.

What do you wish for the club you support, now and in the future? - *John in Boro.*

Bernie: This season, survival, and for Gareth to stamp his authority as a manager and to get some new talent in. Beyond that, to continue the progress that has seen the club playing in Europe and reaching cup finals.

Eric: It would be great if Sunderland could stop just saying it and finally prove that they are a great club.

Malcolm: Not so long ago, Newcastle finished third in the Premier League. From there, they've just nosedived. It would just be nice to see that come back again.

•BAN'EM? What do the Legends think?